icons of
rock

JOHN LENNON

icons of
rock

JOHN LENNON

Terry Burrows

THUNDER BAY
P·R·E·S·S

First published in 2000 by
Thunder Bay Press
An imprint of the Advantage Publishers Group
5880 Oberlin Drive, San Diego, CA 92121-4794
www.advantagebooksonline.com

Library of Congress Cataloging-in-Publication Data
Burrows, Terry.
  John Lennon / Terry Burrows.
      p. cm. -- (Icons of rock)
  Includes index.
  ISBN 1-57145-469-1
  1. Lennon, John, 1940–1980. 2. Lennon, John, 1940–1980--Pictorial works.
  3. Beatles. 4. Beatles--Pictorial works. I. Title. II. Series.
ML4420.L38 B87 2001
782.42166'092--dc21
[B]   00-064886

Produced by **Brown Partworks Ltd**
8 Chapel Place, Rivington Street, London EC2A 3DQ, UK
www.brownpartworks.co.uk
Managing Editor: Lindsey Lowe
Project Editor: Rob Dimery
Design: Wilson Design Associates

Printed and bound in Hong Kong
2 3 4 5 04 03 02 01

Contents

Introduction

Late on December 8, 1980, news of an earth-shattering event filtered across the airwaves of the world. John Lennon, one quarter of the most famous pop group the world has ever known, was dead. Aged 40, he was murdered by a fan outside his New York home. The chilling broadcasts were hard for many to comprehend. John Lennon was loved and respected the world over—and now a shaken world mourned its loss.

Lennon was not just a popular musician. By the end of the 1960s he had also become one of the most prominent standard bearers for world peace—even if his methods did not always meet with the wholehearted approval of the Establishment. Accompanied and inspired by his partner, controversial performance artist Yoko Ono, Lennon instigated a series of protests and publicity-grabbing events to put the issue of peace on the world's front pages.

John Lennon was born in a maternity ward during a lull in the fierce bombing of Liverpool by Germany's Luftwaffe in World War II. His early childhood followed a traumatic path until he was adopted and brought up by his mother's sister, known to him throughout his life as Aunt Mimi. From a young age John's comic writing, witty artworks, and sharp tongue marked him out as an independent thinker. However, he singularly failed to channel his undoubted intelligence into schoolwork, becoming ever more disruptive and troublesome to his teachers. In his mid-teens, like so many others of his era, John found a new and exciting means of salvation from the terminal boredom of the classroom—rock and roll. When the music of the first great wave of American rock stars, such as Elvis Presley, Little Richard, and Fats Domino, made it across the Atlantic he was instantly and completely captivated.

In an age when pop and rock music has long lost its ability to shock, it can be difficult to appreciate the impact that the musical revolution of the mid-1950s had on disaffected youngsters such as John Lennon. Before rock and roll, teenage culture barely existed—you were a child until you left school, at which point you abruptly became an adult. But with rock and roll, teenagers finally had a style of music they could call their own. It was widely condemned by the adult world, and as a result, the generation gap was born.

Although Britain spawned a handful of its own rock-and-roll stars, they were largely inferior copies of the real thing. Of greater interest to John Lennon was the "skiffle" fad, spearheaded by Lonnie Donegan. Skiffle showed that anyone with a guitar and the patience to learn three chords could get up on stage and do their thing—a principle that would re-emerge 20 years later with punk rock. John was ripe for the calling, and quickly formed his own school skiffle group, called The Quarrymen.

By all accounts a shambolic unit, John's band played wherever and whenever they could find a gig. It may all have been fun, but The Quarrymen were heading nowhere until a momentous event took place on Saturday, July 6, 1957, when they played at a local village fete. The band's performance that day was inauspicious, but this time they were watched intently from the side of the stage by another young skiffle fan. After the show, John's friend Ivan Vaughan introduced him to this fellow aficionado—a 15-year-old called Paul McCartney. History was now in the making.

In December 1962 "Love Me Do," The Beatles' debut single, entered the national charts. Hearing them for the first time, people presumed they were a new group. Most people were unaware of their trips to Hamburg, their seven-hour stints on stage in the nightclubs on the Reeperbahn. Stints that had turned The Beatles from an ordinary group of teenage musicians into a tight-knit combo. No one who heard them had any idea of how they would affect popular culture during the next seven years. Their music apart, the world was completely unaware that everything connected with the group—their hairstyles, their suits, and their attitudes—would define the new decade. Right up to their miserable demise in 1970, the fortunes and activities of The Beatles' camp mirrored the path of an entire decade. For many—and that includes some of us who were too young to know about it at the time (or had not even been born)—the 1960s remain such special years because they were touched by the genius of The Beatles, and especially that of John Lennon.

Although it's well over a quarter of a century since they made their final recordings, The Beatles remain the most famous pop group of them all; their classic recordings increase in stature with the passing of time. John Lennon's later solo recordings didn't always shape up to the impeccable standards of the Fab Four, but songs such as "Imagine" remain consistently popular. What's more, Lennon's uncompromising stance continues to inspire many successive generations of young musicians. That he is one of the great icons of rock music is now taken as read. In future years there can be little doubt that John Lennon will be remembered simply as one of the twentieth century's most significant icons.

1 The Early Years

Born in 1940, during a lull in the German bombing of
Liverpool, John Lennon's early years are traumatic. He is
a smart child, but school can offer no useful outlet for his
talents. His vivid imagination is only truly captured by one
thing: rock and roll. From the age of 16 he channels all his
energy into his school band, The Quarrymen. Six long years
later, The Quarrymen have transformed themselves into The
Beatles. They learn their craft playing long sets in the clubs
of Hamburg's seedy Reeperbahn district. When they return
to Liverpool, they are ready to take on the world.

War baby

The city of Liverpool was not the safest of places to live in Britain during the early days of World War II. As one of England's major points of embarkation to America, the naval shipyards and miles of commercial dockland along the River Mersey made it a particularly valuable target for the Luftwaffe—Nazi Germany's airforce—which was by then making regular bombing sorties over mainland Britain.

During the summer of 1940 Liverpool had been devastated by a series of night raids, although the first week of October had seen an unexpected lull in enemy activities. German hostilities, however, were the last thing on the mind of young Julia Lennon as she lay in Liverpool's Oxford Street Maternity Home preparing for the arrival of her first child. Late in the afternoon of October 9, Julia went into labor and at 6:30 p.m. she gave birth to a son. In a fit of patriotic fervor she named him John Winston Lennon, after the country's wartime prime minister, Winston Churchill.

Julia had been born in 1914, one of five daughters. Her father, George Stanley, was employed by the Glasgow and Liverpool Salvage Company, a firm that thrived during World War I—the Mersey's geographical importance meant that no expense was spared in the effort to clear blockages in the river resulting from mounting shipwreck debris. The steady work made the Stanleys slightly wealthier than most other "Scousers" (natives of Liverpool).

Julia was the least conventional family member. She met her future husband—a ship's steward named Freddy Lennon—in Liverpool's Sefton Park. Julia made fun of a hat he was wearing; to make her laugh, he sent it skipping across a lake. Much to her family's dismay, the pair became an item, and eventually married in December 1938. However, theirs was not to be the closest of relationships. Freddy worked on the great passenger liners that journeyed between Liverpool and New York City, and the couple routinely spent months apart.

When war broke out in September 1939, Freddy's liner was berthed in New York; he evidently wanted no part in the war, for he promptly jumped ship. As a result he was arrested, and the maintenance checks that he had been sending to Julia ceased—the couple's marriage soon fell apart as a result. Freddy returned to Liverpool for a few brief conjugal visits but these became increasingly rare. Something of a "ne'er-do-well," he eventually ended up serving a sentence for desertion at a British military prison in North Africa. He returned a couple of times—once in 1940 and again in 1942—before disappearing from Julia and John's life, apparently for good. It was only when John became famous as a Beatle that his father emerged from obscurity.

Wartime Liverpool. Due to its importance as one of England's most strategically valuable dockyards, the city was devastated by the Luftwaffe's bombing raids.

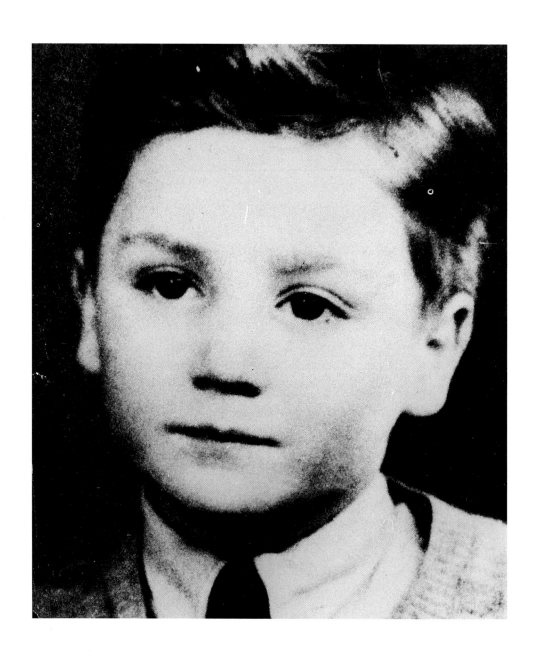

Aunt Mimi

Wartime was especially tough for young single mothers, whose numbers steadily increased as the war progressed. Julia became unsettled; the footloose and fancy-free times she had enjoyed before the war began to seem a lifetime away. And now she had the added responsibility of looking after young John. The burden of childcare often fell on the rest of her family. It was clear that her elder sister Mary Elizabeth—known to the family as Mimi—was forming a close relationship with John. Although happily married, Mimi and her husband George Smith had no children of their own, and she doted on Julia's son.

After the Allied victory in the Battle of Britain during 1941, the Luftwaffe bombings became rarer and life in Liverpool slowly began to return to normal. Julia was still young and attractive and soon had a new man in her life.

She was working at a café in Penny Lane when she met a waiter named John Dykins, and quickly decided to move in with him. Julia saw her life with Dykins as a new beginning, a chance to start a new life. However, the problem remained of what to do with her son; Dykins did not want the responsibility of bringing up another man's child.

Although Julia's refusal to face her maternal responsibilities angered her family, a satisfactory solution soon became clear: John would be adopted by Aunt Mimi. Thus it was that at the age of nearly five John Lennon went to live with his aunt and uncle at "Mendips," a semidetached house at 251 Menlove Avenue, Woolton—a pleasant middle-class suburb three miles outside of Liverpool's city center. From that moment onward, Mimi took her responsibilities as John's guardian very seriously indeed, forging a close, loving relationship with him that would last for the rest of his life.

John Lennon's artistic leanings were self-evident from an early age. He was a bright boy and could read by the age of four. His education started at Dovedale Primary School, near Penny Lane. Mimi would drop John off every morning and pick him up at the end of the school day at a bus stop by Penny Lane roundabout. One of John's earliest interests were the "Just William" stories, which were widely popular at the time. Richmal Crompton's tales of a disruptive 11-year-old boy appealed to young John's sensibilities. John also excelled in art at Dovedale and soon began writing and drawing his own books and comics. He also began to develop a taste for the petty mischief that would get him into trouble time and time again in the future.

Opposite: Dovedale Primary School pupil, John Winston Lennon.
Right: John's Aunt Mimi, who raised him from a young age.

Young teenage rebels

In September 1952, when he was 12 years old, John was sent to Quarry Bank High School, a traditional English grammar school that could boast a distinguished record of academic success. John started at the school with high hopes and good grades. However, with his friend Pete Shotton there to aid and abet him, his academic performance soon started to suffer. As Shotton remembers, "We started in our first year at the top and gradually sank together into the sub-basement." Lennon and Shotton soon found themselves in the company of Quarry Bank's least distinguished pupils, close to the bottom of "C" stream. By the age of 14, the pair had become notoriously disruptive troublemakers and detention became a weekly event for them. Mimi came to dread the periodic phone calls from the school secretary telling her of John's latest misdemeanor.

Although John loved Mimi, his mother had always remained in close contact with him and visited most weeks. As he grew older he began to see more and more of her, often playing truant to do so. John treated Julia more as an older sister than as his mother. For her part, Julia always encouraged John to have fun rather than worry about the future, and his irreverent sense of humor clearly stemmed from her.

When the American phenomenon of rock and roll hit Great Britain during the mid-1950s, John's life was changed forever. The most fervent fans of this new music were the notorious "Teddy Boys," young rebels who wore outlandish draped jackets, frilled shirts, and skintight "drainpipe" trousers; their greased locks formed quiffs, known as "DAs," which flopped down over their foreheads. John loved the music, the look and the sense of rebellion that rock and roll provided. Along with thousands of other young British teenagers, he fell under the spell of the U.S. rock and rollers, especially Elvis Presley. He nagged at Mimi and Julia to buy him rock-and-roll clothes and records, and set about turning himself into a teenage Teddy Boy.

The British scene had its own rock-related fad—skiffle, which was popularized by ex-jazz musician Lonnie Donegan, who covered American folk songs by the likes of Woody Guthrie and Huddie Ledbetter. Based around the simple sound of an acoustic guitar and/or banjo, a stand-up double bass (or a homemade equivalent, fashioned from a pole, a string, and an old tea chest), and a washboard rhythm, skiffle groups sprang up overnight all over the U.K. And John Winston Lennon was not going to be left out of the new craze.

Opposite: John, the teenage rocker.

Right: Lonnie Donegan, the leading light of the skiffle trend that swept through the U.K. during the early and mid-1950s.

The Quarrymen

From the moment he first heard Lonnie Donegan launching into the million-selling "Rock Island Line," John became fixated with the idea of getting a guitar. Even the frugal Mimi eventually had to give in to his persistent demands. One Saturday morning, she accompanied John down to Hessy's music store in the center of Liverpool and paid 17 pounds (approximately $25) for a cheap, steel-string acoustic guitar. She had a warning for him, though: "The guitar's all very well, John, but you'll never make a living out of it."

Her words fell on deaf ears. With all the enthusiasm that they'd failed to put into their schoolwork, Quarry Bank's resident teenage rebels, Lennon and Shotton, formed their own skiffle group—The Quarrymen. John sang and played the guitar while Pete played along on the washboard. They were joined by a variable assortment of skiffle enthusiasts that at one point included schoolfriends Nigel Whalley and Ivan Vaughan on "tea-chest" bass, Rod Davis on the banjo, guitarist Eric Griffiths, and drummer Colin Hanton.

Like many other teenage skiffle groups, The Quarrymen performed Lonnie Donegan's songs alongside American rock-and-roll hits such as "Blue Suede Shoes." The Quarrymen started to get engagements at school dances and youth clubs, though they rarely brought the house down. In fact, it was only John's enthusiasm that kept the band going—most of the others were only doing it for a laugh. But John had found something that he could give himself to heart and soul. He would often strum his guitar so hard that he would break a string; when this happened, he would borrow Rod Davis's banjo and play that while Rod set about trying to fix the string.

On July 6, 1957, The Quarrymen were booked to play at St. Peter's Parish annual church fete in Woolton. They were due to perform on the back of a lorry during the parade, and then afterward on stage at the fete itself. The event turned out to be highly significant—not only for John Lennon, but for the future of pop music.

Ivan Vaughan, no longer playing with The Quarrymen, turned up at the fete with a schoolfriend from the neighboring Liverpool Institute. Ivan was keen for John to meet his friend—he felt sure that they had a lot in common. So, as The Quarrymen played their set that day, Ivan's young friend Paul McCartney watched intently from the side of the stage. Afterward, Paul met up with the group backstage in the Church Hall and ran through the Eddie Cochran classic "Twenty Flight Rock" as well as a few Little Richard numbers. A mildly inebriated John Lennon assiduously studied Paul's guitar-playing skills.

The Quarrymen at the Woolton Village Fete, July 6, 1957. Left to right: Eric Griffiths, Colin Hanton (seated in the background), Rod Davis, John Lennon, Pete Shotton, and Len Garry. Paul McCartney watched their set that day from the side of the stage.

The Fab Three

The first meeting between John and Paul was a shy and awkward one in which little was said. However, though he might not have shown it at the time, John was very impressed by Ivan Vaughan's friend. Paul McCartney could not only tune a guitar, he also knew a wide selection of chords; John was still limited to playing variations on the banjo chords that Julia had taught him. Paul had also learned the words to numerous rock-and-roll hits by heart; John had recently taken to making up his own lyrics, principally because he could never remember the real ones all the way through.

The arrival of Paul presented John with a problem. The Quarrymen had been an extension of his school gangs, in which he had obviously been the leader. Paul was remarkably self-assured, and John realized that he wouldn't be able to boss him around as easily as his other friends. At the same time, Paul was simply too good not to be in the band. It is difficult to imagine two more different personalities—John, rebellious with his dry wit always ready to issue a sharp put-down, and Paul, ambitious and hardworking, with a desire to please everyone around him. Nevertheless, despite their differences, the two quickly became friends.

By the late 1950s, the face of pop music had changed once more. Electric guitars were now taking over from the acoustic instruments favored by skiffle bands. Paul and John also became aware that rising stars from across the Atlantic, such as Eddie Cochran and Buddy Holly, were writing their own songs. (Previously, singers had mostly relied on professional songwriters to provide them with material.) This inspired a highly competitive period that saw John and Paul each writing new songs as if their lives depended on it.

Around the same time, Paul had struck up an uneasy friendship with a fellow pupil at the Liverpool Institute. Young George Harrison, who was already a talented guitarist, soon began hanging around at Quarrymen gigs. George was only 14 years old at the time and when Paul suggested letting him join the band, John was horrified. But when he heard George play, and when the youngster told The Quarrymen that they could rehearse at his parents' house, John began to change his mind. Before long, George was in.

From the moment The Quarrymen first spluttered into life, John's fate was sealed. First skiffle and then rock and roll became his new teachers, and his schoolwork deteriorated sharply as a result. However, the arrival of a sympathetic new headmaster at Quarry Bank, William Pobjoy, temporarily extended John's academic future. Pobjoy realized that the only subject John had any interest in was art. He therefore used his connections to arrange a place for the teenager at Liverpool College of Art, where John duly arrived in September 1957.

Even at the age of 12, George Harrison was a gifted guitarist. Less than three years after this photograph was taken he joined The Quarrymen.

Art school

Although English art schools have nurtured many of rock's big names, including Pete Townshend of The Who and The Kinks' Ray Davies, John found the experience a sobering one. He'd been a hopeless pupil at Quarry Bank, but he'd been popular with his classmates and his anarchic behavior earned him a certain kind of respect. But Liverpool College of Art seemed to him to be filled with goatee-bearded jazz fans. And they weren't too impressed by the Teddy Boy in their midst. "When I was at art school they'd only allow jazz to be played," John later recalled, "so we had to con them into letting us have rock and roll on the record player by calling it 'blues.'"

John struck up an unlikely friendship with another "outcast" student at the college. Stuart "Stu" Sutcliffe was an outstanding young artist—one of his tutors claimed he was the most talented artist the college had ever produced. Moreover, he possessed a markedly intense personality and an unorthodox dress sense—skintight jeans, pointed boots, and brightly colored shirts—that was more outrageous than John's by far. He also adopted a pair of dark glasses that, along with his swept-back hair, gave him a strong resemblance to James Dean. Stu's unconventional dress sense aroused suspicion among his fellow students, but his obvious talent forced the college authorities to turn a blind eye to his appearance. John and Stu quickly became close friends.

Drawn by Stu's unique outlook and sheer coolness, John decided that he had to have him in his band. There was a problem, however: Stu had never played an instrument and showed no evidence of musical ability. But John's persistence paid off. One of Stu's paintings had been selected for the biennial John Moores Exhibition in Liverpool, a considerable achievement. It was bought by John Moores himself, for the princely sum of 65 pounds. Stu went to Hessy's music store with the money and bought a Hofner "President" bass guitar.

Paul McCartney could see why John would want someone like Stu in the band, but had misgivings about the new bassist. McCartney was talented and ambitious and felt that Stu's lack of musical ability would hold the band back. During much of Stu's time with the band, John would feel compelled to protect him from Paul's carping.

On July 15, 1958, John's world was turned upside down. Following a visit to Mimi's house, his mother Julia was knocked down and killed in a road accident. John was devastated. Julia had been a carefree spirit who had always indulged his moods and attitudes and her death haunted him for much of his life. John later dedicated many songs to his mother, and named his first son, Julian, after her. Paul McCartney had lost his mother as a teenager, and the shared experience rapidly brought the two closer together.

John's close friend Stuart Sutcliffe—talented artist, flamboyant dresser, and early Beatles bassist.

Germany calling

Progress was slow. The Quarrymen needed a drummer and regular work. In 1959 they entered a talent competition in Manchester as Johnny and the Moondogs, but met with no success. Then, early in 1960, the band contacted local promoter Alan Williams to see if they could get gigs supporting the U.S. stars who played at the Empire, one of Liverpool's main venues. Williams was not that impressed by The Quarrymen, but did offer advice and occasional work. When he told them to get a new name, "something like The Crickets," Stu jokingly suggested The Beetles, after Marlon Brando's biker gang in the 1954 film *The Wild One*. John's adaptation—The Beatles, a pun on the "Beat music" that Liverpool's bands played—was initially rejected. They settled on The Silver Beetles.

Above: John the rocker in Hamburg, 1960.

The band's first break came when they were asked to back minor English rock and roller Johnny Gentle on a short tour of Scotland. They returned to find that Williams now had a lucrative deal with German strip-club owner Bruno Koschmider, and was sending local groups to play at Koschmider's clubs in Hamburg. One band dropped out in July 1960 and Williams offered the job to The Silver Beetles, who promptly recruited a drummer—Pete Best, whom they met at a Liverpool venue called the Casbah Coffee Club, run by Best's mother. And by the time they reached Hamburg, the band had settled on The Beatles. John finally got his way.

Their first residency was at the tiny Indra club, in the middle of Hamburg's notorious red-light district, the Reeperbahn. The Beatles' home for the next two months was a seedy room at the back of a cinema also owned by Herr Koschmider. The workload was heavy. Sets often lasted for several hours and the band usually played more than one set per day. Permanently exhausted, their employers gave them amphetamine pills ("speed") to pep them up. During the first month, The Beatles honed their stage act and often slipped original Lennon/McCartney songs into their set. The arduous schedule made them a tight and powerful rock-and-roll band, and they were soon promoted to play at Koschmider's larger Kaiserkeller club.

However, disaster struck in November 1960. A routine police inspection revealed that, at the age of only 17, George Harrison was too young to be playing in a nightclub after midnight. He was immediately deported. Days later, McCartney and Best were arrested, allegedly for trying to burn down Koschmider's cinema, and were also deported.

Opposite: The band formerly known as The Silver Beetles in Hamburg, 1960. Left to right: Stu Sutcliffe, John Lennon, an unknown friend, George Harrison, Paul McCartney, and Pete Best.

The Cavern

The Beatles had gone to Hamburg with high hopes, but their dramatic premature return left them feeling dejected. Stu was hit the hardest. While in Hamburg he had fallen in love with a young photographer, Astrid Kirchherr, who had taken a number of striking photos of the group during their stay. It was Astrid who influenced The Beatles to comb their hair forward in the style favored by her German student friends. This was to give rise to the famous Beatle "mop top" haircut.

On their return, The Beatles discovered that Liverpool's beat scene had developed, creating its own style and sound. They also found that they now had something of a reputation as a live powerhouse in Liverpool, spread by other "Merseybeat" bands who had visited Hamburg and seen them play. The Beatles had left Liverpool as a bunch of no-hopers and returned as one of the city's hottest acts.

At the heart of the Merseybeat scene was The Cavern jazz club in Mathew Street, and at the end of January 1961, The Beatles began a legendary residency there. They were paid 25 shillings per day for two 45-minute sets—easy money for a band used to playing nonstop for five hours. Their set featured covers of often obscure American rock-and-roll and rhythm-and-blues hits, brought across the Atlantic by merchant seaman—one of the reasons why Liverpool's musicians often got to hear new music before anyone else in Europe. It was at The Cavern that teenage girls first started to scream at The Beatles. And initially, the object of most of the female attention was drummer Pete Best.

Above: John photographed by Astrid in her Hamburg loft.

In April 1961, The Beatles returned to Hamburg's Top Ten club, but while the band seemed to be going from strength to strength, internal pressures between Paul McCartney and Stuart Sutcliffe were growing. Over the weeks that followed, Stu gradually eased himself out of the band, ostensibly to study at Hamburg State Art College under Eduardo Paolozzi, one of his idols. He was to play no further part in The Beatles' story. Tragically, Stu died a year later from a brain hemorrhage, just days before The Beatles were due to play at the Star Club, a major new rock venue in Hamburg. Astrid told The Beatles of Stu's death when she met them at Hamburg airport. John was devastated, though his initial, shocking reaction was to laugh hysterically. "It was his way of not wanting to face the truth," Astrid explained later.

Opposite: John at The Cavern, clad in Hamburg leathers and playing his first Rickenbacker guitar.

Under new management

By the middle of 1961, rock and roll was such big business in Liverpool that the city had its own music paper—*Mersey Beat*—and several stores that specialized in selling beat music. The city's best record store was NEMS (North End Road Music Stores), an electrical retail outlet that boasted the "The Finest Record Selection in the North." The store was part of a chain run by the Epsteins, a wealthy Jewish family. The record department had been built up successfully by the owner's son Brian, a 27-year-old former drama student.

Brian Epstein was proud to claim that he was able to obtain any out-of-stock records his customers wanted. He was therefore somewhat annoyed when, on October 28, 1961, a teenager named Raymond Jones came into the store to ask for The Beatles' recording of "My Bonnie." Epstein had heard of neither the group nor their record. In fact, the song had been recorded in Germany by a singer called Tony Sheridan, who had used The Beatles as his backing group on the session. (At the time it was only available in Germany and was credited to Tony Sheridan and The Beat Brothers.) A couple of days later, two girls came in to ask for the same record. When one of Epstein's customers told him that The Beatles were a local group who regularly performed at The Cavern, he felt compelled to investigate further and on November 9, accompanied by his assistant Alistair Taylor, he headed down to the club.

The sweaty, noisy atmosphere of a Cavern lunchtime session was a new experience for Brian Epstein, but he was immediately struck by the power of The Beatles' music and their sense of humor on stage. Epstein returned to The Cavern several times to watch the group and gradually an idea began to form in his mind. Seeing the effect The Beatles were having on The Cavern's lunchtime crowds, Epstein could see no reason why this phenomenon should be limited to Liverpool. In early December 1961, he asked the band if they'd like him to be their manager, and on December 15, they signed a management contract with him. Although he agreed to play no part in their musical direction, Epstein henceforth took control of every other aspect of the band's day-to-day existence.

His first task was obvious enough. As far as the Merseybeat bands were concerned, The Beatles were now at the top of the pile. But outside the area—even just up the road in Manchester—they were more or less unknown. Brian Epstein knew that the only way of promoting The Beatles was to bring them to the attention of the big London record companies. Getting his band an audition wouldn't be difficult: as the manager of one of the biggest record stockists in the north of England, no label would want to risk upsetting Brian Epstein unnecessarily. As far as he was concerned, The Beatles' music would do the talking.

Brian Epstein, The Beatles' suave but fragile manager. In the background is London's Saville Theatre, which Epstein leased in the mid-1960s as a venue to showcase his acts.

Meeting George Martin

The first label Epstein approached was Decca, one of the most powerful record companies in the U.K., who arranged an audition with the group for January 1, 1962. In the space of three hours, The Beatles recorded 15 tracks. The band was not really satisfied with the performance, but Epstein was convinced it would be enough to secure a deal. However, Decca felt otherwise, rejecting The Beatles because they sounded "too much like The Shadows." Dick Rowe, the head of artists and repertory at Decca, told Brian Epstein that guitar bands were on the way out, a rebuff that John and Paul referred to in a later interview:

Paul: He must be kicking himself now.
John: I hope he kicks himself to death.

While Epstein was furious at Decca's rejection of The Beatles, the band itself was more sanguine: "Don't worry Brian, we'll have to sign to Embassy," John wisecracked. (Embassy was an albums-only label owned by the Woolworth's chain that released out-of-date, low-quality LPs that sold for the price of a single.)

The band's fortune soon changed, however. Epstein hit on the idea of using the Decca audition tapes to make a demonstration disc to play to prospective labels. He paid a visit to the famous HMV store on London's Oxford Street, where it was possible to have one-off records cut from a master tape. The engineer who processed the record took a liking to The Beatles' sound and suggested that Epstein take it to EMI's publishing wing. That same day, Epstein visited EMI's head of publishing, Sid Coleman, who listened to the record and also liked what he heard. He agreed to publish two of the songs—the Lennon/McCartney compositions "Love Of The Loved" and "Hello Little Girl." Furthermore, Coleman agreed to set up a meeting with George Martin, an EMI talent scout and producer.

George Martin was unusual in the pop field in that he'd had classical music training, and had studied at London's Guildhall School of Music. He'd also worked with Spike Milligan and Peter Sellers, two of The Goons—stars of a legendary British radio show of the 1950s. But as rock and roll was the record industry's biggest money-spinner, Martin had reluctantly begun looking for talent among the countless newly formed beat groups. It was with few expectations that he sat down to listen to the latest demo tape to come his way. On the evidence he heard, The Beatles seemed to have little to distinguish them from many other well-rehearsed groups. But he was sufficiently interested to offer them an audition. As he later recalled, "I thought to myself: 'There might just be something there.'"

An impressed George Martin hears a run-through of an early Beatles song at Abbey Road Studios.

The Fab Fourth

The Beatles' Parlophone audition took place on June 6, 1962, at EMI's Abbey Road Studios. Parlophone is one of EMI's subsidiary labels, and up to the early 1960s was best known for producing comedy records. As well as working with Peter Sellers, George Martin had also produced LPs by Peter Ustinov and the cast of the comedy revue *Beyond The Fringe.*

As before, The Beatles concentrated on their usual mix of standards and original material, including an interesting new song called "Love Me Do." George Martin remained unconvinced: he quite liked what he heard, but didn't find it especially exciting. He felt that the old songs the band chose to cover were dull, and that their own material was not obviously commercial enough. However, he was sure about one thing: although Pete Best was fine for live use, he was not a tight enough drummer to use on recordings. If The Beatles were to make records, Martin would insist on using Andy White, his own session drummer. One month later Parlophone signed The Beatles to a one-year contract.

The problem of what to do with Pete Best immediately became a major issue. When the other members found out Martin's views, Paul and George were keen to get rid of Pete just to get the matter out of the way; John was less happy to toe the line. Nevertheless, on August 16, Pete Best was called to Brian Epstein's office and unceremoniously fired, allegedly because his drumming wasn't up to scratch. From then on Best would always be known as pop's ultimate "nearly" man. Unsurprisingly, the incident caused consternation among the band's primarily female fan-base—the drummer was widely regarded as the best-looking Beatle. John, Paul, and George said little about the whole affair.

Once again, The Beatles were drummerless, though not for long. Top of their most-wanted list was Richard Starkey, widely viewed as one of Liverpool's top beat drummers, and better known to *Mersey Beat* readers as Ringo Starr. John later recalled: "Ringo was a professional drummer who performed with one of the top groups in Liverpool before we even had a drummer." Ringo had made a name for himself playing with Rory Storm and the Hurricanes. Like The Beatles, the Hurricanes had honed their craft in the clubs of Hamburg. But Ringo had tired of the discomforts of life on the road and had returned to Liverpool.

He had briefly rejoined the Hurricanes for a summer season in Skegness, northeast England, when he got a call from John Lennon inviting him to join The Beatles. He was told that he'd have to shave off his beard and change his Teddy Boy quiff for a Beatle mop, but that he could keep his sideburns. He agreed.

Ringo made his debut behind the drums for The Beatles on Saturday August 18, 1962, at the Hulme Hall, Port Sunlight, Birkenhead. The "Fab Four" were now complete.

Ringo, bearded and quiffed, during the Hurricanes' residency at Butlin's holiday camp, Skegness.

The beginning of something big

The recording sessions for the first Beatles single were booked for September 6 and 11, 1962. George Martin had already decided that the best way to launch the band would be to use original Lennon/McCartney compositions. He duly selected two tracks from their audition, "P.S. I Love You" and "Love Me Do." The latter, which was to be the single's A-side, featured a harmonica introduction and solo from John.

Since The Beatles' original audition, nobody had thought to tell George Martin that Pete Best had been replaced, so when the group arrived at Abbey Road recording studios they were introduced to Andy White, their drummer for the session. Much to Ringo's distress, his first session with The Beatles was restricted to watching the proceedings from the control room. When Martin eventually heard Ringo drum, he was sufficiently impressed to let him play on the second session, although it still irks Ringo to this day that he wound up playing maracas on the record while Andy White took over on drums. At one point, The Beatles' new drummer started to worry that the rest of the group were willing to sacrifice him as they had Pete Best less than a month before.

On October 5, 1962, "Love Me Do" hit the streets. However, reaching the whole of Britain remained a problem—outside of northwest England, The Beatles were still largely unknown. Brian Epstein came up with a solution. Knowing the number of sales required to get a record into the charts, he bought 10,000 copies of the single through his NEMS record store, enough to earn an appearance in the national *New Musical Express* chart at number 27. By the middle of December "Love Me Do" had reached number 17. A subdued beginning, but at least it brought the group to the attention of a national audience for the first time. In late 1962 the charts were packed with solo singers, mostly American, including Carole King, Bobby Vee, and Little Eva. For a time it must have seemed as though, just as Dick Rowe had predicted, groups with guitars were becoming a thing of the past.

On a more positive note, The Beatles' roadshow was now beginning to build up momentum. Their first Top 20 hit gave them greater confidence in their own material, which henceforth underwent an extraordinary and rapid improvement. From that point on, the songwriting team of John Lennon and Paul McCartney would become ever stronger, eventually developing into the most successful pop partnership of all time. The success of "Love Me Do" also forced George Martin to reassess his opinion of the Liverpudlian foursome. He was now convinced that there was something unique about the group after all, and offered them a five-year contract with Parlophone. Together, George Martin and The Beatles would change the face of popular music forever.

On the brink of success. The Beatles in London, 1962, at the time "Love Me Do" was released.

2 Beatlemania

John Lennon's life is turned upside down in 1963. With
hits such as "I Want To Hold Your Hand" and "She Loves
You," The Beatles establish themselves as an important new
force in pop music. What's more, they stand apart from their
contemporaries in that they write most of their own songs.
As The Beatles' success spirals out of control, their public
appearances are greeted by hordes of screaming teenage
girls. The press immediately come up with a new name
for this phenomenon: Beatlemania.

The top spot

With "Love Me Do" still in the lower reaches of the Top 30, it was time to record the vital follow-up single. Both Brian Epstein and George Martin were keen on a song brought to them by publisher Dick James. They were convinced that "How Do You Do It?" would be the song to take The Beatles to the top of the charts. But The Beatles themselves had other ideas. John Lennon and Paul McCartney wanted to persevere with their own material, especially their newest number, the bright "Please Please Me," a song that showed off the band's tight vocal harmonies. The track was originally intended as a slow number in the style of Roy Orbison, before Martin suggested the band speed it up. When he heard the results he knew immediately that it was going to be a massive hit. The recording took place on November 26, 1962, and at the end of the session Martin said to the group "Gentlemen, you have just made your first number 1."

When the single appeared in the middle of January 1963, The Beatles made their national TV debut on the Saturday night pop show *Thank Your Lucky Stars*. Further exposure followed on *Juke Box Jury*, a pop show that reviewed new releases.

In the 1960s, the U.K. had several record charts, each of which was based on the sales from selected record stores across the country. Different charts occasionally showed the same single at different positions, depending on the sales registered at a particular store. Most chart guides state that "Please Please Me" reached number 2; however, several of the U.K.'s published record charts, including those in music weeklies *Melody Maker*, *Disc*, and *New Musical Express*, showed the record at number 1, confirming George Martin's prediction. Whatever the position, one thing was clear: with "Please Please Me," The Beatles became a musical force to be reckoned with.

Capitalizing on the momentum of a massive hit single, The Beatles embarked on their first major British tour, though they still found the time for more recording. On February 10, the band traveled down to Abbey Road to record their debut album. George Martin's aim was to capture the energy of their live set. By today's standards the band's work rate was incredible: they began at 10 a.m. and carried on until 11 p.m. In the space of barely 13 hours they recorded an astonishing 79 takes of 14 songs. Eight tracks were Lennon/ McCartney originals; the remaining six were covers from their live show. The session was said to have cost 400 pounds (approximately $600)—a fairly small sum for such a session, even in 1963.

On March 23, 1963, The Beatles' debut album—entitled *Please Please Me* after their hit single—was released. It went straight to the number 1 spot and had sold over half a million copies by the end of the year. The madness had started.

Pop's premier songwriting partnership in the first flush of fame, 1963.

John and Cynthia

Please Please Me was now a national hit. Although The Beatles had broad appeal, Brian Epstein knew that the screaming teenage girls were vital for the group's sustained success and he worked hard to create the illusion that The Beatles were "attainable" to their young female fans. For this fantasy to work, there could be no girlfriends on public display. This was to be a problem for John Lennon. In spite of his wise-guy image and reputation as a rebel, back home in Liverpool John had a wife.

Cynthia Powell had enrolled at Liverpool College of Art at the same time as John. Coming from Hoylake on the Wirral, John quickly marked her out as a "posh kid," though that didn't stop him fancying her. When he asked Cynthia to dance with him at an art school party, she abruptly told him that she was already engaged. "I didn't ask you to marry me, did I?" he shot back. Almost despite herself, Cynthia became increasingly intrigued by this Teddy Boy with a razor-sharp tongue. Her engagement was soon over and before long she and John were dating. The relationship came under stress during The Beatles' spell in Hamburg, when Cynthia would only see John on her occasional visits to Germany, but it really became an issue when The Beatles began to take off. At Brian Epstein's insistence, she was forced to stay in the background.

In August 1962, Cynthia discovered that she was pregnant. Although the timing couldn't have been worse–The Beatles' first single was to be released within two months–John insisted that they be married at once. As unorthodox as he might have been in other respects, John felt compelled to "do the right thing." Thus it was that John Lennon and Cynthia Powell were wed at Mount Pleasant Registry Office on August 23, 1962. Brian Epstein obtained a special marriage license, confident that he could still stop the news from leaking out. Paul was best man; George, Brian, Cynthia's brother Tony, and his wife Marjorie were the only other guests. John's Aunt Mimi, who was furious both at the unplanned pregnancy and the abrupt marriage, which recalled Julia's wedding to Freddy Lennon some 24 years previously, refused to attend. A pneumatic drill outside made much of the wedding ceremony inaudible, causing the participants to become increasingly hysterical with laughter.

On April 8, 1963, Cynthia gave birth to a baby boy–Julian. When The Beatles began the process of moving down to London, it was planned that Cynthia and Julian should return to her mother's home in Hoylake. Before the end of the year, however, Cynthia was tracked down by a reporter and the story of John's marriage and the Lennons' young son broke in the newspapers. Epstein was furious, but John was somewhat relieved that his family no longer had to stay a hidden part of his life.

John and Cynthia, captured as John was becoming one of the most famous pop stars in the world.

Yeah, yeah, yeah!

Nineteen sixty-three was the year that Britain capitulated to the charms of John, Paul, George, and Ringo. Their third single—"From Me To You"—was released on April 11. It went straight to the number 1 spot, selling over half a million copies.

Two weeks later, The Beatles played their biggest gig to date in front of a crowd of 10,000 people at the *New Musical Express* Poll Winners Show, at the Empire Pool, Wembley. The Beatles hadn't actually topped any polls, as the votes were made in 1962, before they'd become a national phenomenon. However, the success of "Please Please Me," "From Me To You," and their debut album meant that their inclusion was a must. And although they were second on the bill to Cliff Richard and the Shadows, the screaming frenzy indicated that much of the audience was there for the Fab Four.

The same thing happened on the national tour that followed. This time The Beatles were supporting Roy Orbison—a true rock-and-roll original and one of their all-time heroes. Within days, however, audience reaction made it clear who the real stars of the show were and the billing order was changed. The Beatles were now a major headlining act.

The British media couldn't get enough of the group. At press conferences each of their distinctive personalities shone through, but more often than not it was the dry scouse wit of John Lennon that captured the headlines. There was also considerable interest in the burgeoning songwriting partnership of Lennon and McCartney. It was unusual enough for a group to write their own songs, rather than having them provided by professional songwriters, but now John and Paul were also scoring hits for other artists. That really was breaking new ground, especially in the U.K.

In August, The Beatles notched up their biggest-ever hit. Indeed, for nearly 20 years "She Loves You" remained the biggest-selling British hit record of all time. (EMI had pressed over 250,000 copies of the single in the month before its release, to cope with demand.) Like many of their classic songs, "She Loves You" was written in a hotel room while the group were on tour. As John and Paul talked and fiddled with their acoustic guitars, John made a crucial suggestion. Instead of writing about "me and you," he reasoned, they should try to come up with something about a third person. As Paul recalled: "We hit on the idea of doing a reported conversation—'She told me what to say, she said she loves you'—giving it a dimension that was different to what we'd done before."

"She Loves You" had all the features that made The Beatles so popular in the first place, plus the instantly memorable "yeah, yeah, yeah" chorus—one of the most famous hook lines in pop history. By the end of the year it had become The Beatles' first million-seller.

The taste of pop, 1963-style. The Beatles' collarless jackets were one of their earliest trademarks.

The Mersey invasion

The buzz surrounding Merseybeat was strong in Liverpool, and it wasn't long before the big London-based record labels heard the sound. Without doubt it was the work of Brian Epstein that gave the new music scene its identity and brought it to national attention.

By early 1963, Epstein's record store was only a small part of his business. He now had a management offshoot, NEMS Enterprises, and signed some of Liverpool's premier acts. At its peak in the early 1960s NEMS represented almost all the major bands in British pop music.

The first Merseybeat band to join The Beatles in the national charts was Gerry and the Pacemakers. Like The Beatles, they had been on the Liverpudlian music scene for a while, having started out as a skiffle act. They even managed to get a number 1 single a few weeks before The Beatles. Ironically, it was their version of Mitch Murray's "How Do You Do It?," the song that The Beatles had turned down in favor of their own "Please Please Me." In an astonishing coup, Gerry and the Pacemakers saw their first three singles—"How Do You Do It?," "I Like It," and "You'll Never Walk Alone"—all go to the top of the national charts.

Other Liverpool bands prominent on the scene at the time were The Fourmost, and Billy J. Kramer and the Dakotas, both of whom achieved several hits, some penned by Lennon and McCartney. The Searchers also enjoyed a substantial career, mostly playing unknown American hits—"Sugar And Spice," "Sweets For My Sweet," and "Needles And Pins" were all Top 2 hits. Another major NEMS artist was Cilla Black, who had a string of U.K. hits before becoming a major TV celebrity later in the decade.

However, Brian's stable of artists faced the problem that he was primarily occupied with The Beatles and had little time to devote to his remaining performers. Within two years most of his other Merseyside acts found that their chart hits had dried up.

Above: The pride of Merseyside. Brian Epstein's stable of NEMS acts in 1963 included The Beatles, Gerry and the Pacemakers, and Billy J. Kramer and the Dakotas. Epstein himself is seated far right.

Opposite: Ex-Cavern cloakroom girl Priscilla White found fame as Cilla Black, scoring a number of hits as a solo singer and becoming a major show business star in the U.K.

It's Beatlemania!

By now, The Beatles had become big news. On Monday, November 4, 1963, they played at The Royal Command Performance, regarded by many entertainers at the time as the peak of professional achievement. For this annual British showbiz outing, a cast of top variety artists—singers, comedians, magicians, dancers, and others—perform in front of members of the British royal family. In its heyday, the show was broadcast on a Sunday night and regularly attracted some of the highest annual TV audience figures. Indeed, it was so popular that in a spirit of fair play that characterized the early days of British TV, the two major networks took it in turns to broadcast the show.

The event took place at London's Prince of Wales Theatre in the presence of the Queen Mother, Princess Margaret, and Lord Snowdon. The Beatles' appearance caused a sensation, and not just because of their music. In fact, there were no screams at all from the crowd when they played their opening song, "From Me To You." Paul made the audience titter with a crack about Sophie Tucker being their "favorite American group" before the band played "Till There Was You." However, it was John's comment before their closing number that really stuck in the mind. Before playing their final song, "Twist And Shout," he made a request for audience participation: "On this next number I want you all to join in. Would those in the cheap seats clap their hands. The rest of you can rattle your jewelry." In an environment of social deference, John's comment was considered quite shocking, but it was delivered in such a tongue-in-cheek manner that it could not possibly cause offense.

They had charmed the Establishment. The other acts might just as well have gone home—the newspaper coverage of the evening's performance was mostly devoted to the cheeky Liverpudlian rock-and-roll group. "Beatles Rock The Royals" announced a *Daily Express* headline the next day, while the *Daily Mail* trumpeted a "Night Of Triumph For Four Young Men." John Lennon's line was widely regarded as a piece of good-natured irreverence, a welcome breath of fresh air in the otherwise rather stuffy atmosphere of the Command Performance. The Queen Mother in particular was taken by the group: "They are so fresh and vital. I simply adore them," she enthused. Meeting The Beatles after the show, she asked them where they were performing next. When she was told they were playing in Slough, Her Majesty mischievously replied, "Oh, that's near us." (The royal residence at Windsor Castle is only a short distance from Slough.)

Outside the Prince of Wales Theatre, hordes of screaming teenage fans waited for a glimpse of their idols. Reporting on the mayhem, the *Daily Mirror* coined a new word to describe this latest pop phenomenon—"Beatlemania."

John on stage in 1963, still tantalizingly within reach of the fans, but only just.

John and Brian

Nobody could deny the major part that Brian Epstein played in The Beatles' success; in turn, their success had made him a very wealthy young man. Brian enjoyed the fame and recognition as much as the healthy bank balance; he liked being a public figure. But the public enjoyment of his wealth was in complete contrast to the secrecy with which he conducted his private life. Although his family and friends knew that Brian was homosexual, in such unenlightened times the consequences of that news becoming public knowledge could have had a disastrous effect on his career and on those whom he managed.

There has been much speculation about Brian's relationship with and feelings toward John Lennon. One famous account of The Beatles' story suggests that he fell in love with the leather-clad John when he first saw The Beatles performing at The Cavern and that this had been his motivation for signing the band. While plausible, this theory has been widely refuted by those close to Lennon.

Nevertheless, mystery still surrounds a short holiday that the two men spent together at the end of April 1963. With a break in The Beatles' heavy schedule, but barely three weeks after the birth of his son Julian, John and Brian flew off together to Torremolinos, Spain. Nobody knows for certain what took place during their break, but there has been speculation over the years that the two had a brief affair. Again, nobody who was close to The Beatles' camp believes this to have been true, although that hasn't stopped books and films being based on the idea. At the time, rumors about the holiday subsequently led to one of the ugliest incidents in The Beatles' early career. In June 1963, at Paul McCartney's 21st birthday party in Liverpool, Cavern DJ Bob Wooler teased John about the Spanish holiday, suggesting that he was homosexual. Drunk and in a confrontational mood, John turned on Wooler and beat him up so badly that he had to be hospitalized. Brian drove the battered DJ to the hospital himself, and later made John apologize to Wooler.

In truth, although Brian was only six years older than the oldest Beatle, the band tended to view him rather as a nervous teacher trying to keep a class of unruly kids in order. When his business was a simple matter of getting The Beatles to gigs or recording sessions, there were no problems, but as their popularity spread, Brian found himself increasingly stretched. Although excellent as the band's manager, Brian's inexperience of big business soon became evident. He found that he had less and less time to deal with the details of the band's affairs. Moreover, under pressure, his business decisions were sometimes unwise: for instance, he signed away The Beatles' exclusive merchandising rights for a mere 10 percent, losing himself and the band a hefty fortune in as much time as it takes to give a signature.

Epstein and Lennon; manager and head Beatle talk business during rehearsals for a TV appearance.

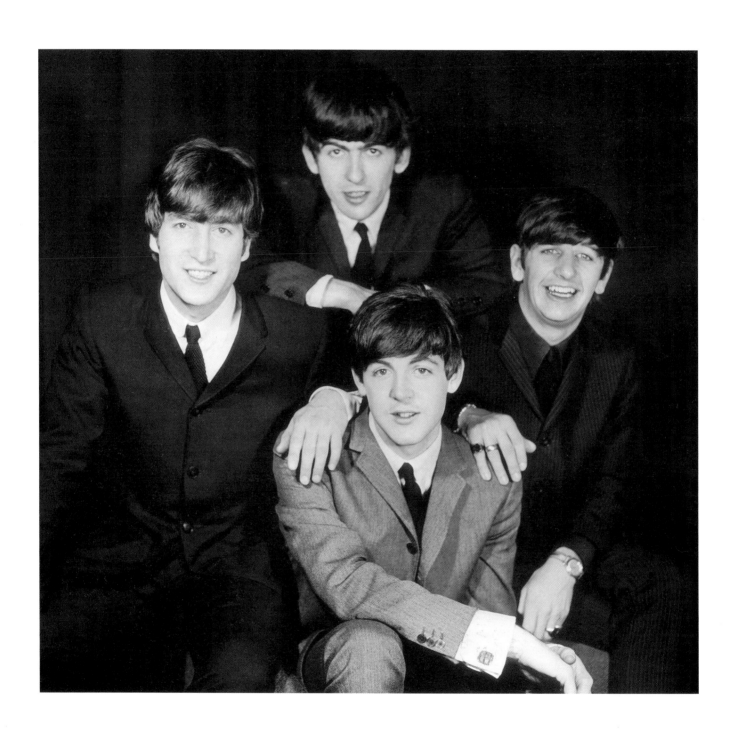

With The Beatles

In August 1963, with "She Loves You" at the top of the singles chart and *Please Please Me* outselling every other album in Britain, The Beatles took time out to record some new material for their second album. Once again, Abbey Road's Studio Two was the home for the sessions. This time the band was given the luxury of three days to finish the entire album. The group was now noticeably more at ease in the studio and John in particular was keen to learn about recording techniques, especially those, such as double-tracking, that could strengthen and improve the sound of his own voice.

Three months later, on November 30, The Beatles' debut album was finally dislodged from the top of the U.K. album charts. The new best-seller was their follow-up, *With The Beatles*, which had received advanced orders of more than a quarter of a million copies. The Beatles' first two albums set a precedent that no other artist has come close to matching: 50 consecutive weeks at the U.K. number 1 spot. *Please Please Me* held out at the top for an incredible 29 weeks, while *With The Beatles* notched up 21 weeks.

With The Beatles was a pioneering album, and the critics again noted the quality of Lennon and McCartney's songs. (Although many of their songs were solo compositions, they were contractually obliged to publish them jointly.) One song, John's "Not A Second Time," was singled out by William Mann, music critic of *The Times*. Mann compared the track to Mahler's "Song of the Earth," observing "One gets the impression that they think simultaneously of harmony and melody, so firmly are the major tonic sevenths and ninths built into their tunes, and the flat submediant key switches, so natural in the Aeolian cadences at the end ...." "I thought Aeolian cadences sounded like exotic birds," John quipped.

The album's cover also set it apart from other pop releases. Brian Epstein commissioned one of Britain's top fashion photographers, Robert Freeman, to provide a jacket image. Freeman produced four moody black-and-white portraits of The Beatles, each one half in shadow. The photographs were arranged on the four quarters of the jacket. In hindsight, the photographs were eerily reminiscent of some of the pictures taken of the five-piece Beatles by Astrid Kirchherr during the group's time in Hamburg.

The Beatles ended an unreal year with another big hit single. "I Want To Hold Your Hand" hit the U.K. top spot with advance orders of over one million copies. In just 12 months the group had stormed the British pop scene and media in a way never seen before or since. They had best-selling records, their haircuts had started a new fashion trend, and the press loved them. But the biggest challenge in Brian Epstein's game plan was still to be faced. As yet, The Beatles meant nothing in the U.S.

By the end of 1963 the Fab Four had become the biggest thing to ever hit the U.K. pop scene.

The Beatles are coming!

Why any American teenager would care about an English pop group was anyone's guess. Pop history offered little in the way of proof that they even knew there was a U.K. music scene at all. Skiffle had remained entirely a British phenomenon, while Cliff Richard and the Shadows, at one point the most popular group in the U.K., meant nothing across the Atlantic. After all, the U.S. had the king of rock and roll, Elvis Presley. They didn't need pallid English imitators such as Cliff, let alone his less successful peers Billy Fury or Marty Wilde. By the end of 1963, The Beatles had conquered their home country, but were far from confident about the chances of their success Stateside. "They've got everything over there," an apprehensive Ringo Starr told the *Liverpool Post*, "will they want us too?" First indications seemed to be that the U.S. didn't much want The Beatles at all.

The Beatles' British label, Parlophone, was part of the mighty EMI corporation that also owned Capitol, one of the biggest labels in the United States. It might have been assumed, therefore, that the mechanism for releasing The Beatles' records in the U.S. was already in place. However, in the days that preceded the "global village" of the modern entertainment industry, there was little in the way of international coordination between Capitol and EMI in the U.K. Capitol Records had heard The Beatles and didn't think much of them. In the end, Brian Epstein took the decision to place the group's first three U.K. hits on small independent labels in the U.S. The singles all sank without trace.

Things took a significant turn when Brian made his first visit to New York and played John and Paul's demo recording of "I Want To Hold Your Hand" to Capitol Records' executives at the company's offices. They remained unconvinced but, given the group's extraordinary success in the U.K., Capitol agreed to give The Beatles a chance.

Help for Brian's efforts to introduce The Beatles to America came from an unexpected source. Ed Sullivan had a nationwide television show that for the previous 10 years had launched many celebrities, including Elvis Presley, into the national consciousness. Whereas Capitol seemed unaware of the pandemonium that surrounded The Beatles in the U.K., Sullivan had experienced it firsthand when a flight he was on from London had been delayed by fans awaiting The Beatles' return from a European tour. Sullivan was impressed that a pop group could have such an impact and could see no reason why the same thing shouldn't be repeated across the Atlantic. He offered to book the group on two of his shows in February 1964. The Beatles' fee for the performance was $3,000. Although Brian was unaware of it at the time, this was a small figure, even for an unknown band. However, it turned out to be one of the most important steps in the band's career.

All set for the States: The Beatles and Brian Epstein at Heathrow Airport on February 7, 1964.

Beatles in the U.S.

The Beatles began 1964 with a low-key tour of France. On January 16, while they were in Paris, Brian Epstein received a telegram from Capitol Records in New York. After making steady progress in the lower reaches of the U.S. charts, "I Want To Hold Your Hand" had suddenly leaped from number 43 to the top position. Although now accustomed to breaking the pop rule book, The Beatles were stunned by the news. With their appearance on the *Ed Sullivan Show* booked for February, they hardly knew what to expect.

Across the Atlantic, a massive publicity campaign was being launched. Posters and windshield stickers everywhere proclaimed "The Beatles Are Coming." English businessman Nicky Byrne, who had bought the exclusive merchandising rights to The Beatles, set up an office in New York, determined to make the best of his new deal. Byrne wanted the band to arrive in a blaze of publicity and had planned his own campaign accordingly. He had thousands of T-shirts printed and took out adverts on prominent New York radio stations. The final touch was a tempting offer to New York's youth: any teenager who went to John F. Kennedy airport to greet The Beatles would receive a free T-shirt and a dollar bill.

The scenes that greeted Pan Am flight 101 as it arrived in New York on February 7 were unprecedented. As The Beatles began to climb down the steps from the plane, they were greeted by 5,000 screaming fans. A 100-man police cordon was called in to hold back the surging mass. At first the Fab Four could not believe that the reception was for them—they presumed the President must be landing. The group was immediately led to a press conference, to face a crowd of 200 New York journalists. Despite the chaos surrounding them, The Beatles fielded every question with their trademark sharp-witted humor. Exchanges were bright and friendly, with each of John's one-liners being met with laughter or even applause. The Beatles had made a good impression at their first meeting with the American public. When the questions were over, the Fabs were lifted into a chauffeur-driven Cadillac by two policemen and whisked off to their hotel, the Plaza, facing Central Park.

On Sunday, February 9, 1964, two days after their arrival, The Beatles gave their first performance on American soil, and in so doing effectively conquered the U.S. The chosen venue was Studio 50—The Ed Sullivan Theater. The show began at 8 p.m. with a dramatic announcement from Mr. Sullivan himself:

"Yesterday and today our theater has been jammed with newspapers and hundreds of photographers from all over the nation. These veterans agree with me that this city never has witnessed the excitement created by these four youngsters from Liverpool who call themselves The Beatles ... Ladies and Gentlemen, THE BEATLES."

Ed Sullivan tries out Paul's bass guitar at rehearsals for The Beatles' U.S. TV debut.

Storming the States

Before the end of Sullivan's introduction a massive scream erupted from the studio audience. Paul counted the band in and they launched into "All My Loving," quickly followed by their cover of "Till There Was You," and then "She Loves You." During their second song, the camera gave each of The Beatles an individual close-up, displaying his name on the screen. John's introduction came with an additional line of information: "Sorry girls, he's married." Later on in the hour-long program, they played "I Saw Her Standing There" and their U.S. chart-topper "I Want To Hold Your Hand."

The Beatles were thrilled by the crowd's reaction, but the pièce de résistance came after their first set. Sullivan held up a telegram from Elvis Presley sent by his manager Colonel Tom Parker, wishing them success on their first visit to America.

The program made television history. The Nielsen Ratings system calculated that the *Ed Sullivan Show* had been watched by 73 million people in 24 million households. This meant that more than 60 percent of all TV viewers in the U.S.—the world's largest TV audience—had tuned in to watch them play. At the end of their first U.S. jaunt, George Harrison commented: "Afterwards they told us that there was no reported crime. Even the criminals had a rest for 10 minutes while we were on."

Not everyone was convinced by the group, however. Ed Sullivan's musical director, Ed Block, saw nothing new in the Fab Four: "The only thing that's different is the hair, as far as I can see," he grouched to the *New York Times*. "I give them a year." Sullivan himself reprimanded Block for his comments.

While they were in the U.S., The Beatles also played a series of high-profile concerts at Washington's Coliseum and New York's famous Carnegie Hall. All met with the same rapturous response. After their Carnegie Hall appearance, U.S. promoter Sid Bernstein tried to secure The Beatles for an appearance at Madison Square Garden a few days later. Bernstein offered Brian Epstein $25,000 and a $5,000 donation to the British Cancer Fund, but Epstein declined, telling the promoter "Let's leave this for next time."

During February 1964 America became besotted with The Beatles. The early singles that had bombed on release were now being repromoted. By the beginning of April, the *Billboard* charts had been besieged by Britain's top group. Not content with holding numbers 1 and 2 in the album charts, The Beatles also had the top five best-selling singles in the U.S., as well as entries at 31, 41, 46, 58, 65, 68, and 79. That's 12 singles in the *Billboard* Hot 100. No artist in the history of popular music had come anywhere near this level of domination. And it's difficult to imagine that it could ever happen again.

The Beatles leave New York's Carnegie Hall after a triumphant performance on February 12, 1964.

And now the world

Having conquered the U.S., in June 1964 The Beatles took on the rest of the world, which succumbed to them as completely as the States had. Dates in Scandinavia were followed by a flight to East Asia and Australia. The chaotic scenes that greeted them were by now becoming familiar. On their flight from Hong Kong to Sydney, The Beatles made an unscheduled refueling stop at Darwin in the north of Australia. Here, even at 2 a.m., a crowd of 400 screaming fans appeared as if from nowhere to greet them.

In the middle of August, after spending a few days at Abbey Road recording tracks for another new album, The Beatles set off on their first major tour of the U.S. The reception awaiting them there was even more hysterical than before. When their plane touched down in San Francisco, they were met by 9,000 ecstatic fans and had to be transported from the airport in a massive iron crate for their own safety. On a more positive note, by now they were reaping the rewards of their unprecedented success and were able to move from city to city in a hired jet plane.

The band were already beginning to view their concerts as something of a joke—they were rarely able to hear themselves play above the constant screams of their fans, and their music suffered as a result. The situation began to affect John in particular. In the odd off-guard moment, the Beatle pleasantries would slip, and the cynical side of John Lennon emerged: "It wouldn't matter if I never sang. Often I don't anyway," he revealed in one interview. "I just stand there and make mouth movements .... I reckon we could send out four waxwork dummies of ourselves and that would satisfy the crowds. Beatles concerts are nothing to do with music anymore. They're just bloody tribal rites."

For the moment, all four Fabs were willing to play the game, but their lifestyle was becoming increasingly abnormal. Feted wherever they went, the group was showered with the kind of adulation more usually reserved for royalty, or gods. As George Martin recalled, "in some places they'd wheel in paraplegics who were brought in to touch them—it was like Jesus, almost." Their private lives were nonexistent and the four young men began to feel more and more like prisoners of their own success: "The only place we ever had any peace was when we got back to the hotel suite, and went to the bathroom!" George Harrison recalled, somewhat ruefully, when the tour was over.

The Beatles stayed in the U.S. for just over a month. They played 25 dates in 34 days in 24 cities, created havoc, and then went home. With only enough time to slot in overdubs for the new album and to record a new A-side, their phenomenal workload continued with another major British tour. Sustaining Beatlemania was proving to be a full-time job.

The eye of the hurricane: The Beatles and Brian Epstein savor a rare moment of peace, 1964.

A Hard Day's Night

By 1964 The Beatles were pop music's biggest act, but Brian Epstein was already preparing the next phase of his master plan. He felt that the time was now right for The Beatles to hit the silver screen, and quickly agreed a three-film deal with the United Artists company.

The working title for The Beatles' debut film, "Beatlemania," was later dropped in favor of "A Hard Day's Night"—one of Ringo's many idiosyncratic phrases. Director Richard Lester was given the task of transferring the group's knockabout humor to the big screen. John Lennon in particular was pleased with the choice—the director's best-known work so far had been an 11-minute feature entitled *The Running, Jumping And Standing Still Film* (1959), featuring Spike Milligan and Peter Sellers, two of John's radio heroes, from *The Goon Show*. The film script was written by Alun Owen, a playwright with a reputation based on a series of gritty TV dramas set in Liverpool.

The storyline was a simple one. The Beatles were to play themselves in a series of scenarios that mimicked incidents in their own hectic lives. *A Hard Day's Night* included many aspects of The Beatles' inimitable style, such as their familiar press conference wisecracks and Marx Brothers-like clowning. The film skillfully created the impression that audiences were seeing The Beatles making the whole thing up as they went along. In reality, the film was tightly scripted and John fought hard to get his own contributions included: "We were a bit infuriated by the glibness of the dialog and we were always trying to get it more realistic, but they [Lester and Owen] wouldn't have it," he complained later.

Both before and since The Beatles, most films built around pop stars have been something of a letdown—witness Elvis Presley's string of movies, which after a promising start degenerated into formulaic flops. By contrast, *A Hard Day's Night* proved to be both a critical winner and an international hit, earning $14 million on its first release. A number of foreign-language versions of the film went out under alternative titles. In Germany, where The Beatles had enjoyed two hits in translation—"Komm, Gib Mir Deine Hand" and "Sie Liebt Dich"—the film was issued as *Yeah Yeah Yeah, Die Beatles*. Italians saw the film as *Tutti Per Uno*, and the French as *Quatre Garçons Dans Le Vent*.

Accompanying the film was the inevitable soundtrack album, which this time featured The Beatles' first set of entirely self-penned numbers. It was clear that John in particular was finding a more serious voice as a songwriter. Widely perceived as the band's leader, he was largely responsible for seven of the eight new numbers. The album *A Hard Day's Night* and the single of the same name sold in vast quantities the world over, while the film's success suggested that The Beatles might become significant as more than just a pop group.

Man in the mirror: John meets John in a reflective moment from *A Hard Day's Night*, 1964.

Meeting Bob Dylan

The Beatles became a global phenomenon in 1964. However, the exhausting lifestyle that they now led was beginning to tell on their music. The year ended with a new album—*Beatles For Sale*—which many critics regarded as something of a disappointment. John and Paul didn't have enough high-quality original material for the LP and so reverted to filling the holes with cover versions.

John's contributions to *Beatles For Sale* revealed a darker side to his writing. This can be heard clearly in the album's three opening tracks: "No Reply," "I'm A Loser," and "Baby's In Black." The pressure of Beatlemania was beginning to tell.

A new influence was detectable in some of the songs on *Beatles For Sale*. The Beatles had their introduction to the music of Bob Dylan when they first hit the U.S., and he made a big impact on them. John remembered their initial meeting, on August 28, 1964, at New York's Delmonico Hotel: "He was always saying 'Listen to the words, man' and I said 'I can't be bothered. I listen to the overall sound.'" But John was the first to admit that Dylan had helped him to think more seriously about his lyrics. John had always thought of himself as something of a wordsmith, but in his eyes Dylan was in a league of his own. This was to be the start of what John himself called his "Dylan period," during which his songs became more introspective. His singing voice even acquired something of Dylan's nasal whine.

The meeting with Dylan was to have further consequences. It was he who introduced The Beatles to marijuana—a drug that hadn't made much of an impact in Britain thus far. Ironically, Dylan had taken The Beatles' breakthrough U.S. single, "I Want To Hold Your Hand," as proof that the Fab Four were already hip to joints. He had misheard the lines "I can't hide, I can't hide" and thought The Beatles were singing "I get high, I get high." After Dylan gave The Beatles their first taste of marijuana, John developed an appetite for any substance that might provide an altered state, boost his creativity, or—when he felt the need—obliterate the pressure of being a Beatle. Shortly afterward, the hallucinogenic drug lysergic acid diethylamide, better known as LSD, was to make a major impression on him; its influence can be heard in much of The Beatles' later music, especially their crowning glory, *Sgt. Pepper's Lonely Hearts Club Band*.

John's wife Cynthia had little interest in sharing her husband's new pursuits. Indeed, to her mind, drugs played a big part in the subsequent breakup of their marriage. "We were on different mental planes," she later reflected. "John's thoughts would always be more expansive than mine ... he kept saying that on his trips he was seeing beautiful things."

Folk troubadour Bob Dylan in 1964. His groundbreaking approach to lyrics made a major impact on John Lennon, whose songwriting fell heavily under the influence of Dylan in the mid-1960s.

Second thoughts

Nineteen sixty-five was to be a year of transition for the group. The Beatlemania frenzy that had characterized the previous two years was beginning to slow down. As far as the group's manager was concerned, though, there was to be no letting up. The coming year was to include another major tour of the U.S. as well as a second feature film. However, for the first time in the band's career, The Beatles themselves were beginning to have second thoughts about the whole business and to wonder how they might break the unrelenting treadmill of new albums followed by grueling tours.

The Beatles had paid their dues as a live band in Hamburg and Liverpool, and when the first wave of Beatlemania broke, they initially enjoyed the experience. After all, they'd earned the adulation. However, by mid-1965 they had lost their enthusiasm for live performances. Whereas once they had been proud of being a tight, accomplished band, nowadays all they could hear when they performed was the incessant screaming of the audience. As The Beatles began to take less of an interest in playing live music, the quality of their onstage performances began to deteriorate. Ringo took to drumming on the offbeat, to keep himself interested. John, who had always jokingly told the screaming fans to "Shaddup!," was more inclined to yell obscenities at the audience when he was away from the concert microphone.

Behind closed doors, The Beatles all agreed that changes were needed. They wanted to reduce the amount of time they toured; significantly, they wanted to devise more time for songwriting and recording. The Beatles had been studio novices when they first met George Martin. Now, over two years later, they were comfortable enough at Abbey Road Studios to want to experiment at greater length with the possibilities of recording. These seeds of discontent would soon transform The Beatles from mere teen idols into, arguably, the greatest artists in the history of popular music.

When he wasn't on the road, John settled into "Kenwood," his newly acquired mock-Tudor mansion in Surrey, with Cynthia and his young son Julian. Although to the public he was the most controversial and provocative Beatle, John was a home bird at heart, happy lounging on a sofa watching TV, reading, or listening to records. In reality, he was feeling more uncomfortable with Beatlemania than the others. He began to lose interest in his public persona and started putting on weight, developing a puffy roundness to his face. At first Cynthia interpreted this as a sign of domestic contentment, but even though he seemed to have the world at his feet, John Lennon was not happy with his life. His feelings were summed up neatly in a new song he'd just written—"Help!"

The Beatles' second U.S. tour, 1965—despite the smile, Beatlemania was starting to wear John down.

Help!

A Hard Day's Night had proved to be more successful—both commercially and artistically—than anyone involved in the film could have hoped for. But The Beatles' next movie, *Help!*, was to be a much less satisfying experience.

Richard Lester was once again at the helm, and a new scriptwriter—the highly rated Marc Behm—was brought in. But unlike *A Hard Day's Night* author Alun Owen, Behm had little understanding of The Beatles' native scouse humor. What he produced may have been funny in its own right, but it failed to capture the essence of the band's laconic in-jokes.

Above: Filming *Help!* in Austria, March 1965.

The plot centers on a religious cult that discovers a sacrificial ring has gone missing—in fact, it has been sent to Ringo by a fan. Ringo is unable to remove the ring from his finger and so The Beatles are pursued for the rest of the film by members of the cult, who seek to recapture the ring, by fair means or foul.

The Beatles acquitted themselves capably enough, their relaxed performances doubtless influenced by their habit of sneaking off for a quick joint between takes. But as far as John was concerned, "*Help!* was a drag, because we didn't know what was happening ... we were on pot by then and all the best stuff is on the cutting-room floor, with us breaking up all over the place." On another occasion he declared that the film was "just bullshit."

Help! was The Beatles' last feature film—at least, the last in which they acted. Contractually tied to a third film, Brian Epstein commissioned a script from British playwright Joe Orton, at the time the toast of London for scandalous comedies such as *Loot* and *Entertaining Mr. Sloane.* The project failed to get off the ground, as much due to The Beatles' refusal to drag themselves through the filmmaking process one more time as to any problems with the script itself, although the latter was sexually and politically controversial. After Orton's violent death in 1967, the script was published as *Up Against It.*

The U.K. album that accompanied *Help!* was structured so that only the first side featured songs used in the film. The LP featured two multimillion-selling singles, the title track and John's memorable "Ticket To Ride," a song he subsequently described as "one of the earliest heavy metal records ever made." Among the lesser fare on the flip side sat Paul McCartney's "Yesterday." Although the latter was not released as a single in Britain at the time, it has since become one of The Beatles' most famous songs, ending up as the most recorded song of the twentieth century.

Opposite: The Beatles in a promotional film for their single "Help!," 1965.

Man of words

John had always been interested in creative writing. Even in the bottom-stream English class at Quarry Bank, he amused himself with his own nonsense verse and short stories that were kept in an exercise book he called the "Daily Howl." In Liverpool, as the pop scene and The Beatles were taking off, his poems, spoof personal ads, and musings were often published in the city's own music paper, *Mersey Beat.*

By 1965, John had forged a reputation as the Beatle who gave his group an edge. At press conferences all four were lively and sharp-witted, but John was always prepared to go one step further, his statements shot through with a bluntness rare in pop stars of the mid-1960s:

"I don't suppose I think much about the future. I don't really give a damn. It's selfish but I don't care too much for humanity."

"I get spasms of being intellectual. I read a bit about politics but I don't think I'd vote for anyone. No message from any of those phony politicians is coming through to me."

Above: A page from John's notebook, the "Daily Howl."

At the height of The Beatles' fame, John produced two books of his own poetry, prose, and doodles; both became best-sellers, enhancing his status as the "intellectual" Beatle. The inventive wordplay of *In His Own Write*, published in March 1964, was inspired by The Goons, Lewis Carroll, and the English linguistic comedian "Professor" Stanley Unwin, who made a career out of spouting indecipherable gobbledygook. *The Times Literary Supplement* called it "Worth the attention of anyone who fears the impoverishment of the English language and the British imagination." The follow-up, *A Spaniard In The Works*, was published the following year and was a more considered collection. Whereas John's debut had been a compilation of pieces created for his own amusement, the second was written to order. Once again, however, his sense of the ridiculous was well to the fore, with stories such as "Snore Wife and Some Several Dwarts" and his "Last Will and Testicle."

John's approach to writing echoed that of his attitude to making music. He summed it up in an interview for BBC radio's *World Of Books* program: "publishers sometimes say 'Should we leave this out or change that?' And I fight like mad because once I've done it, I like to keep it ... I seldom take something out, so it's spontaneous."

Opposite: The Beatles are apparently divided over the literary merits of *In His Own Write*.

Fame and fortune

Wealth and fame brought about enormous changes for The Beatles. They were all now millionaires. John and Ringo both had mansions in southeast England, where most of their neighbors were lawyers, stockbrokers, and businessmen. George bought a bungalow in a similar area. Only Paul broke the pattern, keeping a London base by buying a property in St. John's Wood, a few minutes' walk from the Abbey Road studios.

On the whole, John adapted easily to the upmarket lifestyle. His home on St. George's Hill in Weybridge was a genuine pop star's mansion, complete with swimming pool. Parked outside was a Rolls-Royce fitted with tinted black windows. The interior decoration at Kenwood reflected both John's wealth and his unorthodoxy, with rooms lined in purple velvet, as well as one painted in bizarre stripes of pink and green. On one wall hung two pictures by his old friend Stuart Sutcliffe.

John enjoyed using his wealth to indulge himself, and others too, gaining a reputation as an extremely generous tipper in restaurants and clubs. However, he occasionally worried that he was never able to tell how much money he was really worth, and that he might be overspending. At one point, concerned that he'd been too extravagant on his car collection, he put his Mini and Ferrari up for sale—"Then one of the accountants said I was all right, so I got the cars back from the showroom."

However, the extent of The Beatles' success still occasionally caught even them by surprise. After their conquest of the U.S., Liverpool's four most famous sons were given a civic reception at the city's Town Hall. When The Beatles arrived, John was stunned to find that 100,000 screaming fans had turned out to greet them. Returning secretly to see his Aunt Mimi, he was horrified to discover that Mendips—his childhood home—was now a shrine, sought out by fans and journalists from across the globe. His aunt no longer had any privacy whatsoever: "I kept changing the phone number, but the fans would keep discovering the new one within a few days," she remembered years later.

Eventually, John invited Mimi to stay with him at Kenwood and told her that he wanted to buy her a new home. He asked her where she wanted to live; the first place that came into her head was Bournemouth, on the south coast of England. That same morning, John and Mimi set off in his chauffeur-driven Rolls-Royce to visit properties in the area and within hours he had bought her a bungalow overlooking Poole Harbour. He gave her a plaque to put on the wall, inscribed with her old warning to him: "The guitar's all very well, John, but you'll never make a living out of it."

As well as a Rolls-Royce, John already owned a Ferrari and a black Mini Cooper before he passed his driving test on February 15, 1965. Cars were always to be a major passion in his life.

The new "establishment"

Each year, the Queen of England's official birthday is accompanied by an announcement of those Britons who are to receive knighthoods and other honors. Typically, the list of recipients includes military men, politicians, civil servants, and businessmen. However, in 1965, four unlikely awardees were singled out for attention. Each of The Beatles was to receive the MBE—The Membership of the Most Excellent Order of the British Empire.

The popular press approved the decision—"She Loves Them, Yeah! Yeah! Yeah!" ran a *Daily Mirror* headline. Other members of British society, however, were less enthusiastic about the announcement. One military hero, Colonel Frederick Wagg, was furious at the award. In his anger he returned 12 of his medals, resigned from the Labour Party (Labour prime minister Harold Wilson was responsible for suggesting to Her Majesty that The Beatles receive the awards), and canceled a large contribution to party funds. Ex-RAF squadron leader Paul Pearson returned his MBE "because it had become debased."

The Beatles themselves were rather baffled by the award. "I thought you had to drive tanks and win wars to get an MBE," a bemused John Lennon confessed. But he was clearly irritated by the protesters. As far as he was concerned, army officers were given the award for killing people: "We got ours for entertaining. On balance I'd say we deserve ours more."

Lennon remained ambivalent about the award: "Taking the MBE was a sellout for me," he later admitted. "Before you get an MBE the Palace writes to you to ask if you're going to accept it, because you're not supposed to reject it publicly .... Brian and a few other people persuaded me that it was in our interests to take it ... but I'm glad, really, that I did accept it because it meant that four years later I could use it to make a gesture." (In 1969 he would return the medal as, among other things, a protest at British foreign policy.)

The Beatles' investiture took place at Buckingham Palace on October 26, 1965. Outside Buckingham Palace 4,000 screaming fans were held back by the police. After the ceremony The Beatles displayed their silver crosses to the press. Paul said that the Queen was "very friendly. She was like a mum to us," and that the Palace was a "keen pad."

In 1970, during an interview with French magazine *L'Express*, John claimed that The Beatles had all smoked marijuana in the toilets of Buckingham Palace before the ceremony—an episode that the other three have always strenuously denied.

Opposite: The Beatles receive their MBEs—October 26, 1965.
Right: Storming the gates. The Beatles' investiture provoked frantic scenes outside Buckingham Palace.

Back in the U.S.

A matter of days after the premiere of *Help!* The Beatles returned to the United States for the third time. Although they were only away for two weeks, and their departures and arrivals were now creating slightly less havoc, it was still an arduous ordeal.

The first date, Sunday, August 15, took place at the William A. Shea Municipal Stadium, home of the New York Mets baseball team. Since both the concert and surrounding events were being filmed for a TV documentary, the producers planned to make the band's entrance as dramatic as possible. The original idea was to have the band flown into the stadium by helicopter, but the authorities saw this as potentially dangerous. Instead, the Fab Four rode in a limousine from their hotel to a helipad along the Hudson River. From there they were flown to the site of the World's Fair, in Queens, not far from the stadium. They completed their journey in a Wells Fargo armored truck. At 9:16 p.m.—to the deafening screams of over 55,000 fans—The Beatles entered the arena by running through the players' tunnel, climbed the steps onto the stage, plugged in their guitars, and launched into the opening riff of "Twist And Shout." Seemingly swept along by the spectacle, The Beatles gave one of their most powerfully energetic performances ever that night. The resulting film of the occasion, *The Beatles At Shea Stadium*, is a unique record not only of The Beatles performing some of their greatest hits, but also of the very essence of Beatlemania.

The Shea Stadium concert represented the pinnacle of The Beatles' popularity as performers and the statistics surrounding their appearance were a catalog of superlatives. The crowd of 55,600 fans was at that time the largest ever assembled for a concert. The box-office receipts, $304,000, were the highest yet taken and the band's own share of the takings, $160,000, was the most any artist had earned for a single concert.

Unsurprisingly, the remainder of the tour lacked the zest of that opening triumph. John in particular had begun to hate touring. It didn't matter where in the world The Beatles went, they were now far too famous to travel as ordinary citizens. The routine was always the same: airport; police convoy; hotel room; police convoy; stadium; police convoy; hotel room; police convoy; airport. As John later observed: "The bigger we got, the more unreality we had to face, and the more you were expected to do."

There was also the very real danger that they would be physically harmed. Arriving in Houston at 2 a.m. on August 18, The Beatles' airplane was surrounded by fans as it taxied in. The fans clambered onto the plane to be near their heroes; some were even smoking next to the plane's fuel tanks. And every new city brought more of the same madness.

The Beatles' appearance at Shea Stadium in 1965 saw them play to the largest audience that had ever gathered for a pop concert up to that time.

A new sophistication

After their latest conquest of the States, The Beatles were allowed the luxury of a six-week holiday. Although George and Ringo were able to get away for a bit, the break was not as relaxing for John and Paul. Less inclined than ever to compose new material during their U.S. tour, they now found themselves with another album to write.

The result was the transitional *Rubber Soul*. As George Martin observed: "It was the first album to present a new, growing Beatles to the world." It also clearly showcased the diverging talents of the band's creative axis. Paul McCartney had now become a classic tunesmith in his own right, but it was John who seemed to be making the more interesting moves. Compositions such as "Norwegian Wood (This Bird Has Flown)" were evidence of his continuing fascination with Bob Dylan, featuring strummed acoustic guitars and increasingly personal lyrics. Few people realized quite how personal they were: "I was trying to write about an affair without letting me [sic] wife know," he later confessed, discussing "Norwegian Wood." "I was sort of writing it from my own experiences, girls' flats, things like that." Similarly, on "Nowhere Man," with its rich vocal harmonies and sophisticated arrangement, John's lyrics speak volumes about the boredom, lack of direction, and lack of faith that were increasingly creeping into his life. Songs such as "Girl" and "Run For Your Life" attracted much critical flak for their supposed misogyny, an accusation that John was to spend many years trying to shake off. The album also featured one of his very best songs—the wonderfully understated "In My Life"—in which he reflected fondly on past loves and friends. George Martin added a harpsichordlike keyboard solo in the middle, providing the song with an unexpected but memorable twist.

Rubber Soul was also notable in that it featured no album "filler." All the songs were strong, most were innovative in their use of instrumentation or in their structure, and there were no cover versions or previously released tracks. Brian Wilson of The Beach Boys was so impressed with the high standard maintained throughout the record that he set about creating his own filler-free LP, and came up with *Pet Sounds*, generally regarded as The Beach Boys' masterpiece and one of the finest pop albums of all time.

Years later, John saw *Rubber Soul* as a crucial stage in The Beatles' development, arguing that both technically and musically they felt themselves to be improving, until at last they became the dominant force in the studio: "In the early days we had to take what we were given ... we were learning the techniques on *Rubber Soul*. We were more precise about making that album, and we took over the cover and everything ...." The Beatles were taking pop music and making an art form out of it.

By 1965 The Beatles were no longer merely teen pin-ups; they had become pop pioneers.

3 From Pop to Art

With the release of *Revolver* in 1966, The Beatles reach a
new peak of creativity. For the first time, critics begin treating
the work of a pop group as serious art. It is the start of an
unprecedented string of definitive recordings that include
Sgt. Pepper's Lonely Hearts Club Band—still viewed by many
as the greatest album of all time.

Serious young men

Although they were only in their mid-twenties, the four Beatles had experienced three chaotic years of unrivaled success. And just a passing glance at the cover of *Rubber Soul* was enough to see that changes were in the air. Photographed through a then fashionable "fish-eye" lens, the happy-go-lucky mop tops of old had become four serious-looking young men, unsmiling, and coolly decked out in suede. The pressure to keep on supplying the product was visibly taking its toll.

Nevertheless, 1965 ended in triumph for the group. On the same day that *Rubber Soul* was released, a classic, double A-sided single emerged: John's "Day Tripper" backed with Paul's "We Can Work It Out"—unusually, neither track appeared on the album. The title of the former was a knowing reference to those who were not as initiated into drug culture as The Beatles and their peers—a "Sunday driver" by another name. "We Can Work It Out" was primarily Paul's work, though John supplied the world-weary middle eight of "Life is very short" as a complement to his partner's upbeat, optimistic sentiments in the rest of the song. To satisfy the expected demand in the U.K., EMI pressed 750,000 copies of the record.

As was now traditional, both single and album leaped straight to the number 1 spot on both sides of the Atlantic. Furthermore, *Rubber Soul* scored unanimous critical acclaim from the serious music press. In America, the album broke all sales records, selling 1.2 million copies within the first nine days of its release. Beatlemania may have been on the wane, but the fans were still queuing up outside the record stores and The Beatles seemed to be able to effortlessly combine commercial success with critical acclaim—a rare achievement.

Of course, it was hardly exceptional for a group of teenage idols to want to produce work of greater sophistication as they matured. More often than not, however, such moves resulted in derision from music critics and the alienation of the group's audiences. As in so much else, The Beatles were to prove a significant exception to the rule. The widespread critical praise heaped on *Rubber Soul* gave the group vital encouragement and the confidence to expand their music into uncharted territories. The group's music was growing up and, if sales were anything to go by, the fans were growing with it. The Beatles were now beginning to appeal to a wider, more culturally aware audience.

Significantly, the day "We Can Work It Out"/"Day Tripper" and *Rubber Soul* were released in the U.K., the group began their last British tour. More than ever, the four Beatles were now convinced that it was the recording studio, rather than the stage, on which their future triumphs would depend. *Rubber Soul* proved to be the first in a run of classic albums that no other band has come close to matching.

John Lennon in the mid-1960s, when The Beatles abandoned the stage for the recording studio.

Bigger than Jesus?

The first half of 1966 was relatively quiet by Beatle standards. Much of the time was spent in the studio working on a follow-up to the massively successful *Rubber Soul*. In July 1966, however, John Lennon hit the news headlines as never before. And this time the publicity had nothing to do with his music.

Six months earlier, John had given an interview to the *London Evening Standard*'s Maureen Cleave, a long-standing friend of The Beatles. During their conversation, John talked openly about his views on organized religion, remarking: "Christianity will go. It will vanish and shrink. I needn't argue with that …. We're more popular than Jesus now." The interview was published in January 1966, to little reaction from the British public.

The problems started when an American teenage magazine, *Datebook*, bought Maureen Cleave's interview and published John's comments under the banner "I don't know which will go first—rock and roll or Christianity." His quote caused an uproar that quickly swept through the United States. Stoked by support from the right-wing Christian lobby, thousands of American church-goers were encouraged to take matters into their own hands. Radio station after radio station—and not just those in the traditional Bible Belt—banned The Beatles' music. In addition, many right-wing churches organized public burnings of Beatle records and magazines featuring the group.

Arriving in the States at the start of August for what no one at the time realized would be their final tour, The Beatles held a press conference as usual. This time, however, the assembled journalists had only one question to ask. John explained what he had meant by his comments several times over, but the press simply wanted to know whether the head Beatle was prepared to retract his words. Looking pale and harried, John set about trying to put his words into some kind of context:

"I'm not anti-God, anti-Christ, or antireligion," he stressed. "I was not saying we are greater or better … I said 'Beatles' because it's easy for me to talk about Beatles. I could have said 'TV' or 'the cinema' or anything popular and I would have got away with it." Clearly the wave of anger aroused by his comments had shocked the usually cocky Lennon. With as much good grace as he could summon, he finally conceded "I'm sorry I said it."

A British interviewer later asked John why he'd chosen to make an apology when he'd clearly said nothing wrong. "If I were at the stage I was five years ago I would have shouted 'We'll never tour again' and packed myself off—Lord knows, I don't need the money," he replied. "But the record burning? That was a real shock. I couldn't go away knowing I'd created another little place of hate in the world … not when I could do something about it."

Teenagers from Jackson, Mississippi, engage in a "ban The Beatles" bonfire, fall 1966.

Revolver

August 1966 saw another milestone for The Beatles, with the release of *Revolver*. Earlier in the year, they had spent three months working on the album at Abbey Road. These days, of course, it can take some artists that long to make a single, but in 1966 such an approach was practically unheard of. Nevertheless, it was time well spent. *Revolver* represented an incredible leap forward from the songs the band had produced just a few years earlier.

As a part of the London "scene," The Beatles now moved in sophisticated circles, and their outlook had changed. "We've all got interested in things that never used to occur to us," Paul McCartney revealed in an interview earlier that year. So it was that under the influence of the fledgling hippy underground, LSD, electronic music, experimental cinema, and the avant-garde art scene, The Beatles' music took a new direction.

Revolver was full of experimentation. Many of the songs were actually "created" in the studio, the recording process itself shaping the final compositions—witness the tape loops used in John's psychedelic masterpiece "Tomorrow Never Knows." Little thought was given to how a four-piece beat group might perform the songs in concert: McCartney's "Eleanor Rigby," one of the album's many highlights, consists only of voices and a string quartet.

And the songs themselves had changed, both in subject matter and form. As writers, Lennon and McCartney were now producing music for a whole new audience—hip, culturally aware young people, no longer just screaming teenage girls. "Dr. Robert" was an in-joke reference to the physician who had given an unknowing George and John their first taste of LSD, while "Love You To" revealed George's burgeoning interest in Indian music. "Taxman," featuring a scorching raga-style solo from Paul, satirized the Labour government's tax policies. And John and Paul still found time to write one of the most popular children's songs of all time, "Yellow Submarine," for Ringo to sing.

Revolver also saw the birth of the idea of an album as a coherent body of work, not just a selection of songs randomly thrown together. The world now readily accepts the idea of pop music as an art form, but *Revolver* was perhaps the first album by a pop group to be regarded as such. And with its release, The Beatles took pop music into uncharted territory.

In spite of the album's experimentation, there were still more than enough fans to take *Revolver* straight to the number 1 spot, both in Britain and the United States. It went on to sell well over 2 million copies during that year and its reputation continues to grow with time. As new generations discover The Beatles, it is most often *Revolver* to which they respond most warmly. Indeed, in 1995, readers of British music magazine *Q* voted it the best album ever made; many who voted were not even born when the album was released.

John and George take time out from recording at Abbey Road to pose for the cameras, May 1966.

End of the road

The summer of 1966 saw The Beatles give their last paid public performances. Although by now Brian Epstein had realized that they had increasingly little interest in touring, he nevertheless committed them to a series of concerts around the world. Among these were the band's only dates in East Asia.

The reaction from their Japanese fans came as quite a shock to all four Beatles—they experienced something approaching delayed Beatlemania there. They were greeted at Tokyo airport by 1,500 ecstatic fans, but were shocked at the heavy-handed treatment meted out by a Japanese police force unused to such wild behavior from their teenagers. A total of 35,000 security guards were employed throughout The Beatles' three-day trip. Each of their shows at the Nippon Budokan was attended by an audience of 10,000 fans, and manned by 3,000 police officers. Throughout their stay in Japan, The Beatles were "imprisoned" in their luxury suite at the Tokyo Hilton. Armed police guards stood by every possible entrance. Bad though it was, there was worse to come.

On Sunday, July 3, The Beatles flew on to play two shows in Manila, the capital city of the Philippines. Newspapers widely reported that President Ferdinand Marcos and his family were to be guests of honor at the concerts, and that The Beatles would be invited to their palace the following morning. Unfortunately, nobody had informed the group of these arrangements. When a government official arrived at The Beatles' hotel to pick them up, he was told by Brian Epstein that they were sleeping and that under no circumstances could they be disturbed. This was reported by the local media as a deliberate snub. Chaos ensued. Both The Beatles' hotel and the British Embassy were inundated with bomb threats. In trying to leave the country, The Beatles' entourage faced every form of delay that petty bureaucracy could conceive. When the controversy first broke, President Marcos had all official security withdrawn and as The Beatles made their way through the airport to board their plane, they were kicked, spat at, and jostled by angry Filipinos. In retrospect, the violence of the reaction and the condemnation of the group in the local press may not have been entirely unconnected with the fact that Marcos was a ruthless dictator. It would be an unwise subject indeed who failed to rally to the flag under such circumstances.

Compared to the Philippines, the U.S. tour that took place the following month was a breeze. But it was increasingly difficult for the band to find the enthusiasm to play their famous hits; they didn't even bother to rehearse for the tour. On August 29, at San Francisco's Candlestick Park, The Beatles shuffled off stage having played a 33-minute set to the usual ecstatic reaction. They would never set foot on another stage together again.

Back in the U.K. after their tour, John sounds off about the group's treatment in Manila, July 1966.

An actor's life

When The Beatles returned to London from the States in August 1966, everyone—Brian included—knew that from then on things were going to be different. With the highly acclaimed *Revolver* at the top of the charts, they decided to take a break from being Beatles. There were no plans to record any new material for at least three months.

John spent a lot of time away from the other members of the band, most of it at Kenwood with Cynthia and Julian. His wife observed a less strident manner about him following the end of the tour, and interpreted John's mood as contentment at winning the battle for The Beatles' future direction.

The chief Beatle was by no means idle throughout this period, though. In spite of his reservations about *Help!*, John had remained friends with the American director Richard Lester. With a break in his schedule, Lester offered John a role alongside Michael Crawford in his new film, *How I Won The War*. Although he had no illusions about his talents as an actor, John couldn't resist the idea of a solo film role: "I was flattered at being asked," he confessed later. "The ego needed feeding, with The Beatles at a kind of crossroads."

The film was a cynical antiwar black comedy set during World War II, a theme that appealed greatly to John. To play his character—Private Gripweed—John had to make a few significant changes to his appearance. His Beatle mop was shorn in the British military style and he adopted National Health "granny glasses." Although he did not keep the shorter hairstyle, the specs stayed with him, creating yet another Beatle-inspired fashion.

Shooting took place in Germany and Spain. John was alone most of the time, but broke with tradition when he invited Cynthia to stay. In early October, Ringo and his wife Maureen also flew out to Spain to visit him. But although the experience of acting without the other Beatles had been a novelty, John felt little enthusiasm for the project. "The thing I remember is Dick Lester had more fun than I did," he later commented.

After completing work on the film, John opted to try his hand at TV, appearing in Peter Cook and Dudley Moore's satirical sketch show *Not Only ... But Also*. Lennon was a good friend of Cook, and had already appeared on the show the previous year, reading excerpts from *In His Own Write*. This time he appeared in a comedy sketch as the concierge of a public convenience, still wearing his "granny glasses."

Opposite: A shorn, bespectacled John on location in Almeria, Spain, 1966.

Right: John joins Peter Cook (far left) in a sketch from *Not Only ... But Also*.

Let me take you down ...

The Beatles resumed business on Thursday, November 24, with George Martin at the controls in Studio Two of Abbey Road. They would spend much of the remainder of 1966 recording just one song. While on location with Richard Lester, John had written a song that harked back to his childhood. It was named after a Salvation Army children's home in Liverpool just around the corner from Aunt Mimi's house—Strawberry Field.

"Strawberry Fields Forever" was the most complex recording The Beatles had ever attempted and required George Martin to bring new techniques to his armory of production skills. The song was originally written as an acoustic ballad, but as its arrangement evolved, it took on a much heavier tone, reminiscent of bands that were emerging from San Francisco at the time, such as the Jefferson Airplane. After a break of a few weeks, and worried that the song may have moved too far away from his original idea, John suggested an alternative version and asked George Martin to come up with some orchestral arrangements.

Ultimately, John liked both finished versions and asked Martin if there was any way the two versions could be combined. Since the tuning and tempo of each track were slightly different the prospects of successfully "splicing" them together seemed remote. Nonetheless, when Martin's engineer Geoff Emerick tried he was amazed to find that by speeding up the first version and slowing down the second, both tuning and tempo matched perfectly.

"Strawberry Fields Forever" came out in February 1967 backed by another classic, "Penny Lane"—Paul McCartney's own paean to a part of Liverpool familiar to all four Beatles. Both songs were intended to be part of an ambitious album concept, linked by songs inspired by the band's childhood. However, under pressure from EMI to release a new single, the two tracks were plucked from the album sessions and released as a double A-sided single.

Critical acclaim for the two tracks was taken as evidence of The Beatles' astounding artistic development. Over the years, "Strawberry Fields Forever" has grown in stature, and for many it stands as the greatest seven-inch single ever produced. The group also recorded a short promotional film for both songs, an early video in effect, incorporating color negative images and backward-running film. The combination of music and visuals remains electrifying, concisely evoking the psychedelic era.

Ironically, in spite of the lofty pronouncements of the music literati, "Strawberry Fields Forever" became the first Beatles single in almost five years *not* to top the U.K. charts. It stalled at number 2, behind "Release Me," a schmaltzy ballad by cabaret singer Engelbert Humperdinck. In the States, however, Humperdinck's track stalled at number 4, while "Penny Lane" topped the charts; "Strawberry Fields Forever" reached number 8 separately.

A mustachioed John during filming for the "Strawberry Fields Forever" promo film, January 1967.

Sgt. Pepper

For the first four months of 1967, The Beatles worked solidly in Abbey Road's Studio Two. Throughout this time they meticulously crafted what is arguably the most influential album in the history of popular music—*Sgt. Pepper's Lonely Hearts Club Band*. The record was conclusive proof of a supremely confident group working at the peak of its creative powers.

Continuing The Beatles' desire to produce a cohesive body of music, *Sgt. Pepper* is a concept album of sorts. It was Paul McCartney who came up with the idea of creating a mythical band: "Why don't we make the whole album as though the Pepper band really existed, as though Sgt. Pepper was doing the record?" he suggested.

The album took a total of five months and 700 hours of studio time to record. It cost £25,000 (approximately $37,000)—an unprecedented figure by 1967 standards. But the music throughout reveals a complexity never before heard on a pop album. *Sgt. Pepper* was rapidly lauded as a new benchmark in modern music.

The high point of the album was the closing track, "A Day In The Life." Unlike many of The Beatles' songs over the previous years, this was a genuine Lennon/McCartney collaboration, with John writing the opening and closing sections, and Paul penning the segment in between. The first two parts were linked by a 40-piece orchestra playing, at John's request, "a sound building up from nothing to the end of the world."

As with *Revolver*, the Lennon and McCartney contributions are relatively easy to identify. John's lyrics, influenced by his heavy consumption of LSD, stumbled down an ever more oblique path. Both John and Paul were open to inspiration from any source, however unlikely. The words of "Being For The Benefit Of Mister Kite" were drawn almost verbatim from a poster that John found in an antiques shop, while "Lucy In The Sky With Diamonds" was inspired by a painting his son Julian brought home from school. Famously, the song's title was misinterpreted as a reference to LSD, an early example of both fans and critics scouring Beatles songs for hidden references or "clues." (The "help" in "With A Little Help From My Friends," a song John and Paul wrote for Ringo, was thought by some to be another reference to drugs.) Paul's contributions were more traditionally melodic offerings, such as "When I'm Sixty-Four" and the plaintive "She's Leaving Home," while George's "Within You, Without You" reflected his growing interest in all things Indian. The group's continuing desire to experiment with sound made huge demands on George Martin, but the results were central to the new genre of "psychedelic" music.

Often critical of his Beatles work, this was one album that John had few doubts about: "*Sgt. Pepper* is the one. It was a peak. Paul and I were definitely working together."

Psychedelic bandsmen: The Beatles as pictured on the inside cover of *Sgt. Pepper*.

Cultural leaders

Although the heady days of Beatlemania were long gone, The Beatles were now in a league of their own, and each new stage in their development was eagerly scrutinized by the popular press. Such was their cultural dominance in the mid-1960s that each new single and album was viewed as a landmark release, casting a shadow over the rest of the pop scene. What The Beatles did one month would be copied by thousands of other bands the next, even to the point where inferior cover versions of Beatle album tracks made the charts.

However, the reaction to *Sgt. Pepper*—by both public and critics—was unlike that inspired by any other record before. It was no surprise that it topped the charts all over the world, but the magnitude of its success amazed everyone. On its U.K. release it went straight to number 1 and stayed there for six long months. Even after it left the Top 30 almost a year later, it continued to make occasional reappearances. By the early 1980s, it had sold over 10 million copies worldwide. The publicity surrounding the album's release on CD in 1992, on its 25th anniversary, took it high into the charts all over again.

The critics were unanimous in their praise, declaring *Sgt. Pepper* to be a genuine work of art. *The Times Literary Supplement* called it "a barometer of our times," while in the U.S., *Newsweek*'s Jack Kroll went further, comparing the LP with T. S. Eliot's work—in his eyes, "A Day in the Life" was The Beatles' "Waste Land." Just as there are those who remember exactly what they were doing and where they were the day John F. Kennedy was assassinated or the day Elvis died, a whole generation can still remember the first time they heard the album. Indeed, henceforth an artist's best work would often be referred to as their "Sgt. Pepper."

Moreover, the album's impact wasn't limited to just the music, groundbreaking though it was. *Sgt. Pepper*'s sleeve has become a Pop Art classic, crammed with images of The Beatles' heroes and other cultural icons, including Bob Dylan, Lewis Carroll, Karl Marx, and Aleister Crowley. Even The Beatles' own waxwork dummies from Madame Tussaud's made an appearance. Designed by British Pop artist Peter Blake, the sleeve showed the real Fab Four festooned as psychedelic bandsmen, a reflection of the craze for Victoriana that swept through London in the mid- to late 1960s. The lyrics to each song were printed on the back of the album—another first for a rock release.

The Beatles had pulled off the coolest of tricks. They were the darlings of the middle-class media, their peers watched their every move, they were still loved by their original teenage pop audience, and their commercial tunes appealed to young and old alike. Meanwhile, acid-heads and stoners found an "underground" subtext to the music too. At the time of *Sgt. Pepper*'s release The Beatles had truly become all things to all people.

John at Brian Epstein's house in London, May 1967, for the launch of *Sgt. Pepper*.

ALL
LOVE
L'AMOUR
IHR
LO
IS
C'EST
BRAUCHT
QUE
YOU
POUR
ALS
ES
NEED
VOUS
LIEBE
AMOR

Love is all you need

Sgt. Pepper dominated the charts the world over. However, the dust had barely settled before The Beatles were ready to make history all over again. The first worldwide satellite TV link-up, which took place during the summer of 1967, was a pivotal moment in communications technology and a special pageant, called *Our World*, was planned to celebrate the event. It was to be a six-hour live TV broadcast with 26 participating nations. The total simultaneous television audience would be 400 million, by far and away the largest ever reached. Each nation was invited to nominate its own cultural ambassadors to take part in this historic event. The Beatles were called upon to represent Great Britain.

Brian Epstein decided that it was the perfect forum for a new single to receive its world premiere. The song chosen—"All You Need Is Love"—was primarily John's work. It gave ample proof, were proof needed, that as the most famous group in the world, The Beatles now felt no artistic constraints whatsoever. John's composition was a ponderous, heavily orchestrated piece, the verses of which were played seven beats to the bar—unheard of in most popular music. That The Beatles managed to turn all of this into the greatest singalong anthem of the "Love Generation" is testament to their consummate skills as songsmiths.

On June 25, 1967, the broadcast took place as planned, with The Beatles singing "All You Need Is Love" live accompanied by a prerecorded backing tape. They were joined in the studio by other pop notables, including Mick Jagger, Keith Richard, Marianne Faithfull, and Eric Clapton. The single went straight to the number 1 spot and—appropriately—occupied the top of the charts throughout what is now fondly remembered as the "Summer of Love."

By mid-1967 the "flower power" era had peaked. What began spontaneously in San Francisco's Haight-Ashbury district a few years earlier was now a worldwide phenomenon. However, "Love and Peace" became more a fashionable slogan than the heralding of a radical new lifestyle. "All You Need Is Love" gave hippies a certain amount of cultural legitimacy. During that summer it seemed that everyone was growing their hair, dressing in swirling psychedelic colors, and sporting flowers, beads, and bells.

Ultimately it was not a revolution; it was just another fad. But for many who lived through the time—even those with no great interest in music—"All You Need Is Love" will be remembered as a song that all but defined the high-water mark of 1960s optimism.

Opposite: John's "All You Need Is Love" became a 1960s anthem.
Right: The Beatles promote their single for the "Summer of Love" at Abbey Road Studios, June 25, 1967.

Meeting the Maharishi

Although his efforts as a songwriter were overshadowed by Lennon and McCartney, The Beatles' lead guitarist George Harrison had been slowly developing his own songwriting talents in the background. (His first solo Beatles composition—"Don't Bother Me"—was on their 1963 album *With The Beatles*.) During 1965, just before the recording of *Rubber Soul*, George had acquired a sitar—a traditional Indian stringed instrument—signaling what would be a lengthy infatuation with all things Asian. George had first used the instrument to play the solo on John's "Norwegian Wood." Thereafter he had taken lessons and befriended the sitar virtuoso Ravi Shankar. This developed into a genuine love and understanding of Indian music that colored George's contributions to *Rubber Soul*, *Revolver*, and *Sgt. Pepper*.

During April 1967, George's wife Pattie had noticed a poster announcing a public lecture featuring the Maharishi Mahesh Yogi. The Harrisons and their friends had already become intrigued by Transcendental Meditation. At Pattie's request George persuaded the other Beatles to join them at the lecture. John in particular was keen to know more about it.

Thus it was that on Thursday, April 24, The Beatles joined a small crowd at the Hilton Hotel, in London's Park Lane. There they watched and heard a middle-aged, bearded, long-haired Indian gentleman wearing only a robe describe, in a high-pitched voice, how a person could achieve true inner peace through the practice of meditation. It was a message that John, with his increasingly turbulent life, was all too ready to take on board. After the lecture, The Beatles sent word that they would like a private meeting with the Maharishi. Clearly such high-profile disciples could not be turned away. The Beatles were invited to join the Maharishi on a course of indoctrination at University College, Bangor, on the coast of North Wales. The Beatles asked Brian Epstein if he would like to join them but, as he had already made other plans, he said no.

The media noted this exotic and strange new direction that The Beatles were taking, and were out in force to see the group and their entourage—including Pattie Harrison, actress Jane Asher (then dating Paul McCartney), Mick Jagger, and his girlfriend singer Marianne Faithfull—leaving on a specially chartered train from Paddington station, west London. But Cynthia Lennon missed the train—she was held back by a policeman who thought she was one of the many fans who had joined the crowd to see off the group. Cynthia eventually made her own way to Bangor, but the incident seemed somehow symbolic of the growing distance between herself and her husband, who increasingly seemed to be heading for places where she couldn't follow.

Followers of the Maharishi: The Beatles at the Bangor seminar weekend, August 1967.

Brian's death

The Beatles were now scaling new heights of creativity. But with their continued commercial success assured, Brian Epstein was beginning to feel increasingly insecure. His influence had once been absolute: if he wanted The Beatles to wear suits, they wore them; if he wanted them to change their set list, they changed it; if he told them to tour for months on end, they toured. But things were different now. George Martin recalled one occasion during the *Sgt. Pepper* sessions that illustrated the change. John was laying down a vocal track, and when he had finished, Brian switched on the studio intercom and said: "I don't think that sounded quite right, John." Looking up at him, John replied, "You stick to your percentages, Brian. We'll look after the music." Epstein's word was no longer law.

Other areas of Brian's life were in disarray too. The Merseybeat "boom" was over, and apart from The Beatles, only Cilla Black was still enjoying U.K. hits by 1967. Moreover, his private life was becoming increasingly turbulent. His taste for "rough trade"—potentially violent male prostitutes he picked up at locations such as London's Piccadilly Underground station—had resulted in numerous blackmail threats and "silence" payments.

Although to those on the outside, Brian seemed the epitome of conservative respectability, he had embraced the whole "Swinging London" scene with just as much energy as the four Beatles themselves. However, while pot and LSD provided John with new inspiration, Brian's haphazard cocktails of pills and alcohol were, more often than not, taken as a means of escape. Increasingly unhappy, at the end of 1966 he deliberately took an overdose of pills. The suicide attempt was not successful. He sought psychiatric help and checked into a "drying out" clinic. At first it seemed to have helped him, but a few months later he tried to end his life once more.

In August 1967, while The Beatles visited the Maharishi in North Wales, Brian left London to spend the weekend with some friends. However, he soon became bored, and decided to return to his house in Belgravia. His body was found in bed the following Sunday; he had died from an overdose of Carbitrol, although whether deliberately or by accident is unclear.

The Beatles heard the news while they were still in Bangor and returned to London immediately. They were met by a huge crowd of journalists and TV reporters. The looks on their faces told the whole story—they were devastated. In his way, Brian had been as much a Beatle as John, Paul, George, and Ringo. John was hit particularly hard by Brian's death: "I liked Brian and I had a very close relationship with him for years" he revealed. "As close as you can get to somebody who lives a sort of [gay] life ... We'd never have made it without him ... Brian contributed as much as us in the early days."

Brian Epstein, the man who gave the world The Beatles, photographed not long before his death.

Roll up ...

The Beatles' next project was to be a TV musical, *Magical Mystery Tour*. However, after the triumph of *Sgt. Pepper*, it was to give the band's collective ego a sizable dent. Following Brian's death, The Beatles opted to manage their own affairs, and although John was still popularly perceived as the "leader" of The Beatles, Paul now began to assert himself with increasing authority. He launched himself enthusiastically into the project—the group were to write, produce, direct, star in, score, and edit the film themselves.

The difficulties started immediately. The Beatles decided to hire the famous Shepperton Studios, but didn't realize it had to be booked months in advance. For the storyline, Paul had an idea inspired by West Coast legend Ken Kesey who, two years earlier, had attracted notoriety by taking a bus troupe of assorted oddballs on an LSD-soaked tour of California. In the hands of four working-class Liverpool lads, this became an outing through the English countryside in a bus populated by sideshow freaks and music-hall renegades. Paul's plan was that the plot would effectively generate itself as they drove along.

So The Beatles hired a luxury bus, selected actors from agency directories, and set off to make a film. It all sounded so easy. With no itinerary planned, the bus would go wherever any Beatle wanted it to go. In the event, however, the filming was a catastrophe. The group gave little thought to the mayhem that might be caused to other road users when the bus ambled along tiny country lanes creating traffic jams, or at the end of a day's filming when nobody had remembered to book a hotel for the large entourage. Brian certainly wouldn't have let such things happen.

At the end of their mystery tour, The Beatles had over 10 hours of material and booked an editing suite for one week to put the film together. In the end it took 11 weeks to create a one-hour show, broadcast by the BBC on December 26, 1967. About 15 million viewers tuned in for what many had hoped would be a visual equivalent to *Sgt. Pepper*. Most were disappointed. Matters had not been helped by the fact that although the film had been made in color, the BBC broadcast it in black and white. The following day the British press gave the film a unanimous thumbs-down—one dismissing it as "blatant rubbish."

Magical Mystery Tour was largely Paul's work. John was not wholly behind the project: "George and I were sort of grumbling about the fuckin' movie and we thought we'd better do it and we had the feeling that we owed it to the public to do these things," he later grouched. For his part, the ever-optimistic Paul has always remained unapologetic about *Magical Mystery Tour*: "I think it was a good show. It will have its day, you know."

"I am the eggman ..."—John filming *Magical Mystery Tour*, September 1967. His famous psychedelic Rolls-Royce is visible in the background.

Apple Corps

By Beatle standards, *Magical Mystery Tour* had been a failure. However, still impervious to the need for outside management, The Beatles decided to push their entrepreneurial flair to the limit. The next move would see the birth of The Beatles as alternative businessmen.

In December 1967, The Beatles gave two young Dutch designers £100,000 (approximately $150,000) to open up a clothes store. Known collectively as The Fool, Simon Posthuma and Marijka Koger had worked almost exclusively for The Beatles for the past year, designing their clothes, their home interiors, and even the psychedelic patterning for John's Rolls-Royce.

Located on a corner in a four-story house at 94 Baker Street, London, the Apple Boutique was to be "a beautiful place where you could buy beautiful things." This was only the start. The Beatles aimed to create a new type of business empire of which *they* were in control.

The boutique was to be followed by other exciting new projects such as Apple Electronics, Apple Records, Apple Films, Apple Music, and Apple Books. The whole operation came under the umbrella Apple Corps Ltd. Based in a five-story Georgian building in the heart of London's Mayfair, 3 Savile Row would become headquarters for one of the most absurdly unsuccessful business ventures of the 1960s. Nevertheless, it's perhaps worth remembering that the idea was one clearly born out of the skyscraping optimism of that decade and represented a heartfelt desire to encourage creative artists.

Perhaps the most extreme development was the birth of the Apple Foundation for the Arts —as Paul put it: "We're in a happy position of not needing any more money so for the first time the bosses are not in it for the profit. If you come to me and say 'I've had such and such a dream,' I'll say to you, 'Go away and do it.'" Predictably, the Foundation was immediately overwhelmed with every type of business proposal imaginable, most of them unworkable.

With the exception of the record label, which enjoyed considerable success, by the end of 1968 every other aspect of Apple's activities had shed a small fortune. Apple Films and Apple Books had yet to come up with a single product; in spite of the heavy subsidy, Apple Electronics looked incapable of manufacturing a viable product.

One by one, the failing divisions folded. When the boutique closed, some seven months after its opening, Paul simply told the press: "The Beatles are tired of being shopkeepers." One evening, The Beatles and their families visited the store and helped themselves to anything they wanted. The following day they announced that everyone else could do the same. (Ironically, the boutique had been plagued by shoplifting and many people had been doing exactly that for some time.) Hundreds of shoppers, held in check by a dozen policemen, stormed the doors and made off with anything they could lay their hands on.

Beatles in the high street—the Apple Boutique brought psychedelia to central London.

Meditative times

The time The Beatles had spent with the Maharishi had provided them with a valuable recuperative retreat from the pressures of being the world's most famous pop stars. February 1968 saw them embark on what was intended to be a three-month period studying meditation at the Maharishi's Indian ashram in Rishikesh, overlooking the River Ganges. The Maharishi lived in the relative luxury of a fenced compound. The Beatles, their wives, and girlfriends were accompanied by a selection of fellow celebrities in search of enlightenment, including The Beach Boys' Mike Love, actress Mia Farrow, and the U.K. pop star Donovan.

The intensive religious tuition and chanting sessions, combined with the restrictive diets, proved a testing time for people used to life's luxuries. Ringo, who had been more than a little cynical even at the start of the episode, was the first to crack. He and his wife Maureen made their exit after only 10 days, claiming they had eaten enough of the spicy vegetarian food (they had allegedly taken a large supply of Heinz baked beans with them). A month later Paul McCartney and Jane Asher also made their excuses and left.

John and George stayed on, although they gradually started to become suspicious about their host. It was rumored that the Maharishi's interest in Mia Farrow was rather more physical than might be expected of a guru. Somewhat bitterly, they also decided to leave. It's worth noting that the remaining two Beatles departed Rishikesh without giving the Maharishi the chance to deny the accusations of misconduct or to defend himself. Certainly, he had never stipulated that he was sexually abstinent. Moreover, hindsight suggests that at least one member of The Beatles' entourage may have engineered the rumors in the first place to prevent the Maharishi from becoming too influential with the Fab Four.

It seemed that, like the Apple Boutique, the Maharishi was simply another new toy that The Beatles had grown bored of and were now throwing away. The media had a field day when the news broke. The Beatles themselves were offhand about the episode. "We made a mistake," Paul told the press. "We thought there was more to him than there was. He's human. We thought at first that he wasn't." Although the trip to India could have been looked upon as a public humiliation, John always viewed it in a positive light. The new environment had helped him come through what had become an escalating dependency on certain drugs. Moreover, he had returned from Rishikesh with over 20 new songs, many of which would find their way onto The Beatles' new album. One of them was written about the Maharishi, although, in John's own words, he "copped out" and changed all the direct references to the holy man. The world would hear the song as "Sexy Sadie."

The Indian trip, March 1968. Left to right: Pattie Harrison, John Lennon, Mike Love, the Maharishi, George Harrison, Mia Farrow, Donovan, Paul McCartney, Jane Asher, and Cynthia Lennon.

4 The Dream Is Over

Although their artistic triumphs continue, the four Beatles become increasingly isolated from one another as the decade draws to a close. John has apparently lost interest in the band he created and is increasingly following his own direction. Along with his new wife, Yoko Ono, he takes the first tentative steps along what will be an eccentric solo path. The end of the decade sees John making news headlines because of his prominent peace campaigns rather than for his music.

John and Yoko

Nineteen sixty-eight was to be a turbulent year for both John Lennon and The Beatles. Over the previous year John's relationship with his wife Cynthia had become increasingly strained and they struggled to find common ground. Moreover, his private life was soon to be thrust into the public arena due to the appearance of Japanese artist Yoko Ono. It was a relationship that one way or another would last the rest of his life.

John had always been the Beatle most open to experimentation. He had wholeheartedly embraced marijuana, and had become a frequent user of LSD by the beginning of 1966. This thirst for novelty also saw a burgeoning interest in the world of avant-garde art. It was while attending an exhibition at London's Indica Gallery in November 1966 that John first encountered Yoko Ono, the show's featured artist. He was immediately intrigued. Yoko's work was confident and provocative. For one of her exhibits she asked John to climb a ladder and hammer an imaginary nail into a wall. This, she said, would cost him five shillings. Slightly bemused, John dryly replied "I'll give you an imaginary five shillings." The connection was made. John would later say of the meeting:

"Imagine two cars of the same make heading towards each other and they're gonna crash head-on ... they're doing a hundred miles an hour ... they both slam their brakes on ... and they stop just in the nick of time, with their bumpers almost touching. That's what it was like from the moment I first met her ... I had no doubt I'd met The One."

Cynthia had always known that John was no saint when it came to fending off advances from the many groupies inevitably drawn to the world's most famous pop group. But she took faith in the fact that it was always to her that he would return, commenting later: "Whatever John did outside our marriage, he didn't flaunt anything." But John's honesty could sometimes be brutal. On one occasion he casually told her: "I want to get it off my chest, Cyn. There have been hundreds of other women."

In the middle of May 1968, with Cynthia away on holiday, John invited Yoko to his Surrey home, supposedly to work on a series of sound collages. From that day onward John and Yoko became virtually inseparable. The other three Beatles had seen nothing like it before: their private and working lives had always been totally separate—no one had ever managed to break their way into a Beatle's creative life. John and Yoko's affair moved at a rapid pace. On November 8, 1968, following acrimonious legal wrangling, Cynthia was awarded a decree nisi divorce on the grounds of her husband's adultery.

Early in 1969, John sold Kenwood, his home of the past five years. He and Yoko moved into Tittenhurst Park, a secluded mansion near the town of Ascot in Berkshire.

John and Yoko at John's first proper art exhibition, *You Are Here***, July 1968.**

Crises and cartoons

From the moment John and Yoko became an item, Yoko's influence made itself felt, even spreading into the heart of The Beatles' most hallowed territory—the recording studio. In the past, wives and girlfriends had often visited The Beatles while they were recording at Abbey Road, but they were invariably kept at a distance from the creative decision making. When Yoko appeared, all that changed. Although John attended all the sessions, made suggestions, and played his guitar as he had always done, now he had a constant companion at his side, whispering into his ear. From that point onward, Yoko was always present, a sounding-board for John's music-making.

The recording sessions for the next album were accompanied by a great deal of bad feeling. Yoko's presence certainly affected the studio atmosphere between the four musicians, but at the same time Paul McCartney now began to assert his own "leadership" of the group, often in a heavy-handed way. On August 20, Ringo walked out on the band for two weeks after Paul criticized his playing. Paul, now more than competent on most instruments, took over the drumming in his absence. When Ringo returned, he found that the others had covered his drums with flowers to welcome him back. However, Ringo wasn't the only Beatle to feel he was being talked down to. Things were similarly fractious between Paul and George, who felt that Paul was all too often trying to tell him how he should play his guitar. Only John seemed oblivious to all of this bad feeling.

The year 1968 also saw the conclusion of a project that had been hanging around for nearly two years—a Beatles animation film. The band all hated the idea at the time—possibly because they had disliked the U.S. Beatles cartoon series, which had been handled by the same producer, Al Brodax. The film was a contractual obligation to United Artists as far as The Beatles were concerned, and they deliberately had very little involvement in it, agreeing only to supplying four new songs and a live-action sequence for the ending. In spite of this, the end result, *Yellow Submarine*, was something of a cinematic triumph. The psychedelic style of animation perfectly captured the mood of the late 1960s while the story, crafted from lyrics and characters in songs from the *Rubber Soul, Revolver,* and *Sgt. Pepper* albums, was entertaining and surprisingly coherent. The finished film was a visually stimulating cartoon for children that also had a foot in the "underground" subculture of the decade—a sort of *Alice In Wonderland* for the 1960s.

The Beatles attended the premiere of the film, on July 17 at the London Pavilion cinema in Piccadilly Circus. John used the opportunity to make his first high-profile public appearance with Yoko Ono at his side.

Still smiling, John, George, and Paul work on their new album at Abbey Road Studios, 1968.

The White Album

From May until October of 1968, The Beatles worked solidly in the studio. Sometimes they worked in several studios at the same time. Although the band played together on most of the backing tracks, it was invariably the composer who added the finishing touches to his own song. Many of the songs were strikingly simple and based around acoustic guitars—most had been written in this way while The Beatles were sitting around the ashram in Rishikesh. The jacket, too, was about as basic as it could be—a plain white gatefold—in marked contrast to the dense, colorful sleeve of their previous LP, *Sgt. Pepper*. The album's official title was simply *The Beatles*, though it soon became known popularly as *The White Album*.

For all their personal differences, the recording sessions yielded well over 30 new songs, providing the group with two complete albums' worth of new material. Producer George Martin wanted the material pared down to the 14 best songs, but The Beatles remained convinced that the work was good enough to be released as a double album set.

Given the spirit in which it was made, *The White Album* is certainly the most fascinating of The Beatles' collections. Indeed, there are many who rate it as their best work, among them John Lennon: "it was our first unselfconscious album ... I always preferred the double album because *my* music is better on that album."

Among the album's high points were John's "Glass Onion"—a song aimed at the critics and fans who read unintended meanings into his songs. The album also featured one of his personal favorites, "Happiness Is A Warm Gun." It was interpreted by some as being about heroin—which John was now regularly using—although he refuted the idea: "I think it's a beautiful song. I like all the different things that are happening. It wasn't about 'H' at all."

Another significant track is John's "Revolution 9," a disturbing eight-minute sound collage assembled by himself and Yoko. John had wanted it released as a single; the other three Beatles had been opposed to it even appearing on the album. According to John: "It was an unconscious picture of what I actually think will happen ... like a drawing of revolution. All the thing was made with loops. I had about 30 loops going, fed them into one basic track ... chopping it up, making it backwards ... Number 9 turned out to be my birthday and my lucky number. There are many symbolic things about it, but it just happened you know ... I was just using all the bits to make a montage. I really wanted that released."

When it was released in October 1968, *The White Album* became the fastest-selling album up to that date, going on to sell almost 10 million copies throughout the world.

During September 1968, The Beatles took time out from their sessions for *The White Album* and appeared on David Frost's TV show to premiere their new single, "Hey Jude." In fact, the song was originally titled "Hey Jules," and was written by Paul McCartney for John's son Julian.

Get Back

With John's attentions firmly sidelined, Paul McCartney was now the motivating force behind The Beatles. Concerned at the apparent apathy of the others, he felt they needed something on which they could focus. He came up with the idea of turning the rehearsals and recordings for their next album into a television documentary, the climax of which would be a one-off live performance.

The taped rehearsals started in January 1969, but tensions were apparent from the start. These were partly due to the fact that Yoko was always there with John. The real problem, though, was that Paul seemed to be the only Beatle who *really* wanted to be there at all. His annoyance at the antipathy surrounding him spilled over into arguments about playing. Equally, the other three were clearly beginning to tire of Paul's assertiveness. On January 10, George walked out—in addition to his difficulties with Paul, John had criticized his songwriting two days before, and George had simply had enough of it.

The idea for the new album—still unnamed, but with a working title of "Get Back"—was to capture a spontaneous live recording. The sessions were scheduled to take place at the new Apple Studios in the basement of The Beatles' Savile Row office. However, when the group turned up to start work they found chaos. The studio—designed by Apple's in-house boffin whom John had dubbed "Magic Alex"—resembled a home-built electronics laboratory with dozens of tiny loudspeakers placed all around the studio. The briefest of test recordings proved that the new environment would be useless for The Beatles' needs. The next week was spent undoing Magic Alex's handiwork and bringing in equipment from Abbey Road.

Meanwhile, another problem emerged. New songs were taking longer than anticipated to develop, and it was becoming clear that the budget for filming The Beatles' performance couldn't stretch through the recording of the album, which looked as though it might last up to six months. So it was decided that The Beatles would perform an unannounced concert on the roof of their Savile Row headquarters, which would be filmed.

On Thursday, January 30, 1969, The Beatles took to an impromptu stage at the top of the building, surrounded by family, friends, and film crews. As they struck up the opening chords to "Get Back," local office workers came out to investigate the noise. Gradually, the narrow roads around Mayfair in central London became congested, and the police arrived. After 42 minutes of playing, and distracted by the number of police officers who were by now trying to get them to stop, The Beatles ended the show with another version of "Get Back." With the guitar chords fading, John quipped: "I'd like to say thank you on behalf of the group and ourselves and I hope we passed the audition." The Beatles' final public performance was over.

The end—The Beatles perform a free concert on the roof of the Apple office, January 30, 1969.

Experiments in the avant-garde

Sgt. Pepper represented both the peak of John and Paul's partnership and the last time that the two were to collaborate closely. Yoko Ono effectively took over as John's creative partner from the start of their relationship in 1968. Under her influence, John felt encouraged to indulge his growing interests in alternative or experimental art forms. As a conceptual artist, Yoko taught John that an idea could be more important than a tangible artifact, such as a song or a record. Or, as John put it, "She encouraged the freak in me."

Paul McCartney was at close hand to see Yoko's impact on his friend:

"Once he met Yoko ... he let out all these bizarre sides to his character. He didn't dare do it when he was living in suburbia with Cynthia."

"Yoko would say 'This is very good art, we must do this' and she gave him the freedom to do it. In fact she wanted more: 'Do it double. Be more daring. Take all your clothes off.' She always pushed him, which he liked. Nobody had ever pushed him before."

John and Yoko's first collaboration had been *Unfinished Music No. 1—Two Virgins*, which was recorded and released in 1968. A series of sound collages in a similar vein to "Revolution 9," the music aroused little consumer interest. Few regular Beatles fans would have even considered it to be music at all. The sleeve, however, did create some notoriety—it was a full-frontal nude photograph of John and Yoko. Eventually, the album was made available only in a brown paper bag. Surprisingly, given the huge popularity of The Beatles, if not the uncompromising music, the album only sold around 5,000 copies in Britain on release.

The following year, the duo recorded a similar album, *Unfinished Music No. 2—Life With The Lions*, released on Apple's experimental offshoot label, Zapple, but this one too met with public indifference. One side of the album was recorded on a cassette during Yoko's failed pregnancy at Queen Charlotte Hospital. The flip side featured music from a set that the two had performed during an avant-garde musical evening at Cambridge University on March 2, 1969. Again, the confrontational material failed to attract much interest.

Such esoteric activities cut little ice with The Beatles' traditional fans, many of whom saw Yoko as a corrupting interloper or gold digger. Few realized that she actually came from a background of wealth and privilege, and had little need of a share in John's fortune. Nonetheless, many people felt that it was Yoko Ono who was directly responsible for breaking up The Beatles. And to Beatles fans, that was an unforgivable sin.

Yoko and John performed a set of free-form, avant-garde material at Cambridge University in 1969.

John Ono Lennon

When John Lennon and Yoko Ono first became involved with each other, they were both married to other partners. After an acrimonious six months, Cynthia divorced John in November 1968. Three months later, Yoko was divorced from her estranged husband, the American jazz musician and film producer Anthony Cox.

By stark contrast to John's childhood, Yoko Ono was born into luxury. Her father Eisuke Ono was president of a Japanese bank in San Francisco, while her mother was from an aristocratic family that could lay claim to being one of the wealthiest in Japan. Yoko grew up in an environment of maids and private tutors; money was never a cause for concern.

At the age of 18 Yoko dropped out of New York's prestigious Sarah Lawrence College to elope with her first husband, Toshi Ichiyanagi. Together they immersed themselves in the burgeoning avant-garde art scene. However, Yoko's early efforts met largely with apathy until she met up with Anthony Cox. Together they formed a formidable duo and it was during this time that Yoko learned the art and importance of self-publicity. She made her first appearances as an experimental artist in London in 1962 and over the years preceding her first encounter with John Lennon, she became known as a cutting-edge artist.

Although Yoko's association with John made her well known outside of the art world, her work was never treated with respect beyond her own circle. This was a source of great annoyance to John and, he claimed, a major factor in his eventual decision to abandon his home country: "She's a serious artist, you know!"

Above (top half): The marriage certificate—it was John's second wedding, and Yoko's third.

Yoko's relationship with Anthony Cox had evidently always been a difficult one, and although highly productive in artistic terms, it was never destined to be long-lasting. Yoko had little difficulty getting a divorce when she realized that she wanted to spend her future with John, although problems were later to arise over whether she or Cox were to have custody of their daughter, Kyoko.

On March 20, 1969, John and Yoko took a flight from Paris to Gibraltar where they were married by the Registrar at the British Consulate. They remained in Gibraltar for just 72 minutes before taking a return flight to Paris. One month later, after a discussion in which Yoko lightheartedly told John that she objected to the idea of having to take his surname, he symbolically changed his middle name by deed poll from Winston to Ono. Clearly, in his own mind, John Lennon was entering a new phase in his life.

John and Yoko on their wedding day—March 20, 1969—in front of the Rock of Gibraltar.

Giving peace a chance

"I've always been politically minded, you know, and against the status quo," John once commented. His stance had remained that of an outsider, whether as a teenage Teddy Boy or as the most unpredictable element in The Beatles. "It's pretty basic when you're brought up like I was, to hate and fear the police as a natural enemy and despise the army as something that takes everybody away and leaves them dead somewhere."

Even at the height of Beatlemania, John had always been prepared to speak his mind on political or moral issues. But by the end of the 1960s, having staged a succession of highly publicized propaganda stunts, John and Yoko had carved a role for themselves as the world's most prominent campaigners for peace.

Their first public gesture took place as early as June 1968 when they participated in the National Sculpture Exhibition in Coventry. They each planted an acorn in the grounds of the cathedral; one pointing to the east and one to the west, symbolizing the meeting of two cultures. For the occasion John coined the slogan "Plant an Acorn for Peace."

They stepped up their efforts in 1969 with a series of bizarre "Bed-ins" and offbeat attention-grabbing stunts such as concealing themselves within a giant bag—they called it "bagism." Inevitably, the stunts grabbed headlines and when interviewed about their latest act, John and Yoko would invariably bring the subject round to the need for peace. Their most famous event took place at the Queen Elizabeth Hotel, in Montreal, Canada. For 10 days the Lennons' suite became the centre of all manner of bizarre media activity. They enjoyed high-profile visits from supporters such as Dr. Timothy Leary, and attracted TV crews from all over the world. It was also the location they chose to record their first single—an anthem for their peace protest, "Give Peace A Chance." That it was crudely recorded and performed was not the point. In his mind, John was turning the tables on the media that had for so long fed on The Beatles. "Give Peace A Chance" was the first single attributed to John's new group—The Plastic Ono Band.

The single was an immediate success, and has since become the definitive peace anthem throughout the world. John certainly succeeded in his original aim for the song: "In my secret heart of hearts I wanted to write something that would take over from 'We Shall Overcome.'" He later admitted that "one of the biggest moments of my life" was when he saw a news program in which half a million anti-Vietnam War protesters were shown standing outside the White House singing his song.

Opposite: The Lennons bed down for peace in the Amsterdam Hilton, March, 1969.

Right: It's in the bag—John and Yoko on the U.K.'s *Today* program, April 1, 1969.

Introducing Mr. Klein

Although The Beatles were still best-selling artists, their business affairs had been spiraling out of control since the death of Brian Epstein. No one had taken control of Apple, and despite The Beatles' healthy record sales, the company had been losing money for some time. The group were desperately in need of new management.

There was no shortage of offers to take up the mantle. Ultimately, it was Allen Klein, America's premier showbiz lawyer, who halted the decline of the Apple business empire. The Beatles had first been told about Klein by Mick Jagger in 1966. Although The Rolling Stones—for whom Klein had been employed as a business adviser—sold far fewer records than The Beatles, they were making considerably more money.

Klein had publicly expressed an interest in representing The Beatles on several previous occasions after Brian Epstein's death, but at that time they had been keen to handle their own affairs. However, by early 1969, with a small fortune leaking out of Apple, it was John who took the initiative and arranged a meeting with Klein. Impressed by the fact that the lawyer knew his songs, and wasn't a "suit" like the other businessmen he'd come across, John convinced George and Ringo that Klein should represent them.

However, this decision was a difficult one for Paul McCartney. He was currently engaged to New York photographer Linda Eastman, whose father Lee Eastman was also a well-respected entertainment lawyer. Paul wanted Eastman's firm to represent The Beatles. The scene was set for the first serous rift in the band's ranks. At an Apple board meeting, Paul McCartney was outvoted by three to one. But Paul stood his ground. Although Allen Klein was now in control of Apple, Paul hired Eastman to manage his own personal affairs.

An uneasy alliance was now in place, though it seemed unlikely to hold for long. At every possible crossroads the interests of Paul and the others now seemed to be at odds. These irreconcilable differences would ultimately provide the spark for the demise of the Fab Four.

In the meantime, Allen Klein ruthlessly set about clearing up the aftermath of the Apple debacle. Any activity not directly related to The Beatles or their music was terminated, and many members of the Apple staff were sacked. Later, with his customary honesty, John more or less wrote off The Beatles' attempt at "Western Communism":

"Apple was a manifestation of Beatle naivete, collective naivete," he admitted. "We really didn't get approached by the best artists in the world ... we got all the ones who everyone had thrown out." The Beatles had failed as enlightened businessmen and seemed to have stopped caring about the one thing that had made them great in the first place: their music.

Hard-nosed showbiz lawyer Allen Klein (far left) stepped in to sort out Apple's problems in 1969. Klein had the backing of John, George, and Ringo, but Paul McCartney stood firm against him.

One more time

After having spent much of February trying to finish off the "Get Back" project, the band's enthusiasm for the album had begun to wane. They decided to hand over their backing tapes to producer Glyn Johns. As John remembered, interest in the project was at an all-time low: "We didn't want to know about it anymore, so we just left it and said 'Here, mix it' ... Nobody called anybody about it, and the tapes were left there."

The results were not impressive. Twenty-nine hours of music had been mixed down to a single album. The Beatles had wanted the album to sound spontaneous, but the tapes from the sessions merely sounded rough. John was still keen for the LP to be released as it stood: "I didn't care. I thought it was good to let it out and show people what had happened to us ... 'We don't play together anymore, you know, leave us alone.'" He was voted down by the others. They decided to put the project on the shelf for a while.

Then, in June 1969, Paul McCartney contacted George Martin with an unexpected request. He said that The Beatles wanted to record an album with him again, just as they had on previous highlights such as *Revolver* and *Sgt. Pepper*. For the first three weeks of July, they block-booked Abbey Road Studios. Miraculously, all four Beatles managed to put their personal differences behind them to concentrate on recording together again.

The resulting album was named after the home of all of their classic recordings—*Abbey Road*. Seized upon by fans and critics alike as undeniable proof that The Beatles were still a viable working group, the album sold in phenomenal quantities, even by Beatle standards. It went straight to number 1 in the U.K., and did not budge from the top spot for the next five months. To date, it has now sold over 10 million copies worldwide.

Abbey Road showed that despite having already recorded many of the benchmark singles and albums of the 1960s, The Beatles were still developing as musicians and songwriters. George Harrison, who had always struggled hard to have his own songs included on Beatles albums, penned two of the LP's most beautiful and striking songs—"Something" and "Here Comes The Sun." Side two of the record was mostly devoted to a superb medley masterminded by Paul, but John provided the raunchy "Come Together" and the extraordinary bluesy workout "I Want You (She's So Heavy)," a stark declaration of love for Yoko that ended with a grim repetitive riff and squalls of white noise.

The high standard of *Abbey Road* led many to believe that The Beatles were capable of dominating the forthcoming decade every bit as decisively as they had the 1960s—a period they had all but defined. Instead, it was to be their final gift to the world, an against-all-odds triumph by four men who by now really had given all they had to give as a group.

Smiles for the camera: The Beatles pull together one last time for *Abbey Road*.

Plastic Ono Band

By the time The Beatles were recording *Abbey Road*, John had already decided that he'd had enough. He wanted to put the Fab Four behind him and "leave all that for The Monkees," as he told *Melody Maker* music paper. His interests now lay in the idea of The Plastic Ono Band. He envisaged his new project as being the complete antithesis of The Beatles. He wanted to record swiftly and spontaneously, and have the results in the shops as quickly as possible. The idea drew inspiration from his new partner's avant-garde sensibilities:

"Plastic Ono Band was a concept of Yoko's," he told the press, "an imaginary band ... some pieces of plastic and a tape recorder ... her idea was a completely robot pop group ... there's nobody in the band."

John and Yoko only ever got round to making some miniature plasticine models, and in practice The Plastic Ono Band became a loose pool of musician friends who would sometimes also include George Harrison and Ringo Starr. The band was kick started when John and Yoko offered to perform at a rock concert in Toronto in September 1969. John literally put a band together overnight, comprising himself and Yoko, session drummer Andy White, Eric Clapton on guitar, and Klaus Voormann—a friend from the Hamburg days—on bass. They rehearsed a set, predominantly made up of old rock-and-roll standards, on the flight to Canada the day before the concert. On stage, the music was rough and ready. The critics were not that impressed, but the spontaneity of the performance was perfectly in line with John's new ideas. The event was documented on the album *Live Peace In Toronto 1969*.

Back in England, John continued his peace campaign with one of his most controversial stunts. Always uncomfortable with the "honor" of having been awarded the MBE, he took the decision to return it, on November 25, 1969, as a way of publicly protesting about British foreign policy. In the letter that accompanied his medal, he told Her Majesty the Queen: "I am returning my MBE in protest at Britain's involvement in the Nigeria-Biafra thing [and] against our support of America in Vietnam." Immediately there was an outraged reaction from the British Establishment, the very people who had protested when The Beatles were awarded their MBEs back in 1965. John's Aunt Mimi, with whom he'd left the medal, was also furious: "Over my dead body would I have given you that medal to insult the Queen with," she raged, later admitting, "He broke my heart over that." In fact, in an audaciously irreverent gesture, Lennon added a further reason for returning the medal: as a protest against his latest single, "Cold Turkey," slipping down the charts.

Toward the end of the 1960s, Yoko replaced Paul McCartney as John's musical collaborator.

Primal screaming

By 1969 John Lennon's relationship with Yoko Ono had become pivotal to his entire existence. But away from Yoko, John had a number of problems to resolve. Not least of these was his escalating use of heroin. "Cold Turkey"–The Plastic Ono Band's second single–was a powerfully harrowing document of his ongoing battle to kick the drug. The single was awash with disturbing moans and screams from John; Ringo played drums on the track, and sometime Plastic Ono Band member Eric Clapton contributed searing guitar lines. John had been naturally drawn to experiment with drugs, but had always felt in control of them until he started to take heroin. He was disturbed to find that unlike the other substances he'd indulged in, heroin was a drug that was difficult to give up.

From the start of their relationship, John and Yoko had decided that although they each had a child from a previous marriage, they also wanted one together. In August 1969, when Yoko became pregnant, John decided it would be a good time to get himself "clean." Fearing the adverse publicity that would accompany any revelations that he was being treated in a hospital or clinic, he attempted to end his addiction himself, as suddenly and completely as possible. Such an abrupt termination of heroin use results in certain distinct side effects– clammy skin and periodic outbreaks of gooseflesh. For this reason the treatment is sometimes known as "cold turkey." However, this time around John's resolve failed. In October, Yoko was rushed to hospital where she miscarried. Hurt and bitterly disappointed at another failed pregnancy, John started using heroin once more.

Refuge of a sort came in an unlikely form. That same year, John read the book *The Primal Scream (Primal Therapy: The Cure For Neurosis)*, written by Californian psychiatrist Dr. Arthur Janov. The principles of primal scream therapy work on the assumption that every person has a series of defenses that when stripped away reveal the individual as they truly are. According to Janov, every personal issue or problem that an individual faces can be isolated and overcome through an often intense dialog–i.e., they can quite literally be "screamed away." In John's case, many of his psychological problems were linked to his difficult childhood–the death of his mother and the absence of his father from an early age. In April 1970, John and Yoko flew to the U.S. to undergo four months of primal therapy. It was a cathartic experience that resulted in an increase in John's self-awareness and helped him lay to rest some of the demons that had plagued him throughout his life.

The therapy didn't help him end his drug problems–they would linger for some time. But it was an important inspiration for the soul-baring that would characterize his songwriting over the next few years, in particular his 1970 album *John Lennon/Plastic Ono Band*.

Pop's ambassador for peace, looking distinctly Christlike, in 1969.

The end of the Fab Four

Although *Abbey Road* had been an artistic success, John had not found it a rewarding experience. Still keen to keep the band going, Paul proposed to get The Beatles back on stage, but John and George steadfastly refused. Finally, at a meeting with Allen Klein, John dropped his bombshell: "The group is over. I'm leaving." Since Klein was in the process of improving The Beatles' record deals, he asked John not to go public with his announcement until he had completed his negotiations. Reluctantly, John agreed.

Klein had discovered that The Beatles' contractual affairs were still far from clear. They had mistakenly believed that *Yellow Submarine* constituted the final film of their original three-film deal with United Artists—indeed, that had been the only reason they'd agreed to their minimal involvement with the project in the first place. Evidently they had been mistaken, and still owed United Artists one more movie. Klein saw an obvious solution: the "Get Back" project could be resuscitated and turned into a feature-length film.

The four Beatles continued to have very little to do with the "Get Back" project—now retitled "Let It Be" after one of Paul's songs on the album. With The Beatles' consent, Allen Klein handed the master tapes over to Phil Spector to see what he could come up with. The results were not uniformly appreciated. While John didn't much care what happened to them, Spector's elaborate doctoring of the album—in particular his use of lush orchestration—angered Paul McCartney, who publicly declared that he would have preferred the original versions to have been left on the album. In March 1970, Paul contacted John to tell him that he now intended to leave the group. With John having maintained his silence for six months, it was Paul McCartney who, on April 10, 1970, notified the world's press of his decision to quit The Beatles. The news was confirmed on the press release accompanying his own debut album, *McCartney*, which was issued seven days later. John was cynical about the timing of Paul's announcement, but admitted to feeling a grudging admiration for Paul's tactics: "I was a fool not to do it ... to use it to sell a record," he later carped.

The Beatles were now dead, though few were completely surprised by the time the official announcement came. The group had been immensely popular, both in critical and commercial terms. Each member was world-famous and inspired a great deal of public affection. It was therefore almost inevitable that the individual ex-Beatles would enjoy successful solo careers. Indeed, although John Lennon enjoyed immense success during the 1970s, his former partner (and rival) Paul McCartney would become arguably the most successful solo artist of the decade. Even if much of that success was due to his peddling what John disparagingly referred to as "grandma music."

The end of the Fabs: The Beatles during their final photoshoot together, August 1969.

Kicking over the traces

While The Beatles limped toward an inevitable breakup, John Lennon channeled his creative energy into The Plastic Ono Band. For their third single, John hired legendary producer Phil Spector, who was in London to discuss sorting out the "Get Back" tapes with Allen Klein, now officially acting as The Beatles' manager. The single "Instant Karma!" was the result of this fascinating collaboration. It was the closest John ever came to achieving the spontaneity he now sought in his music-making. He wrote the song one morning in late January 1970, and recorded it a few days later with Alan White, Klaus Voormann, George Harrison on lead guitar, and Billy Preston—who had played keyboards with The Beatles during the "Get Back" sessions—on electric piano. Within two weeks it was in the shops.

To promote the single John appeared on *Top Of The Pops*—the first Beatle to do so since 1966. His appearance came as a shock to many of his ardent fans: both he and Yoko had ushered in the new decade by cropping their long hair. They gave their locks to Black Power leader Michael X, in exchange for a pair of bloodstained boxing shorts once owned by Muhammad Ali. The Lennons later auctioned the shorts for a peace cause.

At the end of September 1970, John moved into Abbey Road with Phil Spector to record The Plastic Ono Band's first studio album. Featuring Ringo on drums, Klaus Voormann on bass, and Billy Preston on keyboards, the album took barely four weeks to complete and was issued two weeks before Christmas 1970. John's public was by now a little wary of the unpredictability of his new offerings. However the album, released as *John Lennon/Plastic Ono Band*, abandoned his experimental leanings in favor of a brutally stark and intense set of songs; Dr. Janov's therapy was a clear influence. Songs such as "Mother" and "My Mummy's Dead" drew on his childhood loss to produce a belated public mourning, while "Working Class Hero" was a sarcastic attack on the values instilled into him during that childhood. It is perhaps the album's central piece—"God"—that gives the clearest picture of Lennon's outlook on life at this time. The song is a dry-eyed rejection of everything from religion and mysticism to Elvis Presley and, ultimately, The Beatles. The dream was over.

Opposite: John and a blindfolded Yoko on *Top Of The Pops*, 1970.
Right: On February 4, 1970, John and Yoko cut their hair and gave the shorn locks to Black Power leader Michael X in exchange for a pair of Muhammad Ali's boxing shorts. Both the hair and the shorts were later to be auctioned for peace and other good causes.

Imagine

John Lennon/Plastic Ono Band was a qualified commercial success, reaching number 11 in the U.K. albums chart. At this point in his life, its position mattered little to John—if the public still wanted to listen to his music, then it would have to be on his terms.

The year 1971 kicked off with a promotional trip to the States. While he was there, John upped his growing credibility with the political "underground" by mixing with controversial radicals such as Jerry Rubin and Abbie Hoffman, often raising money for their causes. If any further proof of his growing politicization were needed, it came in the form of the single "Power To The People," which was no less than a call for mass proletarian action. In the eyes of the U.S. authorities, John was now seen as an "undesirable," a situation that would create numerous practical difficulties for the Lennons over the years that followed. As a footnote, John would later disown the track, claiming that it was a "guilt song" written to appease radical figures who were skeptical of a multimillionaire celebrity with such views.

In July of 1971, John turned his home Tittenhurst Park into a makeshift recording studio where, once again under the guidance of Phil Spector, a new album was recorded. This time the sound was somewhat mellow—lavish, even—and the harsh, cynical lyrics that made its predecessor so hard-hitting were toned down. Credited simply to "John Lennon," it would turn out to be his most famous album: indeed, the title track would be one of the most popular songs ever written—"Imagine."

The inspiration for "Imagine" came, unsurprisingly, from Yoko Ono. In 1964 she published a book of poetry called *Grapefruit* (republished in 1971) in which each piece asked the reader to "imagine" a given scenario. John later admitted that he should have given Yoko a co-writing credit for the song that would eventually become his most famous solo composition, but "I was still full of wanting my own space after being in a room with the guys all the time, having to share things."

Many people have commented on the irony of a fabulously wealthy young man sitting in his mansion, asking the rest of the world to "Imagine no possessions ...," but John repeatedly claimed that the song was a sincere statement. And whatever the personal circumstances of the songwriter himself, the song's simple beauty undeniably still hits home.

In spite of its melodic tunefulness and lush strings, John nevertheless saw the album as coming from the same source as its more "difficult" predecessor: "The first record was too real for people, so nobody bought it ... " he reasoned. "You see, *Imagine* was exactly the same message, just sugar-coated ... Now I understand what you have to do. Put your political point across with a little honey."

John recorded probably his best-loved album, *Imagine*, at his Tittenhurst Park home in 1971.

John versus Paul

With *Imagine*, John Lennon became the potent commercial force that most people expected an ex-Beatle to be. Both the album and the single of the same name became massive global hits. But although The Beatles were now dead and buried as far as John was concerned, his relationship with Paul McCartney was becoming increasingly fractious and public.

Even back in the days of The Quarrymen there had been rivalry between John and Paul. Paul's superior musical skills represented a threat to John's unequivocal authority. Throughout the haze of Beatlemania, Paul had always resented John's perceived role as the band's unofficial leader, and the way John's extracurricular activities resulted in him being dubbed the "intellectual Beatle" by the media. Paul didn't much care for the influence Yoko Ono had over John's work either. For his part, John came to resent the way Paul thrust himself into the driving seat following the death of Brian Epstein.

By the time of *The White Album*, the two were also pursuing different musical aims. John was keen to mine the depths of his soul for inspiration and catharsis, irrespective of whether his public wanted to hear it. Paul seemed happy to continue being one of the greatest pop songwriters of the century and a gifted multi-instrumentalist. The bust-up over The Beatles' management was the first sign of bitterness between Lennon and McCartney. The timing of Paul's debut LP and the announcement of his decision to leave The Beatles—even though he'd known that John had effectively left six months earlier—clearly rankled with Lennon. A public squabble was born between the two that soon found its way into their music.

Paul's solo career got off to a flying start. He wrote and played virtually every note of his 1970 debut album, *McCartney*; it had been a big seller and a critical success. However, his 1971 follow-up, *Ram*, included a number of lyrics that John saw as jibes at himself and Yoko, notably the song "Too Many People (Going Underground)." John's stinging response was the bitterest track on the *Imagine* album. "How Do You Sleep?" was an extraordinary personal attack in which John cast the ultimate insult: "The sound you make is Muzak to my ears." As a final, childish gesture, the album featured a photograph of John grappling with a pig—a parody of the cover of *Ram* showing a rustic Paul posing with a sheep on his Scottish farm.

The sparring spilled over into the music press, when Paul made some derogatory remarks about his ex-partner in a *Melody Maker* interview. Two weeks later, John contacted the paper's editor, requesting that his vitriolic response be printed in full.

The wounds created by the encounters ran very deep. It would be four years before the two men came face to face again, and thereafter they enjoyed only periodic contact.

Like John and Yoko, Paul and Linda McCartney (seen here in 1970) made music together. Both pairings attracted critical flak, though Paul's group Wings was hugely successful in the 1970s.

5 The Final Years

In 1971, John and Yoko set up home in New York City, where they mix with artists, intellectuals, and political revolutionaries. John's music changes, but a new hard edge alienates many of his former fans. A turbulent period sees him estranged from Yoko, but after they are reunited, he retires into domesticity, concentrating on raising their newborn son. Returning from a recording session on December 8, 1980, John Lennon is shot dead outside his home. The life of one of the most extraordinary artists of the twentieth century is over.

War is over!

After the breakup of The Beatles, John and Yoko spent more and more time in New York City, ostensibly fighting for custody of Yoko's daughter, Kyoko Cox. Early in 1971, the duo decided to live in the U.S. permanently. John welcomed the move:

"It's Yoko's old stamping ground, and she felt the country would be more receptive to what we're up to ... in the United States we're treated like artists. Which we are! But here I'm like the lad who knew Paul, got a lucky break, won the pools, and married the actress."

"In New York there's these 20 or 30 artists who all understand what I'm doing and have the same kind of mind as me. It's just like heaven after being here ... you've seen how they treat me in the press."

On September 3, 1971, John and Yoko caught a flight to New York from London's Heathrow Airport. Unknown to John, he would never set foot on English soil again.

John and Yoko's first New York recording session took place little more than a month later. They called on Phil Spector's production skills for what has since become a Christmas classic—"Happy Xmas (War Is Over)." The chorus, sung by John, Yoko, and children from the Harlem Baptist Choir, first appeared as part of their peace protests in 1969—in 11 major cities across the world, the couple hired billboards to display their own personal Christmas card: "WAR IS OVER! IF YOU WANT IT. Happy Christmas from John & Yoko."

After the success of *Imagine*, John's first U.S. album came as a major disappointment. A return to the spontaneity of his early efforts, *Some Time In New York City* was completed in just 19 days. And it showed. Much of the album contained trite political sloganeering, taking on a cross section of the popular issues of the day: sexual inequality ("Woman Is The Nigger Of The World"); Northern Ireland ("Sunday Bloody Sunday" and "The Luck Of The Irish"); and jailed political activists ("Angela," "John Sinclair," and "Attica State"). They may have been sincere statements, but they were not eloquently made. Packaged with the almost unlistenable *Live Jam* free album, *Some Time In New York City* barely made the Top 50 in the U.S. The criticisms that his lyrics had become simplistic and that he was just churning out received opinions from the intellectuals in his circle were hard for Lennon to swallow.

He later acknowledged that the album nearly wrecked his career. Although the U.S. would forgive and forget when it came to each new Lennon release, his popularity in the U.K. dived.

In December 1969, John and Yoko had paid for their slogan "WAR IS OVER! IF YOU WANT IT" to be displayed on 2,000 billboards in 11 cities worldwide in time for Christmas.

Public enemy

John Lennon loved New York City and the seemingly boundless opportunities that the United States offered. Indeed, he went as far as making his thoughts on the matter very public. "I profoundly regret that I was not born an American," he announced shortly after his arrival, doubtless further alienating members of his U.K. fan-base in the process. Lennon disliked the petty-minded way in which the U.K. press treated Yoko and himself. Moreover, as a couple of tracks on *Some Time In New York City* indicated, he was angry at the British government's attitude to the "Troubles" in Northern Ireland. However, dark forces had been at work in an effort to keep him out of the U.S. ever since he and Yoko had first visited the country.

John's open association with radical Marxists, Black Panthers, and other revolutionary groups had created powerful enemies, most notably President Nixon and FBI chief, J. Edgar Hoover. His phones were tapped and he became aware that intelligence officers were shadowing his private life, constantly digging for "dirt" that could be used as evidence against him. Because John had a 1968 drug conviction on his records, obtaining a visa to remain in the U.S. was always going to be difficult for him. At the end of February 1972, his temporary visa ran out and he was informed that a new one would not be issued. He was given two months to leave the United States.

The root of the problem lay in a report from a Senate subcommittee dealing with internal security, which claimed that in 1968 John Lennon had bankrolled a "revolutionary" group that had sabotaged the 1968 Democratic Convention. He was now thought to be financing a plot to have President Nixon ousted at the 1972 Republican Convention. Although John denied the charges, it was clear the U.S. government viewed him as a highly unwelcome guest. At the time, the FBI suggested that a narcotics charge would be the easiest grounds on which to have Lennon deported. Why this threat was never carried out is something of a mystery, as it was the one area in which John Lennon was clearly in violation of U.S. law.

His lawyers fought a fierce campaign to have his visa renewed. However, John's trump card was an appearance on the nationally televised Dick Cavett chat show, in which he described the extent of the government's harassment to a sympathetic U.S. public.

There were frequent legal battles over the next four years, and it was not until July 27, 1976, that John Lennon was awarded the coveted Green Card, allowing him unlimited stay in the United States. Prior to that date he had been too scared to leave the country in case he was not allowed back in. But even after securing permanent residency, he still never found the will to return to England.

Dark days: John arrives at the offices of the Immigration and Naturalization Service on May 12, 1972, to fight moves for his deportation.

Beatles to get back?

The success of The Beatles cast a long shadow over each of the members' solo careers. In public, John, Paul, George, and Ringo usually only discussed The Beatles when journalists asked that one burning question—would the Fab Four ever get together again?

It's clear that none of the ex-Beatles would have gained much from a reunion, short of bolstering their already swollen bank accounts. And in any case, by 1973, all four were successful solo performers. John Lennon and Paul McCartney were chart regulars, while George Harrison had scored a handful of hits, among them "My Sweet Lord," the biggest-selling single of 1971. Even Ringo, who as the drummer might have been expected to fall by the wayside, enjoyed a splendidly eccentric pop career of his own in the early 1970s.

The talk of reunions was often fueled by occasions that featured various permutations of the band. The first came in 1971 when George Harrison and Ravi Shankar organized a benefit concert for UNICEF, the charity that at the time was struggling to bring aid to starving children in Bangladesh. The aim was to raise $25,000. George arranged for some of rock's top stars to perform for no fee and, as a matter of course, the other three ex-Beatles were all invited. At first it looked as though they might play—albeit not as "The Beatles." However, the speculation about it in the music press proved too much for Paul McCartney, who pulled out. Then, when it became clear that Yoko had not been invited, John also withdrew.

Ringo Starr's 1973 album *Ringo* was the closest the four Beatles ever came to recording together (at least until the posthumous recording of John's "Free As A Bird" in 1994). But while each Beatle made an appearance on the LP, no single track featured them all.

Toward the end of the 1970s there were several attempts to revive The Beatles. One was initiated by Paul McCartney—by then the only ex-Beatle still having regular hits. In 1979, proposing a concert for the benefit of Kampuchean refugees, Paul said he would be prepared to share the stage with his three former colleagues. George and Ringo agreed to the idea, but John wanted nothing to do with it. Although their personal differences were now long in the past, John dismissed the idea with the line "we'd just be four rusty old men."

In September of the same year, promoter Sid Bernstein made a public appeal to The Beatles in the pages of the *New York Times*. He wanted to put on a series of benefit concerts for the Vietnamese Boat People, which he believed could raise up to $500 million—The Beatles were to be his star attraction. Two weeks later Kurt Waldheim, then General Secretary of the United Nations, joined in the plea. It was all to no avail. Only John's murder on December 8, 1980, put a permanent end to speculation about a Beatles reunion.

Ringo and George (left and center) teamed up for the charity Bangladesh concert in 1971. A number of other stars appeared, including Bob Dylan (right).

Mind Games

When John and Yoko arrived in New York City, they first headed for the hip artistic atmosphere of Greenwich Village. However, by 1973 John was tiring of his image as a radical and becoming disillusioned with figures such as Jerry Rubin and Abbie Hoffman who, he felt, were "all talk." In March 1973, he and Yoko abandoned the easygoing Village in favor of the celebrity stylings of the Dakota Building, a luxury apartment overlooking Central Park.

For the first time in their five-year relationship, the Lennons were no longer an inseparable couple. Still smarting from the failure of *Some Time In New York City*, John frittered his time away while Yoko pursued her own artistic career. The rumors doing the rounds were that rock's most famous couple were not getting on too well.

John's record contract dictated that he must have a new album ready for release each year. But in 1973 he was feeling no great desire to go into the studio. During the sessions for his new album he confessed to an interviewer: "It's getting to be work. It's ruining the music ... Every time I strap on a guitar it's the same old jazz." And it's a mood that comes through on much of the resulting album.

Released in November 1973, *Mind Games* came as relief to most Lennon fans, as it signaled a return to the lush melodicism of *Imagine*. Gone were the political rantings of its predecessor that some had found a little embarrassing. Gone, too, were the rough-edged performances of old—John had opted to surround himself with some of New York's top session men. (Ironically, the lead guitarist on *Mind Games*, David Spinozza, had also played on Paul McCartney's *Ram*, the album that prompted John to pen the vitriolic "How Do You Sleep?") But although *Mind Games* contained gems such as the title track and the gentle ballad "I Know (I Know)," the overall feeling was that John Lennon was treading water. John himself seemed to agree as he defensively justified the LP's existence: "It's just an album ... there's no very deep message about it. The only reason I make albums is because you're supposed to." The problems in the Lennons' relationship were subtly mirrored in the album's sleeve. The front cover shows Yoko's face in profile, forming a mountainlike background, in front of which is a photograph of John. On the back cover, the image of John is much larger. May Pang, the Lennons' personal assistant, later alleged that John saw this as a metaphor for him walking away from Yoko.

For all its flaws, *Mind Games* went some way to repairing the commercial damage of *Some Time In New York City*. The album and "Mind Games" the single became minor hits on both sides of the Atlantic.

John and Yoko were experts at generating publicity and frequently held press conferences to promote their latest artistic endeavor or to draw attention to a deserving cause.

Leaving Yoko

Mind Games had emerged in the midst of a creative lull. As someone who required constant stimulation, this period made John difficult to live with, especially as Yoko continued to progress with her own work. Moreover, his endless mood swings were made worse by heavy drinking bouts. Realizing their relationship was going nowhere, Yoko told her husband that she felt a temporary separation was necessary. As John would later comment: "She don't [sic] suffer fools gladly, even if she's married to him."

Initially, John was not keen on Yoko's decision: "She kicked me out, pure and simple," he commented, bitterly. Later, he came to respect it, grudgingly admitting: "It was grow up time and I'm glad she made me do it."

Yoko suggested that John move to Los Angeles. There was no question of him leaving the country, due to his continuing Green Card problems, and Yoko felt that John should experience the City of Angels and the Californian lifestyle. She also made the bold suggestion that he take their secretary May Pang to look after him. Born in New York of Chinese parents, 22-year-old May Pang had worked as secretary to the Lennons' company Lennono for several years, and was a trusted employee. Yoko understood that John would be helpless alone in California. Although he could drive, he was invariably chauffeured around wherever he wanted to go. He'd never had to engage in normal activities such as going to supermarkets or paying bills—someone else had always done it for him.

In October 1973, John and May Pang arrived in Los Angeles for what would in many ways turn into a 15-month rampage that saw John transform himself into an appallingly clichéd rock-and-roll animal. In something of an understatement, he would later say of this period, "the feminist side of me died slightly."

Even though John and Yoko would still speak on the phone up to 20 times a day, he quickly formed an intimate relationship with May Pang. She would later write a controversial account of their affair, entitled *John Lennon: The Lost Weekend*. The intimacy that Pang describes developing between the two of them was disputed by Elliot Mintz, John's closest friend in America and one of the few people he knew when he arrived in Los Angeles. Mintz claimed: "To think that John ran off with May to leave Yoko Ono would require a remarkable suspension of logic." As far as he was concerned, "It was not a love affair. It was a relationship born out of the convenience of the moment." However, Mintz did believe that Yoko all but sanctioned the affair: "I suppose Yoko knew it was likely there would be intimacy between them. She took a mature view knowing John: 'Better with May than galloping around with the golden groupies.'"

May and John at the premiere of the musical *Sgt. Pepper's Lonely Hearts Club Band*, November 1974.

The Lost Weekend

John's separation from Yoko resulted in his life spiraling out of control. John later said he felt "like an elephant in a zoo." Whatever the cause, the period that became known as "The Lost Weekend" saw John going well and truly off the rails. Yoko may have hoped that California would help to invigorate John's creative appetite, but on arrival in LA he teamed up with some of rock's most notorious wastrels—Ringo Starr, Keith Moon (drummer with The Who), and singer Harry Nilsson among others—and embarked on one long alcoholic binge.

In fact, the madness may well have been less over the top than posterity records. The problem for Lennon and his Rat Pack was that their scenes of debauchery always took place in public, and so were always reported by the media. According to John, his drug intake had been so vast during the final days of The Beatles that he was left with a low body resistance to alcohol. As his friend Elliot Mintz recalled, he was such a poor drinker that "if he had one glass of wine I'd have to cancel all appointments for the next three days." The booze also made him boorish and argumentative: "He would start an argument and keep it going just for the sake of having a row and winning it," Mintz remembered.

One one occasion, returning from a vodka binge to the house in Bel Air that record producer Lou Adler had loaned him and May, John began to smash the place up. He launched vases at stained-glass windows and trashed the gold discs that hung on the wall. Phil Spector and his bodyguard were present, and wrestled the out-of-control Lennon to his bed, where they bound his hands and feet to stop him from doing any more damage to the house or to himself. John's personal nadir came in March 1974 at the Troubadour Club in Los Angeles during a show by The Smothers Brothers, featuring his old friend Tommy Smothers. Drunk on arrival, his constant foul-mouthed heckling ruined the evening for the rest of the audience. When Ken Fritz, manager of The Smothers Brothers, tried to shut Lennon up he was assaulted. Lennon ended the evening by slapping waitress Brenda Mary Perkins, who tried to take a photograph of the fiasco. Her claim for damages against Lennon was later dismissed in court, but Perkins was sanguine about the experience: "It's not the pain that hurts," she explained, "it's finding out that one of your idols is a real asshole."

Throughout the turmoil John continued his regular telephone dialog with Yoko. According to Mintz: "All of his thoughts, all of his longings had to do with his desperation to get back with Yoko, and to his frustration with her telling him he didn't sound ready." Little did John know that, in spite of his present erratic behavior, Yoko always believed their reunion was simply a matter of time.

Even during his "lost" year with May Pang (in background), John kept in touch with his son Julian (left). However, he always felt guilty that he had not taken a more active role in Julian's upbringing.

Rock-and-roll fiasco

John's arrival in California had coincided with the release of *Mind Games*. Although aware that the album had been a half-hearted effort, he was nevertheless disappointed at the mauling it received at the hands of the world's music press. He felt further dispirited when he realized that Ringo Starr's surprise hit album *Ringo* was outpacing his new offering by some distance. The final ignominy came in 1974 when Paul McCartney's band Wings hit peak form with *Band On The Run*, an album that sold in Beatlesque proportions.

Although he often portrayed himself as tough and impenetrable, at heart John Lennon was a ball of insecurity. He now began to feel that his life—both private and artistic—was falling apart. He needed something to focus on, a project he could become fired up about.

Eventually, he turned to an idea that he'd had in mind for some time, and decided he would record an album of old rock-and-roll classics. His working title was "Oldies But Mouldies"—a parody of a 1966 Beatles hits compilation, *A Collection Of Beatles Oldies ... But Goldies*. As a songwriter, his confidence had reached rock bottom; such a project would take the pressure off having to come up with new material. Furthermore, with a charismatic producer such as Phil Spector at the helm, John wouldn't be forced to make too many artistic decisions of his own.

There was one other benefit to this project. Several years earlier, music publisher Morris Levy threatened to sue John for plagiarism. Levy owned the publishing rights to most of Chuck Berry's classic rock-and-roll hits and claimed that on "Come Together" from *Abbey Road*, John had borrowed heavily from Berry's 1956 hit "You Can't Catch Me." Although the claim was tenuous, John couldn't face more litigation and so agreed out of court to record a number of other Levy-owned Chuck Berry songs for a future album.

The sessions for the album quickly turned into a drunken fiasco. Spector's behavior grew stranger by the day—increasingly paranoid, he would sometimes pull out a revolver and pump the occasional bullet into the studio walls. In spite of an all-star cast that included Dr. John, ace session musician Leon Russell, and members of The Rolling Stones, almost $100,000 was spent on recording and only four of the many tracks laid down were considered usable. Finally, the working relationship between John Lennon and his producer broke down completely, and Spector disappeared, taking the master tapes with him. He returned to his heavily guarded mansion and Lennon was initially unable to get him to surrender the tapes. Even when Spector obliged, Lennon realized they were of dubious quality to say the least. Both his personal and professional lives now seemed to be in stalemate.

Although both men had been called musical geniuses, John's collaboration with Phil Spector on his album of rock-and-roll classics proved to be a disastrous experience for all concerned.

Walls And Bridges

With his album of rock-and-roll covers on hold, and the worst of his LA excesses behind him, John began work on an album of new material. But even though he now lived on the opposite coast to his wife, Yoko Ono remained the principle inspiration for *Walls And Bridges*. Indeed, many of the songs can be easily interpreted as a direct plea for Yoko to take him back and get him out of the mess he now found himself in. Even the album's title may have alluded to the barriers that now separated John from his soul mate, despite the fact that John facetiously claimed it had actually been "sent from above in the guise of a public service announcement."

Walls And Bridges spawned two major hit singles: "#9 Dream," appropriately enough, reached number 9 on the U.S. charts, while the irreverent "Whatever Gets You Thru The Night," featuring Elton John on keyboards and backing vocals, gave Lennon his first solo chart-topping single in the States. However, the album's key moment is the closing ballad "Nobody Loves You (When You're Down And Out)"—the title is a play on that of an old blues song by Jimmie Cox. A cynical (some might say self-pitying) assessment of the state of his world by the middle of 1974, John himself admitted it "exactly expressed the period I was apart from Yoko." Elsewhere on the album, his lyrics were equally revealing. "Scared"—which could almost be "Help!" 10 years on—has its author admitting "I'm so tired of being alone."

In a reflection of its autobiographical nature, *Walls And Bridges* came complete with a lavish sleeve, including a booklet featuring the lyrics and illustrated by drawings and paintings that John had made when he was 12 years old.

Although it gave John his biggest hit since *Imagine*, and restored his public profile, he was never hugely taken with *Walls And Bridges*:

"This last year has been an extraordinary one for me personally. And I'm almost amazed that I could get *anything* out. Musically my mind was a clutter. [*Walls And Bridges*] was the work of a semi-sick craftsman. There was no inspiration and it gave an aura of misery."

John's dismissal of the album is not surprising given that it must have represented a powerful document of a period in which his personal life had reached rock bottom. In truth, *Walls And Bridges* may not have been vintage Lennon, but it was nonetheless a fine record. May Pang has challenged the accepted view that John's life during this period had been one year-long "lost weekend," arguing that he produced some of the best music of his solo career. *Walls And Bridges* does much to back up her claim.

John pictured during a photosession for the cover of the album *Walls And Bridges,* in 1974.

New inspiration

Hanging out with other musicians in LA had not been overly healthy or productive for John Lennon. His early cohorts in drunken mayhem had been Harry Nilsson and Keith Moon—neither being particularly known for their high productivity (nor, for that matter, their sanity). But by the time of the *Walls And Bridges* sessions, Lennon was beginning to get back on track. A key player in this turnaround was Elton John, at that time emerging as the most successful British artist in the U.S. since the heyday of The Beatles. An extremely hard-working and commercially astute musician, Elton provided Lennon with some badly needed stimulation and direction.

The collaboration began when Lennon played Elton a demo tape of the songs that would make up *Walls And Bridges*, and asked him to contribute some piano and backing vocals to a track of his choice. Like many pop stars of the time, The Beatles had been an important inspiration for Elton during his teenage years, and even though he was now a massive star in his own right, he was more than happy to oblige. The number he chose was "Whatever Gets You Thru The Night"—not necessarily the best song in the collection (Lennon himself regarded it as his least favorite), but Elton felt it was easily the most commercial. However, there was a price to pay: if it topped the chart, Elton demanded that Lennon repay the favor by performing at one of his forthcoming shows.

Amazingly, on November 16, 1974, "Whatever Gets You Thru The Night" arrived at the top of the U.S. singles chart, and Elton called in his debt. Two weeks later, at Elton's Thanksgiving Day show at New York's Madison Square Garden, John Lennon appeared on stage as a surprise guest star in front of an ecstatic audience, and performed three songs with the show's star. In addition to his chart-topping single, they duetted on a version of John's "Lucy In The Sky With Diamonds." The brief set ended with "I Saw Her Standing There," a song from The Beatles' first album. As if to signal a gradual mellowing of his spiky character, Lennon poignantly dedicated it "to an old estranged fiancé of mine, called Paul." It would be the last time John Lennon appeared on a public stage.

After the show, Elton's record label threw a party at New York's plush Pierre Hotel. Although Lennon wasn't aware of it at the time, Yoko had been in the audience that night and she was also one of the guests at the aftershow bash; her appearance both shocked and delighted him. That evening marked the start of their reconciliation.

Opposite: The two Johns—Elton and Lennon, Madison Square Garden, 1974.

Right: The concert was to be Lennon's last public performance.

Rock and roller

The year 1974 ended in a whirlwind of activity. With publisher Morris Levy breathing down his neck, chasing the fulfillment of their out-of-court agreement, Lennon had deliberately ended *Walls And Bridges* with a vignette of Lee Dorsey's "Ya Ya"–another song owned by Levy. He had hoped this gesture would be enough to get Levy off his back. He was wrong. Levy demanded that Lennon cover at least three numbers from his catalog.

In an effort to settle the matter once and for all, John retrieved the "Oldies But Mouldies" master tapes from Phil Spector. However, after listening to them again he told May Pang that they were "awful ... I must have felt terrible when I did these." Only three tracks were usable–even for an album driven by contractual fulfillments, John still had certain standards to maintain. At the end of October, in four highly charged days at the Record Plant studios, he recorded and mixed 10 more rock-and-roll classics. The resulting album–now renamed *Rock 'n' Roll*–was less a faithful recreation of the spirit of the 1950s than a nostalgic revisiting of the soundtrack of John's youth. The overall effect was affectionate rather than rip-roaring, but each track has the imprint of John's personality firmly stamped on it.

All things considered, John made the best job of a bad situation. Released in February 1975, only four months after *Walls And Bridges*, *Rock 'n' Roll* was another sizable success, with the single "Stand By Me" becoming a U.S. Top 10 chart hit. In a way, by turning his back on contemporary music for basic rock and roll, John was even mirroring the punk explosion that would soon hit the world.

One of the most attractive aspects of the album was the photograph chosen for the sleeve. Taken by The Beatles' German friend Jürgen Vollmer in Hamburg in 1961, it shows John as a sneering 21-year-old Teddy Boy leaning against the stage door to a club.

Closing the album with Lloyd Price's "Just Because," John parodied one of the clichés of rock-and-roll balladry with a talkover sequence. In the manner of the last song of the evening, as the ending fades away he offers the listener a fond "goodnight." But even as he was recording the song, he found himself wondering "Am I really saying farewell to the music business? I looked at the cover I'd chosen ... I thought, this is some sort of cosmic thing. Here I am with this old picture of me in Hamburg in '61 and I'm saying farewell from the Record Plant, and I'm ending as I started, singing this straight rock 'n' roll stuff."

Having resuscitated his flagging career, John Lennon was now once more a commercial force in the music world. It therefore seems ironic in retrospect that it would be another five years before he set foot in a recording studio again.

John chose a moody photograph of himself taken in Hamburg in 1961 for the cover of the *Rock 'n' Roll* album. He later reflected that he felt he had come full circle with the record.

Reunited

As 1975 got underway, life was looking pretty good for John Lennon. He was once again in the limelight, but now it was for the thing he did best—making music—rather than for troublemaking. Above all, ever since their Thanksgiving Day encounter, his relationship with Yoko was now more positive than it had been at any time since their separation. It came as no surprise to those close to either camp when, in January 1975, John returned home to the Dakota building: "I feel like I've been on Sinbad's voyage and I've battled all those monsters and I've got back," he proclaimed. "Our separation was a failure."

Significantly, in January 1975, The Beatles were dissolved as a business enterprise, breaking another link between John and his past. At first John looked set to carry on the hectic schedule of the past few months. In the middle of January David Bowie invited him to the sessions for what would become the former's *Young Americans* album. John played guitar on Bowie's version of "Across The Universe." While in the studio, John also co-wrote a song with Bowie and guitarist Carlos Alomar—the stripped-down, funky "Fame," a cynical stab at the world of celebrity. The song would shortly provide Bowie with his first U.S. number 1; it looked as if John had rediscovered his golden touch. John and Yoko also appeared with Bowie, Simon and Garfunkel, and Roberta Flack at the 1975 Grammy Awards, the couple's first public appearance together since their reconciliation.

John and Yoko had been trying unsuccessfully to have children since the late 1960s. Seeking advice from a Chinese acupuncturist and herbalist in the early 1970s, they were told that John's hedonistic lifestyle may have lowered his sperm count, and contributed to the problem. He was advised to cut out all drugs apart from cigarettes and to reduce his alcohol intake. John's "Lost Weekend" with May Pang had put paid to such plans, but prior to his reunion with Yoko, he adopted a much healthier lifestyle. It seemed to work: within weeks, Yoko was pregnant. But three pregnancies had resulted in three miscarriages, and the couple were understandably cautious about the chances of a success this time round. Moreover, Yoko's age (she was seven years older than her husband) was not on her side.

It was then that John took the monumental decision to retire from music. He had long since tired of the treadmill of creating an endless supply of "product" and knew that this was the right time for him to act: "I felt boxed in ... the contract was a physical manifestation of being in prison ... I might as well have gone to a nine-to-five job as carry on the way I was carrying on," he later reflected. John eagerly reinvented himself as the perfect father-to-be, channeling his best efforts into caring for Yoko.

John and Yoko appeared alongside a host of musical celebrities at the Grammy Awards in Los Angeles on March 1, 1975. It was their first public appearance together since their reunion.

A big month

October 1975 turned out to be an important month for the Lennons. The ball started rolling on October 8, when John received news about his legal battle to stay in America. The signs were good: New York State's Supreme Court had voted by a two-to-one decision to reverse his latest deportation order. The residing judge was unequivocal in his judgment, stating: "The court cannot condone selective deportation based upon secret political grounds."

America's prevailing political wind was in the throes of change. Two years earlier, former president Richard Nixon had resigned in disgrace under the cloud of Watergate. His successor, Gerald Ford, had finally taken the U.S. military out of Vietnam. Furthermore, a new Democrat administration under Jimmy Carter was preparing itself for office. By the mid-1970s John Lennon was no longer viewed as a subversive—indeed, the authorities were sympathetic to his cause. The court decision enabled John to finally obtain a Green Card in 1976. He was told that after five years he could apply for full U.S. citizenship.

At 2 a.m. on October 9, Yoko Ono gave birth to a son, Sean Taro Ono Lennon. The date also marked John's 35th birthday, and he was ecstatic: "I feel higher than the Empire State Building," he announced, joyously. The first person he called with the news was Aunt Mimi.

John had always been acutely aware of the legacy that his own parental instability had left him. Consequently, he had already tried, with some success, to establish a meaningful relationship with his first son, Julian, who by this time was in his early teens. But John was adamant Sean wouldn't have to face the same hardships that he'd been through himself.

Four months after Sean entered his life, John Lennon's recording contract with EMI/Capitol expired. Heralding his new intentions, he decided not to bother renewing it. For the next four years, John had virtually no involvement in the music world. With Yoko employed in looking after the Lennons' business affairs, John became a self-styled house-husband, channeling all of his energy into Sean's upbringing. While Yoko worked, John and Sean were rarely apart. John took care of the washing, cleaning, and changing diapers—his new domesticity even stretched as far as cookery. This was clearly not the same person who had been screaming for world revolution less than five years earlier.

John's antipathy to the music business also extended to old friends. He was especially contemptuous of the music Paul McCartney and Mick Jagger were making in the mid-1970s. He saw no development in their work and dismissed them collectively as the "Rolling Wings." In a waspish put-down, he also compared Paul to middle-of-the-road balladeer Engelbert Humperdinck. The music-making part of John's life was over. For now.

Beautiful boy. After his son Sean was born in 1975, John dedicated himself to bringing him up. To do so he turned his back on the music business and was not to release another album for five years.

Domestic bliss

Placing his financial affairs in the hands of an avant-garde artist might have seemed like a risk for John, but it turned out to be a wise move. Yoko Ono quickly revealed that she had a phenomenally good head for business affairs, even if her intuitive methods—she was especially fond of using numerology and tarot readings for guidance—were hardly orthodox. Yoko invested in property, agriculture, works of art, and many ecologically sound projects. By the end of the decade, under her guiding hand, Lennono—their joint company—was conservatively valued at $150 million.

Meanwhile, John had turned into something approaching a health freak. He baked his own bread, followed macrobiotic regimes, paid scrupulous attention to his and Sean's diets, and banned alcohol from the Dakota Building. However, he never managed to end his lifelong love of caffeine and cigarettes.

In 1977, secure in the knowledge that they could now safely leave America and be allowed to return, the Lennons embarked on a two-month trip to Japan. John loved the country. He was particularly fascinated by the rituals of a culture that was so alien to him. Moreover, he appreciated the fact that he could walk the streets of Tokyo and remain largely unrecognized. The outside world hardly got a look in during this period in the ex-Beatle's life. John paid little attention to contemporary music, and the changing climate of punk and new wave that was then transforming the world of rock and roll largely passed him by. He and Yoko were enjoying a period of long-overdue domestic contentment.

However, wherever he was in the world, John would invariably phone Aunt Mimi on most days. In July 1980, he gave her a glimpse of his future intentions: "I'm 40 this year. I'm going to make one more record, Mimi, then I'm going to do some writing," he confided.

John had made his decision in July when he was on holiday in Bermuda. He rented a house for a month, during which time he was planning to relax, swim, and sail. However, as it turned out, within a week he was writing songs. Back in New York, John and Yoko spent much of August and September in the studio. But these sessions were like no previous recordings in which John Lennon had been involved—they were civilized affairs, free from alcohol and drugs, both of which were now strictly forbidden. The music that resulted reflected both the relaxed atmosphere in which it was recorded, and John and Yoko's contentment with each other.

During his stay in Bermuda, John visited the Botanical Gardens and came across a freesia that bore a name he instinctively seized upon for the title of the new album. It seemed to perfectly reflect his life with Yoko: "Double Fantasy."

After Sean reached the age of five, John and Yoko began to appear in public more frequently.

End of an era

Fast approaching 40, and with his son Sean now of nursery age, John Lennon rediscovered his thirst to make music: "I swore I'd look after that boy until he was five ... " he revealed in one interview. "He's five now and I feel like getting back to my music. The urge is there. It's been a long time since I wrote a song, but they're coming thick and fast now."

The reports that John was once again in the recording studio caused ripples of excitement in the music media. Unsurprisingly, there was no shortage of music corporations prepared to talk about a new record deal, although the all-out bidding war that might have been anticipated was tempered when the Lennons announced that the new release would be a "John and Yoko" album. Wary at the prospect of uncommercial Yoko offerings, some labels asked to hear demo tapes before committing themselves. John took this as an insult, and eventually signed a deal with the newly created Geffen Records; label boss David Geffen offered the Lennons a deal unconditionally, without hearing any of the new material.

October 27, 1980, saw the much-heralded release of the first new John Lennon single in five years. But "(Just Like) Starting Over" turned out to be an anticlimax for some people. Many had unrealistically high hopes for the return of one of the most important artists of the previous two decades. Even so, on the evidence of this piece of nostalgic whimsy it seemed unlikely the album would break new ground. However, the world welcomed John's return, and within weeks the single had eased itself into the Top 10 of most countries.

Three weeks later, *Double Fantasy* hit the shops, to a largely lukewarm critical response. For many fans of his solo work, John was at his best when he was venting his anger and frustration. The Lennon on display here was a contented man, at one with himself, and happy to tell the world that all that really mattered to him now was his family. Such domestic contentment didn't necessarily make for the most exhilarating music.

Nevertheless, by the start of December 1980, with both the single and album in the upper reaches of the charts, confidence was running high. Work was already progressing on a follow-up and John talked openly about undertaking a world tour in 1981, including a series of dates in Britain. Tragically, none of his plans would come to fruition.

Late on the night of December 8, 1980, returning from a recording session, John and Yoko were about to enter the Dakota Building when a voice called out "Mr. Lennon?" As John turned round in response, five bullets from a .38 revolver tore into his arm and back. Despite his wounds, he managed to stagger up six steps to the office of Jay Hastings, the Dakota desk clerk, where he collapsed, moaning "I'm shot."

Even toward the end of his life John made time for fans' requests for autographs. Occasionally, he and Yoko would even take on the fans who hung around the Dakota as hired help.

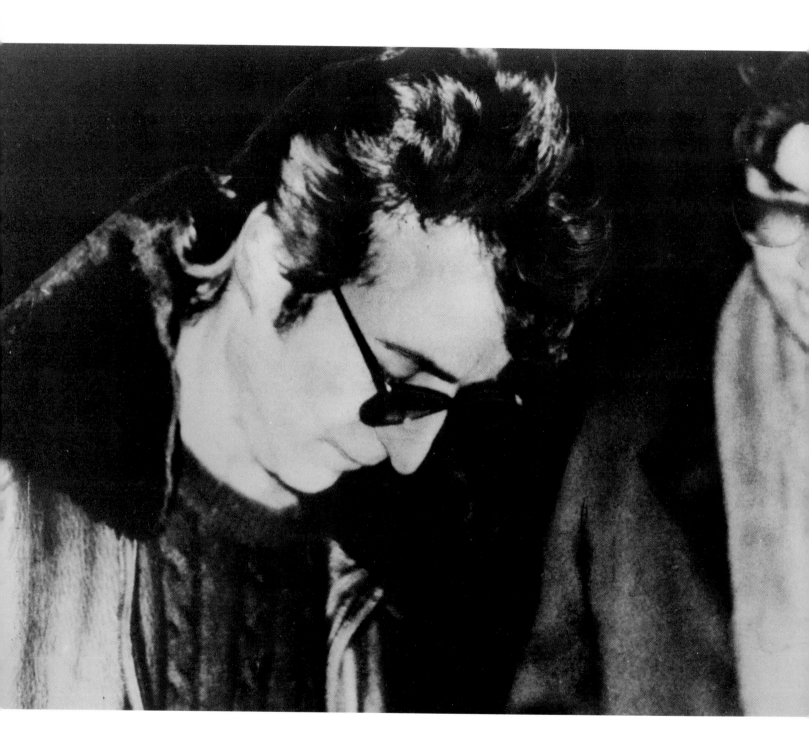

News hits the streets

Scenes of trauma and chaos followed the shooting. Yoko screamed for an ambulance; after covering John with his jacket, Jay Hastings pressed an alarm button that connected the Dakota Building directly with a local police precinct. Some two minutes later, a squad car arrived at the Dakota. There was no time to wait for medical assistance, and John was bundled into the car, which immediately sped off in the direction of the Roosevelt Hospital. Doctors massaged his heart in an effort to get it working again, but it was too late—he had already bled to death. After returning from the hospital, Yoko announced her husband's death to the world, along with a simple plea: "John loved and prayed for the human race. Please do the same for him."

The news of John's murder spread quickly over the world's airwaves. Many bulletins drew attention to the irony that the man who was arguably one of the most famous public preachers for peace since Gandhi and Dr. Martin Luther King, Jr. had, like them, died a sudden and violent death.

On December 10, 1980, John Lennon was cremated at Hartsdale Crematorium, in New York State. He was mourned by millions across the world. On December 14, Yoko requested that his fans observe a worldwide 10-minute silence. Nearly half a million people gathered in New York's Central Park, opposite the Dakota, to pay their respects.

What of his assassin? Mark David Chapman was a 25-year-old former hospital security guard who had arrived in New York several days earlier. A Beatles fanatic, he had stayed at the Olcott Hotel on West 72nd Street—a short walk from John's home. On the day of the murder he had waited outside the Dakota with his copy of *Double Fantasy*, which he managed to get John to autograph for him. Arrested at the scene of his crime, the next day Mark Chapman was charged with murder and sentenced to life imprisonment.

Why would a devoted fan kill his hero? Repeated psychological examinations of Chapman failed to find a satisfactory answer. There were no signs that he was insane, even though he later claimed that God had visited him in his cell and told him to change his plea from not guilty to guilty (in doing so he avoided a trial). Chapman had clearly come to New York City with just one aim—to kill John Lennon.

Lennon's death generated a host of conspiracy theories. One, published by U.K. barrister Fenton Bresler, claimed there was evidence linking Chapman to the CIA. Given John's difficulties with the U.S. authorities, that wouldn't have been impossible. But now most people accept that Mark Chapman was solely responsible for John Lennon's violent murder.

Lennon signs a copy of *Double Fantasy* for Mark David Chapman outside the Dakota on December 8, 1980. Just a few hours later, Chapman shot Lennon dead.

The aftermath

During the media hysteria that surrounded John's death, sales of his music went into overdrive. Indeed, in a sad and ironic twist, the three months that followed saw his greatest period of commercial success as a solo artist. "(Just Like) Starting Over," which had slipped down the U.K. charts to number 21 from its original number 8 peak, did an about-face and leaped to number 1. When it vacated the top spot just before Christmas, 1980, it was replaced by the hastily reissued "Imagine." One position behind that sat "Happy Xmas (War Is Over)." In the new year, "Woman," a track that John himself had thought of as being particularly Beatlesque, provided the third posthumous Lennon U.K. number 1 in three months. "(Just Like) Starting Over" also hit the top spot in the States, while *Double Fantasy* became a transatlantic chart-topper.

Not surprisingly, the period following John's death was extremely painful for Yoko Ono. Radio stations paid tribute to her husband by playing his music endlessly. There was no escaping his legacy—for weeks to come, fans from all over the world held vigil outside the Lennons' home, singing John's songs.

Instead of escaping from New York, Yoko chose the seclusion of familiar surroundings and locked herself away in the Dakota. She closed off the bedroom that she had shared with John and instructed staff to change nothing in the apartment. For three months Yoko went through severe depression, before finally admitting to herself that John would have wanted her to get on with her life. She once again took up the reins of Lennono and, more significantly, returned to the recording studio to make a new album, *Season Of Glass*: "Making the record," she later revealed, "was definitely therapy, the only way I could survive." The record's sleeve was controversial, featuring a photograph of John's bloodstained glasses, which Yoko had picked up after his shooting. Some accused her of tastelessness, although her motives were clearly deeply personal.

After all the criticism that she attracted during the early years of her relationship with John—she was, after all, popularly seen as being responsible for splitting up The Beatles— Yoko Ono at last had the world's sympathy and respect. The Dakota, where she and John shared so many traumas and triumphs, remains her home. She has continued to work as an artist, musician, and performer, often with her son Sean, now also a respected musician in his own right and signed to The Beastie Boys' hip Grand Royal label. But John Lennon still remains an important part of Yoko's life: "We were best friends but also competitive artists. To me, he is still alive. Death alone doesn't extinguish a flame and spirit like John."

After John's death, the Dakota was deluged with floral tributes from devastated Lennon fans.
Despite the trauma of her husband's death, Yoko opted to keep their apartment in the building.

Relics

John Lennon left a legacy of unfinished tracks and half-written songs and since his death a number of these have come to light. The first notable package of unreleased Lennon material, the album *Milk And Honey*, emerged in 1984. It interleaves six of John's recordings-in-progress with tracks written and recorded by Yoko. Although the versions of John's songs are unrefined, they show that he retained his caustic wit and capacity for brutal honesty. The most interesting compilation that followed John's death was simply called *Menlove Avenue*, after the street where he grew up with his Aunt Mimi. This contains out-takes from his solo albums. Many of these recordings possess a powerful raw charm—a quality missing from many of the later releases during John's lifetime.

In 1995, a modest wave of Beatlemania was unleashed. With the market for Beatle rarities and bootlegs as buoyant as ever, the *Anthology* series was conceived. A major television documentary series was accompanied by the release of three double-CD sets made up from out-takes or alternative versions of some of The Beatles' most famous songs.

In January 1994, Paul McCartney, in his capacity as one half of pop's most famous songwriting partnership, had inducted John posthumously into the Rock and Roll Hall of Fame. After the ceremony, Yoko gave Paul tapes of two of John's home demos. The idea was that with the other three Beatles playing along with John's backing track, two "new" Beatles tracks would emerge. George Martin, who played a central role in the *Anthology* series, was against the idea of the new recordings and refused to be involved. However, engineer Geoff Emerick, who had worked with The Beatles during the 1960s at Abbey Road, did lend a hand.

The first new release was "Free As A Bird," culled from two verses of an unfinished song recorded by John while improvising at the piano. Turning back the years, Paul McCartney supplied a middle-eight section. The finished song was vaguely reminiscent of *Abbey Road*-era Beatles. Another song, "Real Love," had been heard in demo form in the 1988 film of John's life, *Imagine*. Some pundits felt that producer Jeff Lynne (formerly of The Electric Light Orchestra) had simply made them sound like ELO. The remaining Beatles themselves had few qualms, though. Paul McCartney pointed out that John and he had often worked on each other's incomplete songs in the past: "It was like John bringing me a song and saying 'Do you want to finish it?'" There were both emotional and technical obstacles to overcome during the recording of the new tracks. Ringo revealed that the remaining three Beatles dealt with John's absence by pretending that he'd simply gone out for lunch, or on holiday. Both singles were worldwide hits, though neither made the top spot in the U.S. or U.K.

Sean Lennon, Yoko, and Paul McCartney gathered to honor John at the Rock and Roll Hall of Fame in 1994. Yoko and Paul embraced during the ceremony, suggesting they had finally made peace.

A man of influence

Now that the old divisions of high and low culture have largely collapsed, it is no surprise to see The Beatles respected as much as the greatest classical composers or jazz musicians. What is surprising is how much The Beatles—both as musicians and personalities—have become a part of our lives. More than 30 years since their last recordings, The Beatles remain the most famous pop group in the world. As the band's creative axis, John Lennon and Paul McCartney's influence on the course of popular music has been profound.

Most major songwriters of the past three decades would cite Lennon and McCartney as important influences, and only Bob Dylan can claim any parity in terms of cultural significance. Producers point to the collaboration between The Beatles and George Martin as a benchmark in the use of the recording studio. Every new generation throws up its own take on The Beatles. Most successful have been The Electric Light Orchestra in the 1970s and Oasis in the 1990s—indeed, the latter's *What's the Story? (Morning Glory)* achieved sales comparable to those of the Fab Four, becoming the U.K.'s second best-selling LP of all time.

Since the demise of the Fab Four, Paul McCartney has emerged as the most successful ex-Beatle in terms of record sales, and remains one of pop's best-selling artists. John Lennon idled away much of the 1970s, but retained critical respect and still took the prizes for serious artistic credibility. After all those years, he was still regarded as the "intellectual" Beatle.

Successive generations of music fans have continued to buy into the legend of The Beatles since their split. Their classic albums—especially those released between 1965's *Rubber Soul* and 1969's *Abbey Road*—continue to sell in large numbers, while John's composition "Imagine" remains one of the most popular songs of the twentieth century.

Some would claim John Lennon was a genius. He himself was characteristically unfazed by the tag, once stating: "If there is such a thing as a genius, I am one. If there isn't, I don't care." Lennon was certainly full of contradictions. While he was capable of exhibiting a hard exterior, those who got close to him spoke of his kindness, and generosity. But while he was capable of acts of cruelty and extreme selfishness, John also publicly stood up for the most positive aspects of humanity. He preached the very spirit of his age—love, peace, and understanding—as vociferously, even belligerently, as anyone.

When asked at the height of Beatlemania how long he thought the Beatles would last, John Lennon's reply was a cautious one: "You can be big-headed and say 'Yeah, we're gonna last 10 years,' but as soon as you've said that you think ... we're lucky if we last three months." It's now over 40 years since his school band, The Quarrymen, played their first ramshackle skiffle concerts, but the legacy of John Lennon will shine on for decades to come.

John Lennon photographed in 1971. An icon of his time, and one of the best smiles in pop.

Index

Brian & Chari,

All the best cruising the med! Have a safe and plea[sant] journey. Hopefully see you over there.

Cheers!

Ken W[...]

Navigational Guide to the Adriatic

Croatian Coast

Leksikografski zavod *Miroslav Krleža*

Zagreb, 2001.

The Miroslav Krleža LEXICOGRAPHICAL INSTITUTE

PRESIDENT OF THE BOARD
Dalibor Brozović, Academician

DIRECTOR
Vladimir Pezo

CIP - Katalogizacija u publikaciji
Nacionalna i sveučilišna knjižnica, Zagreb

UDK 656.61(497.5) (036)
797.1(497.5) (036)
527(262.3) (036)

NAVIGATIONAL guide to the Adriatic :
Croatian coast / <translation Neda
Karlović-Blažeković ; photographs Petar
Kleinoth. . . <et al. > ; editor-in-chief
Anton Simović>. - 3rd ed. - Zagreb : The
Miroslav Krleža Lexicographical Institute,
2001

Kazalo.

ISBN 953-6036-87-8

I. Jadransko more -- Nautički vodič

410604007

Leksikografski zavod *Miroslav Krleža*
Frankopanska ul. 26, ZAGREB, CROATIA

PRINTED BY
GRAFIČKI ZAVOD HRVATSKE d.o.o. - ZAGREB

NAVIGATIONAL GUIDE TO THE ADRIATIC
CROATIAN COAST

Küstenhandbuch Kroatien. - 2. Aufl. - Hamburg:
Ed. Maritim 1999.
(Nautischer Reiseführer)
ISBN 3-89225-338-2 (Edition: Edition Maritim)
NE:EST
ISBN 953-6036-08-8 (Edition: Leksikografski zavod)

Original: Navigational Guide to the Adriatic CroatianCoast,1993.
ISBN 953-6036-06-1

3ʳᵈ edition
ISBN 3-89225-338-2 (Edition: Edition Maritim)
ISBN 953-6036-08-8 (Edition: Leksikografski zavod)

© Leksikografski zavod *Miroslav Krleža*
Frankopanska 26, HR - 10000 Zagreb
Director: Vladimir Pezo

Title of the English original:
Navigational Guide to the Adriatic Croatian Coast
© Leksikografski zavod *Miroslav Krleža*

3ⁿᵈ edition
Navigational Guide to the Adriatic Croatian Coast
ISBN 953-6036-87-8
© Leksikografski zavod *Miroslav Krleža*

Editor-in-chief: Anton Simović
Editorial staff: Žarko Anić-Antić, Đuro Fabjanović, Igor Gostl,
Zvonimir Jakobović, Branka Komadina, Nenad Kunštek, Vesna Kušar,
Ivan Markešić, Vladimir Mesić, Boris Mirković, Ivan Platužić,
Anton Simović, Zdenko Šenoa, Katarina Turkalj, Stjepan Vuk

Cartography and drawings:
Leksikografski zavod *Miroslav Krleža*

Photographs: »Adriatic Croatia International Club« (ACI) - Opatija,
»Edition Maritim« - Hamburg, »Masmedia« - Zagreb,
Photo-documents of the Leksikografski zavod *Miroslav Krleža*,
Photographs of HRT - Zagreb, »Turistkomerc« - Zagreb,
Peter Kleinoth, Igor Michieli, Mato Novaković, Milan Pavić,
Ivan Pervan, Vanja Žanko, Ilija Živanović

Cover: Katarina Turkalj
Translation: Neda Karlović-Blažeković
Desktop publishing: Branka Komadina
Printed and bound: GRAFIČKI ZAVOD HRVATSKE d.o.o., Zagreb
Photo on the front cover: Korčula; photo on the back cover: Mali Lošinj
both by Josip Bistrović (»Masmedia«)
Printed in Croatia 2001.

Marketing: Leksikografski zavod *Miroslav Krleža*, Frankopanska 26, HR, 10000 Zagreb
Tel: ++ 385 1 48 333, ++ 385 1 48 320, Fax: ++ 385 1 48 00 323, M.B. 3211622
e-mail: lzmk@hlz.hr
http://www.hlz.hr

ABBREVIATIONS

(in Croatian navigation charts and publications)

-B	white (light)	kor	coral, coral-reef (seabed)	SE	southeast, southeasterly
Bl	flash(es)	kW	kilowatt	sekt.	sector light
br.	*see* No.	l., L.	port, harbour	sig. mag.	fog signal
c., C	red (signs, light)	LK	Harbour Master's Office	Sj	fixed and flashing lights
C.	cape, point	L. pl.	map (plan) of the port (harbour)	Sl	slipway, shipway
cr.	black (signs)			SS	saints
CRV.	red (sector light)	m	metre	SSE	south-southeast, south-southeasterly
čv	*see* kn	m	mud (seabed)		
D	crane, hoist	M	nautical mile	SSW	south-southwest, south-southwesterly
D.	lower, nether (geography)	M.	small (geography)		
D Bl	long flash(es)	mbar	millibar	Svj. pl.	floating light-buoy
Dir.	directional light	min	minute (time)	SW	southwest, southwesterly
dr., Dr.	inlet, small bay	mm	millimetre	š	gravel (seabed)
dwt	deadweight tons	Mo(A)	Morse code light (A)	šk	shells, conches
E	east, easterly	N	north, northerly	t	ton(s)
ENE	east-northeast, east-northeasterly	NE	northeast, northeasterly	t	sea-weed, grass (seabed)
		NNE	north-northeast, north-northeasterly	tel.	telephone
Ep	electrical hook-up			tfax	telefax
ESE	east-southeast, east-south easterly	NNW	north-northwest, north-northwesterly	tlex	telex
				Tr	car-ferry landing place
FS	pump station (fuel)	No.	number	TS	technical service (repairs)
G.	upper, superior	NW	northwest, northwesterly	u., U.	cove, small inlet
GMT	Greenwich Mean Time	o., O.	island, islet	UK Bl	ultraquick flashing light
Gp	group (flashing light)	Oi.	islands, islets	UTC	similar GMT (see)
gr., Gr.	sunken rock, sunken reef	OZP	Notice to Mariners	v	velocity, speed
GRT	Gross Register Tons	p	sand (seabed)	V.	large, big (geography)
h	hour (time)	P	tenant's registry offlce (reception)	var	variation, magnetic decli-nation
H	hotel				
HHI	Croatian Hydrographic Institute, Split	Pk	occulting light	Vert.	vertical (lights, signs)
		Pl.	buoy, floating mark (bea-con)	Vid.	light visibility
Hor.	horizontal (lights, signs)			Vk Bl	very quick flashing light
hr., Hr.	rock, reef	Plič.	shoal (in a navigation chart)	Vp	water hook-up
HRM	the Croatian Navy			W	west, westerly
i., I.	island, islet	Pm	alternating light	WC	water-closet
IALA	International Association of Lighthouse Authorities	POK.	leading light	WNW	west-northwest, west-northwesterly
		pol., POL.	peninsula		
Izd.	edition	pop.	population	WSW	west-southwest, west-southwesterly
Izo	isophase light	Pot., POTAM.	obscured (sector light)		
J.	lake, small lake	pr., Pr.	passage, straits	z., Z	green (signs, lights)
k	stone (seabed)	PSJM	The List of Lighthouses in the Adriatic Sea, the lonian Sea and on the Maltese Islands	zal., Zal.	bay, gulf
kab.	nautical cable (185.2 m)			zat., Zat.	small bay, small gulf
kam.	oysters			ZEL.	green (sector light)
kan., Kan.	channel			ž.	yellow (signs)
K Bl	quick flashing light	R	restaurant	φ	geographical latitude
kHz	kilo-hertz	s	second (time)	λ	geographical longitude
km	kilometre	S	south, southerly		
kn	knot	S, St, Sv	saint		
KN	kilo-newton	Sam.	monastery		

GLOSSARY

brdo	mountain	močvarno	marshy	sidrište	anchorage
brežuljak	hill	more	sea	solana	salt-pans
dio	part	morski	marine, seaside	spilja	cave
draga	inlet	nacionalni	national	stanica	station
dražica	cove	nudistički	nudist	sveta, sveti (Sv)	saint (St)
dvorac	castle, manor-house	obala	coast	svjetionik	lighthouse
grad	town	otočić	islet	svjetlo	light
gradić	small town	otok	island	šuma	wood, forest
greben	sunken rock (reef)	planina	mountain	tjesnac	strait(s)
groblje	cemetery	plaža	beach	ulaz	entrance
hotel	hotel	pličina	shoal	ušće	mouth
hrid	rock (reef)	poluotok	peninsula	utvrda	fortress
izvor	source, water-spring	potok	brook, stream	uvala	inlet, cove
jezerce	small lake, pond	prevlaka	isthmus	uvalica	small inlet (cove)
jezero	lake	pristanište	landing place, wharf	uzgajalište	farm
kamp	camp-site	prolaz	passage	veliki, veli, velji	great, big
kanal	channel	radio-far	radio-beacon	vrata	strait(s), passage
kopno	mainland	rezervat	protected area	vrelo	spring
kuća	house	rijeka	river	vrh	peak, top
lučica	small harbour	rt	point, cape	zaljev	bay
luka	port, harbour	ruševina	ruin, remains	zaton	small bay
mali, malo	small, little	selo	village, hamlet	žal	beach
mauzolej	mausoleum	sezonski	seasonal		

CONTENTS

FOREWORD

The Adriatic Sea occupies a significant position in Mediterranean nautical tourism. The Croatian seaboard is well-known for its numerous historically significant towns, tourist resorts, beautiful ports and marinas. With its indented coastline fronted by numerous islands and islets, renowned for its scenery, ecologically well preserved, and offering extremely favourable conditions for yachting, Croatian Adriatic seaboard represents a unique area for cruising in Europe.

The Republic of Croatia extends over 56 538 km² of land and 33 200 km² of internal sea waters and territorial sea. The maritime border measures 510 M. It owns 5790.1 km or 73% (mainland 1777.7 km or 47.6%, islands 4012.4 km or 96.1%) of the Adriatic seaboard which totals 7911 km (the mainland accounting for 3737 km and the islands 4174 km). The eastern Adriatic coast has a total of 725 islands and islets, 718 of which belong to Croatia (the inhabited islands - 66 of them - are all Croatian).

Safety at sea is greatly enhanced by a great number of lights and navigational marks, by well organized radio and meteorological services for mariners as well as by service for information and rescue at sea.

The Croats have been living on the eastern Adriatic coast for almost 14 centuries. From the 7th century they have been developing their national identity within the civilisational framework of belonging to the western Europe as well as building their state organization. Numerous archaeological sites and historical and cultural monuments (mentioned in the description of individual localities) bear witness to this.

The Republic of Croatia became a democratic and independent state in 1990, and from 1992 has been internationally recognized state and member of the United Nations Organization. It is our policy to pay great attention to the country's maritime orientation with tourism as an important factor. It is our belief that this Guide will prove a valuable contribution to the development of nautical tourism and especially to the safety in the Croatian part of the Adriatic.

This new edition of the Navigational Guide to the Adriatic (Croatian Coast) is an informative manual for shipmasters of small craft (yachts) cruising in the Croatian Adriatic for pleasure, sport and recreation. While up-dating its contents we stuck to the earlier assumption that only a qualified person who has been issued proper authorization by a pertinent authority (in Croatia this would be Harbour Master's Offices) could be in charge of a vessel which has to be equipped in accordance with the regulations of the internationally recognized institution (in Croatia this is the Croatian Register of Boats).

The introductory part of the Guide contains excerpts from the most important regulations and some other information relevant to safety at sea in the Croatian coastal area.

The main part of the Guide consists of descriptions of ports and marinas and more important minor Croatian harbours and coves. They have been divided into eight natural geographic areas that coincide with the pertinent Harbour Master's Offices. They are accompanied by cartographic illustrations, plans, drafts and colour photographs. The map in the Appendix (scale 1: 400 000) is meant to help select and plan navigational routes and general orientation while navigating. The Croatian Hydrographic Institute in Split publishes special nautical charts for smaller craft. Navigators would be well advised to consult the Lisf of Lights and Fog Signals published by the same Institute when navigating at night.

This Guide contains also pieces of information relating to cultural and historical monuments which will prove invaluable to all tourists on the Croatian seaside.

The Index at the end of the book contains a list of entries dealt with in the main part of the Guide in alphabetical order.

In preparing this edition of the Navigational Guide to the Adriatic (Croatian Coast) we made ample use of publications by the »Miroslav Krleža« Lexicographical Institute and of manuals and maps issued by the Croatian Hydrographic Institute in Split, publications of »Croatian Marinas« Association in Rijeka, Adriatic Croatia International Club (ACI) as well as a number of other foreign manuals. We are taking this opportunity to thank all those who kindly gave us their assistance.

Zagreb, 15.04.2001.   EDITORIAL BOARD

TABLE OF DISTANCES IN THE ADRIATIC SEA (in M)

From \ To	ANCONA	BARI	BRINDISI	DUBROVNIK	DURRËS	HERCEG-NOVI	HVAR	KOMIŽA	KOPER	KORČULA	KOTOR	MAKARSKA	MALI LOŠINJ	OPATIJA	OTRANTO	PAG	PESCARA	POREČ	PORTO CORSINI	PRIMOŠTEN	PULA	RAB	RIJEKA	RIMINI	SHËNGJINI	SPLIT	ŠIBENIK	TRIESTE	VELA LUKA	VENEZIA	ZADAR
ANCONA		216	272	213	303	241	133	121	125	169	254	156	72	109	310	110	80	98	75	107	80	90	111	49	297	131	109	129	149	121	86
BARI			62	108	120	110	125	120	318	113	123	146	232	277	101	237	152	289	289	151	267	239	278	263	130	145	162	322	111	329	194
BRINDISI				123	81	114	169	168	371	145	127	185	286	333	45	288	208	343	342	206	321	295	334	318	104	192	218	375	155	382	243
DUBROVNIK					102	27	82	97	289	49	40	82	208	246	152	207	175	261	282	116	239	206	244	258	85	105	127	293	72	305	160
DURRËS						81	181	190	386	148	94	181	307	349	83	304	248	358	379	215	336	305	347	352	35	202	226	390	172	402	260
HERCEG-NOVI							109	123	317	74	14	107	234	273	138	234	198	289	310	142	267	232	271	286	64	131	154	321	100	333	188
HVAR								23	207	34	122	34	126	165	205	126	110	179	200	35	157	124	164	176	167	23	46	211	19	223	79
KOMIŽA									203	53	136	49	124	162	208	123	90	175	196	35	153	122	161	165	178	36	46	207	32	219	78
KOPER										241	330	228	91	112	410	142	197	28	91	176	54	119	104	107	373	202	170	8	229	60	131
KORČULA											87	33	161	200	184	164	143	213	234	68	191	159	198	214	130	57	79	245	28	257	114
KOTOR												120	247	286	151	247	211	302	323	155	280	245	284	299	77	144	167	334	113	346	201
MAKARSKA													150	189	215	150	137	200	221	55	178	148	187	199	163	29	66	232	47	244	100
MALI LOŠINJ														53	326	55	127	63	95	91	41	31	54	88	291	120	88	95	-146	107	46
OPATIJA															373	68	172	74	112	130	52	44	5	112	332	160	127	116	184	128	86
OTRANTO																335	246	382	382	237	359	335	374	356	112	228	249	414	190	421	283
PAG																	148	114	142	91	92	27	66	133	289	121	87	146	147	158	46
PESCARA																		169	152	103	148	142	177	128	246	116	109	202	117	198	126
POREČ																			72	148	26	91	76	83	345	174	142	32	201	54	103
PORTO CORSINI																				169	72	122	114	30	366	195	163	95	223	62	130
PRIMOŠTEN																					126	89	129	148	201	27	12	180	54	192	45
PULA																						69	54	74	322	152	121	58	179	72	81
RAB																							42	114	289	118	86	123	144	135	46
RIJEKA																								113	330	159	126	108	183	120	84
RIMINI																									345	174	149	111	195	86	117
SHËNGJINI																										187	210	377	155	389	245
SPLIT																											38	206	40	218	72
ŠIBENIK																												174	65	186	41
TRIESTE																													233	62	135
VELA LUKA																														245	100
VENEZIA																															147
ZADAR																															

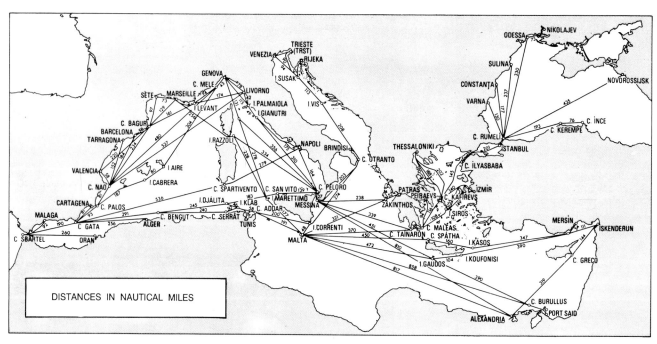

DISTANCES IN NAUTICAL MILES

IMPORTANT NAVIGATION REGULATIONS AND OTHER INFORMATION

INTERNAL SEA WATERS AND TERRITORIAL SEA OF THE REPUBLIC OF CROATIA

The sovereignty of the Republic of Croatia extends over the internal waters and the territorial sea as well as over the air space above them and over the seabed and the subterranean area beneath.

The internal sea waters of the Republic of Croatia include: harbours and bays on the mainland and island coast, parts of the sea between the mainland coast and the baseline of the territorial sea.

Foreign merchant vessels are allowed to navigate in internal waters and enter ports open to international traffic by using the shortest regular routes.

Foreign vessels (yachts) may freely approach and remain in the internal waters of the Republic of Croatia under the condition that they are in possession of a Navigation Permit issued by harbour master's office or its branch office. Legal regulations for foreign vessels apply to foreign pleasure craft as well. In the internal waters of the Republic of Croatia there may be prohibited zones foreign vessels (yachts) may not enter.

TERRITORIAL SEA AND INTERNAL SEA WATERS

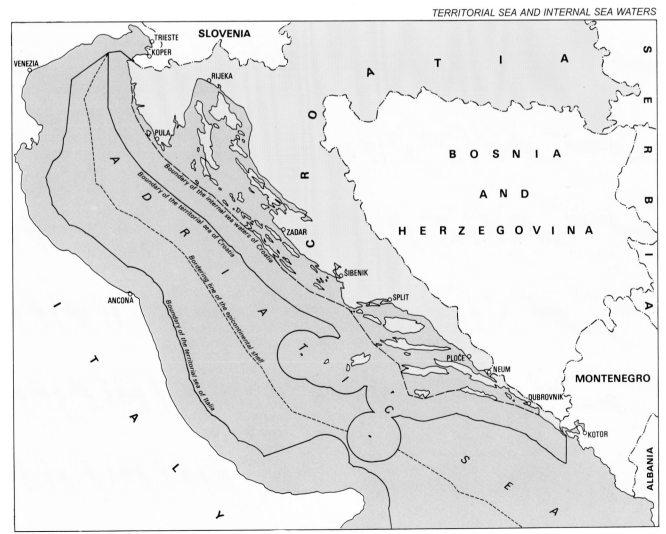

Transport of cargo and passengers from one port to another (cabotage) may be carried out by Croatian vessels only and foreign yachts if they possess a cabotage and concession permit issued by the Ministry of traffic, communications and maritime affairs.

A foreign vessel (yacht) seeking shelter in the internal sea of the Republic of Croatia due to force majeure or danger has to notify the nearest harbour master's office without delay.

The territorial sea of the Republic of Croatia comprises an expanse of water 12 M in width, extending from the starting-line towards the high seas.

The starting-line is composed of:

– the low water line along the mainland and island coasts,

– straight lines closing entrances to ports and bays,

– straight lines connecting legally determined points on the mainland and island coasts.

Vessels of all foreign states enjoy the right of harmless passage through the territorial sea (without entering ports; without endangering order and peace or the security of the Republic of Croatia). Foreign vessel is to proceed without stopping or delay; stopping and anchoring is permitted only if due to some navigational problem, force majeure, imminent danger or rendering help at sea. Foreign fishing craft are obliged to use the shortest route without stopping or anchoring, at a speed not below 6 knots; while navigating they are obliged to exhibit signs by which they may be identified as fishing vessels. They are forbidden to fish, i.e. catch any kind of sea organisms; their catch and their fishing equipment are to be stored inside the vessel or sealed if on deck.

In the territorial sea or in the internal waters special vessels (navy or other vessels and aircraft) are authorized to: investigate whether a vessel has the right to fly its flag; stop any suspicious vessel (yacht); examine the ship's documents and search such a vessel (yacht); chase, impound her and bring to the pertinent authority.

A foreign vessel shall be subject to legal proceedings if the authorities of the Republic of Croatia find reasonable suspicion that the vessel in question and/or its launch have broken laws or regulations relating to the Republic of Croatia sovereignty and jurisdiction or such as imposed by international law. The same applies if a foreign vessel fails to stop after she has been visually or audibly signalled to do so. The pursuit of such a vessel shall last till she stops or enters the territorial waters of its own or some other state.

Offenders are subject to severe punishment ranging from fines to seizure of the vessel (yacht) and equipment, i.e. the catch (in case of fishing craft).

THE EPICONTINENTAL SHELF AND THE COMMERCIAL ZONE OF THE REPUBLIC OF CROATIA

The epicontinental shelf of the Republic of Croatia comprises the seabed and its subterranean area beyond the external border of the territorial sea up to the border of the epicontinental shelves of neighbouring countries. The Republic of Croatia implements its sovereign right to explore and exploit the natural resources of this area (mineral and other inanimate wealth on the seabed and its subterranean area or organisms found exclusively beneath the seabed or in permanent physical contact with the seabed).

The law of the Republic of Croatia defines the commercial zone as the seabed and its subterranean area extending beyond the outer border of the territorial sea towards the high seas up to the borders of the commercial zones of neighbouring countries. Within this zone the Republic of Croatia has the exclusive right to construct, permit and regulate construction work and to use artificial islands, installations and equipment offshore, on the seabed and in its subterranean area. Within this zone vessels are required to respect regulations aimed at preventing pollution of the sea.

ACCESS, NAVIGATION AND STAY OF YACHTS OF FOREIGN REGISTRATION

Regulations about the passport

Tourists from West-European countries can enter Croatia either with their identity card or passport. If one enters with the identity card only his stay is limited to 30 days. When entering with a passport one can stay up to three months. If one wishes to stay longer than that one can apply to the authorities in order to prolong the residence permit.

Police registration

For every foreign visitor staying in Croatia there is an obligation of police registration for which there is a special form.

When staying at a hotel, a pension, a private room or a camping site one is automatically registered at the police by checking in at the reception.

Even persons living on deck of a small craft during their stay in Croatia are obliged to register with the local police. When changing the place of a stay the registration has to be renewed within 24 hours.

Important warning: The obligatory registration of small craft at the harbour masters' branch office does not replace the police registration of any newly arrived passengers on deck: it has to be done separately. It is frequently possible to do the police registration in the marina. If this should not be possible one can register at the local tourist office, hotel reception or police office. When possessing the registration form one avoids any possible problems with regular police controls even anchoring in small bays.

Entering by car with small craft

When entering Croatia beside the personal documents it is also necessary to have the green insurance card for the trailer. One can also close a temporary obligatory insurance for vehicles in Croatia if he can prove his car insurance by means of any other document. Offices in charge of that exist at all border crossings. The price is about 80,00 DM and the trailer insurance is recommended in any case.

The small craft has to be mentioned only when entering the country. Other administration formalities will be done later at the chosen harbour master's office (see special chapter on registration).

Trailers wider than 2.50 m, longer than 18.00 m, and higher than 4.00 m may be driven on Croatian roads only with a special permit. Such permits can be applied for at the local forwarding-offices. Special brochures issued by the Central office for tourism can be obtained by:

phone No. 069 - 25 20 45;

fax No. 069 - 25 20 54.

The procedure for obtaining the special permit takes some time and one should apply on time.

Small craft returning home and leaving Croatia are obliged to register their departure with the local harbour master's office.

Ports of entry

If small craft enter the country at sea it is through the Croatian internal sea waters. Here it has to go through the usual international customs formalities with the passports and pay the corresponding taxes for the craft (see special chapter on registration). Next to that it is necessary to register at the local police.

The following ports of entry are open all the year round as border crossings for international traffic (from north to south):

– Umag,

- Poreč,
- Rovinj,
- Pula,
- Raša - Bršica,
- Rijeka,
- Mali Lošinj,
- Senj
- Maslenica,
- Zadar,
- Šibenik,
- Split,
- Ploče,
- Metković,
- Korčula
- Gruž (Dubrovnik)

During the season (from April, 1st to October, 31st) there are additional ports of entry: Kanegra (Savudrija), Marina Umag - ACI, Novigrad, Sali, Božava, Ravni Žakan (Kornati), Primošten (Marina Kremik), Komiža, Vis (town harbour), Hvar (town harbour), Ubli (Lastovo) and Vela Luka.

Before leaving the internal sea waters one is obliged to go through the customs at the local harbour master's branch office. After that one should abandon the internal sea waters on the shortest route and without delay.

Registration and taxes

Each foreign small craft longer than 3 m should register with a Croatian harbour master's office or branch office as well as foreign yachts with an engine power over 4 kW (independently of its length). When registering it is necessary to enclose the following:

- the registration document;
- the Boat's Leader Licence of Competency (at sea);
- insurance policy.

In case when the registration document is non-existant the harbour master's office can examine the small craft and charge for it.

The insurance policy can also be obtained in the harbour master's office or a branch office.

When registering the craft one has to pay the taxes for its security, a lighthouse tax and a revenue stamp.

The yacht captain, after having paid the taxes in the harbour master's office, gets a registration receipt that is valid throughout one year starting with the registration day. During this period the craft can enter the country as many times as they wish.

With a valid registration the captain and the crew of the yacht can be changed any time, but each change must be reported to the harbour master's office. This rule is referring only to small craft and yachts that are not used for economic purpose (e.g. charter).

Foreign visitors are given a 10% reduction with their insurance charge in case they are visiting the country for the second time in succession as well as a maximum of 30% in case they are coming for the fourth time in succession.

Dinghies

Additional small craft that are used exclusively for sailing between the anchoring place and the nearest coast need not be registered and no extra papers are needed.

If additional boats are longer than 3 m, have an engine stronger that 4 kW (no matter what their length is) and are used for sailing, they need a permit. It can be obtained so that they are registered together with the boat. The owner of the yacht must specify that he wants such registration. By possi-

ble controls one must show the permit with the data about the additional small craft. No special tax is necessary.

Register of boats and small craft

Each boat (according to the category) and small craft (according to its activity, personal use, sport or recreation activity) has to be entered into the Register. The Register is managed by the harbour master's office and its branches responsible for a certain area. They are public documents consisting of data about the identity of vessels and small craft, their owners and consequent rights.

All vessels owned by Croatian corporations or citizens have to be entered into the Register.

Vessels and small craft owned by foreign corporations or foreign citizens have to be entered in the Register if the law requires it. No customs duty is required, only a tax according to the administrative procedure of the Republic of Croatia.

The owner of the vessel need not have domicile in Croatia; however the yacht or small craft must not be entered into a register of a foreign country.

The first registration of a vessel into the Register of boats will be allowed by the harbour master's office, that is in charge of vessels being built, when the papers necessary for the first registration have been provided and enclosed:

- a document proving the owner's right;
- a document proving that the owner is a Croatian citizen or institution, i.e. that all the conditions for registration have been fulfilled;
- an official decision about determining the vessel's name and its description as well as the port of registration;
- a certificate about the gauging;
- a certificate on the technical data of the vessel issued by the Croatian Register of boats;
- a certificate determining the calling signal of the vessel according to the International signalling codex if it is supposed to have such a signal;
- a document about the boat's identification and its technical data; a certificate, issued by the institution that is in charge of the foreign register of vessels, proving that the ship has been cancelled from the register in case when it is going to be entered into the Croatian Register of boats.

The request for the first registration of a small craft into the Register of boats should include:

- a document to prove the ownership of a small craft (purchase contract, bill, customs declaration, report about building the small craft and its launching equipment);
- a document to prove the seaworthiness of the small craft (record about the check-up and the certificate about its building, etc.);
- a document proving the boat's tonnage or displacement and its carrying capacity in cases when the craft is meant to serve for trade or similar activities;
- a certificate about the activity that the craft is to fulfill;
- in case when the launching equipment power is over 15 kW it is also necessary to enclose a copy of the Insurance policy for nonmaterial damage for the craft's owner.

The vessel is cancelled from the Registar of boats:

- if it has been lost or one can suppose it has been wrecked;
- if it is not corresponding to the regulations;
- if it has been called off navigation;
- if it has been entered into another Croatian Register of boats.

The vessel is supposed to have been wrecked if three months have passed since its last message was received. It is considered to have been lost on the day when the last message was taken.

The small craft is cancelled from the Registar of boats:

– if the small craft has been lost or is supposed to have been wrecked;

– if it is not corresponding to regulations;

– if it has been called off navigation;

– if it has become the property of another vessel or any other navigating object or has been rebuilt and shortened to less than 3 m length;

–if it has been entered into another Croatian Register of boats.

The small craft is considered to be lost if three months have passed since its last message was received.

The owner of small craft is obliged to make an application to the harbour master's office about cancelling his craft within 15 days from the day of its wreckage.

SEAWORTHINESS

Seaworthiness of a ship

Ships of the Croatian merchant navy may sail when they have been declared seaworthy and possess all the necessary documents. They are declared seaworthy on the basis of regulations concerning the construction, outfit and maintenance of the ship and on the basis of the required number of qualified crew members (see: »Narodne novine« No. 81/1994). Hrvatski registar brodova (Croatian Register of Boats) in Split is responsible for this in the Republic of Croatia.

Inspections to attest seaworthiness may be initial, regular or special.

Initial inspections are carried out before the ship is registered in Register of Boats of the Republic of Croatia. A request for such inspection is made by the ship-owner or the holder of legal right of use. Initial inspection may be of the entire vessel or of parts thereof.

Regular inspections are carried out every 12 months. In procedure and extent they are the same as initial inspections.

Special inspections may cover a whole vessel or parts thereof. They must be carried out whenever a ship suffered damage, or has been laid up for more than 6 months, when there have been considerable reconstructions or alterations and whenever the owner so requests. The harbour master's office may demand such inspections if there is reasonable doubt as to a ship's seaworthiness.

When a vessel has been passed as seaworthy it is fitted out with the necessary documents (see: »Narodne novine« No. 17/1994).

The harbour master's office is responsible for the security of ships at sea and may inspect whether ships have necessary documents, check that the state of the vessel tallies with the data in documents and if the crew is qualified and sufficient in number.

Similar checks can be made on foreign vessels, that is, on vessels which are not registered in a Register of Boats of the Republic of Croatia.

Seaworthiness of a boat

By maritime boat any vessel is understood up to 12 metres in length or less of 15 GRT which is seaworthy. It may be larger than 15 GRT if it has no deck or if it is not a vessel for technical purposes.

If a boat has several means of propulsion it is classified according to the principal means.

A boat-yacht is any boat so equipped that it can propel itself for a considerable period under its own power.

A speedboat is a boat equipped with an engine which allows it to move with its bows lifted above the water. A motorboat is a boat propelled in normal navigation by inboard or outboard engine.

Sports sailing-boats are boats of special construction with sails. They may be classified according to the classes for this kind of vessels by sailing organizations or may be unclassified.

Boats which must be entered in the Register of Boats can sail within delimited areas on specified purposes: if they have been passed seaworthy (in construction, maritime properties, means of propulsion and equipment) and are in possession of a Navigation Permit and operated by a qualified person. Boats that do not need to be entered in the Register must not sail farther than 1000 m from the coast line.

Boats may be intended for commercial (carriage of cargo or passengers, fishing etc.) or for non-commercial purposes (personal use, sport, recreation).

Passenger carrying boats must be built according to the specifications of the Register of Boats of the Republic of Croatia. Any vessel (boat) carrying 12 or more passengers is called a ship.

A boat is certified seaworthy after inspection by competent harbour master's offices or harbour offices. Such inspections may be initial, regular or special.

Initial inspection is carried out on all boats before they are entered into the Register of Boats, and after any reconstruction has been carried out.

Regular inspections are carried out periodically to ensure that boats are properly maintained. Periods vary as follows:

– boats for transporting passengers or for water-skiing every year;

– other boats used for commercial purposes every second year;

– boats for personal use, sport and recreation every five years (if the boat is longer than 4 m).

Special inspections are carried out if a boat has had an accident, if there is reasonable doubt about its seaworthiness, or if the owner so requests.

Owners must report any accident suffered by their boat within 3 days at the nearest harbour master's office.

NAVIGATION PERMIT

A boat that has been passed as seaworthy is issued with a Navigation Permit. If it is not passed, a Navigation Permit is not issued or is issued for a limited period.

A boat which transports passengers for distances in excess of 500 m must have mechanical propulsion. If a passage lasts for more than three hours continuously then the boat must have toilet facilities and sufficient drinking water.

A boat for transport of passengers and cargo (for commercial purposes) must have a clearly marked loadline:

– up to 6 m long, height 70 cm

– from 6 to 10 m long, height 80 cm

– over 10 m long, height 90 cm.

Small craft lower than that must have an enclosure round the deck. The enclosure height of the covered boats must be at least 80 cm.

The number of passengers that the boat may carry is determined by the harbour master's office and must be clearly marked on the boat. Two children under the age of 10 are equivalent of one adult passenger, but each child must have a life jacket.

BOAT EQUIPMENT

Boats carrying passengers in the territorial sea of the Republic of Croatia must possess the following equipment:

– an anchor of adequate size and anchor rope (25–100 m);

– two 10 m long ropes of adequate diameter, or similar equipment for mooring;

– bitts or similar mooring equipment;

– a spare hand rudder shaft if the boat has separate steering equipment;

– a hand pump or bucket and dipper;

– two oars, four rowlocks or pins (it may have a spare engine or a by-boat instead);

– a boat's compass with illumination;

– an up-to-date chart of the area of navigation;

– the Adriatic Sea Pilot, Part I – East Coast (Peljar Jadranskog mora, I. dio – istočna obala) and the List of Lights in the Adriatic Sea, Ionian Sea and Maltese Islands (Popis svjetionika Jadranskog mora, Jonskog mora i Malteških otoka);

– two nautical triangles or protractor, compasses and other necessary materials for plotting on the navigation chart;

– some means of giving acoustic signals in fog (foghorn or similar);

– six red handflares, three red rockets and two boxes of matches in waterproof wrapping;

– portable fire-extinguisher and an axe;

– a first-aid cupboard or box;

– a life ring (of approved type) with a rope 25 m long and 6 mm of diameter;

– the same number of life jackets (life belts) as passengers that the boat is registered to carry, of which 10 per cent must be of child size;

– an awning to protect passengers from the sun and a boat for the transport of cargo hatches for covering hatchways on the deck and waterproof covers;

– tools and basic spares for the engine and other mechanical equipment;

– navigation lights according to the International Rules for the Prevention of the Collision on the Sea;

– a battery torch;

– a concave rear-view mirror and safety cord for outboard engine (speedboat);

– radio-telephone equipment if passengers are transported outside internal waters.

Boats for other commercial purposes and sailing in a restricted area, if the port authority so decides, do not need a compass, navigational charts, handbooks, flares, rockets and radio-equipment.

Boats of more than 7 m long which are not intended for commercial use must have the following equipment:

– an anchor of adequate size and anchor rope at least 25–100 m long;

– two mooring-ropes of adequate diameter 10 m in length and two bitts or similar equipment for mooring;

– a spare hand rudder shaft;

– a hand pump or bucket and dipper;

– two oars, four pins or rowlocks or a spare engine or a by-boat;

– prescribed lights;

– a boat's compass;

– up-to-date navigation charts with plotting equipment, a List of Lights and Pilot;

– a foghorn or other means of transmitting sound signals;

– fire-extinguisher and an axe;

– a first-aid cupboard or box;

– a complete set of tools and spare parts for maintenance of the engine and other mechanical equipment;

– a battery torch;

– at least two red handflares or rockets and two boxes of matches in waterproof wrapping;

– a sufficient number of life jackets (life belts).

Maritime boats 5 – 7 m need the same equipment as boats of more than 7 m with the exception of: compass, charts and navigation publications, foghorn, flares, rockets and matches, fire-extinguisher, first-aid box and life jackets (life belts).

Foreign speedboats or other craft while sailing in the territorial sea of the Republic of Croatia must have a Navigation Permit and the following equipment:

– an anchor of adequate size and anchor rope of at least 30 m;

– rope of adequate diameter and not shorter than 10 m

– two spare oars;

– prescribed navigation lights;

– a pump or bucket and dipper;

– first-aid box;

– six red handflares and two boxes of matches in waterproof wrapping;

– a rear-view mirror if pulling water-skier.

Other foreign boats must have a Navigation Permit and the following equipment:

– an anchor of adequate size with at least 30 m of anchor rope;

– rope of adequate diameter at least 10 m long;

– bitts or other mooring equipment;

– two spare oars;

– prescribed navigation lights.

Portable fire-extinguisher and an adequate number of life jackets (life belts) are also recommended.

Boats of foreign register can navigate only by persons with an up-to-date Boat Leader's Licence of Competency issued according to the regulations of their own state or who have been issued with a Licence by the competent Croatian harbour master's office or Ministry of traffic, communications and maritime affairs.

Persons who wish to take the test for a Boat Leader's Licence must fulfill the following conditions: be at least 18 years old, has navigated his/her own boat for at least three years or has spent as a seaman on a merchant navy ship at least one year. The test is taken before a commission of the competent harbour master's office and according to a specified programme. An application to take the test must be sent to the harbour master's office accompanied with a copy of the applicant's birth certificate, medical certificate on the hearing and eyesight of the applicant and a certificate of educational level (at least eight years of schooling).

Any boat for the transport of passengers or for commercial purposes up to the outer border of the territorial border of the Republic of Croatia must be navigated by a professional mariner-motorist. Such boats must have at least one other seaman as a crew member. Each member of the crew must have a professional Sailor's Book or Embarkation Permit.

Persons wishing to take the test for a Boat Leader's Licence of Competency (Uvjerenje o osposobljenosti za voditelja brodice) must be at least 18 years old for navigating a speedboat (regardless of the horsepower of the engine) or a motorboat for commercial purposes, and only within a certain limited area. Persons with such a licence can transport passengers within the harbour area only.

Persons who wish to steer a boat with outboard engine of up to 3.7 kW (5 HP) or a boat with a sail up to 5 m long need only pass a test to show their knowledge of the Rules for the Prevention of Collision at Sea and are then issued with a certificate.

Rowing boats for personal use may be operated by persons over 12 years of age without any licence or certificate. They must, however, pass theoretical and practical tests held by a board of the harbour master's office according to a prescribed programme.

Harbour master's offices organize such tests according to their annual plans. All details can be obtained upon written or personal application.

The ship's Navigation Permit and Boat Leader's Licence (according to one of the two above mentioned categories) must always be kept on board.

Boats can navigate in the territorial sea and internal sea waters of the Republic of Croatia. Harbour master's office may delimit or extend the area in which a boat can sail including the right to sail beyond the Croatian territorial seas, or into the territorial seas and internal sea waters of other states.

For safety of navigation and sea-traffic, boats must keep a certain distance from the shore (except in harbours and bathing places): rowing boats up to 30 m, motorboats and sailing-boats up to 50 m, and speedboats, when sailing at speed, 300 m.

Boat regulations stipulate other details on the seaworthiness of the boats as well as the penalties for infringement of the regulations.

Vessels used for commercial purposes must meet the standards set by Croatian Register of Boats or similar foreign register.

ORDER IN HARBOURS AND SHIPPING LANES

Management, maintenance and order in harbours is the responsibility of the administrative body in charge of the harbour. That body must specify the order in the harbour by a special act and proceed it to the harbour master's office that will approve it. The shipmaster or person navigating the boat must abide by all harbour regulations.

Persons navigating a ship or a boat in harbour must take care not to damage shore, piers, harbour installations, moored craft etc.

Vessels (boats) for sport or recreation, as well as boats in general, must not hinder ship's traffic in harbours. They are forbidden to move in the operative part of the harbour (landing-place), especially in parts reserved for international traffic unless they have a special permit. The administrative body in charge of the port (harbour) regulates the mooring and anchorage plan and facilities in a harbour. The master of a boat is responsible for the boat's safety while in harbour.

Fishing, bathing and anchoring in a harbour and its depending area are regulated by the harbour master's office and must not hinder traffic.

It is forbidden to throw garbage or any other kind of refuse overboard in a harbour. Tanks and bilges can be emptied only on the high seas and in places designated by harbour authorities.

Loading, unloading and trans-shipping of cargo must be done by a qualified personnel and in such a way that persons are not endangered, the shore installations are not damaged and cargo does not fall into the sea. After the loading or unloading is finished the responsible persons must clean up the relevant part of the quay.

If dangerous materials (explosive or inflammable matter) are being loaded or unloaded the harbour master's office must be informed thereof and the efficiency of the boat's fire-extinguisher equipment must be checked. When such materials are being handled the code flag »B« (international: Bravo) must be flown as required by international regulations.

SPEED RESTRICTIONS

The following restrictions on the navigation of boats should be noted:

For greater safety and to prevent damage to vessels moored in ports, harbours and marinas on the Croatian coast there are speed restrictions in the following places: Limski zaljev (6 knots); Pula harbour (5 – 8 knots); Cres harbour (7 knots, from Kovačina point): Bay of Bakar (8 knots); Rab harbour (4 knots); the Zrmanja river (8 knots); Novsko ždrilo (8 knots); Mali Ždrelac passage (8 knots); Pašman straits (10 knots); Kanal Sv. Ante, Šibenik (6 knots); Ploče harbour (6 knots); Pelješac Channel (12 knots); Rijeka Dubrovačka (4 knots); and Dubrovnik – Gruž harbour (4 knots).

Boats, other than rowing boats, must not sail immediately off natural bathing places unless they are embarking or disembarking passengers, and then only at designated points and navigating carefully. Wind-surfing is also forbidden within 25 m of bathing beaches.

Boats must keep clear of all places marked by special floating signs as forbidden for navigation, especially when work is in progress. If such places cannot be avoided then boats must go dead-slow.

Speed boating at speed, water-skiing and wind-surfing are forbidden in harbours and their depending areas (especially harbour entrance), in narrow channels, bays, coves etc., also where sea-traffic is intense. In other zones speedboats must keep at least 300 m from the shore and other motorboats at least 150 m. It is also forbidden to drag ski-tows astern without skiers, skiing at night or in poor visibility, skiing behind a speedboat which is already pulling skiers or beside such a boat at less than the length of the ski-tow rope.

When anchoring persons in charge of a boat must be alert to any signs on the shore showing that anchoring is forbidden because of underwater electric or telephone (telegraph) cables or water pipes.

Boat-owners must not allow the use of their boats by persons who do not have the necessary qualifications and papers.

SPORT FISHING

Sport fishing for leisure includes the catching of fish, crustaceans (crabs, lobsters etc.), cephalopoda (squid etc.), and shellfish.

Equipment for this purpose is deemed to be: a fishing line, fishing-hook, rod and line, drag-line or long-line with up to 200 hooks, underwater gun without explosives, harpoon or fish-spear (for use with fishing-boats with lights of up to 400 candelas or without lights). If amateur fishing is organized by a fishing club then larger fishing-boats (leisure-boats) can be used. For fishing with rod and line from shore no permit is necessary and no dues payable. For all other kinds of sport fishing permits are necessary and charges payable according to a scale determined by the local authorities.

Citizens of the Republic of Croatia and foreign citizens with a permanent residence permit in the Republic of Croatia who are members of Croat fishing clubs (associated in the Association of Underwater Activities and Marine Sport Fishing) and who can produce their membership book can without charge or other permit fish in all permitted fishing areas and with all kinds of fishing-tackle except underwater guns. For underwater fishing with guns a special permit is necessary and special charge payable, and such fishing zones are determined by the local authorities. Foreign citizens who have not got a permanent residence permit in the Republic of Croatia need special fishing permits and must pay the relevant charges.

Amateur fishing is restricted by certain regulations. There must be no disturbance of commercial fishing; persons under 16 must not go fishing underwater with guns; aqualungs and other forms of underwater breathing equipment must not be used; underwater guns must not be used between sunset and sunrise. Underwater fishing is totally prohibited between November 1 and March 31 (except in the case of international competitions); a maximum of 5 kg of fish and other sea animals may be caught in any day except during international competitions; the following are not counted in the permitted 5 kg: sharks, rays and individual fish of rare size such as sea--bass, dentex, sea-bream etc. Fish caught for sport may not be sold or exchanged for other items.

In fishing reserves no fishing or hunting of any kind of sea-animal is permitted. Such reserves are the estuaries of the rivers: Dragonja, Mirna, Raša, Zrmanja, Krka, Jadro, Žrnovica (near Stobreč), Cetina, Neretva and Rijeka Dubrovačka, the channel Fažanski kanal, the bays and coves Limski zaljev, Medulinski zaljev, Soline (Krk Island), Bistrina (near Mali Ston) and the lake Mljetska jezera.

The following are authorized to oversee the observance of fishing regulations: fishing inspectors of local municipalities, interior security agencies, harbour master's office authorities, State Inspectorate of Fishing, responsible units of the Croatian Navy and the maritime customs authorities.

Persons breaking the fishing laws can be fined, their fishing-tackle and equipment may be confiscated and so may the catch or any profit made from fishing.

UNDERWATER ACTIVITIES

Diving with diving equipment, underwater photography, filming and all forms of marine research of sea or seabed are understood by underwater activities.

By diving with diving equipment, all underwater activities are understood that require the use of compressed air or breathing apparatus.

By autonomous diving equipment the diving apparatus is understood as well as diving clothes with the complete underwater breathing equipment.

Any taking of photographs (black-and-white or colour) below sea-level is understood to be underwater photography. Underwater filming is all filming with cine-cameras, TV, video or other underwater filming equipment.

By marine research of sea or seabed the collection of all kinds of oceanographic, biological, geological, speleological, gravimetric and other data are understood.

Areas of underwater activity must be clearly marked by a blue and white »A« flag, diving by a red and white flag or some circular marker buoy (in diameter larger than 30 cm) of orange-yellow or red colour. The flags must be fixed to a floating buoy placed in the centre of the area where the activity is taking place.

On those parts of the coastal sea that are not forbidden zones the citizens of the Republic of Croatia can dive with diving equipment and do underwater photography without restriction if they are members of a society or a club for this activity recognized by the Croatian Association for Underwater Activities and Sport Fishing in the Sea and provided that they have the necessary diving qualifications. Persons of foreign nationality may obtain permits from the Croatian state bodies responsible.

Diving with equipment is permitted in the Croatian territorial sea from sunrise to sunset.

The above underwater activities are forbidden in: specially designated zones; in ports and harbours open to public traffic and on the sea-routes normally used for such traffic; 300 m around any naval vessel; in naval harbours and in zones marked as military objects and forbidden for diving of any kind.

Detailed information about the exact location of forbidden zones, esp. coordinates and the boundaries of the zones, can be obtained at all harbour master's offices or their branch offices.

NAVIGATION BEACONS AND RADIO-BEACONS

Sea-lanes are denoted by visual markers, lights, sound warnings and by electronic appliances. Visual markers by day and lights by night are most important for vessels.

Beacons

In the Republic of Croatia the International Association of Lighthouse Authorities (IALA)-system for denoting of sea-lanes is being used: lateral combined with cardinal.

Beacons may be anchored buoys or stationary. Full details are given in Pilot 1 – The Adriatic Sea (east coast) and in Pilot 2 – The Adriatic Sea (west coast) and in the List of Lights and Fog Signals in the Adriatic, Ionian Sea and Maltese Islands published by the Croatian Hydrographic Institute in Split. Light signals are best studied for each case separately.

Navigation lights

Navigation lights with their own source of lighting may be shore-based, located on isolated points for navigation direction or anchored buoys. A special place is taken by lighthouses which have permanent keepers, while coastal lights, harbour lights and light-buoys are unattended.

Lighthouses are located in all places of importance for navigation or at places of special danger. In construction and colour they differ from the surrounding objects and are therefore important also for daytime navigation. They usually have rotating lenses which allows them to emit a powerful light, round the entire horizon. Almost all the lighthouses on the Croatian coast are in radio-telephone contact with centres of information. Almost all important lighthouses emit fog signals which can be recognized by their characteristic sound pattern (length, number of sounds in a group, intervals between sounds).

Coastal lights are positioned on important points, straits, channels, cliffs, rocks, islets, harbours and port entrances etc. Their function is to facilitate navigation in coastal waters. They have fixed lens and are automatically lit and extinguished at sunset and sunrise.

Harbour lights are positioned inside the harbour and at the harbour entrance to facilitate entrance and manoeuvring. They are lit by harbour personnel or automatically.

Light-buoys are floating lights anchored on buoys to show shallows or danger points. Usually they have flashing lights, and are activated by timing mechanism or photocell.

Each light at sea has its own characteristic: colour, character, period, height above sea-level, visibility, number and disposition of lights. Detailed information on this is available in the List of Lights and Fog Signals and on charts.

The colour of lights is B - WHITE (bijela), C - RED (crvena), Z - GREEN (zelena). When these letters are noted beside the light visibility they denote that light shines continuously. If colour is meant to show the approach to a harbour or through straits then red denotes the left side and green the right side. This however is not always sufficient guide and for individual cases the Adriatic Pilot and List of Lights and Fog Signals should be consulted.

Light character shows the way the light is seen: Bl - flashing; Bl (Gp) - flashing in group (i.e. BBl /3/); Pk - occulting; Sj - fixed with flashing; Pm - alternating etc. The difference between flashing and occulting is that with flashing the light periods are longer than the dark and in occulting the other way round. If the light has a special sector then this is noted beside the character of light.

NAVIGATIONAL AIDS AT ADRIATIC SEA: TYPICAL MARKS AND LIGHT CHARACTERISTICS

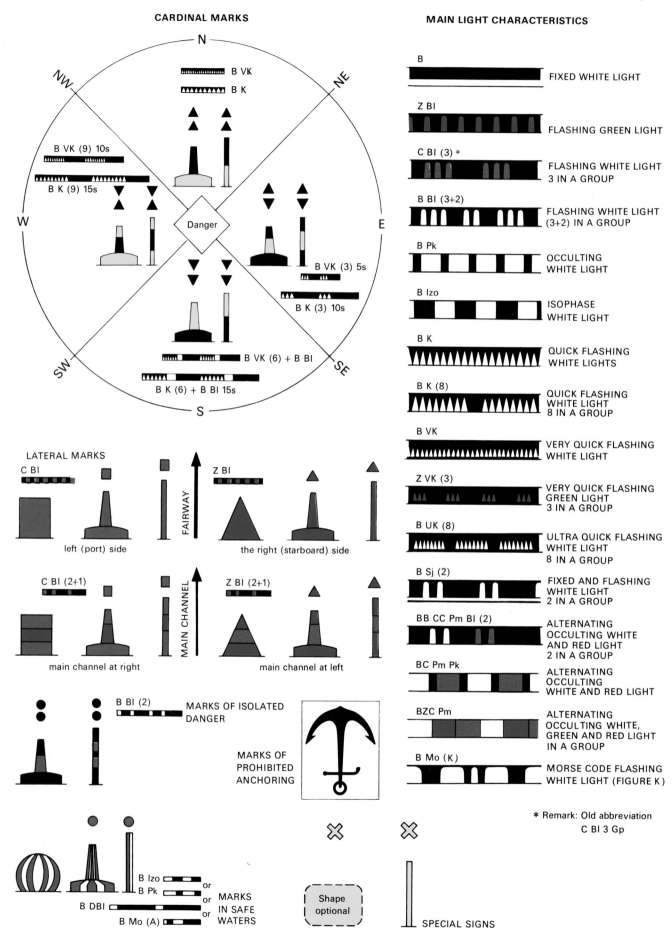

CARDINAL MARKS

N

B VK
B K

NW   NE

B VK (9) 10s
B K (9) 15s

Danger

W   E

B VK (3) 5s
B K (3) 10s

SW   SE

B VK (6) + B BI
B K (6) + B BI 15s

S

LATERAL MARKS

C BI

FAIRWAY

Z BI

left (port) side

the right (starboard) side

C BI (2+1)

MAIN CHANNEL

Z BI (2+1)

main channel at right

main channel at left

B BI (2)   MARKS OF ISOLATED DANGER

MARKS OF PROHIBITED ANCHORING

B Izo   or
B Pk   or
B DBI   or   MARKS IN SAFE WATERS
B Mo (A)

Shape optional

SPECIAL SIGNS

MAIN LIGHT CHARACTERISTICS

B   FIXED WHITE LIGHT

Z BI   FLASHING GREEN LIGHT

C BI (3) *   FLASHING WHITE LIGHT 3 IN A GROUP

B BI (3+2)   FLASHING WHITE LIGHT (3+2) IN A GROUP

B Pk   OCCULTING WHITE LIGHT

B Izo   ISOPHASE WHITE LIGHT

B K   QUICK FLASHING WHITE LIGHTS

B K (8)   QUICK FLASHING WHITE LIGHT 8 IN A GROUP

B VK   VERY QUICK FLASHING WHITE LIGHT

Z VK (3)   VERY QUICK FLASHING GREEN LIGHT 3 IN A GROUP

B UK (8)   ULTRA QUICK FLASHING WHITE LIGHT 8 IN A GROUP

B Sj (2)   FIXED AND FLASHING WHITE LIGHT 2 IN A GROUP

BB CC Pm BI (2)   ALTERNATING OCCULTING WHITE AND RED LIGHT 2 IN A GROUP

BC Pm Pk   ALTERNATING OCCULTING WHITE AND RED LIGHT

BZC Pm   ALTERNATING OCCULTING WHITE, GREEN AND RED LIGHT IN A GROUP

B Mo (K)   MORSE CODE FLASHING WHITE LIGHT (FIGURE K)

* Remark: Old abbreviation C BI 3 Gp

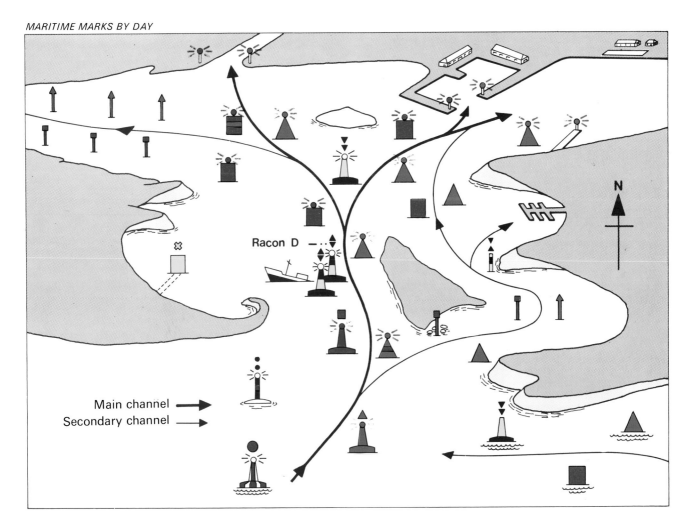

Racon D ─ ·· ·

Main channel ➡
Secondary channel ➡

N

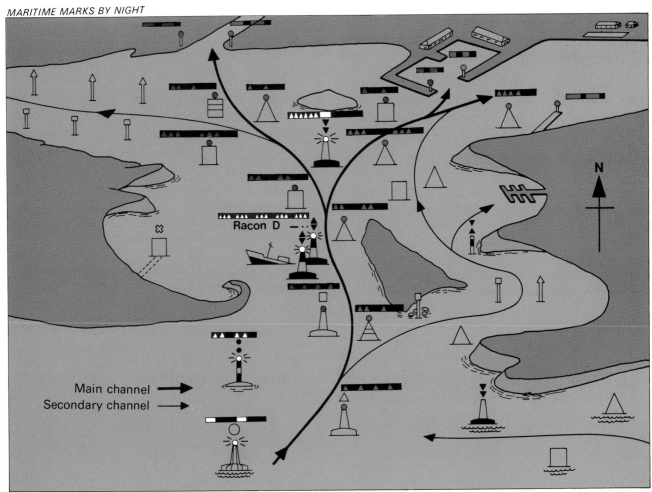

Racon D ─ ·· ·

Main channel ➡
Secondary channel ➡

N

Light sectors denote areas of safety or danger. It cannot be taken for granted that the dark or coloured sector denotes the danger or the safety sector and so each individual case should be separately considered from charts or the List of Lights and Fog Signals. Sectors are marked by the abbreviation »sect« beside the letter denoting the colour (e.g. sect C).

Period of light, the interval between the beginning of one series of light signals and the beginning of the next also provides information. In navigation lights special attention should be paid to the time period of the light either with a stop-watch or, after experience, counting the seconds.

Visibility of lights is expressed in nautical miles (M) in which the light can be seen from a position 5 m above the sea-level. Distances are given for visibility in normal weather conditions and for clear nights and are entered on charts and in the List of Lights and Fog Signals. For example, if the following appears on a chart, B Bl 3 Gp 10 s 16 M or B Bl (3) 10 s 16 M this denotes: white light flashing three in a group, period 10 seconds, light over middle sea-level visibility 16 miles.

Radio-beacons

These are radio-stations which transmit signals around the whole horizon. They have exact positions on navigation or radio-navigation charts (RC for short). Some radio-beacons intended for aircraft may also be used (marked RC Aero). Each radio-beacon has its own station number; name; geographical coordinates; range (mostly about 100 M, local about 20 M); kind of transmission (A1A - unmodulated radio wave length; A2A modulated wave length; intermittent radio signals); frequency (standardly 285-325 kHz); identification signal; characteristics (Morse signals); times of starting and duration of transmission and whether it works continuously or only at times of limited visibility (fog); whether it is single or one of a group (in the Adriatic are 3 groups).

The radio-bearing of radio-station can be measured by way of radio direction finder. This bearing is incorrect for radio-deviation and the angle of half-convergence of the meridian (for distances in the Adriatic sea are almost negligible). Data of navigation radio-beacons are given in the manual of Radio-Navigational Service published by the Croatian Hydrographic Institute in Split.

MARITIME CHARTS

Besides the mariner's compass, all mariners must have up-to-date maritime charts and the standard equipment for plotting course.

Maritime charts provide topographic and hydrographic information. In the upper corner is the name of the chart and general information; in the right bottom corner the chart number; the name of the institution which published it, date of issue, name of institution which drew up the chart (in the middle below the frame of the chart); it also gives the »magnetic rose« with annual declination (in several places in the hydrographic part); details of »minor corrections« (left bottom corner); linear measurements in miles (M) and km (in a suitable place on the chart) etc.

Before the chart is used the information in the title should be read carefully.

The charts published by the Croatian Hydrographic Institute in Split give depths and heights in metres, i.e. depths to level of the chart (Chart Datum) and heights from the medium sea-level. The Croatian Hydrographic Institute in Split takes as level of the chart the medium height at low water during periods of maximum tidal activity (Mean Lower Water Spring). The sea in the charts is printed in several shades of blue for maximum ease of reading. Depths of less than 5 m are in deep blue, between 5 – 10 m in light blue and the rest of the sea section is white.

RADIO-BEACON GROUPS ON CROATIAN COAST (A2A)				
Name	Kamenjak	Movar	Cavtat	Molunat
Position	44°47,2'N 013°54,9'E	43°30,3'N 015°58,3' E	42°35,0'N 018°13,0'E	42°27,1'N 018°25,6'E
Freqency	289,8 kHz A2A	289,6 kHz A2A	397 kHz A2A	305,7 kHz A2A
Identification	YP	YV	CV	YC
Visibility	100 M	100 M	25 M	100 M
In fine weather	h+20, 26, 50, 56	h+16, 22, 46, 52		h+10, 16, 40, 46
Above applicable in fine weather; in fog transmit continuously				

The scale of the chart is expressed in ratio or fractions (e.g. 1 : 100 000 or 1/100 000). Beside the numerical scale the linear scale may also be shown.

The outer border of the chart contains the numerical coordinates of latitude and longitude. Latitude is used in measuring distances (1 M = 1 minute = 1852 m). The length of minutes on the latitude scale of the chart increases as the latitude increases and thus in calculations account must be taken of the position of the vessel. This is because of Mercator's projection of the chart. Distance cannot be calculated by minutes of longitude.

The magnetic roses, usually found in several places on the chart can be used to plot course and azimuth with aid of parallel rulers or set-square. Inside the rose numbers of the magnetic declinations (variations) are drawn-in which should be corrected according to year.

The relief of the land sections of the chart is shown in contour lines (horizontals; usually 40 or 20 m apart), by cross-hatching or a combination of both, some charts are colour-shaded, usually in ocre.

All details important for plotting the course but too small to be convincingly shown on the chart have special identification marks. The exact position of details so marked is taken from the middle of the base of the topographic sign or the centre of a circular mark (for cliffs, buoys etc.). With marks for symmetrical objects (churches, floating docks etc.) the exact position is the centre of the mark. The Croatian Hydrographic Institute in Split has published a summary of all marks and shortenings entitled Symbols and Abbreviations on Maritime Charts (Znaci i skraćenice na hrvatskim pomorskim kartama).

The largest scale and numerically detailed charts recently published and corrected are the best to use. Authorized sellers of nautical charts are bound to sell charts corrected to the day of sale, mariners must further correct them themselves.

Classification of charts

Charts of the Croatian Hydrographic Institute in Split are divided in three classes: informative, navigational and supplementary.

The charts scale is 1: 100 000 and the papers are 34 x 48 cm. The charts, 29 of them, consist of two parts: from Trst to Zadar (MC 1 - MC 12) and from Zadar to Bojana (MC 13 - MC 29).

Informative charts give information important for navigation such as currents, meteorological and hydrological details etc.

Navigation charts are designed for practical navigation, i.e. the plotting of courses, the plotting of a vessel's position. According to scale they may be: general, course, coastal charts and plans of harbours.

General charts present larger area of whole seas with their adjacent shores and they are usually small scale. General charts no. 100, 101, 102 show Adriatic as a whole or in part (scale of 1 : 1 000 000 or 1 : 750 000). Chart no. 103 shows the Ionian Sea and no. 108 and 109 the Mediterranean sea (scale 1: 2 500 000) etc.

General charts can be used for navigation outside Croatian territorial sea if the boat's safety allows it. But their main purpose is to give a more comprehensive view of cruising areas for planning routes and calculating the total distances and duration on the voyage to be covered.

Course charts show smaller areas of sea and include all important details needed for navigation. They are drawn to a scale of 1 : 300 000. The course charts of the Adriatic bear the numbers 300-31 to 300-37 (north, middle and south Adriatic bear the numbers 301, 302 and 303).

The charts with the scale 1 : 250 000 show the coast sections Rijeka – Venezia (3410), Split – Gargano (3412) and Dubrovnik – Brindisi (3414). The Croatian Hydrographic Institute has issued further 18 charts in the scale 1 : 200 000, which present the areas of the Adriatic, Ionian sea and the bay of Tarant (151 – 179).

	0	1	2	3	4	5	6	7	8	9
a	△	○ ⊙	●43	Ckv / Ch	Sp			Ru	(30)	◑
b		Bijelo Crn / B Bl sekt. C / W R								
c		(15)		zeleno	crveno	crn crv crn				N E S W · žuto-crno
d	⊙	RC / RD / RW	R / RG	R / RT / Rst	Ra / Racon / Ramark		·(4) / (4)	(1₆)✳(1₆)		R
e	6 k / 6 Gr / R +(17)	(4) / Wk	Jarb. / (2) Mst			Gr / 15 k / R		Ra 085° / 085°– 265° / 085° DW 22 m	N	Oil / Gas
f		Prohibited Zabranjeno	1m	2m	5m / 2	10m / 10	15m	20m / 20	50m / 50	100m / 100

SYMBOLS AND ABBREVIATIONS ON MARITIME CHARTS

a0 – triangulation point; a1 – fixed point, position; a2 – elevation, hill; a3 – chapel, church; a4 – church tower, belfry; a5 – fort, battery; a6 – monument; a7 – ruins; a8 – tower; a9 - pilot station; b0 – maritime light; light-beacon, lighthouse; b1 – sector light; b2 – light vessel (Aero-nautical light); b3 – anchorage for large vessels; b4 – anchorage for smaller vessels; b5 – breakwater; b6 – mole, pier; b7 – prohibited anchorage; b8 – bollard, loading place with bollard; b9 – floating dock; c0 – draw bridge, rotated bridge; c1 – clearing high 15m; c2 –anchoring berth; c3 – starboard hand buoy; c4 – port hand buoy; c5 – isolated danger buoy; c6 – mooring buoy; c7 – pile, stump; c8 – fixed beacon; c9 – cardinal marks; d0 – radio-beacon (in general); d1 – circular, directional and rotating radio-beacon; d2 – radio telegraph station, radio direction finding station; d3 – radio telegraph, radio telephone and radio broadcasting station; d4 – radar station, Racon beacon, Ramark beacon; d5 - radar reflector, radar conspicuous object; d6 - rock which does not cover (height above chart datum); d7 - rock which covers and uncovers (height above chart datum); d8 – rock awash at the level of chart datum; d9 – dangerous sunken rock - depth unknown; e0 – shoal sounding on isolated rock; e1 – stranded wreck showing any portion of hull or superstructure; e2 – wreck of which the masts only are visible; e3 – sunken wreck dangerous to surface navigation (depth over wreck up to 20m); e4 – sunken wreck not dangerous to surface navigation; e5 – limit of rocky (dangerous) area; e6 – boundary-line of sector light; e7 – radar guided track, deep water route (minimum depth 22m); e8 – underwater cable, underwater power (N) cable; e9 – underwater pipeline; f0 –limit of military practice area; f1 – prohibited (restricted) area; f2 - f9 – depth contours (figures show soundings).

Coastal charts show in detail smaller stretches of the coast and the basic aids to navigation. Their use is obligatory in the immediate vicinity of the coast, and they contain most of the important details to facilitate the navigation. The newest editions (published by the Croatian Hydrographic Institute in Split) have the number 100 plus an additional number which denotes the area covered by the chart (e.g. 100 – 21: Šibenik – Split), drawn to a scale of 1 : 100 000. They often include in larger scale the plans of certain harbours, anchorages and dangerous or important areas, straits, channels etc.

The Croatian Hydrographic Institute in Split publishes special charts for small craft.

Plans cover small areas, usually ports, harbours and anchorages. They are drawn in great detail and to a larger scale (1 : 50 000 and larger). They bear separate scales of measurement for longitude and distance, as they do not indicate latitudes and longitudes at border.

Supplementary charts are drawn for certain special purposes and are not needed for normal navigation.

Charts cannot be used properly without the necessary navigation equipment. The most important items are navigational triangles (protractor) or parallel (slide) rulers for drawing in the vessel's course and azimuth, compasses for plotting distances and coordinates, a magnifying-glass, a soft pencil and a soft eraser.

NAVIGATIONAL PUBLICATIONS

Even charts cannot supply all the information needed for safety navigation. For this reason the Croatian Hydrographic Institute in Split publishes various navigational handbooks with all the detailed information that cannot for technical reasons be shown on a chart.

The Adriatic Sea Pilot (Peljar Jadranskog mora), I - E coast, II - W coast, provides mariners with various details and information about the Adriatic region, i.e. general hydrographic and hydrologic conditions, general navigation directions, especially for navigating in channels and dangerous areas, details of anchorages and sheltered places, various marks, details of water, fuel and provisions and other important information. The pilot book starts with information on legal regulations concerning navigation, instruction on the use of mariner's handbook, charts etc.

The List of Lights and Fog Signals in the Adriatic Sea, Ionian Sea and Maltese Islands (Popis svjetala i signala za maglu Jadranskog mora, Jonskog mora, Malteških otoka) contains all necessary details concerning lighthouses, lights and other important navigation signals.

The Radio-Navigation Service (Radio-navigacijska služba) contains all necessary details concerning radio-beacons and coastal radio-stations as well as other information which refer to safety at sea. It is similar to foreign handbooks of the same kind.

Adriatic Distance Handbook (Daljinar Jadranskog mora) gives the distances in nautical miles between the important coastal ports and harbours on the Adriatic coast. The first part gives the distances between main ports and harbours, anchorages, and places of particular navigational interest. The second part gives distances between smaller harbours and coves arranged in zones.

The Catalogue of Navigation Charts and Publications (Katalog pomorskih karata i navigacijskih publikacija) provides mariners with all information on charts and publications issued by the Croatian Hydrographic Institute in Split. It has an index and a map for selecting the charts needed. The entire Adriatic is divided into quadrangles which shows the zones covered by the charts. The number in each quadrangle is the chart number.

Notice to Mariners (Oglas za pomorce) is a monthly publication. It gives various kinds of information concerning safety at sea in the Adriatic and in part in the Ionian Sea. Its main aim is to give up-to-date information on any changes that should be incorporated into handbooks or navigation charts published by the Croatian Hydrographic Institute in Split.

Before setting on a cruise masters of vessels should study the handbooks, Pilot and charts carefully and in particular take care that they are up-to-date.

VHF RADIO SERVICE IN THE REPUBLIC OF CROATIA

According to the regulations of the International Convention of Safety of Life at Sea - SOLAS Convention of Safety of Life at Sea and the Navigational Law, the Republic of Croatia is obliged to organise radio service for the safety of navigation and the safety of life at sea on all navigable routes in the internal sea waters and territorial sea of the Croatian republic. The service for our country is being organised by the »Plovput d.o.o.« of Split and by help of the mainland stations. The stations in Rijeka (Rijeka radio - 9AR), Split (Split radio - 9AS) and Dubrovnik (Dubrovnik radio - 9AD) are on permanent watch on the international frequency for danger, security and calling of 156,800 MHz (VHF channel 16). Next to the watch on channel 16 the mainland stations are permanently on watch on the given VHF radio channels for public communication, i.e. interchange of radio-telegrams and radio phone calls in the directions mainland – vessel and vessel – maindland.

Besides the above mentioned watch and communication in case of danger (MAYDAY), urgency (pan pan), security (SÉCURITÉ), medical advice (MEDICO) at exactly determined intervals, these stations transmit messages on their official channels with a previous announcement on VHF channel 16, i.e. meteorological reports and navigational warnings for the public corresponding needs the so-called Traffic List.

Also since 1995, in order to fulfill the obligation towards the Global Maritime Distress and Safety System - GMDSS as to the necessary radio facilities on the mainland, an automatic watch has been established through the station Split radio for Digital Selective Call - DSC on VHF channel 70 for sea area A 1.

Since 1992 within the GMDSS System, through the same mainland station also NAVTEX service is working very efficaciously in sending nautical information for navigation security (Maritime Safety Informatoin - MSI) and on the frequency of 518 kHz.

A very favourable geographic position of mainland stations on rather high and conspicuous locations of the coast or the islands secure a complete and reliable VHF communication in directions mainland – vessel and vessel – mainland for the whole eastern Adriatic sea area.

Table 1 A offers the plan of Croatian mainland VHF stations, VHF watch channels and the transmitting time of meteorological reports, navigation warnings and Lists of Traffic, while the data about the NAVTEX service are presented on Table 1 B.

Beside the above mentioned mainland stations VHF calling and working signals have also been distributed to the following services in order to make them work as efficiently as possible as their activity is linked to navigation:

1. Harbour master's offices (Pula, Rijeka, Senj, Zadar, Šibenik, Split, Ploče and Dubrovnik) and all the branch offices in charge of navigation security and activities of search and saving activities at sea

   VHF channels 16 and 10

2. Ports that are in charge of piloting at sea

   VHF channels 09 and 12

3. Marinas

   VHF channels 09 and 12

   VHF channel 17

VHF RADIJSKA SLUŽBA

Table 1A

Mainland station	Calling signal	MMSI	Watch channel	Traffic List (TFC List)		Meteorological and navigational warnings and reports	
				Channel	Time (UTC)	Channel	Time (UTC)
RIJEKA RADIO	9AR		16; 04; 20; 24	24	every uneven hour + 35 min	24	05.35; 14.35;19.35
SPLIT RADIO	9AS	002380100	16; 70; 07; 21; 23; 81	07; 21; 23; 81	if necessary at the end of meteorological and navigational reports	07; 21; 23; 81	05.45; 12.45;19.45
DUBROVNIK RADIO	9AD		16; 04; 07	04; 07	if necessary at the end of meteorological and navigational reports	04; 07	05.25; 13.20;21.20

HARBOUR MASTER'S OFFICE/ VHF CHANNEL/ RANGE

Table 1B

Mainland station	Calling signal	Identification signal B 1	Frequency (kHz)	Range (nm)	Transmitting time (UTC)	Language
SPLIT RADIO	9AS	Q	518	85	02.40; 06.40; 10.40; 14.40; 18.40;22.40	English

For the security of navigation of smaller vessels, yachts and small craft as well as for the advancement of nautical tourism in general it is rather important that meteorological reports are being transmitted permanently during the day and at night, in Croatian, English, German and Italian language. Those reports that include warnings, weather reports and weather forecast are produced within the Nautical meteorological centre in Split, twice a day at 06.00 and 12.00 o'clock and are automatically transmitted through postal telecommunications to harbour master's offices in Pula, Rijeka, Split and Dubrovnik. Further, these offices keep sending the meteorological reports by means of their dislocated VHF radio telephone stations on the given VHF channels.

Table No. 2 shows harbour master's offices, VHF working channels and their range.

MARITIME SEARCH AND RESCUE

Each nautical country is obliged to organise the service of searching and saving at sea based on the regulations of the International Convention on Maritime Search and Rescue, 1979 - SAR Convention.

In the Republic of Croatia, according to SAR Convention and the Law About Harbour's Offices for the maritime search and rescue activites and its organisation in the internal sea waters and territorial sea of the Republic of Croatia, the Maritime Rescue Co-ordination Centre - MRCC has been established in the Rijeka harbour master's office and Maritime Rescue Sub-Centres - MRSC at Pula, Senj, Šibenik, Split, Ploče and Dubrovnik.

Table 2.

HARBOUR MASTER'S OFFICE	VHF CHANNEL	RANGE
PULA	73	Northern Adriatic – Western Coast of Istria
RIJEKA	69	Northern Adriatic – Eastern part
SPLIT	67	Middle Adriatic – Eastern part

In order to function successfully the MRCC in Rijeka and all MRSC in other master's offices are well equipped with:

– rescue units and the staff that is very well organised and instructed for all sort of search and rescue operations;

– their own modern small craft and vessels with all nesessarry equipment for the operations;

– radio stations with permanent watch on VHF channel 16 and 10 and other means of communication.

Next to the listed means of their own, one can engage other vessels of various owners as air-planes that are owned by Croatian auto clubs.

Sound signalling

Sound signalling is slow and today is seldom practised. Sound signals in Morse Code are allowed only in accordance with the Regulations for Prevention of Collisions at Sea.

A vessel or a yacht driven by mechanical propulsion which change course show their intention by:

– one short signal meaning »I am turning to starboard« (right);

– 2 short signals »I am turning to port (left)«;

– 3 short signals »I am going astern«.

If two vessels are near each other and not sure of each other's movements either must show uncertainty by 5 short quick signals.

A vessel (yacht) sailing in a narrow channel and wishing to overtake the vessel in front of it may signal her intention by:

– two long and one short signal if intending to overtake on the starboard side;

– two long and two short signals if intending to overtake on the port side.

The vessel to be overtaken signals agreement by giving a long followed by a short signal twice repeated.

If a vessel (yacht) is approaching a bend in a channel or river, not easy to survey, it signals its presence by one long signal. Any approaching vessel will answer in the same way.

When sailing in limited visibility (fog, mist, strong rain) a vessel longer than 12 m sends the following sound signals:

– a vessel with mechanical propulsion, one long signal with intervals shorter than 2 minutes (while moving), i.e. 2 long signals in the intervals of 2 seconds (the engine is stopped and the vessel is not moving);

– a vessel with limited manoeuvring capability, a sailing-boat, a fishing-craft, a tug-boat, 1 long and 2 short signals in intervals shorter of 2 minutes;

– an anchored ship, quick bell-ringing (above 5 seconds) in intervals shorter than 1 minute (warning signal short-long-short);

– a wrecked vessel, 3 separate bell-ringing and a sound signal like an anchored vessel;

– a tug-boat, as any other, can give 4 short signals.

A vessel (yacht) shorter of 12 m is not bound to follow the given regulations, but must give efficacious sound signals in intervals shorter than 2 minutes.

Flag signalling

Flag signalling is done according to International Signalling Code (ISC). The messages are regularly coded. A signal can be a letter or a figure or a combination of both. More significant of the general (ISC) are: Danger-Urgency. Trouble-Damage. Navigation-Hydrography. Manoeuvring. Various. Meteorology-Weather. Connection. International Health Regulations. A section on medicine is separate.

One-letter signals

A (Alpha) — I have divers below water; keep wide berth or go dead-slow

B (Bravo) — I am loading, unloading, transporting dangerous cargo

C (Charlie) — Yes (affirmative answering signal)

D (Delta) — Give me wide berth, I have difficulty in manoeuvring

E (Echo) — I am changing course to starboard (turning to the right)

F (Foxtrot) — I am disabled, retain contact with me

G (Golf) — I need a pilot (for fishing vessels: I am raising my nets)

H (Hotel) — I have a pilot aboard

I (India) — I am changing course to port (turning on the left)

J (Juliett) — I am on fire and have dangerous cargo; keep wide berth

K (Kilo) — I am trying to make contact with you (signal for need to pass message)

L (Lima) — Stop immediately

M (Mike) — I have stopped and am making no way

N (November) — No (negative reply)

O (Oscar) — Man overboard

P (Papa) — At sea: my nets have snagged (for fishing boat). On shore: all men aboard, we are about to sail

Q (Quebec) — Health on board OK, I am asking free passage

R (Romeo) — Passage beside me free, you can pass

S (Sierra) — My stern engines are working

T (Tango) — Keep your distance, I am towing/trawling

U (Uniform) — You are sailing into danger

V (Victor) — I need help

W (Whiskey) — I need a doctor

X (X-ray) — Stop what you are undertaking and watch for my signals

Y (Yankee) — I am dragging anchor (for Croatian naval

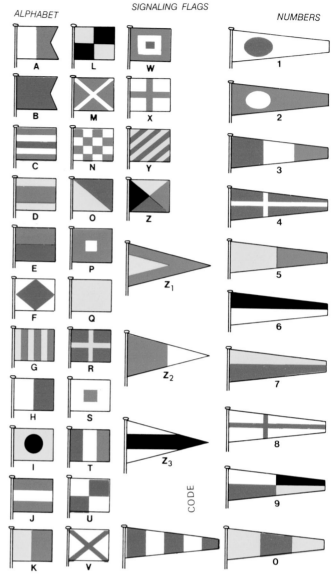

SIGNALING FLAGS

ALPHABET — NUMBERS

vessels: I am leaving/entering port)

Z (Zulu) — I need a tug (for fishing-boats: I am letting down my nets)

Important two-letter signals denoting danger or accidents

AE — I am abandoning boat

AL — I have a doctor aboard

AN — I need a doctor

CB — I need help urgently

CC — I am in danger (then give position)

CP — I am coming to help you

CS — What is the name of your boat?

CV — I cannot help you

DX — I am sinking (then give position)

IT — Fire aboard

JG — I have run aground and am in danger

JM — I have run aground but am not in danger

KF — I need a tug

KG — Do you need a tug?

KM — Can I tow you?

KN — I cannot tow you

VC — Where is the nearest fuel?

VD   You can get fuel at…

VK   Storm imminent from…

THE RULES OF AVOIDING COLLISION AT SEA

The following regulations apply to vessels sailing on the high seas and in internal seaways.

Power-driven vessels (boats) are all those which are moved by mechanical propulsion.

Sailing-vessels are all those which can move by use of sail.

A vessel is considered to be under way if it is not anchored, moored or beached. When sailing at night vessels must show port, starboard, mast and stern lights.

Vessels are considered to have limited manoeuvrability when they are: engaged in work on underwater cables or pipes or with navigation buoys (marks); engaged in dredging or underwater work; loading or unloading persons, cargo or fuel; mine layers at work; tugs or boats towing and unable to manoeuvre to avoid collision.

Ship lights

Navigation lights must be alight from sunset to sunrise, and by day in conditions of poor visibility. Marks need only be shown by day.

White mast light must be visible in sector 112.5° port and starboard of the bows. In vessels 20 m and more the light must be 6 m above the hull. If the vessel is more than 6 m wide, her height is greater than her width but not more than 12 m. In vessels 12-20 m in length their height above the bulwarks must not be less than 2.5 m. In vessels less than 12 m the mast light must be at least 1 m above the side lights.

Port and starboard lights must be visible from the bows in the same way as the mast light: green to starboard (right) and red to port (left). On vessels 20 m and more the side lights must not be forward of the front mast light. Combined green-red lights on vessels shorter than 20 m must be at least 1 m below the mast light.

White stern light must be visible at stern sector 135° (67.5° on each side).

Vessel towing another vessel shows a yellow light with the same characteristics as the stern light. The yellow light is positioned vertically above the stern light.

Light visibility

Vessels 50 m and more: white mast 6 M; side lights, stern light and towing light 3 M.

Vessel 12-50 m: mast 5 M (vessels less than 20 m - 3 M), side lights, stern light and towing light 2 M.

Vessel (boat) less than 12 m: mast light, stern light and towing lights 2 M, side lights 1 M.

Coloured lights (red, green, yellow) that give light to the whole horizon 2 M.

Boats less than 7 m do not need to have navigation lights but must be prepared to show their position at night at least temporarily by showing a white light.

Rules for avoiding collision

When two power-driven vessels approach each other from opposite directions and a collision seems possible each should veer to starboard (right).

When the courses of two power-driven vessels cross and collision seems possible the vessel that can see the other to starboard (right) must change the course, but must not cross the bows of the other vessel.

When a power-driven vessel seems on collision course with a sailing-boat the power-driven vessel must give way.

A vessel about to overtake from astern must pass the vessel on the most suitable side.

When two sail-driven vessels seem on collision course:

– the vessel with wind from port (left) must change course;

– if both vessels are running before the wind then the vessel on the leeward side must give way;

– if the vessel to windward cannot judge the situation with certainty then she must give way to the vessel on the leeward side.

In some navigation situations vessels must give sound signals (see Sound signalling).

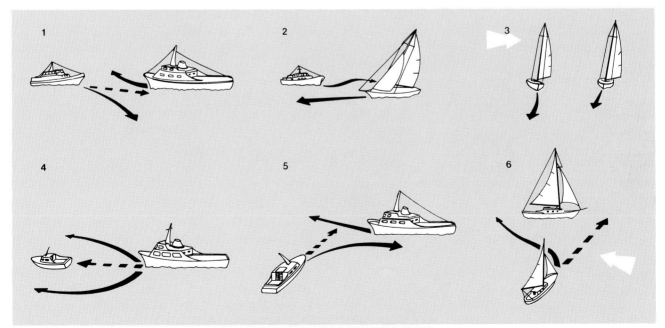

RULES FOR AVOIDING COLLISION AT SEA:

1. both vessels after course to starboard (give one short blast signal); 2. the power-driven vessel must keep off the way of sailing-vessel (give two short blast signals); 3. the sailing-vessel that is to windward must keep out of the way of the sailing-vessel that is to leeward; 4. the vessel overtaking another may pass it on the port side or the starboard side; 5. the vessel must pass away behind the stern of the other vessel; 6. the sailing-vessel that has the wind on the port side must pass away behind the stern of the other sailing-vessel.

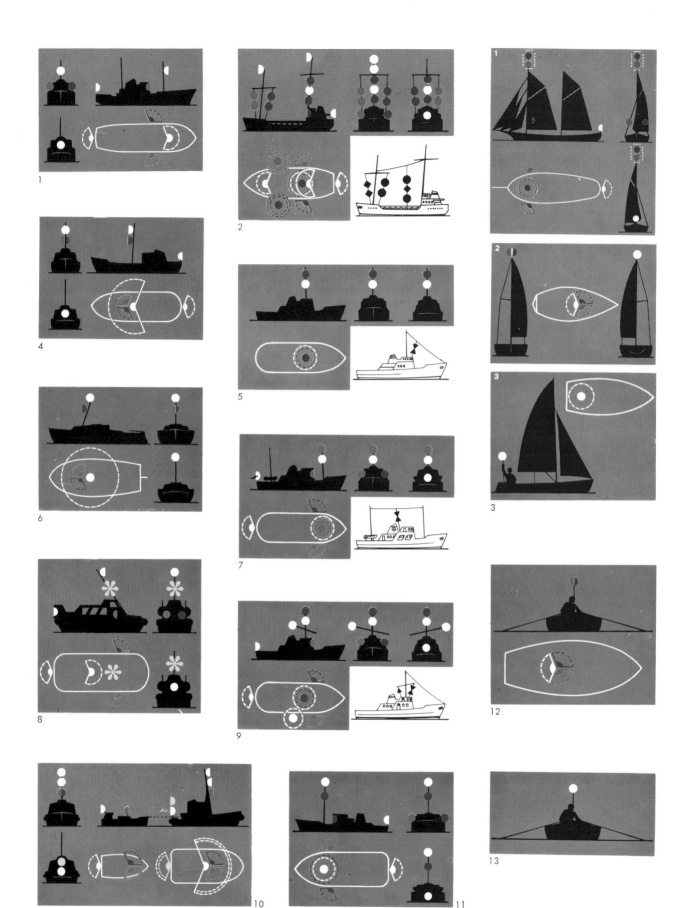

LIGHTS AND SIGNS PRESCRIBED TO AVOID COLLISION AT SEA

1. Power-driven vessel under way (50 metres in length and shorter); 2. Lights and day-marks on a vessel engaged in underwater operations (50 metres or more in length), obstructions leftward; 3. Sailing ship under way: (1) 20 metres or more in length, (2) less than 20 metres in length, (3) less than 7 metres in length; 4. Power-driven vessel under way (length up to 12 metres); 5. Lights and day-marks on fishing vessel under way, the fishing equipment of which extends up to 150 metres distance from hull; 6. Boat under way, up to 7 metres in length (speed not exceeding 7 knots); 7. Lights and day-marks on fishing vessel under way, trawling or dredging (up to 50 metres in length); 8. Hovercraft under way; 9. Lights and day-marks on fishing vessel under way, with fishing equipment extending more than 150 metres from hull; 10. Lights on tug-vessel and towed vessel under way (200 metres in length); 11. Pilot-vessel under way (up to 50 metres in length); 12. and 13. Rowing boat under way;

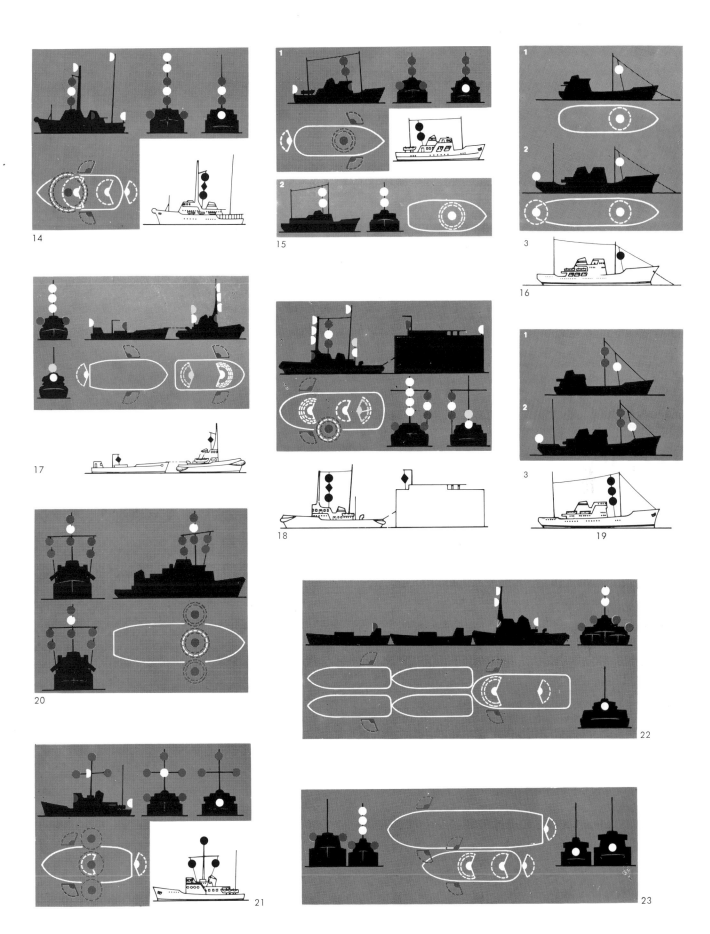

14. Lights and day-marks on vessel under way with impaired manoeuvring capacity (50 metres in length); 15. Lights and day-marks on vessel unable to manoeuvre: (1) under way, (2) under way, standing; 16. Lights on vessels at anchor: (1) up to 50 metres in length, (2) exceeding 50 metres in length, (3) day-marks; 17. Lights and day-marks on tug-vessel (50 metres and more in length) and vessel in tow (exceeding 200 metres) under way; 18. Lights and day-marks on tug-vessel (50 metres and more in length) and vessel in tow (exceeding 250 metres) under way; 19. Lights on vessel aground: (1) up to 50 metres in length, (2) 50 metres and more in length, (3) day-marks for vessel aground; 20. Lights on vessel at anchor engaged in submarine operations (50 metres and more in length); 21. Lights and day-marks on minesweeper under way and in operation (up to 50 metres in length); 22. Lights on power-driven vessel (less than 50 metres in length) pushing barges ahead; 23. Lights on power-driven vessel (50 metres and more in length) towing another vessel alongside.

Avoiding collision in ports and in internal sea waters

Small vessels (boats) give way to larger vessels. Vessels (boats) entering port, river or narrow channel must not hinder vessels coming out.

The vessel that has advantage in manoeuvring must warn with 5 short and quick signals the other craft that are not following the rules.

Fishing-boats are not allowed to fish in ports by means of lights and in places difficult for sailing, they may use only shaded lights. If they are not following the rules they have to switch off the lights when warned by other vessels.

SIGNALLING FOR HELP AT SEA

SHOTS at one minute intervals given from fire-arms or any other explosive device.

CONSTANT SOUND given in any way.

RECTANGULAR FLAG with some circular object like a bell either above or below it flown on the mast or other most conspicuous position.

ROCKETS or FLARES which throw up red lights ignited at short intervals.

ROCKETS WITH PARACHUTE DEVICE or red HAND FLARES:

FLAMES from lighted pitch or oil barrels.

Orange SMOKE SIGNALS.

SOS signal (··· — ···) transmitted by radio-telegraph or in any other way.

MAYDAY signal in open text over radio-telephone.

Signal-flags NC (International Signals Code) flown on the mast or in some other conspicuous position.

OUTSTRETCHED ARMS moved slowly downwards from above.

Radio-telegraph or radio-telephone ALARM SIGNAL.

FLYING OF FLAGS

The flag of the Croatian merchant navy is identical with that of the Republic of Croatia. It is flown from the stern flag-staff or the gaff, i.e. on the mast (the right yard arm). It is normally flown from sunrise to sunset when clearly identifiable: while entering or leaving port, while staying in a port or an anchorage, in sight of naval vessels, fortifications or signal (observing) stations, while exchanging messages (signalling), while navigating through channels or narrow straits, in foreign territorial seas and internal waters as well as on demand by another vessel (station). When entering port between sunset and sunrise the flag has to be lowered after having received permission to establish contact with the shore.

Vessels (yachts) booked in the registers of the Republic of Croatia may fly the flag of their city, port of register, region or »županija« (district) on their bow mast or flag-staff. When entering the territorial sea of a foreign country they replace it with the flag of that country as a sign of respect.

A naval vessel of the Republic of Croatia is paid respect to by lowering the flag to one-third of the mast. The flag is raised again after the naval vessel has replied in the same manner (by lowering and raising the flag).

On festive occasions, state holidays or if so demanded by a harbour master's office, vessels (yachts) are solemnly dressed (gala).

A small ornamentation (gala) consists of the flag of the Republic of Croatia flown on the stern flag-staff, a flag on the bow (the flag of the city or port of register or that of the region or »županija« /district of domicile/), and a flag on the mast (either the flag of the Republic of Croatia or of a club).

A large ornamentation (gala) dressing consists of the flags used for small ornamentation plus strings of International Signals Code flags suspended from the bow flag-staff over the mast head to the stern flags'-staff.

State flag is flown at half flag-staff as a sign of mourning. Vessels of foreign register act in a similar way except that they fly the flag of the country of register instead of the Croatian flag.

WEATHER CONDITIONS IN THE ADRIATIC

Weather conditions are dependent on atmospheric pressure. Weather in the Adriatic is particularly affected by: high pressure (anticyclones) from the Azores and Siberia; low pressure (cyclones and depressions) from Iceland; the position and path of cyclones from the Atlantic take their shape in the Gulf of Genoa and the North Adriatic and depend finally of the geographic relief of the coastal shore. Depending on the above conditions there are mainly three types of weather on the Croatian Adriatic coast: humid – with warm south winds; dry – with cold north winds; and fair settled weather – with a north-west wind called the maestral.

The general features of summer weather are: when there is a high pressure ridge at the Azores, the Mediterranean and the Adriatic are on the edge of extensive anticyclonic air circulation from the North Atlantic. This weakens the effect of Icelandic cyclonic and Siberian anticyclonic activity which do not show reaction on the Croatian coast. So it produces weather in the Adriatic, in which day by day the pleasant NW maestral blows from the sea. Warm light wind from the Sahara intensifies this wind in the South Adriatic. At night in the coastal band of about 12 - 20 M a local wind (burin) blows from land to sea. It blows on both sides of the Adriatic; on the east coast from NNE in the north and mostly from E in its southern part.

In the central Adriatic the most common winds are north-westerlies or winds of light variable direction, producing calm weather.

The situation in winter is completely different. Anticyclones from the Azores withdraw further south which strengthens the effects of Siberian high and Icelandic low pressure. The Adriatic is under the influence of cyclones which move from the west one after another, or else comes under the effect of cold air-masses moving from northeast.

Because of its relative warmth in relation to the surrounding coast the Adriatic is like a long furrow of relatively low pressure with isobars very close to each other on the eastern side. The centre of locally formed cyclones (depressions) is usually off Palagruža island. The normal air circulation is: south-east winds (sirocco) in the south-eastern part of the Adriatic; from centre northwards E winds are more likely, in the Rijeka and Trieste Gulfs the NE bora is most frequent. On the northern Italian coast the winds are mainly NW and south of Ancona down to Otranto Straits mainly W.

The sirocco and bora are the most characteristic winds of the Adriatic and largely responsible for the weather pattern. They mainly blow from October to April. The maestral (NW) mainly blows in the summer months. Weather which is calm or with very light winds is said to be »bora-like« (na buru) or »sirocco-like« (na jugo) according to whether the prevailing air currents come from land or sea.

Bora. It is a dry, cold wind. Since it is a north-easterly it mainly blows from the east coast of the Adriatic from land to sea. It brings fine weather.

Because of the configuration of the land it blows locally with varying force and from various directions ranging from N to ENE. It is under the general influence of the atmospheric pressure over central Europe and the Mediterranean. However, local boras are also frequent. They are caused by the cooling of the air above the karst valleys suddenly pouring down through the mountain saddles to the sea. Boras of this kind are local, short-lived, sudden and they are often violent.

FLAG OF THE REPUBLIC OF CROATIA

FLAG OF THE CROATIAN NAVY

The relief of the east of the Adriatic causes the local boras to blow in violent gusts (refuli) and to begin completely unexpectedly. The force of the bora may vary from a light breeze to a wind of gale force (45-60 knots). All other winds blow horizontally, except the bora. Cold masses of air descend to the sea tearing down the coastal mountains, especially the high saddles, like waterfalls of air. They blow off the crests of the waves and cause spin drift (fumarea) which may also be so thick as to considerably reduce visibility.

The bora blows most fiercely in the following places: the Gulf of Trieste (especially from Cape Savudrija to Trieste close to the shore when it blows ENE), the Kvarner and Kvarnerić (when the bora is strong there is also a 4 knot current), Rijeka Bay and the Velebit Channel (especially between the island of Krk and the mainland, beside Senj and the Senj passage – Senjska vrata), the whole coastal length from Šibenik to Split (Kaštela Bay and particularly Solin) and Vrulja cove (between Omiš and Makarska). The bora blows with less force along the west coast of Istria, in the Zadar Channel, on the lee side of islands of Unije, Dugi otok, Kornati Archipelago and Mljet and on the coastal stretch between Cavtat and point Oštra rt. In the lower course of the River Krka, Zaton, Žuljana

Bay (Pelješac) and at the mouth of the River Neretva the bora blows stronger than in the immediately adjacent areas.

The golden rules of the mariners of this coast are: the naked shoreline of the islands towards the mainland are dangerous and bora-prone; the same holds true for bays and coves where the tree trunks grow leaning towards the south. Such places must never be selected for a stay of any length or for overnight stays if the bora is likely. Coves at the foot of the mountains are no shelter from the bora, on the contrary it often blows there with almost hurricane violence.

The bora blows all the year round but especially in winter when it attains its greater fury. However a fierce bora is not rare in May. In the summer it lasts only two or three days or even a few hours but in winter it may blow for a week or a fortnight. Gale force bora lasts at most two days.

There are not such clear indications of the approach of a bora as there are of sirocco. One indication for bora is the formation of a »cloud cap« over the highest parts of the range of the highest mountains especially Velebit and Biokovo. Such cloud caps may form in any kind of weather, and not only during fair ones. If there are cloud formations on the tops and slopes of the mountains and on the lee side, small clouds

CALM IN TELAŠĆICA BAY

27

HRID GALERA

form which move downward and are dispersed in the wind then the bora can be expected at any moment in the open sea and on the coast is already blowing. If the cloud cap continues to increase this means that the bora is strengthening.

The approach of the bora is not connected with any special time of day but on the whole blows more often in the afternoon than the forenoon. It usually reaches its greatest force between 7 and 11 (especially about 9) or between 18 and 22 hours. It almost always lessens or completely dies around midday and midnight. This is usually after the mountain·»cloud cap« has dispersed. In various parts of the coast, however, the nature of the bora varies.

Following a very strong bora a calm period ensues during which for a few hours during the day a fresh NW wind usually blows, and at night the burin, the wind from shore to sea.

There are two kinds of bora, anticyclonic and cyclonic, according to whether it is caused by an extension southwards of a high pressure area over Central Europe or by a cyclone over the Mediterranean or the Adriatic itself.

An anticyclonic or clear bora brings dry and bright weather, high pressure and cooler days to the entire eastern coast of the Adriatic. It also causes strong gusty winds from NE and N. The clear (anticyclonic) bora is caused by air currents between a high pressure area (maximum) over the northern part of Central Europe and a cyclone over the Mediterranean. Because of local and general climatic conditions these air currents may move with great force, causing stormy winds. Strong gusts are particularly felt from NE to N.

Anticyclonic boras do not only occur in winter but in summer also when a northern anticyclone begins to spread south-east, but in summer the temperature never falls so low as in winter.

The cyclonic or dark bora is a strong and steady NE to E wind bringing dark, rainy weather, and in winter sometimes snowstorms and great cold. It often extends across the west coast of the Adriatic. Boras of this kind move across the Adriatic and as they approach the eastern shores they suck the coastal air down to sea. Before the cyclonic bora begins to blow the sky is covered with a homogeneous layer of cloud which spreads across from the south-west of the horizon. Before this bora begins the air pressure falls, sometimes very low.

It frequently happens that a bora is blowing simultaneously in the North Adriatic and in the central and south Adriatic a sirocco. One of the wind boundaries in such cases are Cape Ploča (near Šibenik) or the island of Vis, and the other is Kvarner Bay.

The typical bora does not cause large waves but very short choppy ones. The bora becomes gradually less violent as one leaves the eastern coast (15-20 M), but as the wind gets less the waves get larger (up to 2 m). Small boats undergo a

RT RAŽANJ

BORA IN THE VELEBIT CHANNEL

special stress in a bora, they are subject to frequent rise and fall or must sail inclined. They should therefore stay fairly close inshore so that the wind path is shorter and the sea less agitated.

The north wind or tramontana is similar to the bora and usually blows from the N. Its force is feebler than the bora, it is less unpredictable and its course is affected by the relief of the coast-line. It is most frequent in the South Adriatic.

An easterly or levanat is the name given to a bora which blows at more or less constant force usually nearer to the east and during rain and cold (bura škura is the name for this wind in Dalmatia). Easterlies of this kind which are something between a bora and a sirocco are more frequent in the North Adriatic.

Sirocco. A warm, humid wind blowing from ESE to SSE. It blows the entire length of the Adriatic coast and brings rough seas. The sky is thickly clouded and there is almost always long lasting rain. It reaches its greatest force in the South Adriatic. It may blow at any time of the year but in the North Adriatic mainly between March and June and in the South Adriatic from autumn until the end of the winter. On average it blows at force 4-5 of Beaufort's scale (16-20 knots) but it may sometimes reach gale force. The sirocco in summer almost always lasts up to 3 and in winter 9 days, though it may in winter blow with shorter intermissions for three weeks.

The sirocco is very strong on those stretches of coast which are exposed to the open sea or where the channel allows the wind direct access. Such areas of strong sirocco are: The Gulf of Venice, the Kvarner and the Kvarnerić, the

SUĆURAJ

STONČICA

open sea around Cape Ploča and the coastline south of Dubrovnik, the outer channels between the islands especially Lastovo Channel and Mljet Channel. As the sea becomes rougher a current of up to 2 knots may develop. Although it is so strong and may last a long time the sirocco is a less dangerous wind in the Adriatic than the bora. It does not come suddenly, it begins gently and develops its full force only after 36-48 hours; it blows with constant force and not in gusts. It only reaches gale force after the third day which allows small boats to seek harbour or refuge sheltered from this wind.

The sirocco is usually preceded by calm seas and light changeable winds, haziness then develops to the south-east, on the horizon. The air seems to become thick and visibility is restricted. The air pressure falls slowly but steadily below normal, temperature and humidity rise. As the sirocco increases in strength general haziness gives way to low vaporous small clouds moving from SE to NW, their path is obstructed by the mountain peaks where they tend to become concentrated while little by little the sky to the NW becomes thick with low grey clouds. Gradually waves begin to develop and an increasingly strong SE current, a heavy swell develops in bays and open anchorages, choppy sea and the level of the sea rises.

The sirocco too has its cyclonic and anticyclonic forms and characteristics, seen in variations of weather and air pressure. Most often it is cyclonic.

SIROCCO

LIRICA

Anticyclonic sirocco mainly occurs in spring and autumn. It is usually caused by interaction between a deep and almost stationary cyclone over North-West or North Europe and an area of high pressure over the eastern Mediterranean. Sky is clear or flecked with high or medium level clouds moving NE, while the SW horizon is always clear. After one or two days of sirocco clouds increase in the North Adriatic. There is only light or no rain. As a result of an increase of dust particles brought from the north African deserts the atmosphere is often turbid.

The cyclonic sirocco is a medium strong to strong ESE to SSE wind often blowing gustily. It brings low, thick clouds, moderate showers and a rough sea. It results in a quick fall of the barometer, often reaching the lowest Adriatic pressure. Especially in the North Adriatic it is a general rule that a sudden fall in the barometer means a quickly passing cyclone and a short lasting sirocco.

The north coast of the island of Vis regularly divides a sirocco zone from a bora zone if the cyclone has a more southerly path. Vessels sailing north in a sirocco from the South Adriatic must, from Vis onwards, be prepared for a sudden wind shift to NE. Vice versa, if there is a bora in the North Adriatic with low pressure a sirocco is very likely blowing in the South Adriatic.

If a sirocco blowing in the South Adriatic gradually weakens and is not replaced by any other wind then what is known as a »rotten sirocco« (trulo jugo) ensues, characterized by quietness and a flat calm (mrtvo more). It is even more sultry than in a normal sirocco. Heavy rain falls with occasional brighter patches.

Besides these general winds the following local ones should be noted: the maestral, a sea-to-land breeze and the burin, a land-to-sea one. They are most frequent in the warm months (late spring and summer). Since they are caused by differences of temperature between land and water they blow more strongly when these temperatures are very different and appear as daily periodical winds. They are felt only along the coast and seldom more than 20 M inland or off-shore.

Maestral. By day the land surface gets more heated than the surface of the sea and as a result air-currents begin to rise up from the land and at a certain distance are drawn down towards the sea thus causing land-sea circulation. In the lowest air-levels a wind comes from the sea called zmorac or maestral. The maestral is usually characterized by white cumulus clouds denoting fine weather.

The maestral normally begins to blow between 9 and 10 a.m. and reaches its maximum force about 2 p.m. It always dies away before sunset (usually about 6 p.m. or after the maximum daily temperature of the sea surface). On the West coast of the Adriatic it is at its strongest at about 4 p.m. and often continues overnight and may create a choppy sea. The maestral is a good weather harbinger and cools the hot days of summer. It is usually wind at force of about 4-5 of Beaufort's scale. It is weakest in the Gulf of Trieste and strengthens towards the south so that in the Otranto Straits it may reach a strength of force 6-7 accompanied with a rather turbulent sea. Sometimes it reaches gale force (the maestralun) which may happen after the passing of a cyclone.

On the Croatian coast this wind mainly blows from the NW, but according to local conditions it may blow WNW. On the Albanian coast it blows from the W and on the Italian coast usually from the E and in some places from SE. During the day maestral varies in direction following the sun.

MAESTRAL

Burin. By night air also circulates in a closed circle in the opposite direction from daytime. The air over the land cools more quickly than that over the water and so the wind blows from the land to sea. The burin starts after the sunset and usually stops before sunrise. On the northern parts of the eastern Adriatic it blows from NNE to ENE and in the southern parts more E. On the western Adriatic coast it blows mostly SW.

The burin is usually less strong than the maestral, but in some places (for example Bol on the island of Brač and Žuljana on the Pelješac Peninsula) it may reach the strength of force 5.

Nevera. The whole length of the coast, apart from the local winds, there may appear various kinds of storms and squalls. Those of a lesser or shorter character are called nevera or neverin – such squalls or storms (mostly from June to September) are more frequent on the northern part of the coast. Most of them originate in Italy, especially in northern Italy, cross the Adriatic and approach the Croatian coast from a NW to SW direction. Mariners treat them with the utmost respect. Nevera moves at speeds of 15-20 M/h, and the faster it moves the more violent are the winds.

Such storms may develop in very varied weather conditions – in fine, clear, warm weather and as part of a cyclone that has already developed. In the first case they are warm or local storms, and in the second dynamic or cyclonic. In winter (cyclonic) storms of this kind are rare but when they occur they cover a wider area than the summer warm ones. Features of every nevera are: thunder, lightning, heavy rain or hail, and violent gusts of wind. They occur most frequently in summer, are short-lived and affect only a limited area. They almost seem to have their own special areas and occur at the same time (following the highest maximum day tem-perature).

Sure signals of the approach of a nevera occur only a short time before it strikes, and it is difficult to foretell them a day in advance. Sometimes storm forecasts will include the information that a nevera is likely. The main forerunners of such storms are: hot and sultry air, storm clouds (cumulonimbus – showing the storm centre), sudden fall in the barometer, rise in temperature, fall of relative humidity, a wind that blows warm and gentle at first but just before the nevera strikes it blows with great strength in the opposite direction from the path of the nevera storm. A sudden change of air pressure brings about a fall in temperature followed by the most violent gusts of wind and a rise in relative humidity. As soon as the nevera has passed the barometer gradually returns to normal and the temperature slowly rises again, the sea calms and it is almost windless or there is only a light shore-to-sea wind.

The sudden nevera may be highly dangerous especially for small boats. Boats at anchor should be bows on to the wind. The narrow passages and high mountains of the coast may make it impossible to notice the approach of a nevera in time. By day the lightning may not be visible nor the thunder audible since the storm is preceded by a wind in the opposite direction to its path. Nor is sultriness a reliable forecast of these storms.

In a gradual nevera the wind begins to be felt at first slightly and gradually with increasing force blowing in the same direction as the path of the storm, with the decrease of atmospheric pressure, thunder will be noticed in good time. Just as the wind and rain reach the maximum intensity the nevera suddenly blows itself out and the weather becomes clear again. It is possible to realize that storms of this kind are approaching and to take necessary precautions to secure boats.

Waterspouts (tromba). The whirling storms of cyclonic origin appearing above the sea. In the Adriatic they occur when a cloud forms a funnel shaped pendant which descends towards the sea and draws up a corresponding amount of whirling water (usually cumulonimbus at a height of about 1000 m). This mostly happens in calm weather when there are a large number of thunder clouds in the sky and in unstable atmospheric conditions. A waterspout looks like a long grey funnel, mouth uppermost, moving across the water. At

GLAVAT

its edges the air whirls with great speed, but inside it is airless with a great difference in air pressure in a relatively small circular area (100 to 300 m) which is the cause of the hurricane speed with which the winds whirl. Waterspouts may move as fast as 60 knots but may also be almost stationary, the speed of movement being regulated by the cloud above.

They most frequently come from the W or SW, cover about 6 miles and then die out. Heavy rain immediately follows, and sometimes a short-lived storm. Waterspouts may occur at the entire length of the coast, especially off the W coast of Istria, from Lošinj to Kornati, around the island of Palagruža, and in the channels of Central Adriatic (i.e. the Brač Channel, Hvar Channel). Vessels and boats are in danger if they come into the path of a waterspout, especially sailing boats and speedboats. Waterspouts can be avoided by turning at a 90° angle from their path.

Lebić (garbina). A gale force SW wind causing high waves and heavy rain.

In summer this is a locally occurring, warm nevera. At other times of the year it is a form of cyclone. It blows when to the south or south-west of the Adriatic there is a strong anticyclone and at the same time a strong cyclone is passing by to the north. Medium strong winds then blow from the S or SW. After a time, as the cyclone moves along the Adriatic coast, the wind veers suddenly to SW and reaches gale force – this is the lebićada known also as the garbinada. The wind strength is regulated by the low air pressure, and when the pressure begins to rise the wind blows itself out. In all other weather conditions other then the above the south-westerly only blows for a short period caused by the normal veering of the SE wind through S to NW if the cyclone which caused it turns to NE or E.

The south-westerly lebićada (garbinada) develops to full force in the central and south Adriatic, on the south side of cyclones between centres of cyclonic and anticyclonic activity. On the Croatian coast this wind brings high seas which are dangerous for harbours and any craft in them that are not protected from SW.

A mark of the arrival of this south-westerly storm is a low hazy line on the south-west horizon with a strongly marked lower margin, the barometer falls suddenly. When the south-westerly is of gale force the white patch on the horizon appears like a segment, and as the wind strengthens the segment widens.

FORETELLING THE WEATHER ACCORDING TO LOCAL CONDITIONS

The radio weather forecasts mainly give general information and do not take account of local conditions. Thus local weather signs, taken in conjunction with the general forecasts, are of great practical importance. It must never, however, be forgotten that isolated indications are seldom in themselves enough, but must be seen in the context of the whole situation. Thus only taking account of cloud formations and a fall in the barometer is not sufficient to forecast the approach of a cyclone. To be reliable the weather signs need to include also changes in humidity, the direction of wind and clouds.

BEAUFORT WIND SCALE

Code	Description of wind	Wind speed m/sec	Wind speed kn	Description of sea
0	Calm	0-0.2	0-1	Like mirror.
1	Light air	0.3-1.5	1-3	Ripples, scale-like.
2	Light breeze	1.6-3.3	4-6	Short wavelets, crests do not break.
3	Gentle breeze	3.4-5.4	7-10	Larger wavelets, crests do not break.
4	Moderate breeze	5.5-7.9	11-15	Moderate waves becoming longer, fairly frequent whitecaps.
5	Fresh breeze	8-10.7	16-21	Moderate waves taking more pronounced long form, many whitecaps, possibility of spray.
6	Strong breeze	10.8-13.8	22-27	Large waves begin to form, white foam crests extensive everywhere, spray.
7	Moderate gale	13.9-17.1	28-33	Large waves breaking in white foam beginning to be blown in streaks in direction of wind.
8	Fresh gale	17.2-20.7	34-40	Moderately high waves of greater length, crests begin to break into spindrift, foam blown in well marked streaks in direction of wind.
9	Strong gale	20.8-24.4	41-47	High waves, crest topple over and break, dense streaks of foam along direction of wind. Spray may affect visibility.
10	Heavy gale	24.5-28.4	48-55	Very high waves with over- hanging crests, breaking crests white sea which becomes heavy and shocklike.
11	Storm	28.5-32.6	56-63	Exceptionally high waves, small vessels lost from sight, everywhere edges of waves blown into froth. Visibility greatly affected.
12	Hurricane	32.7-36.9	>64	Air filled with foam and spray, sea completely white with driving spray. Visibility very limited.

WIND SPEED

Code	Description of sea	Wave height (m) Atlantic	Baltic	Adriatic	Wave length of the Adriatic (m)
0	Calm-glassy	-	-	-	-
1	Calm-rippled	0-0.2	0.05	0.05	2.0
2	Smooth wavelets	0.5-0.75	0.6	0.2	5.0
↓	↓	↓	↓	0.5...	9.5 ...
3	Slight	0.8-1.2	1.0	>0.8	>14
4	Moderate	1.2-2.0	1.5	1.3...	20...
5	Rough heavy	2.0-3.5	2.3	>1.9	>25
6	Very rough	3.5-6.0	3.0	2.6...	32...
7	High sea	< 6.0	4.0	>3.5	>39
↓	↓	↓	↓	4.6...	46.5...
8	Very high sea	>20	5.5	>5.9	>55
9	Phenomenal high sea	>20	-	7.3...	66...
↓	↓	↓	-	>8.8	>79

The following signs indicate that fine or mainly fine weather will continue.

No change of weather as long as there are no clouds.

Clear sky, quiet air, sometimes a few short-lived cirrus clouds which seem to be motionless or to move only slowly mean a continuation of good weather.

The burin (land-to-sea breeze) at daybreak and the maestral (sea-to-land) at afternoon and again the burin in the evening are sure signs of good weather.

When the bora blows in summer rain is far away.

If in the daytime wind follows the course of the sun it will go on being fine.

If there is a clear sunset following fine weather and the sunlight is bright to the end, or if the evening sky is red and the sunset retains all the characteristics of the previous day then the weather next day will almost certainly be fine.

Good weather can be expected if at night the moon is reddish before it sets and not silvery.

When the tides are regular fine weather may be expected to go on.

Weather signs which foretell the approach of bad weather

Cirrus clouds moving across a clear sky are the first sign of worsening weather. The wind direction follows that of the clouds.

When high clouds appear in the south or south-east of the horizon wet weather can be expected in a day or two.

A completely clear sky with clouds about noon is very often a sign that rain will fall before the evening.

If a thick wall of clouds forms on the south-west horizon, especially if it forms in the evening, then rain is to be expected and in the winter a dark (cyclonic) bora within 24 hours.

If there are cumulus clouds at daybreak then worsening weather is to be expected at all times of the year.

If at sunset, after a perfectly clear day, on the western horizon cloud heads rear up then the next day it is likely to be cloudy.

If the sirocco blows more strongly in the evening then it will probably rain.

If in clear weather with a bora the wind veers east the weather will change; the change will be considerable if the wind turns into a south-easterly.

In winter a maestral often comes before a sirocco and wet weather.

If at dawn there is a light bora or burin and the wind then veers to east or south but does not follow the sun, fine weather is not to be expected.

If in the warm months the maestral does not blow but instead a calm ensues at midday, or if the maestral is late or stops blowing sooner than it should, then worsening weather is to be expected.

A hazy sunset foretells wet weather.

If the wind blows from the 3rd quadrant (especially at sunset) this is a sure sign that the weather will deteriorate and it will rain.

A ring around the sun or the moon and a humid wind herald rain. When the sun has a ring in the afternoon in winter a dark (cyclonic) bora is likely.

Red sky or rainbow in the early morning usually means rain shortly.

In the summer months it is almost a rule that if it rains early in the morning it will stop before noon, if the rain begins around noon it will usually last several hours. If it starts raining in the evening it is the beginning of rainy weather.

If the sea level is unusually high bad weather is on the way.

Signs for the coming of better weather

In general, in cloudy weather, if clear patches form on the western horizon the weather will soon clear up.

Clear or red sky on the south, west or north-west horizon foretells good weather.

If, during rainy and cloudy weather, on the southern horizon a SE wind begins to break up the clouds it is a sign that the wind will veer, the rain stop and the sky begin to clear.

As a general rule wind after rain brings good weather.

If after heavy rain lightning is seen in the west the weather will soon get better.

If, in the summer months, after variable and poor weather, the maestral begins to blow at its usual times the weather will get better; in rainy weather if the maestral only blows in the afternoon the next day will be fine.

If the weather is rainy and unsettled, the sky is red after sunset or the clouds are red the next day is likely to be fine.

A marked fall in sea-level means good weather.

Signs of an approaching nevera storm

If in summer the morning breaks sultry, with a hazy horizon, and calm and clouds begin to build up while high clouds come from the north-west then a nevera can be expected in the afternoon.

If, following a nevera a wind, even a light one, blows from the E or SE, or if it is sultry in most cases this presages a nevera next day.

If, after a nevera it gets cooler and a NW wind freshens next day a nevera is less likely.

SEA CURRENTS AND TIDES

Currents in the Adriatic are relatively weak but circulate constantly under the influence of winds and tides.

A branch of the Mediterranean current flows from the Ionian Sea NW up to the Adriatic coast and down the Italian coast in a SE direction. The normal speed of this current is 0.5-1 knot. It is stronger in summer than in winter and stronger on the west coast than on the east. It is strongest on the eastern Adriatic coast during a sirocco and at high tide. Through straits and channels the current is considerably

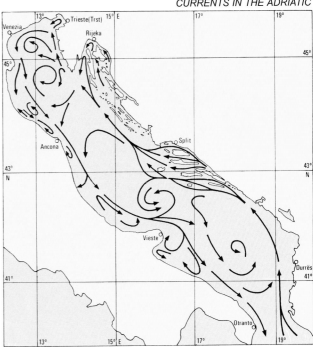

CURRENTS IN THE ADRIATIC

stronger. There are separate signs to mark currents on charts. More detailed information concerning currents is given in Adriatic Pilot 1 and 2, and the publications of the Croatian Hydrographic Institute in Split.

Tides. Tidal changes are caused by the pull of the moon, and to a lesser extent by the sun. The difference between high and low tide in the Adriatic is negligible for small craft. It is least in the central Adriatic (Šibenik–Zadar: 15-30 cm), slightly more towards the south and the north (Istra 60 cm, exceptionally 100 cm, Venice up to 120 cm).

Tidal differences are greater at full moon and new moon, and greatest during the first and last lunar quarters.

Weather also affects tidal action. During periods of high pressure and the bora the water level is lower (as much as 40 cm). Low pressure and southern winds make it higher (to 70 cm).

The Croatian Hydrographic Institute in Split publishes an annual information of tides for some ports on the E coast.

There are stationary waves (known as seš or štiga) in a number of bays and channels caused by weather or proximity to the open sea. These are usually negligible.

SURVEY LIST OF NAVIGATIONAL CHARTS FOR SMALL MARTIME CRAFT

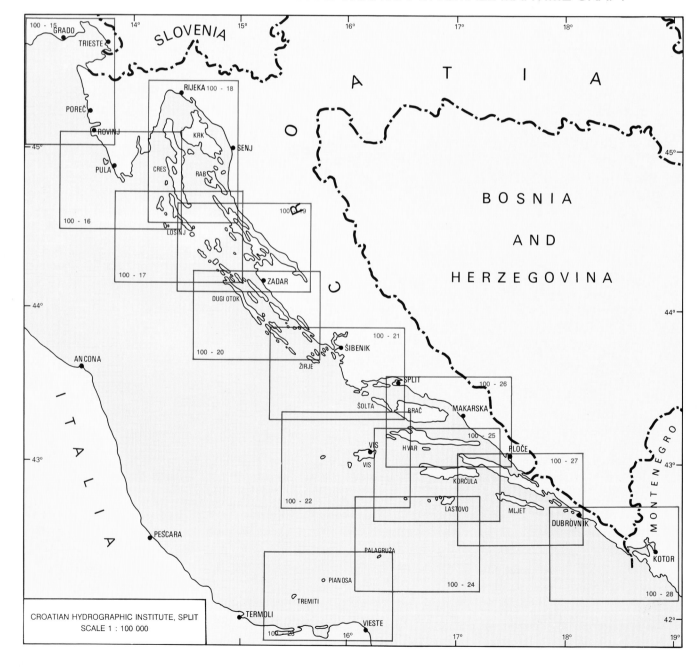

PULA HARBOUR MASTER'S OFFICE AREA

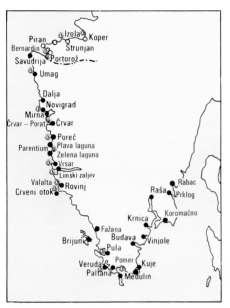

BUDAVA	DALJA	IZOLA	KOPER	NOVIGRAD	PIRAN	POREČ	PORTOROŽ	PULA	RAŠA	ROVINJ	UMAG	TRST	VERUDA	VRSAR	
	52	70	72	48	66	46	67	25	11	35	57	75	19	43	BUDAVA
		17	20	4	13	8	14	33	59	17	5	23	45	14	DALJA
			3	19	4	22	6	47	70	34	12	8	52	30	IZOLA
				22	7	29	9	53	76	37	16	7	60	34	KOPER
					15	6	16	30	53	15	7	26	34	10	NOVIGRAD
						21	2	45	68	30	8	11	49	25	PIRAN
							22	26	52	10	13	32	30	6	POREČ
								46	73	31	9	12	50	26	PORTOROŽ
									33	18	37	56	8	23	PULA
										43	60	78	27	51	RAŠA
											22	41	21	5	ROVINJ
												19	41	17	UMAG
													60	36	TRST
														25	VERUDA
															VRSAR

DISTANCES OF PORTS

SAVUDRIJA

WESTERN COAST OF ISTRIA

SAVUDRIJA

(45°30'N; 013°30'E), small town and harbour N of point of the same name (round, white stone lighthouse, with top gallery, white flashes, 23 M).

A large tourist settlement with motels, bungalows and a campsite is situated near the point.

Mooring. The harbour is exposed to SW and NW wind. In other winds suitable as shelter for small craft only. Mooring at pier (depth 2.5 m), at north part of pier with four-point moor.

Warning. When entering harbour care should be taken to avoid shoals extending about 1.2 M offshore from the point.

UMAG

(45°26'N; 013°31'E), town and harbour on NW shore of Istrian Peninsula, 4 km S of Cape Savudrija.

Approach. Landmarks: the hotel complex N of the harbour, »Adriatic« hotel in the harbour, church belfry surmounted by a pyramidal point, factory chimney S of town, green tower with column (green light) at head of breakwater, red tower with column (red light) and gallery at head of marina breakwater, square white tower (red light) on main pier of harbour.

When entering harbour care should be taken of a number of shoals. The western edge of the Paklena shoal on the north entrance to the harbour is marked by a cylindrical red tower with a column and gallery (white-red sector light) on a white stone base; the southern edge of the rocky Garofulin shoal, also on the north entrance, is marked by a yellow and black post and two cones, points downwards (sea is shallow to about 60 m south of marker).

Incoming vessels should enter harbour passing between the red, conical light-buoy (must be left to port) and the green, conical signal buoy (must be left to starboard). Only after passing the green conical light buoy (leave to starboard) course may be shaped for the pier; at night, until the red light on its head is sighted. Depth of the entrance channel is 4 m.

Mooring. The harbour is sheltered from all winds and sea except N and NNW. The bora may be strong but does not create waves. Summer storms are short but dangerous and form waves in the harbour. Yachts can moor beside the pier and on the east side of the quay. The pier is reserved for coastal and excursion boats; in the summer season it is used by customs authorities. Yachts and smaller vessels are advised to moor in the marina (north part of harbour). There is good anchorage in the centre of the harbour (depth 3–5 m). Larger yachts are advised to anchor about 0.6 M west of the Umag belfry (depth 18 m). At night they should anchor 2 M west of the harbour (depth 27 m). This anchorage provides shelter from the bora but at first signs of a S or SW wind yachts should weigh and leave.

Umag is a permanent port of entry and has harbour master's branch office, customs, post office, hospital, out-patients' department, chemist's, bank, hotels and hotel settlements (Katoro, 1 M north of harbour), casino, campsite for motorists.

Facilities. Water hydrant at base of pier, fuel near pier, supermarket, nautical supplies, charts and nautical publications.

General repairs of yachts in Umag marina.

Every year the traditional »Umag May Festival« is organized.

Sights. Remains of the town walls (14 C, one tower houses the Town Museum); Sv Marija Velika church (Great St Mary, 18 C, Gothic polyptych). – Buje (defence walls, loggia, town mansions) – 13 km. – Grožnjan (town walls, summer art and music centre) – 26 km. – Oprtalj (medieval town walls, 15 C church) – 40 km. – Motovun (walls, towers,

UMAG

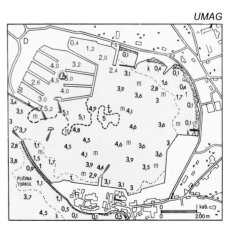

UMAG

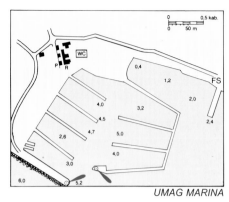

UMAG MARINA

town gate, 16 and 17 C, old houses, fine view across the Mirna valley) – 36 km. – Istarske Toplice (spa with hot radioactive waters, in use since 17 C) – 38 km. – Buzet (medieval necropolis, town walls and gates from 1547 and 1592, Town Museum) – 48 km.

UMAG MARINA (ACI)

(45°26,02'N; 013°31'E) is located in north part of harbour in front of »Adriatic« hotel, road (1.5 km) into town. Protected from all winds except N and NW. In spring and July winds from SW are most dangerous. High seas during summer storms do not last long and come from the west. There is a permanent warning and information service. All weather reports and forecasts are available in the marina offices.

The marina has 550 sea-berths for craft up to 18 m (four-point moor) and area for 350 vessels at the pier. The marina is open all the year round.

It has reception office, restaurant, shops toilets and showers with hot water, water and electricity hook-ups, laundry, telephone; fuel; sports equipment and nautical equipment; car park.

MOTOVUN

Boat hoist (10 t), travel-lift (40 t), slipway. During the season it is a port of entry with the customs office and police station at the E mole.

DALJA

(45°22'N; 013°33'E), small bay and holiday centre about 2.5 M north of Novigrad.

Approach. The bay can be identified by the buildings of the tourist settlement on high ground above the shore and a wide tower with a flat roof in the settlement itself.

Approaching vessels should be careful to avoid the Dalja (Pašador) shoal extending 400 m NW of Dalja point; the northwest edge of this is marked by a yellow conical buoy with black band round the middle. This should be left to starboard.

Mooring. This shallow bay provides good shelter from the bora and the sirocco but is exposed to W wind and sea. Yachts may land in the NE part of the harbour (Špic),

and moor at the head of the small pier (four-point moor), depth 2 m at pier head, or anchor in the middle of the bay (depth 7–8 m) with a good holding bottom.

Facilities. Local shops, water in the hotel centre. Fuel and all other requirements in Umag or Novigrad.

Sights. Ruins of ancient buildings.

NOVIGRAD

(45°19'N; 013°34'E), town and harbour (on the peninsula on the S side of the bay).

Approach. Novigrad can be identified by ruins of the town walls, church belfry and white, eight-sided concrete tower (sector light) at the head of the breakwater and a white tower with column and gallery (green light) on the head of the pier.

Care should be taken to avoid two shoals at the harbour entrance: Val shoal (WSW of harbour) is marked by a cylindrical black buoy with red line round the middle, topped with two black spheres; Meja

shoal (at the root of the outer side of the breakwater). When approaching at night vessels should keep within the white sector of the light on the breakwater head. The Val shoal is covered by its red sector and the Meja shoal by its green sector.

Mooring. The harbour is protected from all winds except W and NW which cause a surge in the harbour. As soon the first signs of N and NW winds are noticed yachts should transfer to Novigrad marina. Yachts drawing up to 3.5 m may moor along the breakwater, near the head, and on the NE side of the pier (four-point moor). The pier is also used by coastal and excursion boats, and in sum-

DALJA

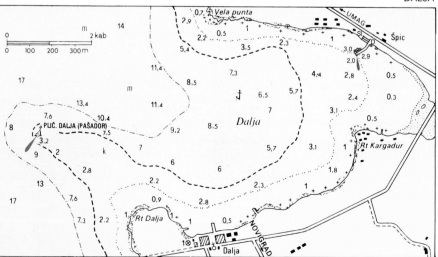

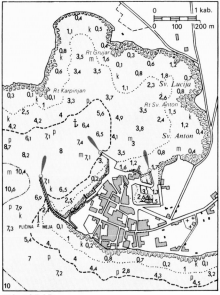

NOVIGRAD

NOVIGRAD

mer for customs. The best anchorage is about 200 m NE of the pier (depth 3–4 m).

Novigrad is a seasonal port of entry; customs, harbour master's branch office, post office; medical service, chemist's.

Facilities. Self-service (groceries), restaurants, navigation charts and publications, water and fuel in marina.

Sights. Part of walls with two towers, Sv Pelagije church (St Pelagius 8 C, with 15 C and 16 C additions, crypt), loggia and Gothic houses, štancija – a typical Istrian country estate (1761) on Karpinjan headland. Town Museum in the Urizzi mansion.

NOVIGRAD MARINA

(45°19,1'N; 013°31'E), is located SE of Novigrad harbour, about 100 m from pier. Provides shelter from all winds and sea.

NOVIGRAD MARINA

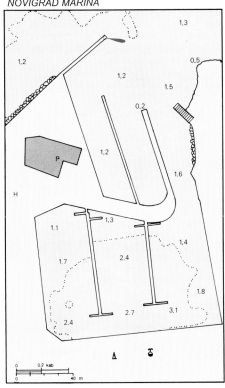

When entering harbour care should be taken of the shoals off Meja point extending about 150 m from shore and of Val shoal about 900 m SW of breakwater.

The marina has 86 sea-berths (four-point moor without anchor) for smaller craft (drawing 1.5 m) and room for about 30 vessels at the pier.

It has reception office; water and electricity hook-ups at the root of the pontoon pier. Slipway for small craft, crane (10 t); lift (30 t); small repairs in marina, larger ones in Pula shipyard. Winter berthing with care and maintenance. Fuel and butane gas available. Other supplies in Novigrad.

ZALJEV MIRNA

(45°18,5'N; 013°34'E), wide bay S of Novigrad, estuary of river Mirna.

Approach. Novigrad lies on the N point at the entrance to the bay. There are steep red cliffs E of Pod Uliki point one mile E of Novigrad harbour and a lighthouse (sector light on the corner of a single-storey house of a lighthouse keeper) on Zub point (Rt Zub).

Vessels approaching from the north should take care to avoid the Val shoal, marked by a cylindrical black buoy with a red band in the middle, topped with two black spheres. At night this shoal is in the red sector of the harbour light (on the breakwater) in Novigrad harbour. Vessels approaching from the south should take care to avoid the Čivran and Veliki Školj shoals lying about 1.6 M south of Zub point.

Mooring. Mirna bay affords small craft shelter from all winds except those from the W which cause rough water. Larger craft are advised to anchor north of Valeta cove (depth 17–18 m) or in front of Stari Tar village. Smaller yachts can anchor near the S shore or in the Tar cove which is shallow

(alluvial deposits). Anchorage about 1.6 M south of Zub point.

LUKA ČRVAR or ČERVAR

(45°17'N; 013°36'E), a long narrow inlet SE of Zub point (Rt Zub). It forms two branches: Lunga and Sveta Marina.

Approach. Vessels approaching from the north will see a lighthouse (single storey building white and red sector light) on Zub point, a holiday settlement S of the lighthouse, the buildings of the hotel centre and the Červar-Porat marina in the S part of Lunga. The large rocky shoal on the S side of the entrance to the inlet, the northern part of which is called Veliki Školj and the southern Čivran, is dangerous for all vessels. NW of Veliki Školj shoal there

is a cylindrical green buoy (green light) topped by a cone pointing upwards. Both shoals are easily spotted because of the waves breaking over the rocks. On the SW edge of the Čivran shoal is a yellow buoy with a black band (white light) in the middle, topped with two black cones, their points upwards. The shoals are in the red sectors of the lighthouses on Zub point and coastal light on Barbaran cliff, and must be left to starboard on entering Črvar. The marina should be approached by a course in the middle of the inlet.

Mooring. The inlet is protected from all winds except those from NW, depth in centre about 18 m, and at marina entrance 14 m. For about 200 m along the north shore the sea is shallow (2 m).

Facilities. Water and provisions in a supermarket in the village. General repairs in Červar-Porat marina.

ČERVAR-PORAT MARINA

(45°16,7'N; 013°36,2'E), lies at the very end of the SE part of Črvar inlet, about 3 M south of Novigrad harbour. It is well protected

ČRVAR

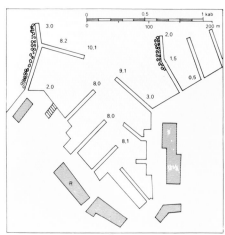

ČRVAR-PORAT MARINA

POREČ, ATRIUM OF THE BASILICA

from all winds except that from the NW which causes a heavy swell in the marina and makes entrance difficult (max. depth 10 m).

The marina has 300 sea-berths for yacht 3–25 m long and about 50 dry-berths for yachts 3–13 m long. Electricity and water hook-ups.

Anchoring in the marina is forbidden. Small craft can anchor N of the marina in Sveta Marina cove (depth 6 m) or N of the cove (depth 15 m).

The marina has reception office, a hotel with a restaurant, snack-bar, coffee-bar, toilets and showers, sports grounds, self-service shop, telephone, petrol station (6 km).

There is a 1.5 km long bathing beach 500 m from the village near to the »Ulika« naturist centre.

Services include a crane (12 t), equipment for transport and berthing of craft on land. A small slipway, maintenance and repair services to hull and engine, electrical installations, repairs to sails and masts.

POREČ

(45°14'N; 013°36'E), town and harbour, protected from S by a small peninsula and islet of Sveti Nikola (St Nicholas).

Approach. Poreč can be identified from a distance by a castle, the ruins of a tower and the campsite on the islet of Sveti Nikola, by the belfry with turret in the town, by a red cylindrical tower (white and red sector lights) on Barbaran cliff and a white concrete tower with green cupola (green light) on the head of the breakwater (islet of Sveti Nikola).

Vessels approaching from the N should take care to avoid the Meja shoal about one mile NNW of the harbour, the middle is marked by a black spar with two red bands topped by two black spheres. At night this shoal is covered by the red sector of the light on Barbaran cliff. About 0.5 M from the Meja shoal care should be taken to avoid the Pical shoal (depth 2.4 m). Vessels should keep well over to the west of the alignment of Zub point and Busuja point until abreast of Pical point. After that course can be shaped for the harbour. Vessels approaching from the south should take care to avoid the Bekarija shoal about 0.3 M south of the islet of Sveti Nikola and marked with a black spar with two red bands and topped by two black spheres. There are underwater pipes and cables between the shore and Sveti Nikola.

There are four approaches to the harbour; the safest being the channel between Barbaran cliff and the head of the north breakwater on Sveti Nikola islet. At night this channel is in the white sector (62° to 153°) of the light on Barbaran.

Mooring. The harbour is protected from NE and to some extent from SW and NW. Winds from S and NW create high waves. The sirocco here is more frequent than the bora wich blows very strongly, especially in autumn. In summer during the sirocco SW squalls may be experienced and these cause high waves in the harbour. Strong sea currents may make manoeuvring difficult in the harbour. Yachts drawing up to 5 m can moor at the quay in front of the »Rivijera« Hotel and those drawing up to 4 m at the pier which also serves coastal and excursion boats and for customs. There is anchorage in the middle of the harbour but it is not recommended as there is no good holding bottom. If strong SW or W winds blow the best anchorage is below the NE shore of Sveti Nikola islet.

ČRVAR

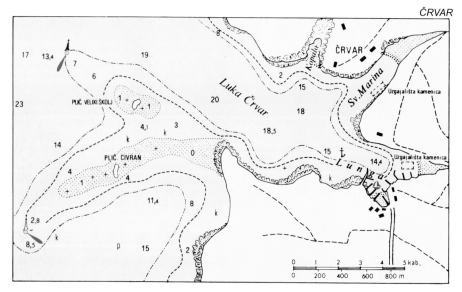

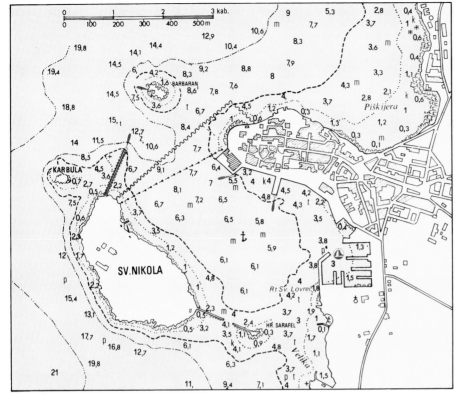

POREČ

Poreč harbour is a permanent port of entry; customs, harbour master's branch office, post office, several hotels and hotel settlements, banks, hospital, medical services, chemist's.

POREČ, GOTHIC PALACE

Facilities. Water hydrants in the E part of the harbour (depth 3 m) and on the foreshore, fuel pumps on the waterfront in front of shops. The shop sells charts and nautical publications. Other supplies may be bought from the town shops. Small repairs to hull and engine available.

Annual events: art exhibitions and summer art festival.

Sights. Ruins of temples of Neptune and Mars (1/2 C), Roman street layout, Eufra-zijeva bazilika (Basilica of St Euphrasius, 6 C, under UNESCO protection, baptistery, atrium, St Maur oratory, mosaics, ciborium), canon's house (1251), Sv Franjo church (St Francis, 13 C, collection), Two Saints' House (12 C, Romanesque/Gothic, exhibition hall), the Sinčić mansion (17 C, Poreč Regional Museum). – On the islet of Sveti Nikola (half a mile from the harbour): remains of an Illyrian building (3 C B.C.), lighthouse (1409, oldest lighthouse on the eastern Adriatic). – Beram (Sv Martin church, 1431, 19 C addi-tions, frescoes, »Sv Marija na Škrilinah« church, frescoes from 1474; Vladimir Gortan's monument) – 27 km. – Pazin (12–14 C castle, Pazin National Museum; Sv Nikola church, 1266, additions in 1441 and in 18 C, frescoes, church museum; Franciscan church 1463–77) – 32 km. – Sv Petar u Šumi (13 C church and monastery, reconstructions in 1459, 1731, 1773, cloister) – 42 km. – Lovreč (church, 9–11 C; loggia, medieval town walls) – 17 km.

PLAVA LAGUNA

(45°12'N; 013°36'E), small harbour and hotel settlement in the bay of the same name about 1.5 M south of Poreč.

Mooring. The 20 m concrete pier largely protects the harbour from the SW and NW. Only vessels drawing up to 3 m can moor. The outer side of the pier is reserved for hydrofoils that ply between Poreč and Plava laguna (the Blue Lagoon).

Facilities. Food and water. Small slipway S of little pier.

POREČ MARINA

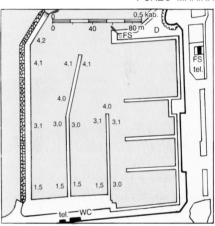

POREČ

39

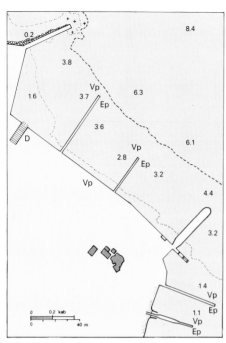

PARENTIUM MARINA

POREČ MARINA

(45°13,8'N; 013°36,2'E). The marina lies 0.3 m SE from the harbour of Poreč. The berths for smaller boats are well protected.

Mooring. Berths for yachts up to 30 m length and 20 for the smaller ones. About 200 small sport and fishing boats can be left in a special section of the port.

Facilities. Water and electricity hook-ups, WC/showers, bathing beach next to it and several good shops in town.

PARENTIUM MARINA

(45°12,4'N; 13°36,2'E), marina and Parentium holiday settlement on the S shore of Mulandarija bay (2 M from Poreč).

Approach. Between Regata rock (NW of the point at the N entrance) and the Žontulin and Žontuja rocks about 500 m W of point at S entrance. The rocks are not marked at night and the approach is difficult.

The marina has 200 sea-berths (up to 20 m length, four-point moor) and 50 dry-berths (up to 12 m length). On breakwater and piers there are water hydrants and electricity hook-ups.

Fuel in pumps in marina, charts and nautical publications in a shop, other purchases in local shops of marina and Poreč and in hotels.

Hoist (10 t) and slipway for small craft, transport of vessels; small repairs to hull and engine, for larger repairs Červar-Porat marina and Pula.

LUKA FUNTANA

(45°11'N; 013°36'E), cove about 3 M south of Poreč. On the south-eastern shore is the little village of Funtana. In the cove Frnažina holiday centre with several hotels and a campsite for motorists.

Approach. Funtana with its church belfry on a rise above the cove is conspicuous and on the main angled pier a red post with red light.

Warning. From Poreč to the entrance to the Limski kanal there are a large number of dangerous shoals and rocks. On the N side of Funtana bay is the Janjci shoal, its northern edge is marked by a black post with two red bands and topped with two black spheres. At the southern entrance, between the islet of Veli Školj and the shore is the Funtana shoal marked by a yellow and black post topped by two black cones, their points upwards. West of the pier, about 200 m from the shore there are dangerous rocks and cliffs. The safest approach is from the west, care being taken to avoid the Janjci shoal.

Mooring. The cove is exposed to W and NW winds and boats should leave as soon as any signs of the W wind are noticed. The depth is 1.5–2 m (four-point moor recommended). There is anchorage in the middle of the cove at a depth of 6–8 m. Landing may be made at the head of the pier of the Frnažina holiday centre (depth 2–4 m).

Facilities. The Frnažina holiday centre has post office, medical service, shops and a restaurant. Fuel at Vrsar (about 4 M); also more complete supplies.

VRSAR

(45°09'N; 013°36'E), small town and small harbour 1.5 M north of entrance to the Limski kanal, sheltered from the SW by the islet of Sv Juraj.

Approach. Vrsar can be identified by the old castle above the town itself built on a steep hillock. On the islet of Galiner, at the entrance to the harbour, there is a square red tower topped with an iron construction (white light) and hotels S of the pier; a white tower (red light) at the head of the main pier.

Care should be taken of a whole chain of shoals 1–1.5 M west of the harbour: Velika shoal (yellow and black cylindrical buoy), Mramori shoal (red cylindrical tower with column and gallery on a concrete base; red flashing light), Lunga rock (yellow cylindrical concrete marker with black band in middle and two black cones on top, points facing), Galopun rock (between Lunga islet and shore), Orlandin rock about half a mile SW of Galiner islet.

The safest approach to Vrsar is from NW leaving the Mramori shoal 300 m to starboard; on entering the bay Galiner islet should be left slightly to port. If entrance is made from SW then the marker on Mramori shoal should be left 200–300 m to port and course set towards Galiner islet. At night approach should be made in the white sector of the light on Galiner islet (sector 50–64° and 100–116°).

Warning. It is forbidden for any vessel to sail between the isle of Sveti Juraj and the shore within a zone marked by: pier in the SE part of Vrsar harbour (sports centre of hotels) – NW shore of Sv Juraj; Fornace point – SE shore of Sveti Juraj. Craft of all kinds are also forbidden to sail within a zone: Bojko point – NW shore of Kuvrsada islet (nets), Šjole point – SW shore of

VRSAR

VRSAR

BERAM, ST. MARY'S CHAPEL AT ŠKRILINAH

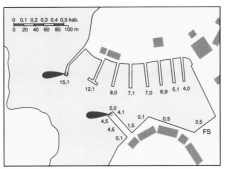

VRSAR MARINA

ROVINJ

Kuvrsada islet. These are forbidden zones from April 15 to October 15 every year.

There is a water-skiing track from Funtana point to Fujaga point.

Mooring. The harbour is protected from all winds except from NW. In strong south--westerlies the whole pier is flooded. Coasters and excursion boats moor along-side the pier, craft may moor along the shore (four-point moor). There is good anchorage between the islet of Sv Juraj and the shore (depth 12–15 m). In strong NW winds anchorage should be made on the lee side of the island.

Facilities. Post office, medical service, chemist's, exchange office, several hotels and hotel settlements, camp for motorists, shop. Food and water (hydrant); fuel pumps, butane gas.

On Kuvrsada there is a naturist camp and bathing beach.

Sights. Traces of a Roman settlement in harbour and islets; Sv Marija church (13 C); Castel Vergottini medieval town gate (18 C). – Kanfanar (Sv Silvestar church with medieval furniture and fittings) – 28 km. – Dvograd (ruins of a medieval town deserted in 1630 because of the plague) – 31 km.

VRSAR MARINA

(45°9,2'N; 013°36,1'E) Is situated on the northern part of the city port. It is open throughout the season.

Approach. The same as for Vrsar.

Mooring. It has 180 berths along the breakwater, the waterfront and sea-berths (everywhere with water hydrants and electricity hook-ups. of 64 A)

Facilities. There is a reception office, a restaurant, a cafe-bar, toilets, a fuel pump. a shop and all other facilities within the tourist settlement Vrsar (a bank, an exchange office, a post office , medical care and a pharmacy).

Hoist (35 t), technical service, parking lots for 100 cars.

LIMSKI ZALJEV,

bay about 5.5 M long and average 500 m wide, about 3 M north of Rovinj. Inland from its head extends the karst valley of the small seasonal river Lim. The sides of the bay are steep and overgrown with macchia. Powerful freshwater springs gush up from the seabed at the shore especially during winter months. The depth at the mouth of the bay is about 30 m and at the head about 10 m. There are underwater pipes and cables across the entrance to the bay. Limski kanal is a legally protected centre for fish breeding and shellfish.

Warning. It is forbidden to sail or anchor in the bay without special permission.

Approach. Hotels on Šjole point are conspicuous. The Lim shoal is marked by a large cylindrical buoy with a red band round the middle topped by two black spheres.

Caution must be exercised when entering the bay to avoid the Kuvrsada shoal north of the bay entrance (marked with a cylindrical buoy with a black post and red belt round the middle, topped with two black spheres). Kuvrsada inland is linked with the mainland by a bridge (on the posts). The Lim shoal in front of the entrance is marked by a cylindrical buoy with a black post and a red belt in the middle topped by two black spheres. The Fujaga shoal on the north side of the entrance is marked by a black and yellow post topped by two black cones, points downwards. If approaching from the S,

about 500 m SSW of Križ point is an unmarked rocky shoal (depth 3.2 m).

Facilities. Very limited (motel and inn on sea front, the seasonal »Viking« restaurant).

Sights. Illyrian remains (4/3 C B.C.), ruins of a Benedictine Abbey (12 C) and Old Christian church (6 C, remains of frescoes); Sv Marija church (St Mary, 1041).

VALALTA MARINA

(45°07'N; 013°37'E) is located in Sveti Feliks cove S of the entrance to the Limski kanal and part of the Valalta nudist centre (open only in summer).

When entering the marina from the W care should be taken of the rocky bottom which extends NW from the root of the breakwater.

The marina has 180 berths either side of the breakwater, by the pontoon pier and along the waterfront. There is only very limited dry-berth accomodation for yachts. Vessels should be four-point moored and

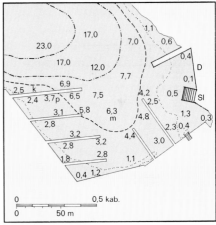

VALALTA MARINA

LIMSKI ZALJEV

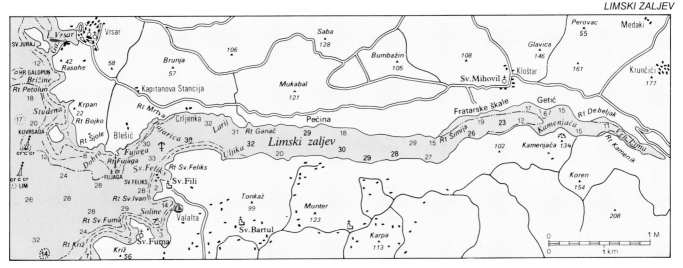

41

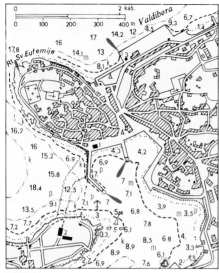

ROVINJ

ROVINJ, CRVENI OTOK

lateral beside both side of the breakwater. There is good anchorage in the W part of Saline cove (depth 4 m).

It has reception office, and self-service shop.

Slipway for small craft. Hydrants and electricity hook-ups. Technical services in Parentium marina and Červar-Porat marina. Fuel in Vrsar.

ROVINJ

(45°05'N; 013°38'E), town and harbour on a peninsula and hill slopes. The harbour has two parts: southern (Sabionera) and northern (Valdibora).

Approach. Rovinj is easily identified from the sea by the belfry of Sv Eufemija (St Euphemia) church on the hill top, the chimney of the sardine cannery in the N harbour, the square white stone tower (white light) on

Sv Eufemija point, and the islet of Sv Katarina S of the town.

When approaching the south harbour the passage between Sv Katarina islet and the cylindrical buoy with a post (black and red, two cones on top their bases together) which marks the E edge of a shoal (E of the islet), must not be used.

In Lon cove there is a submerged ship; its mast 1 m above the surface of the sea.

Mooring. The north (Valdibora) harbour is well protected from the bora and sirocco but exposed to W and SW winds when the sea floods the whole quay. The south harbour is also well protected from the bora and sirocco but exposed to W and SW winds.

In the north harbour yachts drawing up to 5 m may moor along the quay, smaller vessels can berth SW and NE of the quay.

If there is a strong SW wind, and at the first sign of summer gales, vessels should transfer to the south harbour. In the south harbour (Sabionera) the outer side and part of the inner side of the angled breakwater are reserved for passenger and excursion boats; other vessels can berth at the root of

the breakwater at the pier or along the masonry waterfront. It is advisable for smaller craft to berth in the marina. When there are strong E and W winds a powerful current develops along the outer side of the breakwater which makes manoeuvring difficult.

Rovinj is a permanent port of entry; customs, harbour master's branch office, post office; hospital with orthopedic surgery, medical services, chemist's; shops, a large number of hotels, banks.

Facilities. Water hydrants in north and south harbours, all kinds of fuel from pumps in north harbour on the W corner of the waterfront, other supplies in town shops.

In the southern part of Mašćin islet, joined by a narrow sandy causeway to Crveni otok (Red Island) is a naturist camp.

Muntrav Park (under nature protection) with its hotels and bathing beach extends S of the town.

A boatyard is located in the SE part of the south harbour (part of the »Mirna« food processing factory) which can carry out small repairs to wooden craft and servicing. Slipway for vessels up to 400 GRT.

In summer the art colony holds exhibitions in »Grisia« street.

Sights. Sv Eufemija church (St Euphemia, 1736, on the site of an old Christian church), Sv Trojstvo chapel (Chapel of the Holy Trinity, 13 C), Loggia (1592), clock-tower and Balbi arch (1680), Town Hall (17 C, museum). In the graveyard there is an

ROVINJ

ROVINJ MARINA

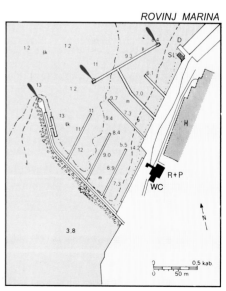

avenue of cypresses which is a natural monument.

A number of areas around Rovinj (the forest and park on Zlatni rt, the islets fronting the town and an area along the coast) are under protection as nature reserves.

ROVINJ MARINA (ACI)

(45°04,06'N; 013°38,04'E), is in the SE part of Rovinj harbour (Monte Mulin), beside the shipyard, surrounded by pine-woods, 1 km by road from the centre of the town. Islet of Sveta Katarina and a breakwater (300 m lenght) protect it from all winds except the SW wind which seldom blows except in late autumn and winter when it is dangerous; the W wind causes a heavy swell.

The marina has 400 sea-berths up to 25 m (four-point moor) and 100 dry-berths. Water and electricity hook-ups are on pontoon piers and on the pier.

The marina is open all the year round.

Anchorage in Valdibora bay (N of the belfry of Sv Eufemija church), depth 20–24 m, 300 m offshore; recommended anchorage in front of the south harbour is 500 m NW of the centre of Sveta Katarina islet, 600 m SW of the islet of Banjol or 300 m SSW of Sveta Katarina. Small boats and yachts can anchor a little further east. If the bora blows wessels should anchor in Sabionera bay (southern harbour) south of Sveta Katarina islet, depth 6–15 m.

The marina has reception office, restaurant, shop, toilets and showers with hot water, laundry, sporting equipment, parking lot and exchange office. Boats can be hired (charter).

Crane (10 t) and a small slipway. Modern workshops for all kinds of repairs to hull and engines. Larger repairs can be carried out in Rovinj shipyard.

Permanent information and warning services concerning weather, storms and tides in the marina offices.

SVETI ANDRIJA or CRVENI OTOK

(45°03'N; 013°37'E), small harbour and hotels on the islet of the same name, about 1.5 M south of Rovinj.

Approach. Vessels may guide themselves by Sv Ivan na pučini lighthouse, the eight-sided tower beside the lighthouse-keeper's single-storey house (white flashes).

On approaching the north shore care should be taken of shoals marked by a yellow spar with a black band in the middle (100 m W of Samer rock), two black cones on top their points towards each other. On the north shore of the islet to the shore at

BALE, CHOIR-SCREEN WITH INTERLACERY DECORATION

Kurent point there are underwater cables and pipes.

Mooring. Small north and south (for landing of small craft) harbours. The pier in front of the hotel in the north harbour is exposed to wind and sea from NE and NW, the southern harbour is exposed only to SW winds. Depth at head of landing stage is about 3 m and at the head of the SW and NW piers of the southern harbour about 2.5 m, the harbour is a shallow one. Four-point moor beside the pier in the northern harbour and lateral berthing on both sides of the south harbour.

Facilities. Water hydrant in south harbour. Other requirements in Rovinj.

FAŽANSKI KANAL,

passage between the shore and the Brijuni islands is marked by a line: in the north of Barbariga point – Kabula reef and in the south Proština point – Pinida (Peneda) point.

Approach. This is a very rocky shore with many shoals and reefs 200–400 m offshore. Beside the islands the sea is shallow. On approaching the channel the Brijuni and its characteristic buildings and vegetation are conspicuous.

BRIJUNI, RUINS OF ROMAN TEMPLE IN VERIGE COVE

Care must be taken to avoid: Kabula reef (black and yellow tower with column and gallery, two black cones, points upwards, white light) on the NW part of Brijuni; the Mrtulin shoal cylindrical buoy with post and two black spheres, coloured black with red band in middle on the eastern side of the north entrance; the shoal S of Fažana (2 green conical buoys); Saluga shoal (cylindrical shoal red tower with post and gallery; sector light – red sector danger) S of entrance to Brijuni harbour; Rankun shoal (cylindrical red buoy with pyramid construction, red light) E of the point of the same name on Veliki Brijun; Kotež shoal (cylindrical green tower with post and gallery) E of Rankun shoal.

There are a number of anchorages in the channel for small craft especially when SW and SE winds blow; in front of Marić cove, in front of Fažana and Brijuni harbours and in the Verige and Rankun coves. A NW wind causes a swell in the N part, and winds from SW and SE in the south part of the channel. There is a constant NW current. During

SVETI IVAN NA PUČINI

PULA, TEMPLE OF AUGUSTUS

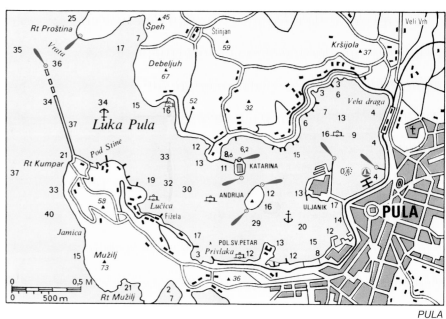

flood tide and when there are S winds the current attains a speed of 3 knots.

Warning. Between Fažana and Brijuni islands there are a number of underwater cables and pipes.

FAŽANA

(44°56'N; 013°48'E), small town and harbour on eastern shore of Fažanski kanal (opposite Veliki Brijun island).

Approach. The church belfry is the main landmark. The harbour is enclosed by a breakwater to the N (at its head a red cylindrical tower with red light) and to the S a pier (on its head a white cylindrical tower with greeen light).

When the harbour is approached from the S care should be taken of the shallow rocky bottom extending 400 m offshore. The western edge of dangerous shoals is marked by two green conical buoys, these should be left to starboard. A number of underwater pipes and cables are laid between Fažana and Veliki Brijun island.

Mooring. The harbour is protected from NE and SE winds and sea; W and NW winds are dangerous because they cause rough sea in harbour. Anchorage is 0.3 M

northwest of the harbour. Only small craft can berth in the harbour moored at the pier. The depth at the smaller pier is about 2 m and at the southern pier 3.5–4.0 m. On the pier there is a hydrant and electricity connnections.

Facilities. Hotel, several restaurants, medical services.

BRIJUNI

(Veliki Brijun, Mali Brijun, 11 small islands and a considerable number of rocks and reefs), islands separated from the mainland by the Fažanski kanal.

It is not allowed to sail within the area of the whole archipelago unless one aims to enter the harbour and stay which is to be paid for. The area is in particular limited with the following lines:

Zone I
A (44°55,6'N; 013°44,4'E)
– cape Vrbanj
B (44°55,9'N; 013°44,1'E)
– cape Kadulja
C (44°55,8'N; 013°44,9'E)
– island Supinić
D (44°54,8'N; 013°42,2'E)
F (44°53,2'N; 013°46,0'E)
G (44°53,6'N; 013°45,9'E)
– cape Kamnik

Zone II
A (44°54,3'N; 013°47,0'E)
– cape Kavran
B (44°54,2'N; 013°46,6'E)
– cape Kozlac

S of the island of Veliki Brijun anchoring is prohibited in a circular zone with a radius of 2 M (in the midst of 44°51,2'N; 013°44,4'E).

Approach. There is a castle on the top of Veliki Brijun, a shore light on Peneda point (white isophase light); black and yellow tower with black post and gallery and 2 black cones, points upwards (white light) on the Kabula rock (see Fažanski kanal).

The islands have been inhabited since prehistoric times and especially in Roman times (from 2 C B. C.). There are the remains of a number of settlements and castles in the cove of Veriga, the remains of a Temple of Venus and of a 6 C basilica. From the Middle Age there is a Byzantine camp ground, the three-nave basilica of a Benedictine monastery. Venetians made extensive use of the stone quarries on the islet of Jerolim and built fortifications in several places. During malaria epidemics in the 17 C the islands were almost deserted but at the end of the 19 C anti-malarial precautions began to be taken (Robert Koch), hotels were built and planting began of Mediterranean and exotic vegetation. Piped water was brought from the mainland and Brijuni became an international leisure centre. The mild climate fosters the growth of Mediterranean plants in natural parks. On Veliki Brijun there is a zoo with many kinds of animals. In 1984 the Brijuni were declared a national park.

PULA

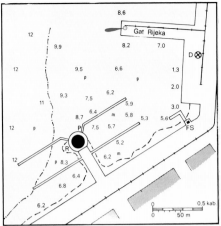

PULA MARINA

VERUDA

PULA

(44°52'N; 013°50'E), city port and marina at the SW end of the Istrian peninsula. It lies in a natural bay sheltered by a peninsula and breakwater.

Approach. The signal station on Mužilj hill (on peninsula S of harbour entrance), the red light on Proština point N of entrance (square stone tower the upper part coloured red), green light on the head of the Kumpar breakwater (green tower with a post and a gallery) and the light on Peneda point (square tower beside house, white isophase light) are easily identified from seaward. When approaching at night keep to the middle of the channel and shape course for the red light on the S side of Sveti Andrija islet; when a clear passage can be seen between Sveti Andrija and Sveta Katarina course may be shaped for the passage between the two islands and between two pairs of light markers (port-red, starboard-green) which lead to the E part of the harbour. The passage between the two islands is marked by two red cylindrical towers with red lights on the NW side, and two green lights on the SE side.

Restricted and forbidden zones. From the alignment Proština point – Kumpar point to alignment Sveti Andrija island – Sveti Petar peninsula vessels must sail at a speed of less than 8 knots, and from this zone onwards at a speed of not more than 5 knots. Vessels must pass the ships moored at »Uljanik« shipyard at the greatest possible distance. Workboats with divers and frogmen on board must be passed at minimum speed and with engines stopped. In the passage between Sveti Andrija and Sveta Katarina islands incoming vessels must give-way to vessels leaving port. In this passage vessels are forbidden to use sail as their only means of propulsion. Vessels must not approach within 50 m of Sveti Andrija and Sveta Katarina islands and the mainland coast E of the end of the Fižela Vela cove (Lučica) and the piers in Pod Stine cove at Kumpar point. Pleasure boats, motor-boats, sailing-boats and speed-boats must not approach within 50 m of bathing beaches and swimming establishments marked with protective nets.

Sveti Petar peninsula and the islets of Sveti Andrija and Sveta Katarina divide the harbour area into an outer and an inner harbour.

Mooring. In the inner (commercial) E part yachts can berth at the Rijeka Pier (Gat Rijeka, depth 3.5–7.9 m), in the marina and

S on the quay (depth 2.5–6.0 m). It is recommended to moor in Pula marina. There is anchorage about 400 m NW of Rijeka Pier (8.5 m).

Pula is open to international sailing and is a permanent port of entry. Harbour master's office, customs, sale of charts and navigation publications (PLOVPUT plovno područje

VERUDA MARINA

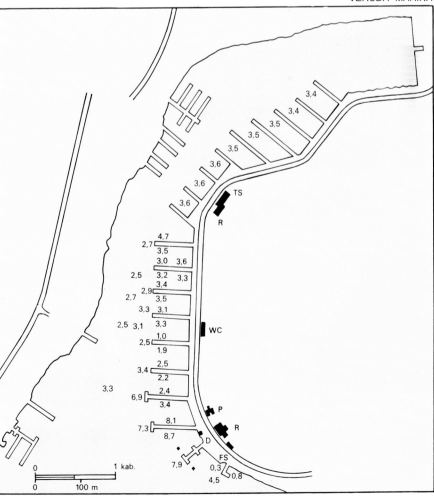

MEDULINSKI ZALJEV

PENEDA

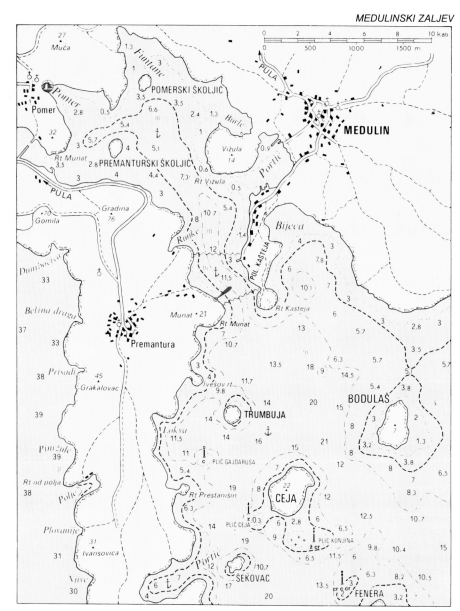

MEDULINSKI ZALJEV

Pula – Sailing in the Pula Area, in harbour master's office building); railway station, post office, medical service, hospital, chemist's.

Facilities. Water from hydrant; fuel station on the small pier in front of the harbour master's office; shop, nautical equipment and storage facilities (Brodokomerc). There is a 15 t electric crane at the shore end of Rijeka pier; »Uljanik« shipyard can carry out all repairs to hulls and engines of all sizes; this work can also be carried out in »Pula« and »Uljanik« shipyards.

Car ferry line: Pula – Mali Lošinj – Silba – Zadar.

At the beginning of July the Istria Regatta is organized in Pula (Pula – Poreč – Umag – Rovinj – Pula), and during July a Film Festival.

Sights. Kaštel (after 177 B.C., alterations in 13 C and 1631), Roman Amphitheatre (1–2 C, 23,000 spectators), Slavoluk Sergejevaca (Triumphal Arch of the Sergians, 1 C B.C.), Porta Gemina (2/3 C), Roman mosaic showing the punishment of Dirce (1 C), Temple of Augustus (1 C), Cathedral (4–5 C, reconstructions in 15 C and in 1640), chapel in the church of Sta Maria Formosa (about 556, mosaic), Sv Franjo church (St. Francis 14 C, polyptych), Town Hall (1296, restored in 1651), Archaeological Museum of Istria.

PULA MARINA (ACI)

(44°52,6'N; 013°50'E) is in the SE part of the city harbour (Istra pier). There are sea-berths for 200 vessels at the pontoons projecting from Istra pier (up to 25 m length, depth 4–8 m). Water, electricity and telephone hook-ups.

The marina has reception office, restaurant, shops, coffee-bar, toilets and showers; laundry; car-park; fuel pumps (300 m from marina).

Small repairs to hull and engine and electric installations can be carried out in the marina. Larger repairs in »Pula« and »Uljanik« shipyards.

The marina is open all the year round.

LUKA VERUDA

(44°50'N; 013°50'E), cove and islet 3.2 M from Kumpar point (about 4 M south of Pula).

Approach. White tower with red top and gallery beside house (red light) on Verudica point, ruins of monastery on Veruda islet; buildings of hotel complex at the NW entrance point and marina offices are all visible from seaward.

Veruda is sheltered from all winds and sea. When approaching care should be taken to avoid a rocky shoal about 150 m

SW of Verudica point. Vessels should hold to the centre of the bay because of shoals along the shore.

Mooring. In Veruda Marina.

VERUDA MARINA

(44°49,8'N; 013°50,1'E) is situated on the eastern shore of the northern cove of Veruda harbour, 3.5 M south of Pula. Provides shelter from all winds and sea, but outer breakwater exposed to S and SW winds. Weather reports and forecasts provided by the marina.

The marina has 17 concrete piers (average depth 3.5 m). There are berths for 630 boats up to 25 m length (four-point moor, bow or stern to pier) and about 150 dry-berths up to 15 m length for repairs and wintering. All berths are provided with water and electricity hook-ups.

There is a good anchorage N of marina (depth 4–5 m).

The marina has reception office, shop, restaurant, supermarket, exchange office, near the W shore of the bay there is a holiday centre (hotel 500 m). Fuel and butane gas available in marina.

Electric crane (50 t); care, maintenance, servicing and cleaning of engine, sails and electrical installations available in marina. Larger repairs at »Uljanik« shipyard in Pula.

»Arenaturist« sports grounds (tennis, basketball, mini-golf, bowling).

PALTANA

(44°49'N; 013°52'E), cove about 5.5 M southeast of Pula; Banjole village.

Approach. The cove can be identified by a stone pyramid topped with post and sphere (mile measurement) and high antennae column on the S entrance point. Two buoys are anchored about 300 m from the entrance to the cove.

Mooring. The cove is protected from all winds and sea except from NE and SW. In the northern part of the cove is a masonry waterfront (depth 2–4 m) beside which vessels may berth and also along the small pier in front of a fish cannery (depth 1.2–3 m). There is anchorage in the middle of the cove at a depth of 4 m.

MEDULINSKI ZALJEV

(44°46'N; 013°55'E – 44°49'N; 014°0'E), bay on the south shore of Istria between points Kamenjak and Marlera; the Kašteja peninsula divides it into two parts. The inner part is shallow and suitable only for small vessels (drawing up to 5 m).

Approach. Premantura village can be identified by a belfry; in Medulin village

LABIN

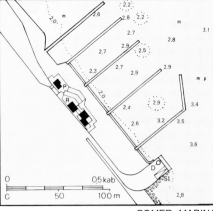

POMER MARINA

there is a church with two belfries; the stone tower above a house on the Porer cliff (white light), a square tower beside house (white light), on Marlera point; the red and white pyramid on Fenera islet.

Great care should be taken because of the many shoals: Fenera, NW of the islet of the same name, marked with red and black iron post topped by two black spheres; Konjina, SE of Ceja islet, yellow and black post topped by two cones, points downwards; Ceja SW of islet of the same name, green post topped by green cone; Gajdaruša WNW of Ceja islet red post topped with red can.

Warning. The safest route for small craft is between Albanež shoal and Porer rock (marked by a light). Approach may also be made between the shore (Kršina point) and Porer rock but great care must be taken of the dangerous (unmarked) rocky shoal of Veliki Balun and of Fenoliga shoal (cylindrical red tower, red light); depth of channel about 8 m. About 250 m S of Kršina point there is a shoal of the same name marked by a post topped by two black cones points downwards. Course may be continued towards Fenera islet. This should be passed on the S side and course may then be shaped toward the channel between the islets of Bodulaš and Ceja (within the white sector of the light on Munat point; red cylindrical tower). Approach may also be made between Kamenjak point and Fenera islet; then E of Šekovac islet, leaving the Ceja shoal to starboard (marked by post topped with green cone), then shape course for Medulin belfry, E of the islet of Trumbuja. In the inner part of the bay it is advisible to keep in the middle of the straits between points Munat and Kašteja; after passing abeam of the Trumbuja islet, hold to the middle of the channel towards Pomerski Školjić islet until the details of the marina become clearly visible. In approaching Pomer marina the Premanturski Školjić islet should be left to port. Should approach be made by night the utmost caution is necessary.

The outer bay is exposed to S winds which cause limited visibility, the bora, too, is rather strong and lasting. Bad weather can be expected when clouds appear over Osorščica hill (Island of Lošinj).

Mooring. Larger boats can anchor between the islets of Ceja and Trumbuja (depth 20 m), smaller craft are advised to use the anchorage protected from all winds in the passage W of Kašteja peninsula and

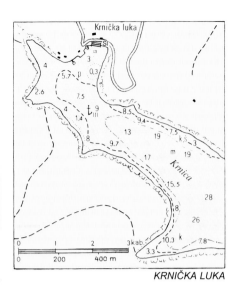

KRNIČKA LUKA

S of Pomerski Skoljić islet. Small craft can berth beside the two piers in Runke cove (depth 3 m) or opposite the E shore beside the path with the hoist (depth 2.5 m); filling station for butane gas, restaurant and supermarket.

Facilities. Food in local places, water on Kašteja point, fuel in Medulin which has post office and medical service.

Sights. Mutila Roman villa rustica; Roman graves and baths on Vižula peninsula.

POMER MARINA (ACI)

(44°49'N; 013°54'E) lies in the NW part of Medulin bay south of Pomer village, 10 km from Pula.

Approaching. In the bay of Medulin, between the cape Marlera and cape Kamenjak there are dangerous shallow

RAŠA

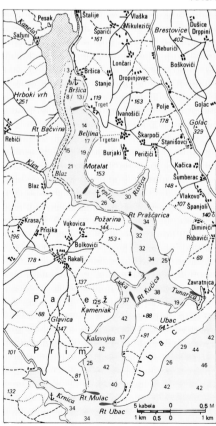

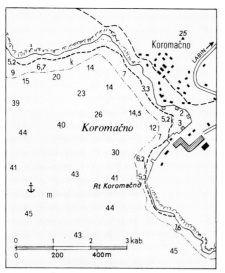

KOROMAČNO

places. That is why one should use the main channel when entering, i. e. pass between the isle of Ferera (E) and the isles of Ceja and Bodulaš. At night the white light of the lighthouse Bodulaš covers the channel.

During long lasting sirocco a swell develops in the marina, the bora and tramontana make sailing difficult. There is good anchorage E of the alignment: Pomerski Školjić – Premanturski Školjić; depth 6–8 m. There are 5 piers with 250 sea-berths (2–2.8 m) up to 25 m in length and 90 dry-berths; electricity hook-ups.

PRKLOG – RABAC

The marina has reception office, restaurant, shop, toilets and showers with hot water; sports grounds; car park; fuel pump, exchange office and supermarket (700 m).

Crane (10 t) and slipway for small repairs to hull, engine and electrical installations.

Permanent information and warning service concerning storms and tide waves, weather forecasts and navigational messages.

The marina is open all the year round.

EASTERN COAST OF ISTRIA

KUJE

(44°49'N; 013°59'E), cove and anchorage for small vessels on the SE shore of Istria (SE of Ližnjan village). The little harbour is sheltered from all winds except those from NE.

In approaching care should be taken of the Sika shoal and rock 600 m offshore, SE of harbour. At night the shoal and rock are in the dark sector of the Marlera lighthouse.

VINJOLE

(44°55'N; 014°02'E), indented bay and shelter for small craff on the SE coast of Istria. Exposed to winds and sea from SE, the bora is also strongly felt.

»Duga uvala« hotel apartment settlement. Hotels, restaurants.

In approaching care should be taken of shoals in the centre of the entrance to the bay (depth 0.3 m).

KRNIČKA LUKA or KRNICA

(44°57'N; 014°03'E), village and cove on W side of entrance to Raša inlet (SE shore of Istria). Sheltered from all winds except SE. Affords good anchorage for small craft at the inner end of the bay (depth 7.5–9 m), small landing stage usually occupied by fishing boats.

Shop and restaurant in the village.

RAŠA

(44°57'N; 014°03'E – 45°02' N; 014°05'E), a long inlet into which flows the Raša river.

Approach. Landmarks: belfry in Krnica village, white iron tower (white light) on Ubac point, cylindrical red tower of open construction (red light) on Mulac point and stone pyramid N of that point.

Care should be taken when approaching to avoid the shoal NW of the pier at Bršica cove and the wreck in Salamušćica cove (about 1.5 km NE of Rakalj village).

Also beware of intensive commercial traffic to the Trget and Bršica terminals. In the coves of Risvica, Salamušćica and Blaž there are shellfish beds.

The bora here blows in gusts and forms whirlpools. When there is a strong sirocco the swell is felt all the way down the inlet to Trget harbour which is the rail terminal of the industrial line from Lupoglav.

Mooring. Yachts drawing up to 6 m can berth in the Bršica cove and smaller ones in Trget harbour. In this harbour its is best to anchor (four-point moor) S or SE of the harbour offices. The best anchorage for large yachts is in Tunarica cove, off the NE shore (about 2 M from the entrance). The bora is somewhat less than in other parts of the

PORER

inlet. Smaller craft are advised to anchor off the E shore of the inlet S of Risvica cove (bollards for stem moorings) and Teplica cove. The bora is felt strongly here and forms whirlpools. Shellfish beds in Risvica, Salamušćica and Blaž coves have no markers and are thus dangerous for navigation.

The harbour is open to international navigation and is a permanent port of entry.

The town of Raša is reached by road from Trget (10 M); it has post office, medical services, chemist's.

TRGET

(45°01,4'N; 014°03,4'E), small village and point at the end of Raša inlet.

Approach. Green tower with post and gallery (green light) on Trget point about 0.2 M northwest of town.

Mooring. Small yachts can berth beside the two small piers (four-point moor). The bora from the E is strongly felt.

Harbour branch office and customs.

Facilities. Water from the mains, shops in Raša and Labin.

BRŠICA

(45°01,8'N; 014°03'E), cove and harbour at the bottom of the Raša inlet serving Raša and Labin. Timber wharf off E shore of cove and livestock wharf at T-pier.

Approach. Steep whitish cutting behind a concrete platform; three harbour cranes, iron tower (light green) on Trget point.

Mooring. There is a masonry waterfront NW of the steep pier. Small craft can only moor at the small number of buoys. The sirocco is felt here with great force, the bora is fierce and blows in gusts.

Harbour branch office, customs and post office in Trget (1.5 km). As a border crossing it is open all the year round.

Warning. Alluvial sediments brought down by the Raša river causes variation in the depth of the sea which may be as much as 1 m. When the river is in spate after rain, currents may make it difficult to manoeuvre and sail into or out of the inlet.

Facilities. Water hydrant on the shore, provisions in shops in Raša and Labin.

TUNARICA

(44°58,4'N; 014°05,8'E), wide cove on the E side of the Raša inlet, SE of Sv Mikula point.

Approach. Landmark: on the entrance point to N is a red column and post with gallery (red light).

Mooring. The cove is sheltered from all winds. Smaller vessels can moor beside the pier or anchor in the N cove (several stone blocks allow four-point moor).

KOROMAČNO

(44°58'N; 14°07'E), village, cove and point on the E coast of Istria, W of Crna punta point. Provides good shelter from the bora but is exposed to strong S winds and sea from SW to SE (if such winds develop, shelter should be sought in the Raša inlet).

Approach. Landmarks: white cage on the corner of a stone house (white light) on Crna point, the chimney from the cement factory, village buildings and silos in the background, quarry in the hill behind and harbour cranes.

In approaching the masonry waterfront care should be taken to keep at least 50 m starboard of the stone blocks before the main, small pier SW of entrance.

The best anchorage for yachts is 0.5 M northwest of Koromačno point.

Facilities. Limited amounts of food and water. Post office and medical service.

PRKLOG

(45°02'N; 014°10'E), cove beside the point of the same name on the E Istrian coast about 2 M south of Rabac; depth up to 39 m. Protected from all winds but those from the S. Yachts may anchor or moor but only in cases of emergency.

Approach. The cove can be identified by the chapel on Sv Marina point.

Mooring. Vessels can anchor here in normal weather conditions and in emergency (good holding bottom), but the bora blows fiercely and S winds cause waves which makes it an uncertain refuge. Small craft can berth (four-point moor) at the bottom of the cove (NE of reefs).

Warning. At the bottom of the bay, just off the W shore, small reefs are above sea-level at low water.

RABAC

(45°06'N; 014°10'E), tourist settlement and small harbour between Sv Juraj and Sv Andrija points on E coast of Istria.

Approach. Landmarks: Labin belfry (NW of harbour), a square stone tower (white light), the buildings of the hotel settlement on Sv Adrija point; NW of the point at the bottom of the cove there are more hotels. When approaching care should be taken of Sv Juraj rock about 300 m NE of the point of the same name.

Mooring. The cove is partially sheltered from the bora which, however, causes a swell. It is open to S winds and waves. On the N part of the E side of the cove there is a masonry waterfront; the N part, to the pier, is used by fishing boats (depth 2–3 m) and the boats of the local people. The pier (5.5–6 m) is reserved for coastal and excursion boats. The built section of the S pier is used by the ferry to Porozina (if the ferry

RABAC

MARLERA

cannot sail from Brestova). Yachts and small boats should berth (four-point moor) at the most southerly part of the waterfront, in front of the hotels. Water and electricity hook-ups. On the NW shore is the wharf of a deserted mine. This is a dangerous place to moor when the bora blows.

The best anchorage for vessels of all size is in the NE part of the harbour.

Facilities. Harbour master's branch office, post office, medical service, chemist's, banks, several hotels and hotel settlements with shops. Groceries; fuel pump 500 m from shore.

Services. The »Oliva« camp for motorists is beside the harbour. Crane (5 t); small repairs can be carried out by Raša workshops.

Sights. Remains of town walls (1587), the site of the Roman town of Albona, buildings from medieval times to the Baroque period. Museum with a collection of stone fragments. About 5 km away is Dubrova where Mediterranean sculpture symposium is held – collection of sculpture.

PLOMINSKA LUKA

(45°06,8'N; 014°12'E), deep cove about 3 M northeast of Rabac. It is very deep and steep sided except at the end where inflowing streams make the seabed variable. The small town of Plomin is situated at the end of the cove.

Approach. It may be identified by the steep NE entrance at Mašnjak point where there is a motel, the belfries of Plomin churches and the chimney of the thermo-electric power plant.

Mooring. The bora here is strong and dangerous and blows in gusts from SW, it blows in summer too, often unexpectedly. The sirocco causes a swell in the harbour. Anchoring is advisable in fine weather only (good holding bottom), anchoring is not recommended at the bottom of the bay because of the shallow rocky bottom.

Facilities. Water from the main. Provisions in local shops.

RIJEKA HARBOUR MASTER'S OFFICE AREA

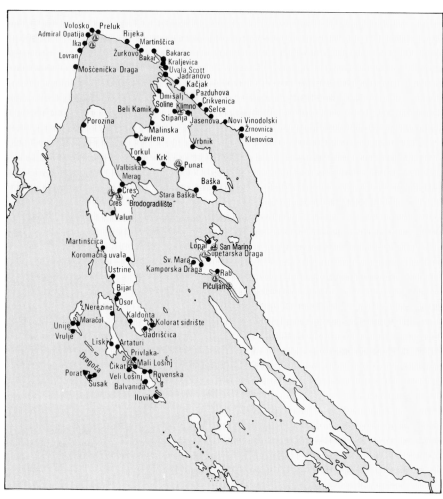

BAKAR	BAŠKA	CRES	CRIKVENICA	KRALJEVICA	KRK	LOVRAN	MALINSKA	MALI LOŠINJ	NOVI VINODOL	OLIB	OPATIJA	RAB	RIJEKA	SELCE	SILBA	
	28	30	11	3	24	15	12	59	17	61	14	42	10	13	61	BAKAR
		43	17	26	12	34	25	42	12	38	36	18	33	16	38	BAŠKA
			34	28	34	23	26	34	40	51	26	51	27	35	47	CRES
				9	27	20	16	57	5	53	20	33	16	2	53	CRIKVENICA
					23	13	10	57	15	59	13	40	8	11	59	KRALJEVICA
						24	15	43	23	40	26	23	24	26	40	KRK
							15	50	26	60	3	41	7	23	59	LOVRAN
								53	22	51	16	33	13	18	51	MALINSKA
									53	22	53	31	54	56	18	MALI LOŠINJ
										49	26	29	21	4	49	NOVI VINODOL
											63	25	61	53	4	OLIB
												44	5	23	63	OPATIJA
													43	33	24	RAB
														17	60	RIJEKA
															53	SELCE
																SILBA

DISTANCES OF PORTS

HARBOURS ON THE COAST

MOŠĆENIČKA DRAGA

(45°14'N; 014°15'E), small settlement in Rijeka Bay, 7.5 M north of the entrance to Plomin harbour.

Approach. Landmarks: the church belfry and buildings of Mošćenica on the hill above the bay, a green tower with post (green light) on the SE corner of the pier, a valley extending from the mountains to the sea, by night the green light from the SE corner of the breakwater.

Mooring. The bay is exposed to all winds except those from NW. In winter a strong ESE wind blows and in summer gales are frequent. Sometimes the maestral blows here strongly from the S which makes landing very difficult. When the Mt Učka is cloud capped bad weather from the S can be expected. Yachts can anchor or moor beside the masonry waterfront (four-point moor) but only in good weather. Only a limited number of small craft can berth in the inner harbour.

Facilities. Harbour master's branch office, post office; medical services in the town; several hotels, marina and camp for motorists. Provisions and water. Hoist (3,5 t) in harbour.

The seat of the »Draga« Sports Club and the »Orion« Yachtsmen Club.

Sights. Mošćenica (medieval walls, tower and town gate, 17 C loggia), Sv Andrija church (St Andrew 1780–90 with baroque interior, museum collection) – 1,8 km.

LOVRAN

(45°17'N; 014°17'E), small town and small harbour S of Opatija.

Approach. Landmarks: the pointed belfry, the red building on the hill above the town,

MOŠĆENICE

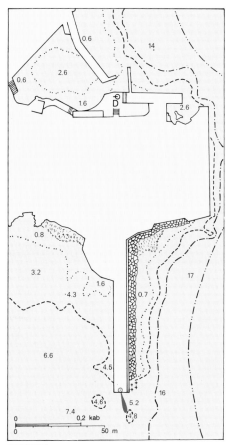

MOŠĆENIČKA DRAGA

LOVRAN

LOVRAN

the hotel on the shore NW of the breakwater, a square green tower (green light) on the head of the breakwater.

Mooring. The harbour is exposed to the bora and sirocco and is not recommended for a long stay. E winds cause high waves (warning signs are a cloud cap on Mt Učka and high sea level). During S winds currents make manoeuvering difficult. Moorings are continuously occupied. There is anchorage about 500 m offshore in a depth of 30 m, the holding is good but the anchorage is exposed to all winds except those from NW quadrant.

Facilities. Abundant water from town supply, fuel pump in town.

Summer and health resort, hospital for bone tuberculosis and medical service; hotels, restaurants and shops, post office.

Sights. Stubica town gate towards the sea and tower (medieval); Sv Juraj church (St George, 14 C, wall paintings dating before 1479), Sv Trojstvo chapel (Holy Trinity, 13 C) on the shore; Baroque buildings on the square.

IKA

(45°18,3'N; 014°17'E), old fishing village lying along the inlet formed by the inundated mouth of the Banina stream.

Approach. Red sphere on a post (red light) on the main pier is a conspicuous landmark. Because of the shoal along the breakwater extension (length about 100 m, width 20 m) it is advisable to approach very carefully. From the bay E of the pier an underwater pipe extends in a SW direction.

Mooring. The small harbour is exposed to all winds except those from the N. South and E winds cause a choppy sea and

yachts are not advised to make an extended stay.

Facilities. Supermarket, fuel in Lovran (1 M). Water from a hydrant on the shore in front of the hotel.

Services. Hoist (3 t) at the bottom end of the pier.

IČIĆI MARINA (ACI)

(45°19'N; 014°17,7'E) is situated between Opatija and Ičići.

The marina has 6 piers. It is protected from the E by a breakwater, depth 2.5 m (near the shore) and up to 10 m (beside the breakwater). It has 360 berths (four-point moor for yachts up to 60 m length) and 100 dry-berths. The marina will be extended north with additional 5 piers.

The speed of the vessel is limited at 2 knots.

The marina has reception office, restaurant, fast-food restaurant, shops, boutiques, sale of nautical equipment, snack-bar, toilets and showers with hot water, laundry services; technical service, car park, slipway, crane (15 t).

The marina is open all the year round.

OPATIJA

(45°20'N; 014°19'E), town and holiday resort; also a small harbour on the NW side of Rijeka Bay, about 4 M west from Rijeka.

Approach. The town can be recognized by the small grey stone church (without belfry with a copper dome), many hotels, the cylindrical white tower with post and gallery (red

51

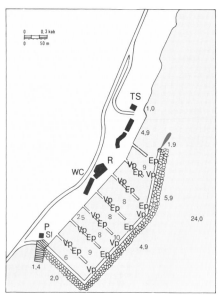

IČIĆI MARINA

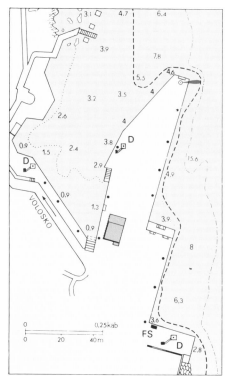

OPATIJA

light, visible azimuth 137° through S to 254°) on the pier head, a red tower with post and gallery (red light) on the breakwater head of the marina in front of the »Admiral« hotel.

Mooring. The outer part of the pier is for excursion and passenger boats and is suitable for mooring in good weather. The inner side of the quay is suitable for boats drawing up to 3 m and is sheltered from all winds except the NE. The bora is moderately felt and always blows from the E. S and E winds cause rough sea. The inner part of the harbour is reserved for boats of local people. The best berth for yachts is in the marina fronting the »Admiral« hotel (0.8 M southwest of the harbour). Anchorage (about 500 m offshore, depth 50 m) is not recommended in strong E and SE winds.

Opatija has harbour master's branch office, customs, post office, medical centre for thalassotherapy, chemist's, medical service, banks, a large number of hotels of all categories, varied shops. It is the centre of the »Adriatic Croatia International Club« (ACI).

»Jadran« Yacht Club can undertake winter care of a limited number of boats. In early spring (March) it organizes an international sailing regatta for the »Opatija Cup« (Finn and Flying Dutchman classes).

Facilities. Fuel pumps on the outer part of the quay, hydrant on quay. Electricity connections by harbour offices. Shops of all kinds in town. Electric crane (5 t) on the inner part of the quay, manual hoist (3 t) on the outer quay. Small repairs can be effected in Admiral Marina, larger in the »Kantrida« shipyard in Rijeka.

Sights. The church of Sv Jakob ad Palum (St Jacob ad Palum, 1506, additions 1774, 1937), Villa Angiolina (1844, the beginning of Opatija as a seaside resort); »Prvi Maj«

park (exotica). – Veprinac (Gothic castello, town gate, loggia, St Mark church) – 13 km. – Mount Učka (1,396 m, sweeping views of Kvarner Bay and Istria) – 20 km by road. – Kastav, little town with medieval remains (15 C church of Sv Fabijan i Sebastijan, 15 C loggia) – 6 km.

ADMIRAL MARINA

(45°12,6'N; 014°18,4'E) is located in Opatija, mainly for »Admiral« hotel guests. The marina operates during the whole year.

Landmarks: the large, white step-like building of the »Admiral« hotel standing above the marina and the cylindrical red tower with post (red light) on the main breakwater are easily visible from seaward.

The marina is protected from all winds and sea, but strong bora and sirocco create a swell especially at the berths beside the breakwater (nearer the sea). This makes entrance very difficult and sometimes impossible. The marina offices provide weather bulletins and forecasts.

It has 160 berths (up to 30 m length) for small yachts and boats. On shore there are 40 dry-berths (up to 8 m length) for repairs and wintering.

Shops in the marina and in Opatija. Fuel available (0,5 M); restaurants, coffee-bars, exchange office etc.

Crane (5 t), electricity hook-ups, water from hydrant, engine servicing, repairs to electrical installations, battery charging, sail repairs. Maintenance during wintering.

VOLOSKO

(45°19,6'N; 014°19'E), a typical old Mediterranean fishing village clustered around a little harbour.

Approach. Landmarks: the church with two pointed belfries, the red iron tower on the south breakwater (red light) and green at the head of the north breakwater (green light).

Mooring. The harbour is well protected from SW and NW winds. Other winds create dangerous waves in the harbour so any long stay by yachts is not recommended. Small craft, drawing up to 3 m, can berth beside the pier.

Facilities. In Opatija.

PRELUK

(45°21'N; 014°20'E), small harbour at the extreme N end of Rijeka Bay, about 0.3 M north of Volosko. It does not provide shelter

ADMIRAL MARINA – OPATIJA

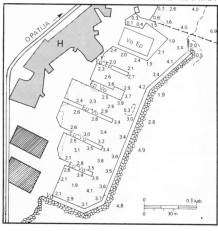

ADMIRAL MARINA

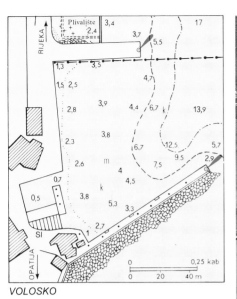

VOLOSKO

RIJEKA

from SE and SW winds and is exposed to the bora. Not even in summer is it recommended for anything but a short stay.

About 120 m from the E point is a shoal (3 m).

Mooring. Larger yachts may anchor in the NE part of the harbour (good holding bottom). Small craft can moor at the operative coast (55 m, depth 1 m).

Facilities. Crane (1,5 t). In Rijeka and the neighbouring camp for motorists (E side of the Preluk cove).

RIJEKA

(45°20'N; 014°25'E), town and largest Croatian commercial port. Rijeka port is open to international sailing and is a permanent port of entry with customs and health authorities.

Approach. Rijeka can be approached from three directions: from Kvarnerski zaljev (Kvarner Bay) through Vela vrata (Vela Straits), between the peninsula of Istria and the island of Cres; from Kvarnerić through Srednja vrata between the islands of Krk and Cres; from Velebitski kanal (Velebit Channel) through Tihi kanal (Tihi Channel) between the island of Krk and the mainland.

The following landmarks are conspicuous when approaching the harbour: the high hexagonal tower of Mlaka lighthouse (black and white bands, white light), the pointed white steeple of the church on Kozala Hill (above the town), the building of the large city hospital, the large travelling crane of the »Treći maj« (Third May) shipyard to the left of the harbour, the green tower with gallery (green light) at the head of Riječki lukobran (Rijeka breakwater).

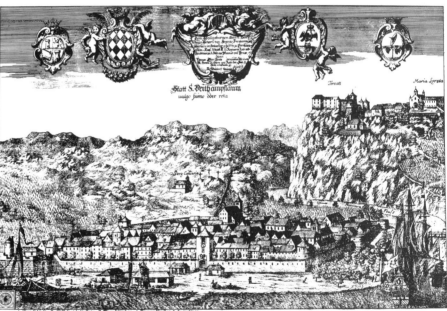

RIJEKA, ENGRAVING FROM 1689

RIJEKA, TRSAT CASTLE

MLAKA

West of the entrance to the main harbour lies Brgud, the harbour of the »Treći maj« shipyard (green tower with post above a house, green light). In the E part of the harbour part of the waterfront is reserved for passenger boats and the berthing of boats. Rijeka harbour does not provide good facilities for yachts and is not suitable for a longer stay. Large yachts will have great difficulty in finding a good berth in the harbour, the only available berths being in the E part of the main harbour.

53

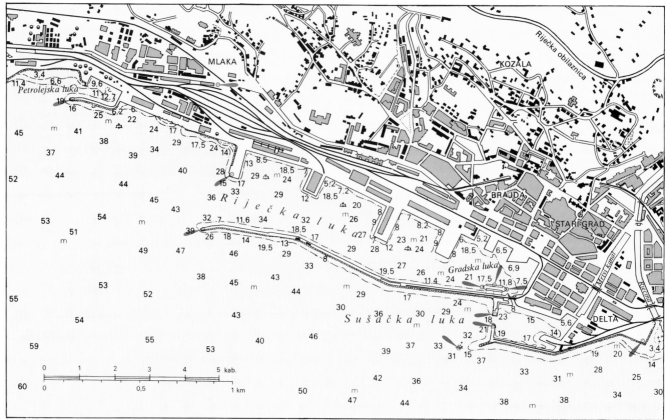

RIJEČKA LUKA (PORT RIJEKA)

In spring and autumn the sirocco frequently blows (foretold by cloud cap on the top of Učka). Nimbus and cumulonimbus clouds above the Velebit mountain range usually herald W and NW winds, accompanied by rough sea and strong slop in the harbour.

On the coast from Preluk to Bakarski zaljev there are several small sports harbours (»Kantrida«, »Treći maj«, »Jeletićevo«, »Grčevo«) but they are crowded during the summer season and it is difficult to find a good berth.

Facilities. Harbour master's office, post office, train and bus terminals, airport (on the island of Krk) and airfield for sports planes (on Grobnik, outside of Rijeka), tourist offices, hotels, several hospitals, extensive medical services (outpatient's department for seamen).

BAKARSKI ZALJEV

Rijeka has a university, shipping companies and shipyards.

The coastal maritime radiostation RIJEKA-RADIO forms part of Croatia Maritime Radio Service.

Provisions of all kinds are available in the town shops and the open market beside the harbour. Drinking water from hydrants and fuel (oil, petrol, gas) on the petrol station. Navigational publications and charts are available.

Repairs of all kinds to hull, engines, and all kinds of refitting available at »Viktor Lenac« shipyard in Martinšćica. Repairs, servicing and installation of engines up to 184 kW (250 HP) at »Kantrida« boatyard.

Car-ferry line: Rijeka – Cres – M. Lošinj – Rab – Zadar – Primošten – Split – Hvar – V. Luka (Korčula) – Mljet – Dubrovnik.

Sights. Sv Marija cathedral (13 C, renovations 1695, 1715–26, leaning belfry 1377), city tower (18 C), Capuchin monastery and church of Sv Jeronim (Baroque 18 C,

Gothic chapel), Sv Vid church (St Vitus, rotunda 1638–1742), theatre (1885– 86), Gospa Lurdska church (Our Lady of Lourdes, in Žabica, 1906 and 1929), Calvary (remains of Roman limes), church (1934) and graveyard on Kozala (view of Rijeka Bay). – Trsat: 538 steps of Petar Kružić (lower part 1531), Frankopan castle (before 1288, additions in 19 C, fine view of Rijeka Bay), church of Marija Lauretanska (12 C, rich inventory). – History and Naval History Museums, Natural History Museum, Modern Art Gallery.

ŽURKOVO

(45°18'N; 014°29'E), small harbour about 2.5 M southeast of Rijeka.

Approach. The red cliff of the stone quarry W of the harbour is conspicuous.

Mooring. The harbour is exposed to SE and SW winds which do not cause waves. The bora may be violent. Small craft can anchor in the middle of the bay.

BAKAR, »TURKISH HOUSE«

BAKAR

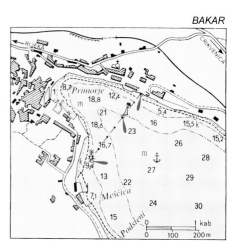

Facilities. Motel and restaurant. Water from hydrant on waterfront, motel and restaurant, supermarket; at the W side of the cove there is a petrol pump.

There is a small boatyard which can carry out repairs to small craft, such craft can also find winter berths. There is a hoist on the head of the main pier and two small slips.

BAKARSKI ZALJEV,

bay about 6.5 miles ESE of Rijeka. It is very deep and the shores are steep and rocky. It offers no hindrances to navigation. The little town and port of Bakar lies the NW part of the bay and to the SE of the village of Bakarac. On the west side of the bay there is a petrol terminal (Urinj refinery). The entrance is through Bakarska vrata. Care should be taken to avoid the shallows around Oštro point (isobath of 5 m extends as much as 80 m from the shore of the point). Bakarska vrata has the following light marks: to the W Babno point (red flashing) and Srednji point (white flashing); to the E there are buoys in front of Oštro point (green flashing) and Kavranić point (white flashing).The sirocco blows across the whole bay but neither it nor the bora form much swell. The bora blows frequently and very fiercely and in the SE part of the bay it changes direction. When the bora is strong it is advisible to sail as near as possible to the N shore of the bay.

Mooring. Yachts can berth in the small harbours of Bakar and Bakarac.

BAKAR

(45°18,4'N; 014°32,2'E), small town and harbour at the NW bottom of Bakarski zaljev (Bakar Bay).

Approach. The appearance of the town is dominated by a hotel and a church, there are facilities for underwater transporters on both shores, two light buoys; green to NE (green light) and red to SW (red light). Entrance course should be made between these two buoys. In winter the bora may hinder or make entrance or exit impossible.

Mooring. Vessels drawing up to 5 m may berth beside Masaryk quay, and smaller craft with four-point moor beside this quay or in the hotel harbour.

Facilities. Harbour master's branch office, post office, medical service, chemist's, a number of restaurants and shops, customs,

KRALJEVICA

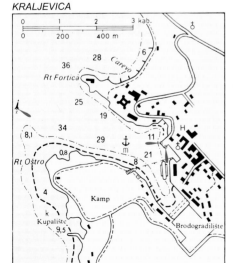

KRALJEVICA, ZRINSKI CASTLE

secondary nautical school. Water from a hydrant on the quay, all provisions from local shops, fuel from petrol pumps.

Crane (5.5 t) for vessels up to 6 m long and slipway for vessels up to 12 m long at the »Luben« Sports Club.

Sights. Castle (16 C, additions 18 C), Sv Andrija church (St Andrew, 1830), buildings of bishopric (1494) and Plovanija (1514), baroque buildings, a Turkish house and a Roman house, Sv Margareta u Primorju church (St Margaret on the Littoral, 17 C), Municipal and Maritime Museum.

BAKARAC

(45°16,8'N; 014°34,8'E), village and small harbour on the SE side of Bakarski zaljev (Bakar Bay).

Approach. Landmarks: the church belfry; red tower with post (red light) on the head of the main pier.

Mooring. Four-point moor in harbour or along the outer side of the breakwater. The bora blows strongly here and always comes unexpectedly.

Facilities. Post office, camp for motorists, motels and several restaurants in the village, water from the main; all other requirements in Kraljevica.

KRALJEVICA

(45°16'N; 014°34'E), small town and harbour on S side of Bakar Bay between Fortica and Oštro points.

Approach. Landmarks: the old church belfry on Oštro point and castle on Fortica point; church belfry; hospital building on N shore; round green buoy (green light topped by cone) anchored NW of Oštro point at depth of 20 m; harbour light. South of Kraljevica the Krk Bridge links the island of Krk with the mainland.

Mooring. Beside the S shore of the harbour and the shore in front of the Frankopan castle vessels can use four-point moor or can lie with four-point moor north of the quay in Dražica cove. Smaller vessels can moor in Carevo cove N of the quay but here they are exposed to bora and maestral.

Facilities. Harbour master's branch office, post office, hospital for bone tuberculosis and paraplegics, medical service, banks, chemist's, hotels and hotel settlement, camp for motorists, a number of private restaurants. Fuel at the petrol station on the Adriatic highway (700 m), water from the shore hydrants.

North of the quay is a small slip and crane (3 t). The »Kraljevica« shipyard can carry out repairs of all kinds.

Sights. The old Zrinski castle (first half 17 C, two courtyards), the new Frankopan

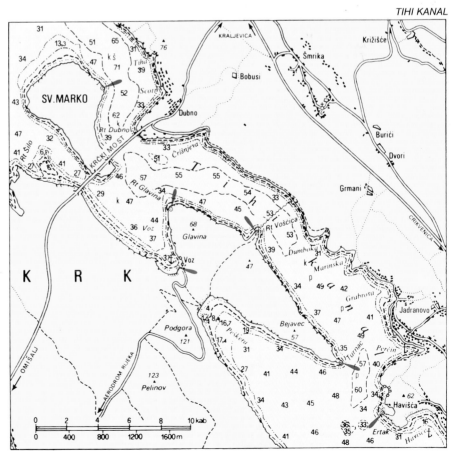

TIHI KANAL

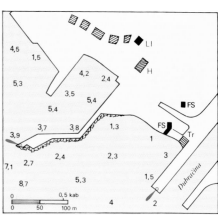

CRIKVENICA

CRIKVENICA

castle (about 1650 with corner towers), Sv Nikola church (St Nicholas, 16 C, storage buildings, since 1790 church).

UVALA SCOTT

(45°15'N; 014°34'E), hotel settlement and cove on the mainland coast E of the islet of Sveti Marko, near the N entrance to Tihi kanal (some 1.4 M south of Kraljevica).

Approach. From NW: between the mainland and the steep islet of Sveti Marko, the entrance to Tihi kanal can be seen. It is bridged by the Krk Bridge (length 1440 m, vertical clearance 67 m; two arches, one linking the mainland and Sveti Marko and the other Sveti Marko and Krk; built 1976 – 1980, opened July 9, 1980). Approaching through Mala vrata, just before the bridge, the Uvala Scott hotel complex can be identified consisting of a group of larger buildings and smaller houses in four levels. When approaching from S: go through Tihi kanal and under the Krk bridge. After Dubno point, Uvala Scott can be seen towards E.

CRIKVENICA, FRANKOPAN CASTLE

When approaching by night, steer for the red light on the NE point of the islet of Sveti Marko and on the Glavina point (the island of Krk).

Mooring. Yachts can moor at the mole by the hotel (depth 3.5 m), at the second mole (four-point moor) or anchor throughout the cove. The cove is exposed to N and SW winds.

Facilities. Water from the hydrant on the quay; provisions in Kraljevica; fuel at the petrol station on the Adriatic highway in Kraljevica.

JADRANOVO

(45°13,4'N; 014°37'E), village and small harbour at the head of Perčin cove, 0.4 M north of Ertak point in Tihi kanal.

Mooring. Yachts can moor alongside the mole. Perčin cove is sheltered from all winds and provides good anchorage for small boats and yachts.

Facilities. Post office. Provisions and water available. Hoist (3 t) for small craft.

PAZDUHOVA

TIHI KANAL,

sea passage (length 3.5 M) between the mainland (Oštro point–Ertak point) and the island of Krk (Šilo point–Bejavec point); the islet of Sveti Marko divides it into the E and W part.

Approach. From NW: the building of the former lighthouse at Oštro; the island of Sveti Marko and the red tower with a column and gallery (red light) on its NE side: the Krk Bridge (vertical clearance 67 m); the Uvala Scott hotel complex; the red tower with a column and gallery (red light) on Glavina headland; the stone tower with a red cage next to the house (red light) on Vošćica point; the red iron column on the white tower (red light) on Turnac point (Bejavec); the white round tower with a column and gallery in front of a small house (white light) on Ertak point. Entering Tihi kanal from SE follow the landmarks in the opposite order.

The bora is violent and blows in gusts developing eddies, which are especially dangerous off the southern point of the islet of Sveti Marko. The sirocco creates considerable waves and a current of up to 3 knots. Uvala Scott, Črišnjeva and Perčin (Jadranovo) provide good shelter.

Directions for navigation. Small yachts can pass between Sveti Marko and Krk; care should be taken of the shoals and two rocks 0.4 M E of Šilo point and of the shoal along the southern shore of Sveti Marko (green light buoy). Yachts entering the passage from NW have right of way.

KAČJAK

(45°12'N; 014°39'E), village, point and anchorage some 2 M southeast of Ertak point.

Approach. A whitish rocky slope and a hotel complex can be easily identified.

Mooring. The anchorage N of Kačjak point is well sheltered from the bora. In the cove are three bollards for yachts drawing up to 2 m.

PAZDUHOVA

(45°12'N; 014°40'E), cove and harbour of the village of Dramalj, some 1.5 M northwest of Crikvenica. It is sheltered from the west by the pier and from the south by the breakwater off the »Lanterna« Hotel.

Mooring. Yachts drawing up to 1.5 m can moor alongside the quay or use the four-point moor. The harbour is open to NW winds and is not safe for a longer stay.

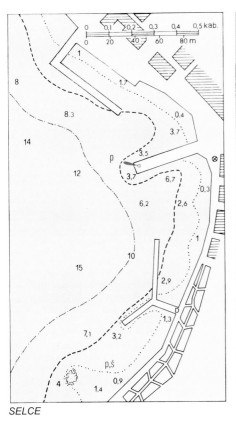

SELCE

SELCE

CRIKVENICA

(45°10,4'N; 014°42'E), harbour and tourist centre of Vinodolsko primorje on the estuary of the Dubračina stream.

Approach. Landmarks: the white viaduct above the town, hotel buildings on a hill above the NW part of the town, and the green rectangular tower with a column (green light) on the head of the breakwater.

When entering the harbour care should be taken of the shoal extending NW of the breakwater, marked by two cylindrical red buoys: the buoys should be left to port and the breakwater to starboard. Do not navigate between the buoys and the mainland. Another shoal extends SE of the head of the breakwater. It is marked by a green conical buoy. Do not navigate between the buoy and the head of the breakwater.

Mooring. The harbour is sheltered from all winds except W and SW winds, which cause a swell. The bora from N blows in gusts and is strongest at the head of the breakwater. The anchorage off the harbour is exposed to all winds, especially the bora, and should be avoided. Small craft can moor alongside the inner side of the breakwater or, using the four-point moor, between the breakwater and the mole.

Some 100 m from the estuary of the Dubračina stream there is Podvorska small harbour where smaller yachts can moor; depth 3–4 m; winter berthing on the mainland. Crane (4 t); electricity and water hookups.

Facilities. Harbour master's branch office, post office, a number of hotels and other tourist facilities and shops, a thalassotherapy clinic, medical service, chemist's.

Provisions can be obtained in the town, water from the hydrant in the harbour, fuel at the pump in the ferry harbour.

Repairs of wooden and plastic yachts. Boat engine repairs: »Automehanika« AMD and a private workshop. Diving cylinders can be refilled here.

Car-ferry line: Crikvenica – Šilo (Island of Krk).

Sights. Kaštel (Castle 1412, later reconstructions; at one time housed the Pauline monastery), Uznesenje Marijino church (The Assumption of the Virgin, 1659). – Drivenik (castle ruins) – 11 km. – Bribir (castle of the Frankopans; parish church, 1740; art collection) – 9 km.

SELCE

(45°09,4'N; 014°43'E), small town and harbour some 1.5 M southeast of Crikvenica, situated in a small cove open to NW.

Approach. Landmarks: the belfry in the town, hotel buildings in the N and S part of the harbour, the white tower with a column

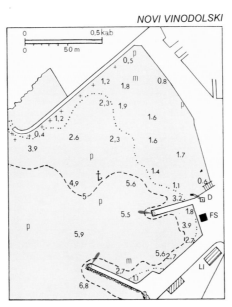

NOVI VINODOLSKI

and gallery (green light) at the head of the N mole.

Mooring. Yachts can use the four-point moor alongside the quay between the moles. Small craft can berth behind the breakwater. The harbour is exposed to winds from the SW and NW quadrants. In the bora moor on the S side of the mole, in the sirocco on the N side of the mole. There is good anchorage for large yachts W of the harbour light (depth 12 m); good holding ground.

Facilities. Harbour master's branch office, post office, several hotels and restaurants, tourist office, medical service, a number of shops. Water from the local waterworks; fuel in Crikvenica and Novi Vinodolski.

JASENOVA

(45°08'N; 014°44'E), cove some 0.3 M northwest of Tokal point, SE of Selce.

Good shelter from all winds, especially the bora. Small yachts can anchor at the entrance to the cove or moor (four-point moor) in front of the »Zagori« hotel complex SE of Tokal point.

Facilities. In Novi Vinodolski.

TRSTENIK

PRESTENICE

NOVI VINODOLSKI

(45°07,4'N; 014°47,4'E), town, small harbour and popular seaside resort on the estuary of the Suha Ričina periodic stream.

Approach. Landmarks: the belfry, the islet of Sveti Marin with a chapel SE of the harbour, the water supply tower on the hill E of the harbour, the rectangular green tower (green light) on the head of the breakwater and the white tower with a column (red light) on the head of the mole in the harbour.

Warning. While entering the harbour keep to the middle of the fairway (a shoal and rocks near the head of the breakwater).

Mooring. The harbour is exposed to SW and NW winds; westerlies are particularly dangerous. Yachts can moor along the inner side of the breakwater, along the quay and on the E side of the mole. During the bora and W winds it is advisable to use the anchorage some 200 to 300 m W of the harbour; good holding ground.

Along the Adriatic highway there is a 200 m stretch of the shore where smaller vessels can moor; depth 0.5–1 m.

Facilities. Harbour master's branch office, post office, medical service, several hotels and restaurants, tourist office, a variety of shops and a camp-site.

Water from the hydrant, fuel at the petrol station on the quay. Hoist (3 t) and a slipway; boat engine repairs at »Marjan Belošević«, Povile; repairs of wooden and plastic vessels (boats).

Sights. The Lopar ruins (Roman?), Kvadrac Tower (14/15 C, ruins of a castle); Sv Filip i Jakov church (St Philip and Jacob, 1520), the Town Museum, the ruins of the Pauline monastery on Osap hill.

OSOR

ŽRNOVNICA

(45°06,5'N; 014°50,3'E), cove some 2 M southeast of Novi Vinodolski at the NW entrance to Velebitski kanal.

Mooring. A good anchorage for small craft when the sirocco blows; it can be dangerous with SW winds. Good holding ground (mud). The Teplo cove (0.4 M southeast from Novi Vinodolski) also offers good shelter; 30 m of coast, average depth 4 m.

OSOR, ENGRAVING FROM 1571

KLENOVICA

(45°06,5'N; 014°50,3'E), village and cove 0.4 M southeast of Žrnovnica.

Approach. Landmarks: Sv Anton rock, the stone tower (white light) and the village.

Mooring. Alongside the mole. The bora is violent and blows in gusts but is not dangerous for secured yachts. SW winds are dangerous.

Facilities. Post office, hotel, several restaurants. Water in the village. Provisions available in shops. Boat crane (3 t).

ISLAND OF CRES

MERAG

(44°59'N; 014°26,5'E), village and car-ferry harbour in the small cove of the same name on the NE coast of Cres Island.g

Approach. Landmarks: Sveti Bartul hill (374 m), the church in the W part of the village and the green tower with a column and gallery (green light) on the head of the mole (in the E part of the cove). One mile to NW of the harbour is a stony reef.

Mooring. The cove is partially protected from S winds but is exposed to N wind. Larger yachts can anchor in the cove too.

Warning. When casting anchor care should be taken of underwater cables extending in the direction of the island of Krk.

Facilities. Provisions available in the local shop and restaurant.

Car-ferry line: Merag – Valbiska (Island of Krk); the shortest connection of the central and southern parts of islands of Cres and Lošinj with Rijeka.

KOROMAČNA

(44°47'N; 014°27,5'E), cove and anchorage on the E coast of the island, W of Sv Duh point; the steep slopeswhich are easily identified when approaching the cove.

Mooring. The cove offers shelter only from N winds. The small harbour on the W coast of the cove is sheltered from all winds except the north-westerlies. Smaller vessels can anchor (only with the northerlies) in the NW part of the cove. The cove is not safe in the sirocco.

KOLORAT

(44°38,6'N; 014°31,5'E), anchorage in the indented cove on the SE coast of Cres.

Approach. Care should be taken of Kolorat shoal (4.5 m) some 500 m N of the point of the same name and Matešić shoal some 750 m NW of Tanki point. The dangerous area is marked by the red sectors of the coast lights on Suha point and Bik rock.

Mooring. The anchorage is sheltered from all winds. Smaller craft can anchor off the NE coast in depth of 3.5 m; good holding.

JADRIŠĆICA

(44°37'N; 014°30,4'E), cove in the SE part of the island.

OSOR

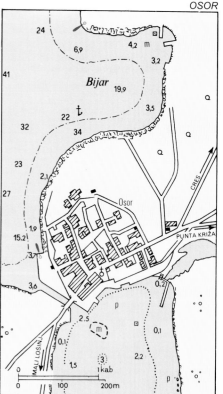

Approach. When approaching, care should be taken of the 5-metre deep shoal S of the W side of the entrance.

Mooring. The cove is protected from all winds. With the sirocco a slight swell enters. Larger yachts can anchor stern-to NW off the first cluster of houses of Bokinić hamlet, to the right of the entrance, in a depth of 12 m. Smaller vessels can anchor off the second cluster of houses of Pogana hamlet, stern-to the waterfront (also NW), or moor on the inside of the small breakwater (depth up to 2.5 m).

Facilities. The »Baldarin« campsite and post office at Punta Križa, 2.5 km SE of the cove; restaurant, sports grounds and shops.

MARTINŠĆICA

(44°37,5'N; 014°27,8'E), cove on the island of Cres, SE of Kaldonta; it is well sheltered from the bora but exposed to the sirocco. Stretching from Plantur point southwards is a submerged reef; there is another reef in the cove. Yachts can anchor at the entrance to the cove in depth of 10–20 m; good holding.

KALDONTA

(44°38,3'N; 014°27'E), cove and point in Lošinjski kanal on the SW coast of the island of Cres.

Mooring. The cove is sheltered from all winds and offers good anchorage to smaller yachts, which can anchor in the middle of the cove or use the bollards (four-point moor) at the far end of the harbour, bows--to SW.

OSORSKI TJESNAC and OSOR

narrow straits (100 m long, 12 m wide) between the islands of Cres and Lošinj connecting the Bay of Osor with the Lošinj Channel. It is navigable for vessels drawing up to 2.6 m. The village and small harbour of Osor.

On the S part of the straits there is a turning bridge (vertical clearance 1.5 m); the islands of Cres and Lošinj are connected by road. The bridge is opened from 9 am to 5 pm toll-free. The speed of the vessels is limited to 5 knots. Vessels coming from the south must be given right of way. Vessels waiting at the N entrance may moor along the waterfront for passenger ships. On both entrances to the straits there are underwater cables and in the middle of the straits there is a pipeline.

Currents in the straits are variable and attain a rate of up to 6 knots. The bora is strong at the N entrance and the sirocco at the S entrance. They cause a considerable sea. Winds from NE and SE quadrants make the approach to the S entrance difficult. Five white stone markings at this entrance should be left on the W side.

Mooring. Boats can moor along the E waterfront (for the passenger ships) in front of the N entrance to the straits (depth 3.5–4.5 m), which is reserved for passenger ships. Vessels can anchor in the Bijar cove, somewhat N of the straits.

Facilities. Post office, tourist office, shops, restaurants and coffee-bars.

Water from the main, provisions in shops.

Sights (in Osor). The remains of Roman town walls near Bijar cove (dating from the time when the straits were constructed);

foundations of temples and public buildings; the ruins of an early Christian cathedral (6 C), of a Benedictine abbey (11 C) and of the Romanesque churches of Sv Marko and Sv Katarina; the former cathedral of Sv Marija (1498), the old Town Hall (now the Town Museum with a collection of stone monuments), the ruins of Sv Marija church (late 15 C) in Bijar. The Juraj Dalmatinac Gallery. Archaeological museum in Osor.

Osor summer musical evenings, international event held each year.

BIJAR

(44°42'N; 014°24'E), cove some 0.5 M north of Osor, in the eastern part of Osor Straits.

Mooring. The cove is a good allround shelter. Small yachts can moor at the two moles or anchor in a depth of about 1.5 m. Larger yachts can anchor W of the red light on the N point of the cove in the middle in depths of about 15 m.

There are several bollards on the waterfront.

Facilities. Water, supermarket and restaurant in the campsite in the cove.

USTRINE

(44°45'N; 014°23'E), small cove between Osor Straits and Martinšćica harbour.

Mooring. A good all-round shelter, especially its N part (depth 11–30 m). The S part is exposed to the bora and waves caused by W winds. Anchor stern-to SW, securing bows-to NE to the bollards on the waterfront. Good holding.

MARTINŠĆICA

(44°49'N; 014°21,5'E), village and small harbour in the N part of the small cove of the same name on the W coast of the island, E of Tiha point.

Approach. From S: Zeča (light on the SW side) and Visoki islet (light), the round red tower with a column and gallery (harbour light) on the head of the mole.

GALIOLA

Mooring. Smaller yachts (drawing up to 2.5 m) can moor along the mole (the outer part is used by passenger ships). Good anchorage in the middle of the cove (depth approx. 5 m). Larger yachts can moor at the entrance to the cove (depth approx. 40 m). Good shelter from the bora; SW wind causes big waves. In the Tiha cove (campsite for motorists) there are berths for smaller vessels (depth 1–3 m).

Facilities. Water from a hydrant; provisions in the local shop; fuel in Cres.

Sights. The ruins of a Roman villa rustica, the Franciscan Glagolitic monastery (16 C) with votive pictures donated by seamen, the Sforza summer house (17 C). Vransko Lake (16 m above sea level, maximum depth 84 m, area 5.75 km2) – 4 km by road.

VALUN,

large bay between the points of Pernat and Kovačine. The coast is steep and the depths great, except near the SE coast. In the S part of the bay is the village of Valun and in the cove between the points of Kovačine and Križice is the town and harbour of Cres.

Mooring. Larger vessels can anchor some 0.4 M north of Nedomisje cove, smaller vessels will find good anchorage in the middle of the entrance to the cove. With the bora and NW winds, the cove is dangerous.

In the village of Valun is a small mole; go bows-to, secure using the four-point moor.

Sights. Valunska ploča (The Valun Tablet) in the church of Valun, one of the oldest monuments (11 C) with a carved Glagolitic inscription.

CRES

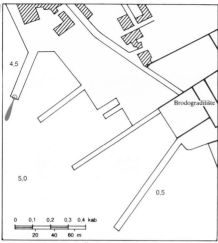

»BRODOGRADILIŠTE CRES« MARINA

CRES

(44°57'N; 014°24'E), town and harbour in a cove in the bay of Cres.

Approach. Landmarks: Pernat point; the red tower on a block (white light) on Kovačine point; the green tower (green light) on Križice point; the red tower with a column and gallery on a concrete base (red light) on Melin point; the white tower with a column and gallery (green light) on the head of the S pier.

Approach through the narrow access channel (width 400 m). Care should be taken of the shoals extending up to 100 m on each side of the channel. Off Melin point (light) is a submerged reef. Do not exceed 5 knots between Kovačine point and Cres harbour.

Mooring. The harbour offers shelter from all winds, but a strong sirocco causes waves up to 1 m high that flood the waterfront. It is recommended to moor in the Cres marina. In the Priprajena cove there is 25 m stretch of the mainland for yachts drawing up to 3 m. Yachts can use the following anchorages: Gavza cove, some 0.8 M north of Kovačine point (depth 12–15 m) and

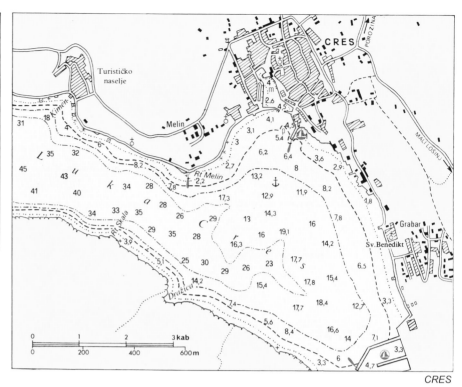

CRES

Nedomisje cove (depth 8–10 m), some 1 M south of Križice point.

Warning. Mooring along the damaged parts of the waterfront is prohibited.

Facilities. Harbour master's branch office, post office, medical service, chemist's; several hotels, campsite, tourist office, shops.

Water from the hydrant in the harbour, fuel at the petrol station on the waterfront.

Repairs and hauling out of vessels up to 400 GRT can be carried out in Cres shipyard, which specializes in wooden vessels; situated in the harbour, it also carries out engine repairs and provides dockage over the winter; dock for vessels up to 1000 t; hoists (5 and 7 t).

Car-ferry lines: Porozina – Brestova (Istria) and Merag – Valbiska (island of Krk).

Local passenger lines (only in summer): see Rijeka and Mali Lošinj.

Sights. Parts of the old town wall with a round tower and a loggia (15/16 C), the church of Sv Marija Velika (St Mary the Great, built in 1554, renovated in 1829), the Romanesque church of Sv Sidar (St Isidore), the church of Sv Marija Magdalena (1402), the monastery of the Minorites (14–15 C, cloisters), the Benedictine nunnery (1527, renovated after the fire in 1764), Fontik (15 C, now a hotel), Town Hall (16 C, art col-

CRES MARINA

CRES MARINA

lection), the Arsan-Petris (15 C, now Town Museum) and Rodinis (15 C) mansions.

»BRODOGRADILIŠTE CRES« D. D. – MARINA

(45°57'N; 014°24'E) is situated next to the shipyard of the same name.

Mooring. 50 berths for yachts up to 30 m length and 100 dry-berhs.

Facilities. Reception office, harbour master's branch office, electricity and water hook-ups, telephone, WC, showers, parking-lot, exchange office, post office, tourist office, shop.

Service: The shipyard repairs yachts up to 400 GRT, lift (100 t), cranes (5 t and 7 t).

CRES MARINA ACI

(44°57'N; 014°24'E) is situated in the S part of the Cres harbour cove. Capacity: 460 sea-berths along the pontoon quays and the pier (up to 25 m length), and approx. 200 dry-berths (winter berthing with care and maintenance; 2,5 m length), electricity, water, telephone and TV hook-ups.

The marina operates the year round.

It has reception office, restaurants, skipper's bar, appartments, supermarket, shop and various boutiques (sports equipment, boat shops, drug store); sports courts, toilets and showers; laundry; petrol and gas pump; car park; charter fleet.

Hoist (10 t), travel-lift (30 t), slipway (15 t), crane for masts (20 m); complete mechanical service (repairs).

POROZINA

(45°08'N; 014°17'E), small harbour and ferry quay in the cove of the same name on the NW coast of Cres (Vela Vrata Straits), some 1 M northeast of Prestenice point.

Approach. Landmarks: the stone tower with a gallery on the house (white light) on Prestenice point, the house on the hill above the harbour, the red tower with a column and a gallery (red light) on the head of the pier.

Mooring. The cove is protected from all winds except the south-westerlies and westerlies. Yachts can anchor in the cove or secure along the head or the outer side of the pier (depth 4.9 m), on which there is a red tower with a column (red light).

NEREZINE

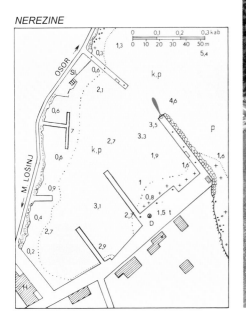

PROLAZ PRIVLAKA

Facilities. Post office, restaurant; accommodation in private rooms.

Car-ferry line: Porozina – Brestova (peninsula of Istria).

ISLAND OF LOŠINJ

NEREZINE

(44°40'N; 014°24'E), village and small harbour some 2 M south of the Osor Straits on the Cres–Lošinj road.

Approach. Landmarks: the belfry of the monastery N of the harbour and the red column with a red light on the head of the S breakwater.

Mooring. Yachts drawing up to 2.5 m can moor on the inner side of the S breakwater and along the piers.

Facilities. Post office, medical service, hotel and other facilities in the village. Water from a hydrant, provisions in local shops.

Crane (1.5 t) and slipway for smaller vessels; the boatyard carries out repairs of wooden vessels and engines.

Sights. Franciscan monastery (1509–15, cloister) with church (1510), the Draža family defense tower (16 C), Sv Marija Magdalena church (13 C). Mt. Televrina (588 m, the highest peak on the island, panoramic view).

PRIVLAKA

(44°33'N; 014°27,5'E), passage (length 70 m, width 8 m, depth 2 m) NE of the harbour and marina in Mali Lošinj; it links the bay of Mali Lošinj harbour and Lošinjski

VELI LOŠINJ

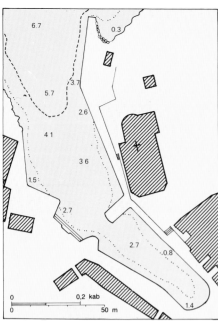

VELI LOŠINJ

kanal (Channel of Lošinj). The bridge opens every day at 9 am and at 6 pm; it is toll-free. Vertical clearance 2 m.

With strong winds, the current in the passage can attain a rate of up to 3 knots.

VELI LOŠINJ

(44°31'N; 014°30'E), village and a small harbour on the E coast of Lošinj, some 2.2 M southeast of the Privlaka passage. Nearby is Rovenska.

Approach. Landmarks: the church on the Kalvarija hillock (231 m), red column (red light) on the E entering point into the harbour.

Mooring. Along the landing ground at the entrance into the small harbour and on the stretch of the coast (four-point moor). The sirocco causes strong waves that flood the inner part of the harbour. It is not recommended to enter Rovenska during bora.

Warning. Mooring along the central, protruding part of the waterfront is prohibited.

Facilities. Post office, tourist office and several hotel establishments and shops, medical service, hospital for allergic diseases and

ČIKAT

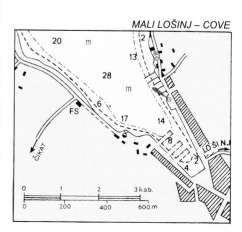

health resort during the winter. Provisions and water available; fuel in Mali Lošinj.

Sights. The round defense tower (1445), the churches of Sv Nikola (Romanesque, late Baroque and Classicism), Sv Antun opat (St Antony the Abbot, 1450, renovated in 1774), Sv Marija (1510, renovated in 1732).

ROVENSKA

(44°31'N; 014°30'E), cove and small harbour on the SE coast of Lošinj, separated by a small peninsula from the harbour of Veli Lošinj; forms part of the village of Veli Lošinj.

Approach. Care must be taken of the reef fringing the northernmost part of the breakwater – give it a berth of at least 100 m.

Mooring. Smaller yachts can moor by the mole in the harbour (depth 2 – 3.4 m). The cove is sheltered from all winds except the north-westerlies. With a strong north-easterly, waves splash over the breakwater, sometimes over the mole too.

The area between the islet of Orjule and Lošinj is a good all-round shelter except with SSE winds blowing. Smaller vessels can anchor W of the island of Male Orjule (between two islets) in a depth of 20 m; the Batelić shoal 0.25 M from the island of Male Orjule.

Facilities. Provisions and water available.

Car-ferry line: see Mali Lošinj.

On the islets of Vele and Male Orjule there is the »Orjule« nudist hotel complex.

BALVANIDA

(44°29'N; 014°30'E), cove on the SW coast of Lošinj, some 3 M southeast of Čikat.

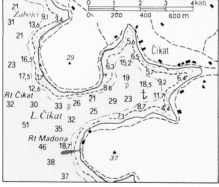

ČIKAT

Mooring. A good shelter for yachts, but SW and W winds send in a swell. Depth in the inner part of the anchorage 2–4 m.

KRIVICA

(44°29,8'N; 014°29,5'E) small cove, 2.5 M S of Madona point on the SE coast of Lošinj.

Mooring. Protected from all except SW winds. Depth 1–3 m on the eastern coast, 6–10 m on the north and south coast of the cove. Good anchorage ground for yachts (four-point moor).

Facilities. Restaurant in the cove of Balvanida (15 min on foot), shop in Veli Lošinj (1 hour walk).

ČIKAT LUKA

(44°32'N; 014°27'E), small cove and well-known tourist resort some 0.7 M west of Mali Lošinj.

Approach. Landmarks: the polygonal stone tower with a green gallery (green light) on Madona point, the chapel N of it and the buildings in a pinewood.

Mooring. The cove is protected from all winds except the westerlies which cause a considerable sea. Smaller vessels can anchor in the middle of the cove (depth 14—25 m) or moor along the pier (only for embarking or disembarking) in front of the hotel (depth 3.5 m) in the NE part of the bay.

Facilities. In the pine wood fringing the cove are several hotels and a large camp for motorists. Shopping for provisions in Mali Lošinj.

Warning. From May 1 until September 30 it is prohibited to moor, anchor and run speedboats at full speeds and waterski in the cove.

MALI LOŠINJ

(44°32'N; 014°28'E), town and harbour in the SE part of the bay of the same name; one of the best shelters in the northern Adriatic for ships and yachts of all sizes.

Approach. From W-landmarks: Mt Tovar and the ruins on it (opposite the entrance to the bay) and the church in the town; the islet of Zabodaski and the stone tower with a red top (red light) on it; the islet of Murtar and the white tower with a gallery in front of the house (white light) on it; the red tower on a white base (light with white and red sectors) on Torunza point; the green tower on a white base (green light) at the S end of Križ point (the N end of the islet of Koludarc); the light on Poljana point – a red tower with a latticed structure on a white base (red light); the red tower with a column and gallery (red

MALI LOŠINJ – COVE

light) on the NW end of the mole in Mali Lošinj.

Mali Lošinj is usually approached by passing between the islets of Zabodaski and Murtar. It can also be approached by going between Beli rat point and the N coast of the islet of Zabodaski (by night in the white sector of the light at Torunza point). Enter the bay by passing between the points of Torunza and Križ. When you sight the harbour light at Poljana point, shape course for the Mali Lošinj harbour; enter on the right side of the bay; from the harbour light at Poljana to the Privlaka bridge it is allowed to sail at 6 knots, further on at the smallest possible speed. The same holds when you leave the bay.

Warning. It is prohibited to go at speeds that cause waves on the stretch between Poljana point and the SE part of the harbour. Mooring is prohibited along the piers on the W coast of the bay on the stretch between the Most straits (Koludarc Island – Lošinj Island) and the petrol station. It is prohibited to approach the coast, anchor or moor in Kovcanja cove (NW part of the bay) and the E coast in Artaturi cove. Also, it is prohibited to anchor at the inner part of the harbour and along the coast up to 100 m from it.

Mooring. Moor alongside the mole and the quay or use the four-point moor in the E part of the harbour or alongside the three floating fingers in the S part of the harbour.

The mole is reserved for passenger ships and customs inspections.

Facilities. Port of entry, harbour master's branch office, customs, post office, hospital, chemist's, supermarket, bank, hotels, campsites, various repair shops, meteorological station; the head office of the »Lošinjska plovidba« shipping company; Maritime School Centre. Water from the hydrant on the waterfront, fuel from the petrol station in the NW part of the cove. Repairs are carried out by the »Lošinjska plovidba« boatyard and the workshops in the marina.

Car-ferry lines: Pula – Mali Lošinj – Zadar; Porozina – Brestova; Merag– Valbiska.

Local passenger lines: Mali Lošinj – Srakane Vele – Unije – Ilovik – Susak – Mali Lošinj; Mali Lošinj – Susak – Unije – Martinšćica – Cres – Rijeka; Pula – Mali Lošinj – Silba – Zadar (see Zadar); Mali Lošinj – Trst.

Mali Lošinj is the venue of the annual international competition in underwater fishing (January 1).

Sights. Mali Lošinj has many Late Baroque and Neo-Classical buildings; the churches of Sv Martin (at the cemetery, 16 C) and Porođenje Marijino (The Nativity of Our Lady, 1761, renovated in 1961), the Venetian Watch Tower (15 C).

MALI LOŠINJ MARINA
(44°32,4'N; 014°28,2'E) is situated on the NE side of Mali Lošinj harbour, between the quay for passenger ships and the Privlaka passage (W of the boatyard).

The marina has 130 sea-berths for vessels up to 20 m in length; there are 120 dry-berths, 60 of which are in hangars. Moor along the quay and the piers (four-point moor). Bigger yachts moor along the outer longitudinal pier (depth 10 m) bows-to

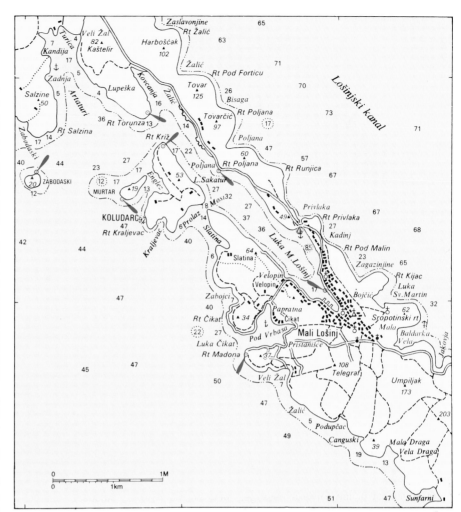

MALI LOŠINJ

the buoys. Smaller yachts can also moor along the inner piers and quay (four-point moor), where it is much less deep. The berths for yachts in transit are in the W part of the marina by the customs pier.

The facilities in the marina include reception office, restaurant, shop, toilets and showers, laundry, car park for 100 cars with trailers; electricity points (220 V) and hydrants on the piers and the quay; fuel at

MALI LOŠINJ

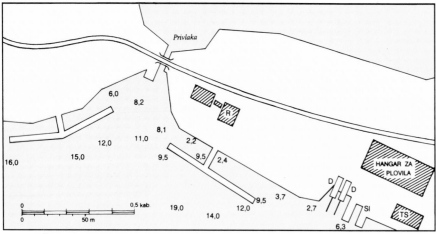

MALI LOŠINJ MARINA

SUSAK

the petrol station on the SW waterfront, on the road leading to Čikat (0.5 M).

Hoists (2 t), several travel-lifts (12 t), a slipway for vessels up to 30 tons. The »Lošinjska plovidba« boatyard carries out repairs of hulls and sails. The shops in the marina undertake repairs of wooden, metal and plastic parts and of marine engines, electrical work, battery charging, and painting of vessels.

ARTATURI
(44°34'N; 014°24,6'E), cove N of the entrance to the bay of Mali Lošinj.

Mooring. The cove is exposed to N winds. Smaller yachts can moor on the W coast of the cove (four-point moor) or anchor at the head of the cove; larger vessels can anchor in the middle of the cove in 17 m.

Facilities. In Turica (N end of the bay).

LISKI
(44°35,8'N; 014°23'E), cove on the W coast of Lošinj, some 5 M north of the entrance to the bay of Mali Lošinj, E of the point of the same name.

Approach. The house with a small tower can be easily identified. Approaching from S a wide berth should be given to Karbarus rock (shoal).

Mooring. The cove is protected from S winds but open to the bora. The anchorage is at the head of the cove (depth 3–6 m); good holding. Yachts can moor on the W pier and the bollard off the small harbour.

ISLAND OF UNIJE

UNIJE
(44°38'N; 014°15'E), village and small harbour on the W coast of the island of Unije.

Approach. Shape course for the belfry and chapel on the hill SE of the village and the red round tower with a column and gallery (red light) on the head of the breakwater.

By night approach in the red sector of the light on the breakwater. Školjić rock is in the red sector of the light on Vnetak point (a round stone tower above the attendant's house).

Mooring. The harbour is sheltered from the sirocco but exposed to SW and NW winds, which send in a big swell. Larger yachts can anchor SE of Školjić rock, some 500 m from the coast (depth 20–25 m); good holding. Yachts drawing up to 3 m can moor on the inner side of the breakwater, which is also used by passenger ships.

After the first heralds of W and NW winds leave the cove and go to Podkujna or Vognišća cove on the N coast of the island.

Facilities. Post office, medical service, several restaurants and a shop. Limited provisions and water.

Coastal passenger lines: see Mali Lošinj and Rijeka.

VRULJE
(44°37'N; 014°15'E), cove on the E coast of the island. It is well protected from the bora; small vessels anchor along the coast E from the Vnetak point.

MARAČOL
(44°38,6'N; 014°15,4'E), cove on the E side of the island of Unije.

Mooring. It is well protected from all winds, except the sirocco. Small vessels can moor at the head of the pier or in four--point berths (there are bollards on the mole). Anchorage lies SE from the pier (depth 7–9 m).

ISLAND OF SUSAK

DRAGOČA
(44°31'N; 014°18'E), cove in the NE part of the island, the small harbour of the village of Susak.

Approach. Landmarks: the Susak lighthouse, the belfry in the village, the factory chimney in the W part of the cove and the round green tower with a column and gallery (green light) on the breakwater.

UNIJE

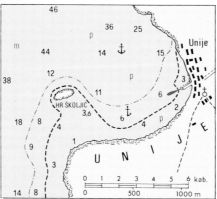

Dragoča is accessible only to smaller vessels (depth 2.5 m). When entering the harbour keep to the middle of the fairway, between the light on the head of the breakwater and the red round buoy marking the E edge of the remains of the old breakwater.

Mooring. The cove is protected from S and W wind; NE wind causes an unpleasant sea, while SE wind whips up a strong chop. Moor on both sides of the pier or along the masonry breakwater. With NE wind and the sirocco leave the moor at the head of the breakwater. Four-point anchoring in the SW part of the cove only offers full safety.

Facilities. Harbour master's branch office, post office, shop and medical service. Limited provisions and water (drinking water should be boiled). Fuel and other shopping in Mali Lošinj.

Coastal passenger lines: see Mali Lošinj and Rijeka.

Sights. Sv Nikola biskup church (St Nicholas the Bishop, 1770), next to it the ruins of the Benedictine monastery (11 C).

The island is interesting from the ethnographic point of view. The islanders live in isolation (endogamy) and their dialect, customs and costume differ from those found on the neighbouring islands.

PORAT
(44°31'N; 014°17'E), cove on the NW coast of Susak.

Mooring. The cove is sheltered from the bora; it is exposed to SW and NW winds and a longer stay is not advisable even in the summer (maestral).

Larger yachts can anchor some 300 m off the W coast of the island (depth 30–40 m), in line with the lighthouse (elevation 100 m, white flashes, visibility 23 M) on Mt Garba, bearing 210°.

ISLAND OF ILOVIK

ILOVIK
(44°28'N; 014°33'E), village and small harbour on the NW coast of the island of Ilovik. The middle fairway between the islands of Ilovik and Sv Petar (bearing NW–SE) is navigable for yachts drawing up to 6 m.

Approach. Landmarks: shape course for the white tower with a column and gallery (white light) on the islet of Sv Petar and the belfry of the church in Ilovik.

Mooring. The harbour is sheltered from all winds; a strong sirocco sends in an unpleasant sea. The best anchorage for smaller yachts is in the middle of the fairway, S of the small church on Sv Petar, stern-to NE; several bollards. Moor along the head of the pier (60 m long, depth 3.5 m) off the village; smaller vessels can moor along the pier in the E part of the harbour.

Facilities. Post office. Limited provisions and water.

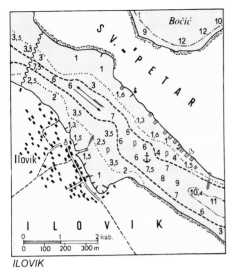

ILOVIK

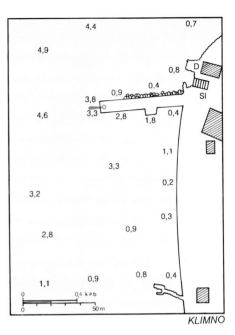

KLIMNO

Coastal passenger lines: Ilovik – Premuda – Silba – Olib – Zadar, Ilovik – Mali Lošinj.

Sights. The ruins of a large prehistoric fortification at Straža. On the islet of Sv Petar are the ruins of a Roman villa rustica and of the walls of the Benedictine monastery St Petrus in Nembis (11 C); also a defence tower, built in 1597 against the Uskoks (1597).

ISLAND OF KRK

SOLINE

(45°09'N; 014°38'E), bay on the NE coast of the island; the largest village and harbour is Klimno, situated on the S coast of the bay. The bay is sheltered from all winds and affords a safe anchorage for smaller vessels.

Approach. Landmarks: the stone tower with a red top (red light) on Glavati point; the round red tower with a column (red light) above the white base on Crni rock (some 0.3 M off the harbour), and the red column (red light) on the head of the breakwater of the harbour of Klimno. When entering the bay keep as near as the SE coast to avoid Solinji reef. Care must also be taken of Crni rock (light), Veli Školjić rock and of the shoal (1.8 m) E of this rock.

Mooring. Yachts drawing up to 2 m can moor on the inner side of the breakwater of the harbour of Klimno or along the mole of the village of Čižići on the W side. The NE part of the bay affords good anchorage in 5–6 m and W of the harbour of Klimno (the anchorage of the Punat marina). The cove and the harbour of Klimno are well protected from all winds.

Facilities. Provisions in a local shop, limited water. Repairs and dockage over the

winter at the local boatyard and at Punat marina (its own facilities).

KLIMNO

(45°09,4'N; 014°37,2'E), village and small port in the cove of Soline on the coast of the island of Krk, max. depth 3,5 m. Dependence of Marina Punat, 50 berths for yachts up to 25 m length.

Approach. When entering the bay one has to pay attention to Solinji reef in the middle. It is best to keep to the south and then continue to NW in order to avoid the Crni shallow.

Mooring. On the inner side of the breakwater berths are protected from all winds. Anchorage in the NE part of the bay Soline (depth 5–6 m).

Facilities. Restaurant, coffee-bar, shop, harbour master's branch office (8 km).

Service: Crane (5 t), slipway, technical service.

STIPANJA

(45°09'N; 014°40'E), cove and anchorage on the E coast of Krk. The small harbour and village of Šilo is situated at the head of the cove.

Approach. The white octagonal tower (white light) at the root of Šilo point and the green tower with a column and gallery (green light) at the head of the breakwater in the small harbour of Šilo are conspicuous. Entering the cove take care of the shoal off Šilo point; when mooring take care of the protruding underwater part of the breakwater.

Mooring. The cove is well sheltered from all winds. Smaller yachts can moor along the inner side of the breakwater of the harbour of Šilo (depth 2.5 m) or along the quay (four-point moor); a part of the breakwater is reserved for car-ferries. There is a good anchorage S of the light on Šilo point and in front of the small harbour of Šilo; care must be taken of the underwater cable.

Facilities. In the harbour of Šilo: harbour master's branch office, post office, tourist office (accommodation in private houses), shops and restaurants. Provisions in a local shop; fuel in Crikvenica.

Repairs on smaller yachts and boats and marine engines, off-season dockage and maintenance services.

Sights. Dobrinj with the church of Sv Stjepan Prvomučenik (St Stephen the

Martyr, built in 1100, renovated in 1903, the embroidered antependium depicting the Coronation of the Virgin, 14 C) and the Ethnographic Museum – 5 km by road.

VRBNIK

(45°05'N; 014°41'E), village and small harbour on the E coast of Krk in Vinodolski kanal.

Approach. The houses and the church belfry on the hill (49 m) and the red tower with a column and gallery (red light) on the head of the breakwater can be identified.

Mooring. The harbour is sheltered from all winds, but the entrance to the harbour is exposed to the bora, which makes approach difficult and dangerous with the bora blowing. Smaller yachts can moor on the inner side of the breakwater (depth 2 m) and along the head of the mole (depth up to 4 m). The inner part of the harbour is occupied by fishing boats.

Facilities. Post office, shops, hotel, medical service. Provisions and other shopping in local shops; mains water supply.

Sights. The remnants of the medieval town wall with towers, Uznesenje Marijino church (the Assumption, 15/16 C, renovat-

VRBNIK

VRBNIK

65

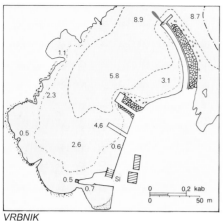

VRBNIK

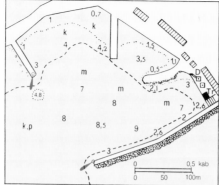

BAŠKA

ed in 1966), Sv Ivan church (St John, 15 C, at the cemetery), Dinko Vitezić's Library (15.000 volumes, illuminated manuscripts, incunabulae).

BAŠKA

(44°58'N; 014°46'E), village, tourist resort and small harbour in the N part of Baš-čanska Draga.

Approach. Landmarks: the coast lights in Senjska vrata: the white tower with a gallery (white light) in front of the house on Stražica point (Prvić Island); the red tower (red light) on Škuljica point (Krk Island); the ruins on Kričin point (E of the harbour); the belfry in the town; the quadrangular tower with a green top (green light) on the head of the breakwater; the red tower with a column and gallery (red light) on the head of the pier.

Mooring. Smaller vessels can moor along the waterfront; the root of the breakwater is reserved for passenger ships and a carferry. Larger vessels can anchor some 400 m off the breakwater bearing SW (depth 20–30 m); good holding. The inner harbour (depth 1.5–3 m) is sheltered from all winds; the anchorage is exposed to the bora and SE winds and is not recommended for a longer stay.

NE of Baška there are Vela luka and Mala luka coves, and SE there is Bracol cove. In Vela luka there is a landing ground (30 m long, 2 m deep); it is well protected from the sirocco and from the bora; during the stormy bora it is recommended to use a four-point moor along the E coast. In Mala luka there is a natural coast, but it is a safe shelter from all winds. In Bracol cove there is a landing ground for small vessels; it is well protected from all winds.

Facilities. Harbour master's branch office, post office, several shops, restaurants, hotels, travel agency, bank, campsite, medical service, chemist's.

Water from a hydrant, provisions in the village. The harbour has two small slipways and a crane (0.8 t).

Car-ferry line: Baška – Senj and Baška – Lopar (Island of Rab).

Sights. Remains and excavations of the Roman settlement and fortifications; the churches of Sv Ivan (St John, early Romanesque), Sv Trojica (Holy Trinity, 1723), and Sv Marko (St Mark, Romanesque); Town Museum (ethnographic and maritime collections). – Jurandvor: a former Benedictine monastery with Sv Lucija church (St Lucia), about 1100, the original site of the Baščanska ploča, the oldest Glagolitic inscription (on a stone tablet, dating back to

ca. 1100) – 2 km by road. Further on there is Baščanska Draga – village and a peasant farm – 4.5 km by road.

Baška is the venue of two traditional events taking place in August: Fishermen's Day (Dan ribara) and the Traditional Baška Wedding (Baščanski starinski pir).

STARA BAŠKA

(44°57,5'N; 014°41'E), cove and small harbour on the SW coast of the island of Krk.

Approach. Landmarks: the village and a church.

Mooring. At the head of a small landing ground (depth 2.5–3.7 m); four-point moor, anchoring towards NE and with a stern at the pier or the mainland. Good anchorage at the Klobučac point (not safe during SW and W winds). The cove is a good shelter from the bora; the harbour is protected from the sirocco.

PUNAT

(45°01'N; 014°37'E), town and harbour in the large but shallow cove of Puntarska draga in the NE part of the Krk Bay. A popular seaside resort.

Approach. Landmarks: the white tower with a column and gallery (white light) in front of the small chapel at the E entrance point of Pod Stražicu; three round green towers (green lights) on concrete bases in the sea and three conical stone marks; the green tower with a column and gallery (green light) on the mole.

When entering, pass between the conical stone marks and the green lights, leaving the lights to the starboard (E) at least 10 m. When entering by day, turn to the harbour of Punat after passing the N green mark (light) by about 70 m, and by night when you see the green harbour light on the mole. Maximum speed 4 knots.

Mooring. The harbour is well sheltered from all winds. Smaller vessels can moor along the quay in the harbour or anchor off the town and N of the islet of Košljun (a safe

BAŠKA

PUNAT

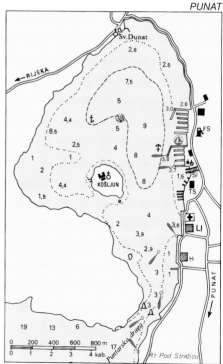

ST. DUNAT, NEAR PUNAT

anchorage in stormy winds from NW); care should be taken of an underwater cable.

Facilities. Harbour master's branch office, post office, several hotels and restaurants, campsite, shops and medical service, chemist's. Good shopping for provisions; water from the hydrant on the quay. Repairs carried out in the »Punat« boatyard and in the marina.

Sights. Sv Trojica church (Holy Trinity, 1773, renovated in 1934). The old olive mill (Stari toš, 18 C). – The islet of Košljun: the Franciscan monastery (formerly an early Romanesque Benedictine monastery, the cloister, defense tower, St Bernardine's chapel); Navještenje Marijino church (Annunciation, 1523, fine collection of sacral art); a collection of stone monuments, ethnographic collection and old library with rare items.

KRK

PUNAT

PUNAT MARINA

(45°01,3'N; 014°37,6'E), is situated on the E coast of Puntarska draga cove, N of the town of Punat, adjoining the »Punat« boatyard.

Capacity: 860 moorings for vessels up to 25 m are laid out along the quay; there are dry-berths for 300 vessels.

The marina is open the year round.

It has reception office, money-exchange, self-service shop, shop, ship chandler's shop, snack-bar, two restaurants and an inn; skipper's club (restaurant, yacht club, medical service, sailing school); a parking lot for 500 cars. The chemist's is in the town of Krk (8 km); toilets and showers with hot water.

Tourist office is 200 m away. Custom-house is at the airport (30 km). A camp- site for motorists is nearby; nudist camp (5 km). Fuel available in Krk (2 km).

Hoists (5 and 10 t), slipway (for vessels up to 30 t), several travel-lifts; services (security, cleaning, etc.) provided; yacht services;

PUNAT MARINA

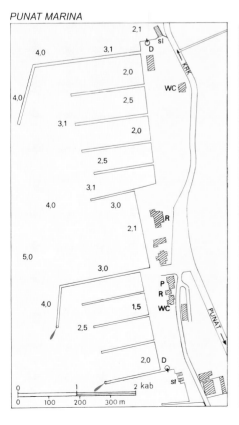

KRK

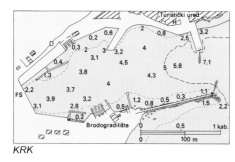

KRK

hull repairs (wood, plastic, metal); regular hull inspection; repair, maintenance and installation of marine engines, electrical installations and battery charging; special varnishing shop.

KRK

(45°10,6'N; 014°34,5'E), town and harbour in the NW part of Krčki zaljev (Krk Bay).

Approach. Landmarks: the church with the belfry surmounted by a statue; the quadran-

gular red brick tower (red light) on the head of the breakwater; the round white tower with a column (green light) on the head of the E breakwater.

Mooring. The harbour is open to the sirocco and partly protected from the bora (E-ENE); it offers very good shelter in all other winds. The safest mooring during the sirocco (waves splash over the breakwater) for larger vessels is on the inner side of the E mole (depth 3.5–4.0 m), which is otherwise reserved for ships of the coastal passengers lines, and for smaller vessels deeper in the harbour. The best mooring during the bora is along the quay between the two moles (four-point moor). The breakwater is not accessible because of shoals and scattered stones.

Facilities. Harbour master's branch office, post office, medical service, chemist's, museum, travel agency, several hotels, campsite, shops; shipyard.

Water from the hydrant at the entrance mole; fuel in the harbour at the small mole and in the W part of the harbour.

The »Krk« d.d. shipyard carries out general repairs including diesel engine repairs; hauling-out service.

Car-ferry lines: Valbiska – Merag; Baška – Lopar (island of Rab).

Sights. Uznesenje Marijino Cathedral [The Assumption of Our Lady, 12 C, built on the site of the Roman thermae (1 C) which was succeeded by an early Christian basilica (5/6 C); an art collection with items ranging from Classical times to the Baroque; Gothic chapel of the Frankopan family], the Bishop's Palace with an art collection, the two-storey basilica of Sv Kirin (St Quirinus, Romanesque, fragments of wall paintings), the churches of Gospa od Zdravlja (Our Lady of Salvation, Early Romanesque, 12 C), and Sv Franjo (St Francis, 1290); the Canon's House (11 C); Kotter House with Romanesque windows, well-preserved town walls (from 11 C onwards) with Kamplin Tower (1191), fort, bastions (15/16 C) and a round tower; Roman cemetery.

VALBISKA

(45°01'N; 014°30'E), cove on the NW coast of Krk Island, 3.4 M west of the harbour of Krk. The hillsides precipitate steeply into the bay.

Approach. Landmarks: the white tower with a column and gallery (green light) on Sv Mikula point, the surfaced road at the root of the cove and the red tower with a column and gallery (red light) on the head of the ferry pier.

Mooring. The cove is exposed to SW winds but is sheltered from NE and SE winds. The bora is violent and blows in gusts.

Car-ferry line: Valbiska – Merag (island of Cres).

TORKUL

(45°03'N; 014°28,2'E), cove in Srednja vrata on the SW coast of Krk, some 2.5 M southeast of the coast light on Manganel point.

Approach. Landmark: the ruins of the tall narrow building at the N entrance point.

Mooring. The cove is sheltered from all winds and affords a good berth to yachts drawing up to 1.30 m. With the bora blowing, go stern-to the waterfront, bows-to NE.

ČAVLENA

(45°06'N; 014°28'E), cove 4 M south of Malinska at the entrance to Srednja vrata straits, sheltered from the bora and easterlies. The anchorage is safe for vessels of all sizes in depth of up to 40 m. Smaller vessels can anchor off the E coast.

MALINSKA

(45°08'N; 014°32'E), village and seaside resort on the W coast of Krk.

Approach. Landmarks: the green spar surmounted by a cone marking the shoal on the SW side of the entrance should be left to starboard; the red tower with a column and gallery (red light) on the head of the mole; the white tower with a column and gallery (red light) in front of the »Haludovo« hotel complex.

Mooring. The harbour is exposed to NW winds, which cause a swell in it; in the summer they are usually shortlasting storms.

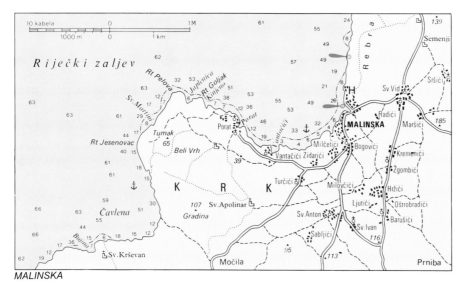

MALINSKA

MALINSKA

Smaller vessels can moor on both sides of the pier and along the mole in the S part of the harbour and the quay E of the pier (depth 2 m).

About 300 m NW of the pier is a 100 m long breakwater. The end of the breakwater is marked by a red buoy. The best anchorage is about 0.5 M west-southwest of the harbour (depth 25–45 m).

Facilities. Harbour master's branch office, post office, several hotels and restaurants, shops, tourist office, medical service, chemist's.

Water from the hydrant on the E waterfront; fuel in the harbour.

In the immediate vicinity of the harbour is the »Haludovo« hotel complex with a small harbour for smaller vessels (a hoist and slipways). It is used mainly by hotel guests.

There is a slipway and a hoist for smaller vessels. The boatyard makes and repairs the wood panelling on smaller yachts and speedboats.

Sights in the neighbouring villages. Porat – the Franciscan monastery (15 C) with Sv Marija Magdalena church. Dubašnica – the belfry of a dilapidated church (1618). Bogovići – the chapel of Majka Božja Karmelska (Our Lady of Carmel, 1644). Zgombići – Sv Andrija church (St Andrew, 15 C). Strilčići – the ruins of Sv Nikola church (St Nicholas, Gothic).

BELI KAMIK

(45°10'N; 014°32'E), anchorage some 3 M north of Malinska; the village of Njivice.

Approach. Shape course for the green round tower with a column and gallery (green light) on the head of the pier in Njivice and the hotel buildings there.

Mooring. The anchorage is sheltered from the bora and the sirocco, but is open to SW and NW winds. Larger yachts can anchor N and W of Njivice in 30–40 m. With the bora and the sirocco blowing, a safe anchorage for smaller vessels is in the harbour of Kijac, S of Beli Kamik anchorage; in fine weather vessels can moor along the inner side of the breakwater in Njivice.

Facilities. Post office, hotels and other facilities in Njivice. Provisions in local shops; water from the hydrant on the waterfront.

OMIŠALJ

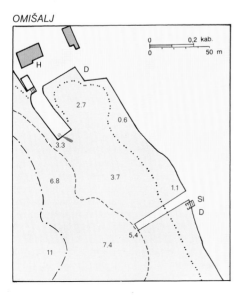

OMIŠALJ

(45°13'N; 014°33'E), town and small harbour on the N coast of Krk Island, in the bay of Omišalj.

Warning. On the W coast of the bay is the oil unloading terminal; vessels are not allowed to come nearer than 500 m to the coast. The sea area around Sapan cove is the industrial zone of the harbour of the INA petroleum company.

Approach. From W - landmarks: the large white oil containers on Tenka peninsula; some 1.5 M northwest of Kijac point is the light buoy with red and white stripes (white light); the round red tower (red light) on Kijac point; several light buoys mark the fairway for tankers and a landing-light in Omišalj marks the approach course 151°; the white tower with the column and gallery (red light) on the head of the pier; the hotel near the pier and the water-supply tower.

Mooring. Only smaller yachts (draught up to 3 m) can moor along the pier in the harbour and the moles in the small harbour SE of the pier. In front of the »Jadran« hotel there is a pier (50 m, depth 3.5 m).

Facilities. Harbour master's branch office, post office, medical service, shops. Provisions, water from the main. Fuel at the pump some 2 km from the waterfront. Off-season dockage facilities. Minor repairs to wooden boats and speedboats can be undertaken. Crane (5 t).

Omišalj is the venue of the »Stomarina« Festival (August 15), the day of all seagoing vessels.

Sights. The town has a Gothic street layout. The churches of Marijino Uznesenje (Assumption of Our Lady, built before 1405, later additions, three-nave Romanesque

RAB, CHOIRSTALLS

basilica), Sv Jelena (St Helena, 1470), Sv Antun (St Anthony, Romanesque) and Sv Ivan (St John, 1442); the ruins of the Rector's palace (14/15 C), the Loggia (1470), Pančirov House (Gothic). In Sepen cove the ruins of Fulfinium (Roman, 1–3 C) with a basilica (6 C).

ISLAND OF RAB

RAB

(44°45'N; 014°46'E), town and harbour on the island of the same name.

Approach. Landmarks: the town walls and four belfries; the round green tower with a gallery (green light) on a concrete base on Frkanj shoal; the quadrangular stone tower with a red top (red light) on Frkanj point; the round red tower on Sv Ante point (red light) and the multi-storey tower with a green top-

RAB (TOWN AND MARINA)

RAB

The marina has 150 berths for yachts drawing up to 5 m and up to 18 m in length; there are dry-berths only for yachts that are being repaired or overhauled. Water and electricity hook-ups at the berths. The marina has a meteorological service (warning and alarm sounding, weather reports and other relevant information).

It has reception office, restaurant, shop, recreation ground, toilets and showers with hot water, parking lot, fuel and gas pump.

Hoist (5 t); slipway; repairs.

SVETA MARA

(44°47'N; 014°40'E), cove some 0.7 M east-southeast of Donja punta point (white coast light) on the SW coast of Rab.

Approach. Landmarks: the small white house on the hill above the ruins of the chapel on the E coast of the cove. The round white tower (white light) on Donja punta point.

Mooring. The cove affords good shelter for smaller yachts from the bora and the sirocco. Smaller yachts can anchor in the middle of the cove, securing stern-to the bollards cut out in the rock.

KAMPORSKA DRAGA

(44°47'N; 014°42'E), cove E of Kalifront point on the NW coast of island of Rab.

Approach. Maman islet, which separates the cove from the neighbouring Supetarska Draga, can be easily identified.

Mooring. Because of the shoals fringing the NE and SW coast of the cove and off the islet of Maman, Kamporska draga does not afford good anchorage. It is exposed to the north-westerlies which cause a considerable sea; the bora and the sirocco are strong but do not create a sea. Smaller vessels can anchor S of Kaštelina point securing stern-to the bollards on the coast.

Facilities. Supermarket in the W part of the village of Ružići.

Sights. Sv Eufemija church (1237) with the Franciscan monastery (1446, library, historical collection, collection of stone monuments) and Sv Bernardin church (1458, later reconstructed in the Baroque style). Nearby the ruins there is a Roman villa rustica. Memorial cemetery, built in 1950–55 on the site of a former Nazi concentration camp (1942–43).

SUPETARSKA DRAGA

(44°48'N; 014°42'E), town, cove and marina in the NW part of Rab, some 2.5 M southeast of Sorinj point.

Approach. Care should be taken of the reef some 50 m N of the islet of Sridnjak, SW of the entrance to the cove. The reef is visible only at low tide and a choppy sea; it is marked by a concrete column.

Mooring. The cove is exposed to N and NW winds, the bora and the sirocco are violent in it but do not cause a sea and are not dangerous for yachts lying at anchor. The best anchorage for smaller yachts (sheltered from NW winds) is in the middle of Dumići cove (S of the islet of Sajlovac). Larger yachts can anchor in the middle of Supetarska Draga (depth 21–28 m).

Sights. The disused Benedictine monastery of St Peter, established in 1059, abandoned in 16 C. Sv Petar church dating from the foundation period.

mark on the islet of Tunera (green light); the white tower with a column and gallery (white light) on Donji point (the islet of Dolin).

Warning. Off the entrance to the outer part of the harbour are two shoals: Vela sika (3.8 m) and Frkanj. Do not exceed 3 knots when entering or leaving the harbour.

Mooring. The inner harbour is sheltered from all winds except the south-easterlies. The sirocco causes a strong swell in the harbour with waves flooding part of the W waterfront. It is therefore recommended for yachts to go to the Rab marina. The best anchorage for larger yachts is in the nearby Sveta Fumija cove (depth 4–28 m) and NW of Tunera islet at the entrance to the harbour.

Facilities. Harbour master's branch office, post office, several hotels and restaurants, various shops, medical service and chemist's. There is a naturist hotel complex on Frkanj peninsula. Provisions are available in shops. Water from a hydrant, fuel from the pump in the Rab marina.

Several boatyards at Banjol make and repair boats, speedboats and small wooden and plastic yachts. The mechanics at Banjol carry out repairs of outboard engines.

Car-ferry lines: Lopar – Baška (Island of Krk) and Mišnjak – Jablanac (mainland).

Sights. The town wall (12/13 C, later reinforced, pulled down in part at the beginning of 20 C), with the Town Tower; Rector's Palace (13 C, later reconstructions), the Loggia (1509), Sv Marija Velika cathedral (St Mary the Great, 1177, renovated in 1278 and 1483, ciborium about 1500, choir stalls 1455, with the parish art collection, the belfry from 1181); the ruins of Sv Ivan church (St John, 10/11 C, with the belfry from 12 C); the churches of Sv Andrija (St Andrew, Romanesque, reconstructed in the Renaissance) and Sv Justina (1573–1578); the residences of the families Crnota (15 C), Cassio (Gothic), Dominis-Nimira (15/16 C), Nimira (16 C, with a portal), Tudorin, Kukulić and Marčić-Galzigna. Komrčar Park, landscaped at the end of 19 C, with Sv Franjo church (St Francis, 1490). In Trg Slobode square stands the Tree of Freedom (Stablo slobode) – a natural memorial. In the NW part of the island is Dundo Wood – a nature reserve.

RAB MARINA (ACI)

(44°45,4'N; 014°46'E) is situated on the E side of the inner harbour, directly behind the breakwater, in the SE part of the harbour. It is sheltered from all winds except the southerlies by the breakwater; SE winds cause a strong slop (especially dangerous in the winter) and raises the sea level by up to 1 m; it can break the securing ropes of vessels and floating fingers.

PIČULJAN

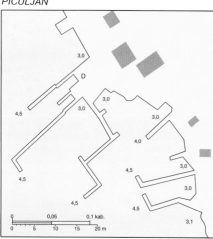

70

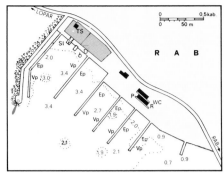

SUPETARSKA DRAGA MARINA

SUPETARSKA DRAGA MARINA (ACI)

(44°48,2'N; 014°43,8'E) is situated on the NE coast of the cove of the same name.

The following landmarks are conspicuous: the white towers (white light) on Kaliront point and Krištofor point; the red tower with a column and gallery (red light) on the head of the breakwater in the marina; the low buildings of the workshops and the main office of the marina. The marina is situated at the edge of a wood and olive groves.

It is protected from NW winds by a 160 m long breakwater.

Capacity: 275 berths along the breakwater and the floating fingers for yachts up to 20 m long. There are 150 dry-berths. Water, electricity and telephone hook-ups at the berths. The shallow water along the waterfront, built at an incline from piled up rocks, increases rapidly in depth 10–25 m in the middle of the cove.

The marina is open the year round. The meteorological service in the marina provides regular weather reports (bulletins and information).

It has reception office, restaurant (tavern), shop, toilets and showers with hot water; laundry; car park; rental of sports equipment; water, electricity and telephone hook-ups. Ample opportunity for water sports.

Fuel at the pump in the Rab marina. Other shopping in the shops in the marina and in the town of Rab.

Hoist (10 t) and a slipway; general repairs.

LOPAR

(44°50'N; 015°43'E), town and small bay on the N coast of the island of Rab.

SAN MARINO MARINA

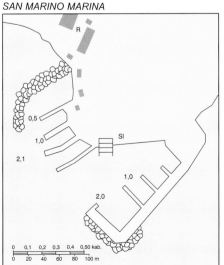

SUPETARSKA DRAGA MARINA

Approach. Shape course for the white tower (white light) on Sorinj point; the belfry of Sv Marija (St Mary) church on the hill above the town; the yellow building next to the pier; the green tower with a column and gallery (green light) on the head of the pier.

Care should be taken of the shoals of Pregiba and Vela sika (cylindrical yellow--black-yellow buoy, 2 cones point to point) in the N part of the bay, W of Stojan point.

The bay is open to NW winds, which cause a sea. The bora and the sirocco are strong.

Mooring. Smaller yachts moor at the head and the S side of the pier in front of the hotel (alongside them or by using the four-point moor); the N and outer sides of the pier are reserved for the ferry. The anchorage for smaller vessels, safe only with the bora, is in Makućina cove in the SW part of Loparski zaljev (Bay of Lopar).

In the San Marino tourist village on the NE side of Lopar there is a small harbour for yachts up to 10 m.

Facilities. Post office and medical service. Provisions and water (from cisterns) available.

Car-ferry line: Lopar – Senj and Lopar – Baška.

Sights. Ruins of walls dating back to the ancient times.

SAN MARINO MARINA

SENJ HARBOUR MASTER'S OFFICE AREA

SENJ

JABLANAC	KARLOBAG	NOVALJA	SENJ	SV. JURAJ	
	14	20	17	13	JABLANAC
		30	31	27	KARLOBAG
			35	31	**NOVALJA**
				4	SENJ
DISTANCES OF PORTS					SV. JURAJ

HARBOURS ON THE COAST

SENJ

(44°59,4'N; 014°54'E), town and harbour in Velebitski kanal.

Approach. Landmarks: quadrangular Fort Nehaj on the hill S of the town, the octagonal stone tower with a white light on the head of the S breakwater Marija Art and the octagonal stone tower with a red light on the head of N breakwater (Sv Ambrož); the white tower with a green light on the head of the Sv Nikola mole in the harbour and the shoal (a pile of stones) off the S breakwater.

Some 500 m NE of the harbour is an underwater pipeline (about 35 m off the waterfront).

Mooring. The harbour is open to the NW; the most dangerous wind is the bora which most frequently blows from ENE and often reaches gale-force. It comes very suddenly and therefore the harbour is not safe. The bora is heralded by a clear blue sky above the harbour and thick white clouds with a clearly outlined horizontal edge over the Velebit Mountains. Sometimes tiny clouds separate from the white cloud and are carried towards SW by the bora.

The best mooring is by the quay between the two moles. When mooring by the Marija Art breakwater, care should be taken of the underwater bank. The best mooring in the sirocco is by the Sv Nikola mole. Other well-sheltered anchorages in the vicinity are Spasovac (1 M south) and Jelena (1 M north).

Facilities. Senj is a permanent port of entry with customs, harbour master's branch

SENJ, NEHAJ CASTLE

office, post office, hospital, medical service, chemist's, hotel, several restaurants and shops.

Water from the hydrant on the mole of Sv Nikola; good shopping for provisions; fuel at the petrol pump some 100 m N of the harbour.

Sights. Remains of the town wall (15–16 C) with Vela Vrata (Big Gate, 1779) and Šabac Tower, Sv Marija cathedral (St Mary, 11 C, reconstructed in 18 C, renovated 1947), the belfry of Sv Franjo church (St Francis, built in 1558, destroyed in a bombing raid in WW II), Kaštel (Fort, 1340, later reconstructed), the Vukasović mansion (15 C, now the Town Museum), Kaštel Nehaj (Nehaj Castle, 1558, renovated in 1966–75, now part of the Town Museum).

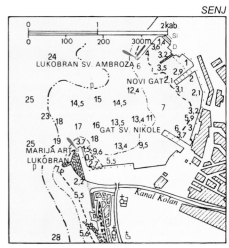
SENJ

SVETI JURAJ

(44°56'N; 014°55'E), small village and harbour on the coast of Velebitski kanal, some 4 M south of Senj.

Approach. The rocky islet of Lisac and the quadrangular tower with a red column (red light) on the head of the L-shaped mole (visible from the NW quadrant) can be easily identified.

Warning. Care should be taken of the Sika od Malina shoal, some 1.3 M south of the harbour (depth 2 m). At the N edge of the shoal there is a column with black and red bands surmounted by two spheres. It is not possible to navigate between the islet of Lisac and the mainland.

Entering the harbour during a strong bora is dangerous.

Mooring. The harbour is exposed to SW and NW wind; it is sheltered from the sirocco. The bora is very strong but does not cause a sea in the harbour. Westerlies can cause dangerous waves. Yachts can moor alongside the L-shaped mole or use the four-point moor closer to the root of the mole.

Facilities. Harbour master's branch office and post office, a hotel, several restaurants and various shops selling food and other provisions. Water from the waterworks.

LUKOVO (OTOČKO)

(44°51,3'N; 015°53,6'E), village and small harbour in Velebitski kanal.

Approach. Landmarks: the whitish Malta point, the church in the village, the quadrangular stone tower (white light) on Malta point, the red tower with a column and a gallery (red light) on the head of the breakwater.

Mooring. The cove is exposed to the bora and sheltered from SE and SW wind. The bora is violent and blows in gusts. The small harbour inside the harbour offers shelter from all winds. Small yachts can moor on the inner side of the breakwater (alongside it or using the four-point moor). Good anchorage some 200 m NW of the church in the harbour.

Facilities. Post office, tourist office, campsite and shop selling food and other goods. Water from the waterworks.

STARIGRAD

(44°48'N; 014°53'E), village and small harbour in Velebitski kanal, some 3.5 M south of Lukovo harbour.

Approach. Landmarks: the chapel N of the harbour, the church in the harbour and the houses in the village.

Mooring. The harbour is only partly sheltered from the main winds, i.e. the bora and the sirocco, and is exposed to SW and NW winds. Yachts can moor alongside the mole (depth 3–4.5 m) or use the four-point moor alongside the quay N of the mole.

Facilities. Post office. Limited provisions.

VELA STINICA

(44°43,5'N; 014°54'E), cove 1 M north of Jablanac; it consists of two small coves.

Approach. Landmarks: the columns of the cable car and the buildings of the former saw mill.

Mooring. The cove is sheltered from all winds. In the N and S cove are bollards for mooring. With the bora the top of the N offers safe anchorage in a depth of 15–20 m.

Provisions in the tourist village.

STARIGRAD

MALA STINICA

(44°43,1'N; 014°53,6'E), small cove S of Vela Stinica.

Approach. A high chimney and several houses can be easily seen.

Mooring. Use the four-point moor off the quay S of the mole or moor alongside the small mole (depth 3–3.9 m). The S part of the cove is a safe anchorage during the sirocco.

Facilities. Provisions in the shop, water from the cistern.

JABLANAC

(44°42,6'N; 014°54'E), village and harbour in the narrowest part of Velebitski kanal.

Approach. Landmarks: several hotel buildings on the NW side of the entrance to the harbour; the red quadrangular tower with a red column (red light) on Gradić point and the chapel on the waterfront; the small white house (white light) on Štokić point; the green tower with a column and gallery (green light) on the S end of the mole.

When entering the harbour care should be taken of the shoal (3.2 m) in the SW part of the harbour.

Mooring. The harbour is sheltered from all winds but the bora sends in a considerable sea. Small yachts can moor alongside the S quay (depth about 3 m) or alongside the small mole (four-point moor). The outer end of the mole is reserved for the ferry.

Facilities. Harbour master's branch office, post office, medical service, three hotels and a hostel. Provisions are available in the local shops. Water from the hydrant on the mole.

Car-ferry line: Jablanac – Mišnjak (Rab).

PRIZNA

(44°36'N; 014°58,3'E), cove and village, some 6.5 M northwest of Karlobag.

Approach. Landmarks: car-ferry landing ground (harbour light); the church on the waterfront, the conical stone structure with black and red stripes surmounted by two black spheres, on Prizna shoal (flashing white light) NW of the cove (the reefs on the shoal are visible during low tide).

Mooring. The cove is well sheltered from the sirocco; the bora is strong and causes a

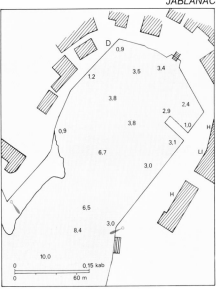

JABLANAC

JABLANAC

swell. Car-ferry landing ground with 2 berths. There is no place to moor boats (yachts).

Car-ferry line: Prizna – Žigljen (Island of Pag).

KARLOBAG

(44°31,5'N; 015°04,6'E), small town and small harbour in the middle part of Velebitski kanal.

Approach. Landmarks: the large hotel complex NW of the harbour, the belfry next to the church, the green tower with a column and gallery (green light) on the head of the S breakwater. When entering the har-

bour, take care of the stone blocks scattered up to 15 m off the head of the S breakwater.

Mooring. The harbour is only partly sheltered from the bora and the sirocco and is not recommended for a longer stay. Small yachts can moor on both sides of the mole or alongside the N breakwater, next to the quay reserved for the Pag ferry. Because of reefs and insufficient depth, the S breakwater cannot be used for mooring. Small yachts can moor in the small harbour in the SE part of the harbour. Bigger yachts can anchor off the harbour (depth 30–40 m) and in Baška Draga cove (0.4 M southeast of the harbour) – sheltered from the bora. On

the coast there are two berths for vessels up to 24 m long and up to 4.5 m of draught.

Facilities. Harbour master's branch office, post office, tourist office, several hotels and restaurants, shops, medical service and a chemist's. Water from the hydrant on the waterfront; fuel at the petrol station on the Adriatic highway (some 300 m from the harbour); provisions and other shopping in local shops.

Car-ferry line: Karlobag – Pag.

ISLAND OF PAG

STARA NOVALJA

(44°36'N; 014°52'E), village in the small bay of the same name on the NE coast of the island of Pag.

Approach. Landmarks: the quadrangular white tower on a base (white light) on the N entrance of Deda point, the hill of Veli vrh (131 m) opposite Deda point and the buildings on the NE coast of the bay.

Mooring. The bay is sheltered from the bora and the sirocco. The sea in it is not dangerous. Vessels drawing up to 3.5 m can moor on the end side of the L-shaped mole just off the village. The best anchorage for larger vessels is S of Drljanda cove, NW of Stara Novalja (depth 27–38 m). A good anchorage for smaller vessels is in the NW part of Drljanda cove, E of the entrance to the cove. It is a good shelter from the bora and the sirocco. With the bora blowing, anchor bows-to SW and secure to the coast bearing NE. The mole in Drljanda cove is reserved for the car-ferry.

Car-ferry line: Stara Novalja (only during the storm) – Prizna (mainland).

Sights. Ruins of walls dating from ancient times, a necropolis dating from the late Roman period, ruins of the Pre-Romanesque church of Sv Križ (Holy Cross).

CASKA

(44°33'N; 014°56'E), cove and village in the NW part of Paški zaljev (Bay of Pag). A very good anchorage sheltered from the bora. The best anchorage for larger yachts is in Zrće cove, some 0.5 M southeast of the village of Caska (depth 17 m). Smaller yachts can anchor closer to the innermost part of the cove, off the village.

Facilities. Limited provisions.

Sights. On the site of the Roman military camp Cissa: remnants of buildings, of a road

NOVALJA

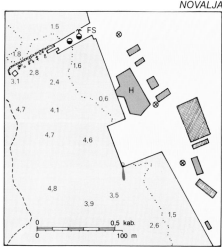

NOVALJA

and aqueduct, the ruins of the acropolis; Sv Juraj church (St George, early medieval).

METAJNA

(44°31'N; 015°05'E), village and cove in Paški zaljev (Bay of Pag).

Approach. Landmarks: Mt Zaglava (117 m), the green tower with a column and gallery (green light) on Zaglava point, the church with the belfry in the S part of the cove and the ferry pier can be easily identified.

Mooring. The cove is well sheltered from the bora and the sirocco. Good anchorage for larger yachts is some 0.5 M west-north-west of the chapel of Sv Marija (St Mary) at the S edge of the village; yachts drawing up to 2 m can anchor closer inshore.

Facilities. Limited provisions and water available.

NOVALJA

(44°33'N; 014°53'E), town and harbour in the small bay of the same name on the NW coast of the island of Pag.

Approach. Landmarks: the belfry and the tall white pole of the HT relay; the red tower with the column and gallery (sector light) on the S end of the pier. When entering the harbour by night, steer for the green sector of the harbour light on the S end of the mole, which indicates the passage safe from the shallow reefs: Gaj and Vrtlic.

Mooring. The bay is sheltered from winds from the NE and SE quadrants; winds from the SW and NW quadrants are very strong.

Yachts drawing up to 2.5 m can moor on the inner side of the breakwater and along the pier, which head is reserved for passenger ships; smaller vessels can moor between the pier and the breakwater (four-point moor). A good anchorage for medium-sized vessels is in the middle of the harbour (depth 5–8 m).

Facilities. Harbour master's branch office, post office, medical service, a bank, camp-site, several hotels and restaurants.

Shopping for provisions in local shops, water from the hydrant on the waterfront, fuel at the petrol station on the waterfront.

Minor repairs can be undertaken; there are hauling-out facilities for smaller vessels. Engine repairs can also be carried out.

Sights. The ruins of a Roman castrum, a 1 km long tunnel of an underground aqueduct (1 C), fragments of columns; near the town is a site with Illyrian graves, early Christian sarcophagi, the ruins of an early Christian basilica (5 C).

TOVARNELE

(44°41,5'N; 014°44,1'E), small harbour in the cove of the same name on the NW coast of the island of Pag, some 0.8 M south of Lun point.

Approach. Landmarks: the quadrangular white tower with a column and gallery (white light) on the south entrance point; NW of the cove is the dangerous Tovarnele reef, marked by an iron spar with red and black bands on a round white base surmounted by two black spheres; it is covered by night by the red sector of the light in Tovarnele cove.

Mooring. The cove is sheltered from N winds. Smaller yachts anchor in the middle of the cove (depth 2–3 m). Anchor bows-to SW, securing the stern to NE. It is also possible to moor offshore, off the restaurant (depth 3 m) or along the L-shaped pier.

Facilities. Provisions and other shopping in the village of Lun; water from the cistern (limited). Smaller repairs in Rab.

Sights. Ruins of ancient walls and of the Romanesque church of Sv Martin.

ZADAR HARBOUR MASTER'S OFFICE AREA

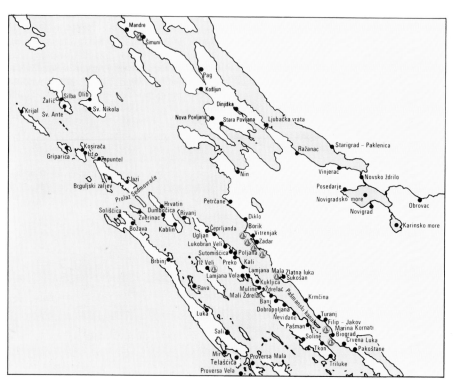

When approaching from SE, care should be taken of the shoals, reefs and rocks extending some 500 m offshore; the S rim of the shoal is marked by a black and yellow buoy surmounted by two black cones points downwards. A shallow reef bank stretches between the buoy and the coast.

Mooring. The harbour is exposed to the bora; the sirocco is moderate but causes waves; the westerlies blow in the summer and are strong and dangerous. Smaller vessels can moor on the E end of the breakwater (depth 2–4 m). In calm weather moor along both sides of the breakwater. The anchorage offshore is exposed to the bora and is not safe.

Warning. Mooring along the damaged E pier is prohibited.

Facilities. Harbour master's branch office, post office, chemist's, medical service, a hotel, travel agency, several shops and restaurants, campsite. Provisions and water in the village, fuel at the petrol station on the Adriatic highway (1 km SE).

Sights. Veća kula (a tower dating probably from the time of Turkish attacks in 16 – 17 C), Sv Petar church (Pre-Romanesque, 10 C), next to it the ruins of the necropolis with 20 medieval tombstones, two pre-historic cairns at the entrance to Velika Paklenica. – The Velika Paklenica National Park, a karst valley stretching for 10 km in the S part of the Velebit mountain range, situated between 450-metre high hills. The cave Manita Peć, the Borisov Dom mountain lodge (550 m), starting point for climbing the peaks of Velebit.

VINJERAC

(44°15,5'N; 015°28'E), village and small harbour 2.6 M west of the entrance to Novsko Ždrilo.

Approach. Landmarks: the red tower with a column and gallery (sector white light) on the head of the breakwater, church on the E entrance point.

When entering the harbour care should be taken of Štanga shoal, some 0.5 M northwest of the harbour, marked by a black and

DISTANCES OF PORTS

BIOGRAD	BOŽAVA	FILIP JAKOV	IST	IŽ VELI	NIN	NOVIGRAD	OBROVAC	OLIB	PAG	PAKOŠTANE	PAŠMAN	POSEDARJE	PREKO	PREMUDA	SALI	SILBA	UGLJAN	ZADAR	ZVERINAC	ŽDRELAC	
	29	2	38	17	40	61	67	43	61	4	3	62	14	46	17	43	19	15	28	9	BIOGRAD
		27	11	11	23	44	50	19	49	33	26	44	16	19	17	18	11	16	2	19	BOŽAVA
			36	16	39	60	66	41	59	6	2	61	13	43	15	41	18	13	26	8	FILIP JAKOV
				20	23	42	48	10	50	41	35	43	23	11	26	10	18	23	10	29	IST
					28	49	55	27	48	22	15	49	13	29	9	27	10	14	11	9	IŽ VELI
						25	31	26	20	44	37	26	27	28	36	25	23	26	22	33	NIN
							8	46	27	65	58	4	47	49	55	45	44	46	43	53	NOVIGRAD
								52	33	71	64	10	53	55	61	51	50	52	49	59	OBROVAC
									53	46	40	47	28	9	34	4	24	28	18	34	OLIB
										65	58	27	48	54	57	53	43	46	47	53	PAG
											7	66	18	48	17	46	23	19	34	13	PAKOŠTANE
												59	12	43	14	40	17	12	26	6	PAŠMAN
													48	50	56	46	44	47	44	54	POSEDARJE
														31	12	28	5	3	17	6	PREKO
															36	11	27	31	18	37	PREMUDA
																34	17	13	18	8	SALI
																	23	28	18	34	SILBA
																		6	12	10	UGLJAN
																			16	7	ZADAR
																				19	ZVERINAC
																					ŽDRELAC

PRE-ROMANESQUE CHAPEL OF ST. GEORGE IN RAVANJSKA

HARBOURS ON THE COAST

STARIGRAD

(44°17,7'N; 015°26,4'E), village and small harbour on the NE coast of the southernmost part of Velebitski kanal.

Approach. Landmarks: the round red tower with a column and gallery (red light) on the head of the breakwater, the church of Sv Juraj (St George) and the multi-storey »Alan« hotel.

yellow spar surmounted by two black cones points upwards. When approaching by night from NW keep within the white sector of the light on the breakwater. Approaching from E, keep off the shallow N of the village; as soon as you sight the red sector of the light on the breakwater, shape course for the light. A number of shoals extend about 800 m offshore between Vinjerac and the entrance to Novsko Ždrilo; they are marked by a conical green buoy surmounted by a radar reflector.

Mooring. The harbour is sheltered from all winds except the bora, which is very strong and a longer stay in the harbour is not recommended. Smaller yachts moor along the inner side of the breakwater and on both sides of the pier. With the bora and NW winds blowing, moor on the NW end of the pier (four-point moor). When securing, take care of the projecting underwater part of the breakwater.

Facilities. Post office, hotel, tourist office and a shop. Limited provisions and water.

Sights. The ruins of an Illyrian settlement (3/2 C B.C.), Sv Marko church (medieval, part of an ancient Pauline monastery), ruins of a Venetian palazzo of the Venier family – hence the name of the village.

RAŽANAC

(44°17'N; 015°21'E), village and small harbour, some 5 M southeast of Ljubačka vrata.

Approach. Landmarks: the ruins of the tower, the hotel, the church and the red column on the breakwater (red light). The low and bare islets of Ražanac Veli (white tower with a column, white light), Ražanac Mali and Donji Školj.

When approaching from SE, care should be taken of the shoals near the outer end of the root of the breakwater.

Mooring. The harbour is protected from all winds except the bora, which is very strong here; a longer stay in the harbour in the bora and the north-westerlies is not recommended. Moor along the breakwater; with the bora blowing, use the four-point moor securing bows-to the breakwater and stern-to the bollards on the opposite coast.

Facilities. Post office, medical service, hotel, campsite and tourist office. Provisions and other shopping in the local shop; water from the main.

Sights. Ruins of an Illyrian fortress and tombs (3/2 C B.C.), Gospa od Ružarija church (Our Lady of the Rosary, 1682, new church 1856, renovated in 1983); in the vicinity (2 km) Sv Andrija church (St Andrew, medieval); ruins of a defense tower against Turkish attacks (near the harbour, 1507).

NOVSKO ŽDRILO

(44°15'N; 015°31'E), passage connecting Novigradsko more with Velebitski kanal, 1.5 M long, 0.15 M wide. The channel is spanned by a bridge (NW of Ždrijac point; destroyed on November 21, 1991 during the Homeland War).

Approach. Landmarks: at the N entrance to the passage: a green buoy surmounted by a green cone (green light) and a red buoy surmounted by a red can (red light); the quadrangular red concrete tower (red light) on the E Baljenica point (conspicuously yellow and brown) and the round red tower with a column and gallery (green light)

on Korotanja point at the opposite side of the entrance. The coast of the passage is fringed by several lights; the green tower with a column and gallery (green light) at Vranine point and the red tower (red light) at Brzac point. At the Ždrijac point there is a loading place reserved for the car-ferry; on the W side of the south entrance to Ždrilo there is a round green tower with a column and a gallery (green light).

The NW going current in the passage attains a rate of 1 knot, but with the sirocco blowing it can attain 4 knots.

Directions for navigation. The speed limit in the passage is 8 knots. Vessels must not pass or overtake each other in the passage. A vessel about to enter the passage must stop off the entrance, 500 m N of the northern point of Baljenica and 500 m off the southern point of Ždrijac and give two 5-second siren blasts. Any vessel already in the passage must reply by giving five 1-second blasts. Vessels waiting to enter the passage will, on hearing the blasts, wait at the above given position until the vessel in the passage comes out. When entering the passage, all vessels must give five short blasts to signal their presence to smaller craft (boats).

Facilities. In the village of Maslenica, on the E inner point of the entrance to Ždrilo, is a cargo terminal (bauxite) and an old ferry landing ground.

On NE side of Novsko Ždrilo (by the bridge) there is a motel with 150 beds, a swimming pool, a supermarket and a tourist office.

Sights. Rovanjska with Sv Petar church (St Peter, early Romanesque, built on the site of a Roman villa rustica); Jasenice with Sv Juraj church (St George, early Romanesque).

NOVIGRADSKO MORE,

stretch of sea connected with Velebitski kanal by Novsko Ždrilo and with Karinsko more by Karinsko Ždrilo.

Its N and E coasts are steep; its S and W coasts are covered with woods and olive groves and slope gently towards the sea. On the E coast is the estuary of the river Zrmanja.

The bora is very strong, the sirocco more moderate. The nearby villages include Maslenica, Posedarje (its shallow coast is fringed by reefs) and Novigrad.

NOVIGRAD

(44°11'N; 015°33'E), village and small harbour in the cove on the S coast of Novigradsko more.

Approach. Landmarks: the stone tower (red light) on Sv Nikola point and the chapel can be easily identified.

Mooring. The cove is sheltered from all winds except the bora, which causes a slop in the harbour (considerable oscillations of the sea level). Smaller yachts can moor along the pier in the cove; with the bora blowing, use the four-point moor, securing to both ends of the cove.

Facilities. Harbour master's branch office, post office, medical service, chemist's, a hotel, several restaurants and shops. Provisions in local shops; water from the hydrant in front of the harbour office.

There is a mussel farm in the cove.

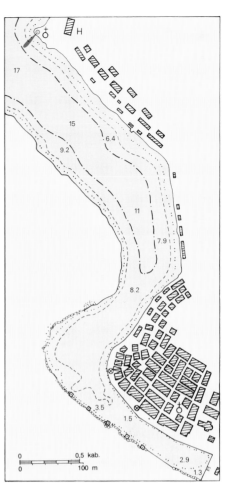
NOVIGRAD

Sights. Queen Elisabeth (executed in 1387), widow of Ludovic of Anjou the Great, King of Hungary, and Maria, later wife of Sigismund of Luxembourg, were imprisoned in the Castle of Novigrad. – Fortress above the town (13 C) with partly preserved town walls; Sv Kata church (St Catherine, fragments of lace ornaments and church furniture. – Pridraga, 6 km SSE (Sv Mihovil church /St Michael/, 10/11 C, six-foil groundplan, Sv Martin church /St Martin, part of it is early Christian, old Croatian necropolis of Goričine) – 6 km SSE; Kugin Čunj (a stone on the hill above the village) – tradition has it that it protects the village from the plague. – Islam Grčki, the redoubt of Stojan Janković, a fighter against the Turks, 17 C.

POSEDARJE

(44°13'N; 015°29'E), village and small harbour in the W part of Novigradsko more.

Approach. Landmarks: the betfry, the »Luna« hotel and the chapel on the islet in the W part of Luka cove.

A 2.5 m deep dragged channel marked by wooden spars leads to the harbour. E of the harbour is Veli Školj rock.

Mooring. The harbour is sheltered from all winds except the sirocco; the bora in it is moderate. Only yachts drawing up to 1.5 m can moor there. The anchorage for smaller vessels is in the middle of Luka cove, between Veli Školj and the small peninsula with the chapel.

Facilities. Post office and medical service. Provisions in local shops.

OBROVAC

LJUBAČKA VRATA

(44°20'N; 015°16'E), passage connecting Velebitski kanal with Ljubački zaljev.

Orientation. Landmarks: the bridge connecting the mainland with the island of Pag, the pyramidal stone tower with a gallery (white light) on Tanka Nožica point, the quadrangular tower with a red top (red light) on Fortica point and the quadrangular tower with a green top (green light) on Oštrljak point.

Approach. Ljubačka vrata passage can be entered only by day and only by vessels with masts less than 30 m high. When approaching Ljubačka vrata from Velebitski kanal, give Tanka Nožica point a wide berth because it is fringed by a shoal.

Special directions for navigation in the passage. Vessels larger than 50 GRT and trawlers regardless of tonnage must give a long signal on the whistle or siren before entering Ljubačka vrata. The ship which has given the signal first has right of way, unless another ship is already in the passage. The latter must in that case reply with at least four short blasts. This signalling does not apply in foggy or overcast weather, when the regulations for avoiding collision at sea apply.

The most dangerous wind in Ljubačka vrata is the bora, which blows with gale force from various directions and causes a strong chop. The current from Velebitski kanal normally attains a rate of 1 knot, exceptionally 2–3 knots.

Sights. Uzašašće Marijino church (Assumption of Our Lady, 12/13 C, later Baroque reconstruction), Gospa od Ružarija church (Our Lady of the Rosary, Baroque reconstruction in 1700) and Sv Duh church (fhe Holy Ghost, 15 C) on the islet in the W cove; 5 km SW on the crossroads is the 150-year old Zeleni hrast (Green Oak tree) - a protected monument of nature.

KARINSKO MORE,

stretch of sea connected with Novigradsko more by Karinsko Ždrilo (1.5 M long, 100 m wide, 10–20 m deep at midpoint). While sailing into the Karinsko more steer clear of the Ždrilo shoal (marked by a pole and a green cone).

The bora is strong. On the S coast there is a monastery with a small mole nearby. Along the NE coast are rocks to which vessels can secure (four-point moor). The whole bay is a good anchorage (depth 11–13 m).

OBROVAC

(44°12'N; 015°41'E), town and harbour on the S bank of the Zrmanja River, 6 M upstream from the estuary.

Special directions for navigation. The river can be entered only by day and only with a permit issued by the harbour master's branch office in Novigrad at the request of the vessel's skipper. The fairway is 40–60 m wide; on both sides are mud banks. All vessels must keep to starboard. Boats must give ships free passage. The speed limit on the river is 8 knots. Stopping, overtaking or anchoring on the river is prohibited.

Mooring. The harbour in Obrovac is sheltered from all winds including the bora, which is very strong in the area. Smaller yachts can moor along the projecting end of the mole (depth about 2.6 m).

Facilities. Post office, medical service and chemist's, a motel. Shopping for provisions in town, water from the hydrant on the waterfront, fuel at the petrol station (100 m from the bridge).

Obrovac is the venue of the summer festival called Noći đerdana (Nights of Necklaces) – gatherings of the local population dressed in picturesque folk costumes.

LJUBAČKA VRATA – PRIVLAČKI ZALJEV – ZADAR

Sights. In the village of Ljubač: an Illyrian castle and several tombs, the early medieval Sv Ivan church (St John). – On Ljubljana point: the ruins of the early medieval residence of the Templars with Sv Marija church (12/13 C).

NIN
(44°14'N; 015°11'E), old Croatian historical town in the shallow lagoon in the bay of the same name. The shallows extend far offshore.

Approach. Landmarks: the chimney of the brickyard NE of the town, the belfry of the church in Nin and the chapel NE of Privlaka harbour.

Mooring. The bay is exposed to the bora and the sirocco, which are very strong but do not cause big waves. The best anchorage for vessels drawing up to 1.2 m is in the E part of the bay; larger yachts can anchor off the NE coast of the bay, in the direction NNE of the belfry of the church in Nin. E from the town (0.5 M) there is Miljašić jaruga (Miljašić gully) where the stream reaches the sea. Along the quay (on the left side) there are berths for vessels drawing up to 2 m.

Facilities. Post office, medical service and chemist's. Limitied provisions and water.

Several sites of medicinal mud (pelloid, with 80% colloid particles). Nin has salt pans (which cover an area of 45 hectares), a brickyard and a tree nursery.

Sights. Neolithic finds; Illyrian and Liburnian finds (town of Aenona): ceramics, a necropolis, tombstones; from the Roman times: town walls, bridges, cemetery, aqueduct, Diana's Temple (about 70 A.D.); medieval churches of Sv Križ (Holy Cross, 11 C?), Sv Bilić (renovated in 1673 and 1965, with the chapel of Sv Ivan Krstitelj /St John the Baptist/), of Sv Ambrozije (Gothic, renovated, built on the site of the former Benedictine monastery), of Gospa od Ružarija on the cemetery (Our Lady of the Rosary, mentioned in a document from

NIN, THE SHOULDER-BLANDE OF ST. ASEL

VIR

NIN, CHAPEL OF THE HOLY CROSS

1228); Sv Nikola church at Prahulje (late 11 C); the Slav necropolis on Ždrijac beach (250 tombs, 8/9 C).

In 1069 king Petar Krešimir issued in Nin the deed of gift known as Mare Nostrum. The remains of an old Croatian ship dating back to the 10 or 11 C have been excavated near the town.

The Statute of the District of Nin regulating shipping and fishing in the region popularly believed to date from 1103 – a more probable dating is 15 C.

VIR
(44°18'N; 015°6'E), small harbour on the S coast of the island of Vir in the N part of the bay Privlački zaljev.

Approach. Through the middle of the bay. One should not approach the coast more than 400 m because of the shallow places.

Mooring. On the head of the mole the boats are protected from all winds except the South ones.

Facilities. water, post-office, restaurant, shop.

PRIVLAKA
(44°16'N; 015°7'E), small port on the SE coast of Privlački zaljev.

Approach. While entering the harbour one should take care of the prolonged breakwater part which is hidden under the sea surface (20 m away).

Mooring. On both sides of the quay (depth 2–3 m).

Facilities. Food shop, water, post office, restaurant.

PETRČANE
(44°11'N; 015°09'E), village and small harbour on the coast of the cove of the same name, some 5 M northwest of Zadar.

BORIK MARINA

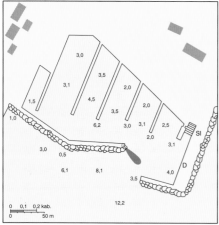

BORIK MARINA

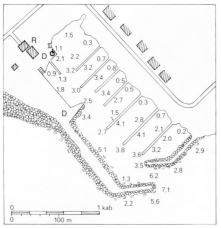

VITRENJAK MARINA

Approach. Landmarks: the quadrangular white tower (white light) on Radman point (forest in the background) and the belfry with a rectangular top and a clock in the middle of it.

Warning. It is prohibited to moor along the mole with the breakwater (S part of the harbour) because it is damaged.

ZADAR

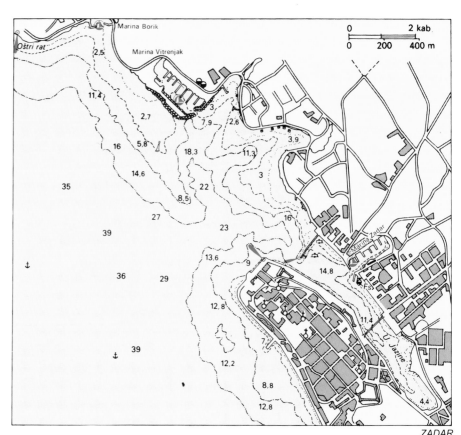

ZADAR

Mooring. The harbour is well sheltered from the bora and the southerlies. Smaller vessels can moor along the pier enclosing the inner harbour and along the jetty E of the N breakwater.

Facilities. Post office and medical service. On Radman point is the »Pinija« hotel and 2 km northwest of the village is the »Punta Skala« camp site and a hotel for naturists.

Water and provisions in the village; fuel at the petrol station by the hotel.

Sights. Sv Bartul church (St Bartholomew, 12/13 C, later converted into a private building).

DIKLO

(44°09'N; 016°12'E), village and anchorage, some 2 M north-northwest of Zadar.

Approach. The belfry and the grove on the hill can be identified when approaching the anchorage. Some 1 M southeast of the town is a dangerous shoal (0.5 m), which should be given an offing when sailing toward Oštri rat point (Punta Mika).

Mooring. The anchorage is sheltered from the bora but exposed to onshore winds and sea. The best anchorage in the bora is SSW of the town (depth 17–20 m), in the sirocco SSW of the town (depth 23 m). A good anchorage for smaller yachts in the sirocco is offshore W of Oštri rat point.

ZADAR, ST. DONATUS

Facilities. Provisions and water can be obtained in the nearby hotel complex of Borik (Zadar); fuel at the petrol station.

Sights. The medieval churches of Sv Martin (St Martin, 12 C) and Sv Petar (St Peter, 13 C).

BORIK MARINA

(44°08'N; 015°13'E) is situated in Uvala fratara cove, 500 m E from the Oštri rat lighthouse. There are five pontoon quays, depth 1.5–5 m.

Capacity. 200 sea-berths and 100 dry-berths (for yachts of 6–20 m in length).

It is sheltered from all winds by two breakwaters; at the head of the W breakwater there is a red tower (harbour light); on the E breakwater there is a 5 t hoist.

VITRENJAK MARINA

(44°08'N; 015°12'E) is situated 0.7 M northwest of the harbour of Zadar. It is protected by two breakwaters and has 8 concrete piers. The depth decreases gradually toward the inner end of the harbour and the roots of the piers: it is about 6 m at the

ZADAR MARINA

bearing 213°, to Kali harbour (0.2 M east of the harbour light). Its NW boundary is the line joining the small jetty on Obala kralja Petra

ZADAR, THE ARCA OF ST. SIMON

Krešimira IV, bearing 220°, with Preko harbour (0.2 M northwest of the harbour light).

- In the area, about 0.5 M in width, between the mainland coast and the coast of the island of Ugljan, its SE boundary being the line joining Oštri rat lighthouse, on a bearing of 230°, with a point some 0.4 M northwest of the light on Sv Grgur point. Its NW boundary is the line extending from a point some 0.7 M to the southeast of the church in Diklo village, on a bearing of 235°, to a point about 0.4 M northwest of the harbour light in Lukoran Veli harbour.

Prevailing weather conditions. The bora is moderate; the sirocco can be strong but does not cause waves. Summer storms with winds blowing from NNW, may send in a swell into the harbour but present no danger either to vessels entering nor to those lying in the harbour. The SW waterfront of the town, Obala kralja Petra Krešimira IV, is exposed to NW and SE winds and waves.

ZADAR MARINA

entrance and about 1.5 m near the waterfront. Berths for 120 vessels (part of which are reserved for the Borik marina).

At the inner end of the cove there is the building of the »Uskok« Sailing Club and a large hangar; two hoists (2.5 and 5.5 t) and two slipways.

Provisions and other shopping in Borik (1 km) or Zadar; fuel at the petrol station in the marina.

ZADAR

(44°07'N; 015°13'E), city and port in Zadarski kanal.

Approach. Landmarks: two belfries in the town, the lighthouse on Oštri rat point, the round white stone tower (white light); the concrete tower with a green dome (green light) on the N corner of Istarska Obala (Istra Quay); the concrete tower with a red dome (red light) on the head of the breakwater.

Warning. Anchoring is prohibited in the following areas within Zadarski kanal:

- In the area, 1.4 M in width, between the mainland coast and the coast of Ugljan Island; its SE boundary is a line extending from the church in the village of Arbanasi,

Mooring. The harbour is protected by the peninsula on which the old part of Zadar is situated and by a breakwater (on the opposite side). The entrance is 70 m wide. Yachts can use the berths laid by Zadar Marina in Vrulje cove. The berths in the harbour are reserved for merchant ships. A good anchorage is some 1 mile S of the Oštri rat lighthouse.

Facilities. A permanent port of entry; harbour master's office and customs, hospital and post office.

Provisions in local shops, water from the hydrant on the watertront, fuel at several petrol stations, one of them in the Marina. Naval charts and other publications can be bought in the PLOVPUT – Plovno Područje Zadar, Airport Zemunik (15 km).

The Maritime Museum (Pomorski muzej) of the Institute of the Croatian Academy of Sciences and Arts (Zagreb) is situated in a park in Brodarica, a suburb of Zadar. The Historical Archives, established in 1625, contain many documents and other material relevant to the history of shipping and fishing in the East Adriatic. Zadar has a secondary marine school. »Tankerska plovid-

ZADAR, ST. ANASTASIA CATHEDRAL

ba« shipping company. NW of the Old Town is Borik, a recreation area with a motel, campsite, beach and several hotels.

During the summer season Zadar hosts a series of concerts in Sv Donat church (Večeri glazbe u Donatu).

Car-ferry lines: Zadar – Preko; Zadar – Zaglav (Dugi Otok); Zadar – Brbinj (Dugi Otok); Zadar – Ancona (Italy); Rijeka – Zadar – Dubrovnik (see Rijeka).

Coastal passenger lines: Zadar – Olib – Silba – Premuda – Ilovik; Zadar – Premuda – Silba – Olib; Zadar – Molat – Brgulje – Ist – Zapuntel – Olib – Silba – Premuda – Ilovik – Mali Lošinj; Zadar – Rivanj – Molat – Brgulje – Zapuntel – Ist; Zadar – Rivanj –Sestrunj – Dragove – Božava – Zverinac – Soline – Veli Rat; Zadar – Iž Mali – Iž Veli – Brbinj – Savar – Mala Rava – Rava; Zadar – Sestrunj – Božava – Zverinac – Molat –Brgulje – Ist – Zapuntel – Premuda – Olib – Silba; Zadar – Mali Lošinj – Pula.

Sights. Remnants of the old Roman Forum (1 C, with foundations of a temple, basilicas, columns and shop walls). The churches: of Sv Donat (with a rotunda from 9 C), of Sv Marija (1091, Romanesque, reconstructed in 16 C in the Baroque style; furnishings from Romanesque to Baroque; belfry from 11 C), of Sv Stošija (St Anastasia, Romanesque cathedral, 13/14 C, choir stalls from 1418–50, crypt), of Sv Krševan-Krisogon (St Grisogonus, Romanesque, from 1175, with apses, Baroque furnishings), of Sv Šimun (St Simeon, first recorded in 12 C, later reconstructions, contains the silver coffin of St Simeon from 1377–80), of Sv Franjo (St Francis, from

ZLATNA LUKA MARINA

ZLATNA LUKA MARINA

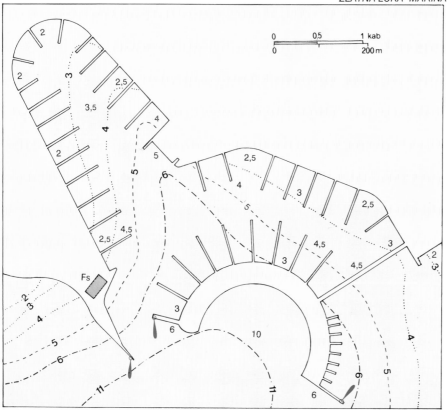

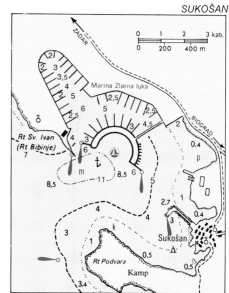

SUKOŠAN

ZADAR, ALTARSCREEN FROM ST. NEDILJICA

1283, reconstructed. choir stalls from 1394, Renaissance cloister).

Remnants of old fortifications along Gradska luka (Old City Harbour) dating from 16 C, Porta Terraferma – the Old Town Gate dating from 1543, the defense tower Bablja kula (13–14 C), Veliki Arsenal (Great Arsenal from 1752), the palace of the Venetian governor (1607), the Loggia (1565), Gradska straža (City Guard from 1562).

Museums and collections: Archaeological Museum, National Museum, Natural History Museum, Ethnographical Museum, Maritime Museum, Art Gallery and permanent exhibition of Sacral Art.

ZADAR MARINA - TANKERKOMERC D.D.

(44°07,1'N; 015°14'E) is situated on the east quay of Gradska luka (Old City Harbour) in Vrulje bay.

The berths are laid on the inner side of the breakwater in the harbour (vessels up to 40 m length), along the quay and pier (vessels up to 25 m in length); there are 200 berths along 5 floating fingers (four-point moor) and 400 dry-berths (in the open and in sheds). The depth in the bay are 3–6 m, along the NE waterfront and the breakwater 1.5–2 m, near the head of the breakwater about 7 m.

The marina operates the year round.

It has restaurants, snack-bar, shop, laundry, toilets and showers, food shop, ship chandler's. Water and electricity hook-ups on the waterfront and the piers, telephones. Fuel pump on the SE entrance to the bay.

Repairs to the hull, marine engines and electrical installations; maintenance and servicing of all types of vessels and engines in the marina. A travel-lift (50 t) and hoists (6.5 and 15 t).

ZLATNA LUKA MARINA (SAS)

(44°03,6'N; 015°18'E) is situated in the bay of Zlatna Luka, 4.5 M south of Zadar (near Sukošan). It is sheltered from all winds.

The marina covers an area of 125 acres; it has 1200 berths (four-point moor) for yachts up to 15 m in length and up to 4 m draught, 600 dry-berths (200 in hangars); a stretch of 400 m on the waterfront is occupied by berths for yachts over 25 m in length and up to 5 m draught. All berths have water, electricity, telephone and television hook-ups.

The marina operates the year round.

It has reception office, harbour master's branch office, customs, a shopping centre, ship chandler's, spare parts, dry cleaner's, medical service, chemist's, toilets, showers; fuel and butane gas pump; specialized service shops; yacht club; casino; hotel (400 beds), apartment settlement (400 beds), villas (on an area of 2000 m3); parking lot; sports grounds with tennis courts and facilities for water sports, an outdoor swimming pool and an indoor Olympic swimming pool. Travel-lifts (30 and 65 t); repair of marine engines (spare parts available), hulls and rigging.

The marina has a charter fleet with over 200 motor and sailing boats, between 6 and 13 m long, the motor boat »Adria 1000«.

SUKOŠAN

(44°03'N; 015°18'E), town and small harbour in the large but shallow cove in the S part of Zadarski kanal.

Approach. Landmarks: the quadrangular concrete tower (white light) on a concrete base off Podvara point; the ruin on the shoal in the S part of the harbour and the church with the low belfry.

Mooring. The harbour is protected from all winds except the south-westerlies, which cause a moderate sea in it. Smaller yachts can moor along the head of the long breakwater (depth 3 m); on the head is a red column with a red light. It is advisable to moor in Zlatna Luka marina.

Facilities. Provisions and water available; fuel at the petrol stations in Biograd na moru or Zadar.

The local boatyard undertakes repairs of wooden boats. A post office, medical service, railway station, several hostels and a campsite on Podvara point.

Sights. Sv Kasijan church (11 C?, renovated in 1673), on the islet in the harbour the ruins of the summer house of M. Valaresso, archbishop of Zadar (1470).

PAŠMANSKI KANAL,

channel between the mainland and the island of Pašman. In its SE part the channel is narrow and shallow with many islets and shoals. The islets of Komornik, Babac, Frmić, Planac and Sv Katarina form two passages in this part of the channel – the western and the eastern – navigable for ships drawing up to 6 metres.

SUKOŠAN, RUIN OF CAPE BRIBIRČINA

The bora is much stronger in Pašmanski kanal than in Zadarski kanal, reaching gale force in the winter. The sirocco is also strong and particularly unpleasant with the current coming from the opposite direction. The SW wind changes direction in the channel and blows from S or SSE. The northwesterlies can also be very strong and cause high waves, especially in the area N of the islet of Bisage. The NW current (high tide) attains a rate of 1–2.5 knots in the channel, and the SE current (low tide) a rate of 1–2 knots. The current attains greatest strength in the narrowest part of the channel and off the villages of Turanj and Sv. Filip i Jakov. Southerly winds influence the direction of the current and often cause very strong eddies.

The ordinance on the navigation of ships (up to 50 GRT) and boats through Pašmanski kanal determines its limits and two fairways.

The limits of Pašmanski kanal:

- in the north, the line joining Tukljačan point the Ričul light structure the Galešnjak light structure the W point of the islet of Bisage Male and the N coast of the islet of Garmenjak;

- in the south, the line joining Soline cove (S of Biograd na moru) with Studenac point (island of Pašman).

The fairways:

The western fairway within the lines joining the NE coast of the islet of Garmenjak Brižine point the harbour light in the village of Pašman light Čavatul the intersection of the alignment of the lights at Čavatul and Babac with the southern border of the channel the intersection of the southern border of the channel with the alignment (SW) of the point of the islet of Planac and the Sv

PAŠMANSKI KANAL – BIOGRAD

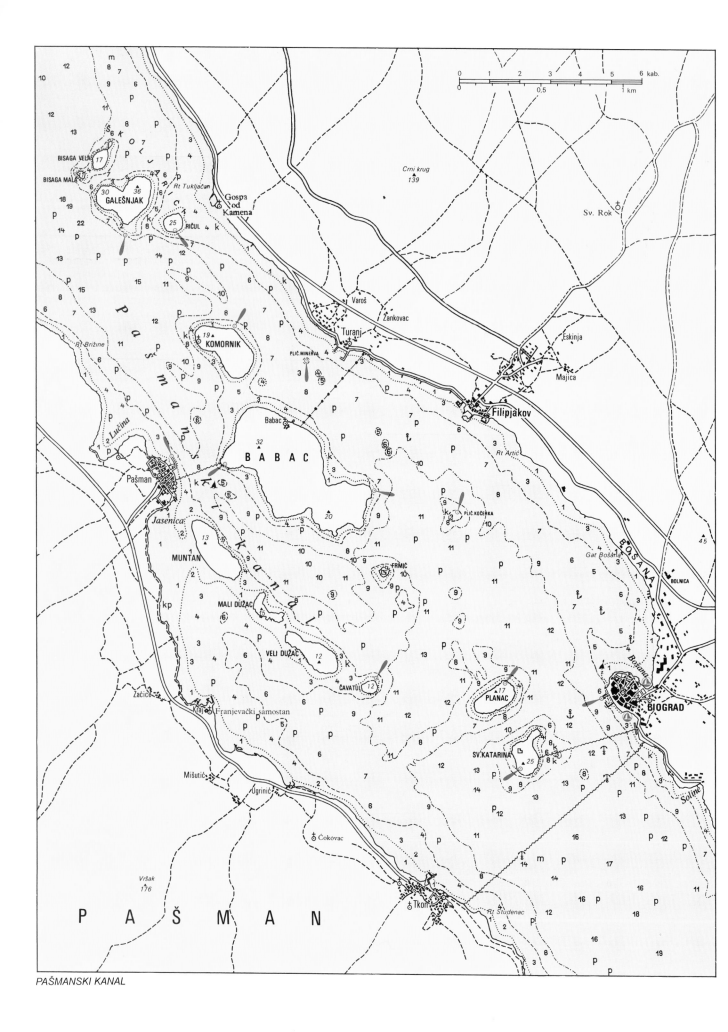

PAŠMANSKI KANAL

Katarina light – the Sv Katarina light the Babac light– the intersection of the alignment of the midpoint of the islet of Čavatul and the Babac light with the northern border of the channel.

The eastern passage lying within the lines joining Soline cove, the Biograd na moru harbour light, the Kočerka shoal light, the Minerva shoal light, the Ričul light, the Galešnjak light, W point of Bisage Male, the intersection of the alignment of the midpoint of Čavatul islet and the Babac light with the northern border of the channel, the intersection of the alignment of the midpoint of Čavatul islet and the Babac light with the line joining the N coast of Garmenjak islet and the Galešnjak light the W point of the island of Komornik, the Komornik light, the light on the E coast of Babac, the Planac light, the N point of Sv Katarina, the intersection of the S border of the channel with the alignment of the SW point of Planac island and the light on the islet of Sveta Katarina.

Vessels over 50 GRT must use the western fairway when going SE, and the eastern fairway when going NW.

Vessels up to 50 GRT and boats can pass from the western to the eastern fairway and vice versa in any part of the channel.

In the fairways of Pašmanski kanal, vessels over 50 GRT can navigate at a speed of up to 10 knots in the following areas:
- in the western fairway from Brižine point to the S border of the channel;
- in the eastern fairway from the entrance to the Komornik light.

Directions for navigation through the channel:

1. Entering the channel from NW, use the western fairway; the course is indicated by the alignment, on a bearing of 143.5° (the western point of the islet of Babac the point of the islet of Čavatul). When abreast of the green tower with a column (green light) on the edge of the shoal S of the islet of Galešnjak, steer 148° which leads through the middle of the fairway between the harbour light (green tower with a gallery, green light) in Pašman harbour and the lighthouse (stone tower and small house, white light) on the islet of Babac. Passing the lighthouse, leave the shoals S of it (4.8 and 5.3 m) to port, steering 131° (the lighthouse on the islet of Sveta Katarina). Keep on that course until abreast of the light marking the shoal (green tower with a gallery, green light) off the N point of the islet of Čavatul; then turn right to the course leading W of the islet of Sveta Katarina (white tower in front of the house, white light).

2. Entering the channel from SE, use the eastern fairway, shaping course for the middle of the line joining the harbour light in Biograd na moru and the islet of Planac, taking care of the shoal (3.5 m) E of the islet of Sveta Katarina. From the middle of this line steer for the islet of Ričul (white tower with a column and gallery, white light) on a bearing of 320° until abreast of the light on the islet of Komornik (red tower with a column and gallery, red light); then steer in the course leading S of the light on the islet of Galešnjak.

Warning. Anchoring off the entrances and exits from the fairways mentioned above and in the fairways themselves is prohibited. All vessels are prohibited from entering and navigating in the channel when visibility drops under 0.2 M.

BIOGRAD NA MORU

KRMČINA

(43°59,6'N; 015°22'E), village and anchorage in Pašmanski kanal, SE of the point of the same name.

Mooring. A good anchorage for vessels of all sizes, sheltered from the bora. Anchor (depth 12 m) S of the village on the S side of the point, characterized by red landslides.

Sights. In the nearby village of Tukljača is the chapel of Our Lady, endowment of Mikuc Mogorović, commander of Prince Miroslav's fleet (memorial inscription on the lintel dated 845).

TURANJ

(43°58'N; 015°25'E), village and small harbour on the mainland coast on the narrowest part of Pašmanski kanal.

Approach. Landmarks: the belfry of the church in the village and the long L-shaped breakwater, on whose head is a green tower with a column and gallery (green light). Off the harbour is Minerva shoal (4.5 m) marked by a green tower with a column and gallery (green light) on a concrete base in the sea.

Mooring. The harbour is not sheltered from the sirocco and should be avoided with this wind blowing. Smaller yachts can moor in the harbour or along the outer end of the breakwater.

Facilities. Provisions and water in the village; fuel at the petrol station in Biograd na moru.

Sights. Roman finds (tombs, remains of various buildings), ruins of a fortress (16 C).

SV FILIP I JAKOV

(43°57'N; 015°26'E), village and small harbour in Pašmanski kanal, some 1.5 M northwest of Biograd na moru.

Approach. Landmarks: the belfry; the round green tower with a column and gallery (green light) on a base on Kočerka shoal

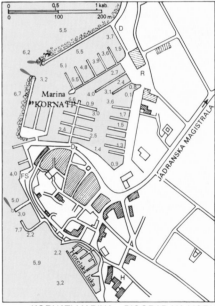

KORNATI MARINA – BIOGRAD NA MORU

(some 600 m south of the harbour); the red tower of the former light on the head of the pier; the belfry with a column in the village and, E of it, glasshouses extending up to the waterfront.

Mooring. The harbour is sheltered from all winds. Smaller yachts can moor along the pier protecting the harbour for fishing boats. It is also possible to moor along the inner end of the W pier (depth 2 m) and along the breakwater (inner side 2 m, outer side up to 4 m).

Facilities. Post office and medical service. Provisions from local shops, water from the hydrant on the waterfront and the pier. Fuel at the petrol station in Biograd na moru.

Sights. Sv Mihovil church (St Michael, 14 C, reconstruction 1707), the ruins of Dvorine castle (former Benedictine monas-

PAKOŠTANE

tery with Sv Rok church, 1374) in Rogovo; Folco Borelli Park – monument of garden architecture.

BIOGRAD NA MORU

(43°56'N; 015°27'E), town and harbour in the S part of Pašmanski kanal.

Approach. Landmarks: the belfry in the town; the semi-circular yellowish hospital building with two quadrangular chimneys on the W side; the white tower with a column and gallery (green light) on the head of the pier; the red tower with a column and gallery (red light) on the head of the N breakwater of the marina; the green tower with a column and gallery (green light) on the head of the W breakwater of the marina; the red tower with a column and gallery (red light) on the islet of Planac; the white tower (white light) on the islet of Sveta Katarina; the green buoy on the shoal W of the ferry harbour; the »Adriatic« hotel.

Mooring. The harbour is sheltered from all winds and seas, except the south-easterlies. The sea raised by the south-westerlies can sometimes be unpleasant. The waterfront in the main harbour is reserved for passenger ships. The hotel harbour next to the »Adriatic« hotel, which has 170 berths for yachts up to 7 m in length, is reserved for hotel guests. The Kornati – Biograd marina is situated some 0.5 M west of harbour and 0.1 M west of the ferry harbour.

Facilities. Harbour master's branch office, medical service, chemist's, orthopaedic hospital, post office, several hotels, motel, campsites (some of them in the environs), restaurants, sports facilities, a fishing net factory, the Centre for Maritime Exploration.

Good shopping for provisions; mains water supply; fuel at the petrol station on the waterfront and on the Adriatic highway (1 km).

Car-ferry line: Biograd na moru – Tkon (Island of Pašman).

Sights. Liburnian and Roman finds (remains of the water mains, villa rustica), remains of houses and churches of the medieval Royal Borough (11–13 C), and archaeological collection (from Iron Age, Roman and medieval times); a special part of the collection is Treasures of the Seabed with glass and bronze items, candlesticks, textiles, copper wire, household utensils, a cannon (1200 kg) dating from 1582–all of which were found on a sunken ship dating from the turn of 16 C, discovered near Gnalić islet.

East of Biograd na moru is the lake Vransko jezero (14 x 4 km, depth up to 4 m) famous for its fisheries and wildfowl shooting. On the northern shore of the lake are the ruins of a fortified monastery of the Templars (13 C) and Maškovića han, a Turkish caravanserai (1644).

KORNATI–BIOGRAD MARINA

(43°56,2'N; 015°26,7'E) is situated in the natural harbour N of the ferry pier in the town harbour. It is protected by two breakwaters.

The marina has 500 sea-berths and 200 dry-berths; depth 2–5 m. Boat rental: about 60 yachts, 40 smaller vessels (for day rental) and family vessels sleeping 4–6 (weekly rental).

The marina operates the year round.

It has reception office, restaurant, shops; harbour master's branch office, customs; showers and toilets, parking lot for 600 cars.

Provisions at the supermarket; nautical items and spares, hardware and tools, sports equipment; fuel at the petrol station on the waterfront and on the Adriatic highway (1 km).

Hoists (10 t), facility for mounting masts, cleaning and rubbing down of boats, security for wintering boats; water and electricity hook-ups laid out on the piers. Maintenance and repair services in the marina; general overhauling of vessels and engines at Zadar Marina.

CRVENA LUKA

(43°56'N; 015°30'E), small bay, hotel complex (13 hotel buildings, 27 bungalows) and small harbour some 2 M southeast of Biograd na moru.

Approach. The white tower with a column (light with sectors) on the islet of Oštarije, SW of the entrance to the bay can be easily identified.

Warning. Between the islet of Oštarije and the mainland is a reef extending 100 m SE of the islet; approach the bay by going south of the islet and giving it a berth of at least 100 m.

Mooring. The bay is sheltered from the bora; the sirocco causes a considerable

PAG

sea. Yachts can moor along the pier (depth off the head 3 m) on the NW coast of the bay or anchor in the middle of the bay (depth 3–6 m); good holding. Leave the bay as soon as you see signs heralding the sirocco.

Facilities. Provisions (in shop and restaurant) and water are available; fuel at the petrol station in Biograd na moru.

In Božakovica cove near Crvena Luka is the Club Méditerranée village with Tahitian-style huts (300 bungalows) and hotel buildings.

PAKOŠTANE

(43°55'N; 015°31'E), town and small harbour at the entrance to Pašmanski kanal.

Approach. Landmarks: the belfry in the village, the string of islets (Babuljaš, Veli Školj, Sveta Justina) off the entrance to the harbour, the green tower with a column and gallery (green light) on the head of the breakwater.

The most convenient of the four passages is the one leading NE of the islet of Sveta Justina (chapel). NE of the islet is a bollard on a concrete base in the sea; between the islet and the bollard is a shoal (1.8 m). Go between the bollard and the mainland coast (keeping as close to the latter as possible) bows-to the head of the breakwater.

Mooring. The small harbour (depth at the entrance 3 m) is only partially protected from the sirocco and open to the south-westerlies. Moor on the inner side of the breakwater small yachts drawing up to 3 m only.

Facilities. Post office and medical service. Provisions, water from the hydrant on the mole. Fuel at the petrol station in Biograd na moru.

Sights. Remnants of a Roman breakwater can be seen in the sea between the mainland coast and the islet inside the harbour. On the islet stands Sv Justina chapel (1670), erected on the site of an older parish church to commemorate the defeat of the Turkish fleet at Lepanto (1571).

ISLAND OF PAG

PAG

(44°27'N; 015°03'E), town and harbour on the SE coast of Paški zaljev (Bay of Pag).

Paški zaljev is entered through Paška vrata passage (between Krištofor and Sv Nikola points). There are several coves in the bay: Slana, Ručica, Metajna, Caska and the harbour of Pag.

The bora in the bay is strong and most frequent in Paška vrata passage and Slana cove; in the NW part of the bay it blows from the E and in SE part from the N. With a strong bora blowing, spindrift and a turbulent sea make it difficult to enter the bay. With the sirocco blowing the sea sometimes floods the coast around the salt-works. Currents caused by the tides attain a rate of 4 knots; their direction is changeable.

Approach. Landmarks: the white tower (white light) on Krištofor point; the red tower (red light) on Sv Nikola point. In the bay: the green tower with a column and gallery (green light) on Zaglava point; the belfry of the church in the town, the large salt storehouse at the head of the harbour and the hotel buildings on the SW coast, the red tower with a column and gallery (red light) on the head of the mole reserved for the car-ferry, the red tower with a column and gallery (red light) on the head of the S pier.

The harbour is entered through a 50 m wide and 4.5 m deep fairway. The axis of the fairway is indicated by the two iron structures (one front, the other back) of the former harbour light with a black triangle and a white vertical line on the top of the each structure. The starboard side of the fairway is marked by two conical green buoys and, further toward the bridge, by two green spars surmounted by a cone. The port side of the entrance is marked by the round red tower with a column (red light) on the head of the ferry pier and the red tower with a column and gallery (red light) on the head of the S pier. When entering, leave the red light on the ferry pier to port, giving it an offing of 15–20 m, and shape course for the light on the head of the S pier. Care should be taken of the current caused by the changing tide (up to 4 knots).

Mooring. The harbour is protected from all winds except the westerlies, which blow infrequently. Yachts drawing up to 3.5 m can moor (four-point moor) on the inner end of the small N mole in the inner harbour or along the quay next to the bridge. The best anchorage for larger yachts is off the E coast, some 1.5 M south of the ruins of the chapel of Sv Nikola (depth 24–48 m). In fine weather smaller vessels can anchor off the ruins of the chapel of Sv Katarina (St Catherine).

Facilities. Harbour master's branch office, post office, several hotels and restaurants, medical service, chemist's, bank.

Good shopping for provisions. Water from the hydrant on the waterfront. Fuel at the petrol station in Pag.

Hoist (1 t) and a slipway in the harbour. The local dairy makes the excellent Pag sheep-milk cheese (paški sir); the well-known Žutica wine is also made locally. The Bašaca camp organizes a traditional summer carnival (July 26–28). The Lokunja thermal spa (radioactive mud used in treating rheumatic diseases) is situated on the SW coast of the bay, opposite the town.

Car-ferry lines: Žigljen – Prizna (mainland) and Pag – Karlobag (mainland).

Sights. The development of the town began in 1433 and was planned by the builder and sculptor Juraj Dalmatinac. Parts of the town wall with the clock tower (after 1433), the Rector's Palace (1467, unfinished), Uzašašće Marijino cathedral (Assumption of Our Lady, 1443–88), the churches of Sv Juraj (St George, Renaissance) and Sv Margareta (second half of 15 C). Starigrad (the centre of the island before the development of the present-day town; 14 C church, next to it the ruins of the Franciscan monastery) – 3 km SE. Climb to the summits of Sv Vid (348 m) and Sv Juraj (263 m) – panoramic view of the area.

Pag has an eight-century-old tradition of lace-making; the lace-making school was established in 1906.

DINJIŠKA

(44°22'N; 015°10'E), village and cove on the SE coast of the island, NE of Ljubačka vrata passage.

PAG

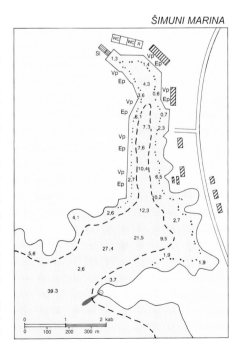

ŠIMUNI MARINA

ŠIMUNI MARINA

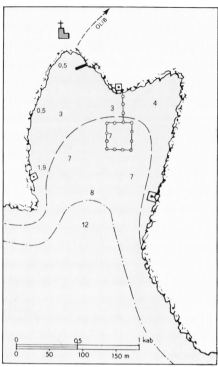

SVETI NIKOLA

Mooring. The cove is a reasonable shelter from the bora; the sirocco is strong in it. Larger yachts can anchor along the NE coast and smaller ones in the cove (depth 13 m). Care should be taken of the rocks on both sides of the entrance to the cove. Vessels can also moor along the pier SE of the village of Miškovići.

STARA POVLJANA
(44°19'N; 015°10'E), uninhabited cove in the SE part of the island of Pag. Sheltered from the bora, it is open to the sirocco, which blows with great force but without causing waves. Larger vessels can anchor at Škamica (depth up to 36 m); smaller yachts can anchor in Gradac cove, SE of the village of Smokvica.

NOVA POVLJANA
(44°21'N; 015°06'E), village and cove on the SW coast of the island of Pag.

Approach. Landmarks: the red round iron tower with a column and gallery (red light) on Dubrovnik point, the hotel complex and the chapel of Sv Nikola (St Nicholas) on the E coast of the cove.

Mooring. The harbour is well sheltered from the most frequent winds, the bora and sirocco, but is open to winds from the SW and NW quadrants. Vessels drawing up to 3 m can moor on the inner side of the breakwater. With the bora and sirocco blowing, larger vessels can anchor only in the middle of the cove and smaller ones closer to the chapel of Sv Nikola.

Facilities. Provisions and water in the village of Povljana, 0.8 km inshore.

Sights. Sv Nikola (early medieval, fragments of frescoes) and Sv Juraj (St George, (18 C) churches.

KOŠLJUN
(44°22,8'N; 015°05'E), village and small harbour in Košljunski zaljev (Bay of Košljun), on the SW coast of the island, between Tihovac and Zminka points.

Approach. Landmarks: the quadrangular white iron tower with the white light on Zaglava point and the white round tower with a gallery (sector light) at the head of the breakwater.

Zminka and Tihovac points are fringed by shoals; by night the green sector of the light

OLIB

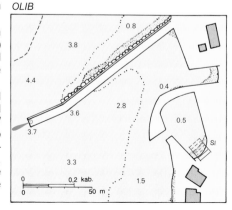

at the root of the breakwater indicates the safe passage.

Mooring. The bay is sheltered only from winds from the NE quadrant (it is therefore the auxiliary harbour of the town of Pag in the bora); southern winds cause a heavy sea in the harbour. Smaller vessels can moor along the head of the breakwater (depth about 2 m), or use the four-point moor on the rest of the breakwater (depth under 1 m). Larger vessels can anchor WSW of the ruins on the NE coast, some 700 m offshore (depth 18–23 m). The harbour is not recommended for a longer stay, especially in bad weather.

Facilities. Limited provisions and water are available.

ŠIMUNI
(44°28'N; 014°57'E), village and small bay on the W coast of the island of Pag in Maunski kanal.

Approach. Conspicuous landmark is the round white tower (green light) on Šimuni point. On the port side of the bay there are submerged rocks and Šimuni shoal (depth 1.3 m) and while entering the bay steer clear of the points on the left side of the bay.

Mooring. The bay is well sheltered from all winds. During the bora, small yachts can anchor in the SE part (depth up to 1.5 m); good anchorage. Yachts drawing up to 2 m can moor (four-point) along the mole in the NE part.

GRUJICA

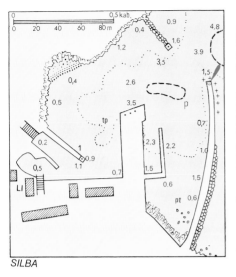

SILBA

Limited provisions and water.

ŠIMUNI MARINA (ACI)

(44°28'N; 014°57'E) is located in the cove on the NW side of the Šimuni bay (Maunski kanal), W part of the island.

The marina has 150 sea-berths (up to 18 m length) and area for 30 vessels (dry-berths); water, electricity, telephone hook-ups. Slipway (for yachts up to 8 m long); crane (15 t).

It has reception office, shop, restaurant, laundry, toilets and grocer's shop (groceries can be delivered to the vessel if ordered so).

The marina is open the year round.

MANDRE

(44°29'N; 014°55'E), village and cove on the W coast of the island of Pag in Maunski kanal.

A good shelter for smaller yachts, which can moor off the mole in front of the hotel. The harbour is sheltered from all winds, except those from the SW quadrant. The depth in the harbour is up to 2 m.

Facilities. Provisions at a shop; water from the main.

ISLAND OF OLIB

SVETI NIKOLA

(44°21'N; 014°47'E), cove on the SW coast of Olib, some 1.6 M southeast of the Tale point.

Approach. Landmarks: the stone chapel and three stone bollards on the points of the cove; the yellow buoy with a black band (white light) on the Tale point.

Mooring. The cove is sheltered from the bora and N winds, but is open to the siroc-co, which causes big waves and makes the cove dangerous. Anchor in the middle of the cove (depth 12 m); smaller yachts can moor (four-point moor) by securing to the bollards at the root of the cove.

Sights. The ruins of the monastery and the church (late 17 C) in the Banve cove.

OLIB

(44°23'N; 014°47'E), village and small har-bour in the cove on the W coast of the island of Olib.

Approach. Landmarks: Sv Stošija chapel (St Anastasia) in the village; the chapel on the N coast of the cove; the red tower with a column and gallery (red light) on the head of the breakwater.

Care should be taken of the shallow S coast. By night steer by the light on the head of the breakwater, which indicates the berth that must be given to Kurjak rock (on the NW side). Approaching the cove from SE, leave the yellow light buoy with a black band (white light) marking the shoal off the Tale point-to starboard.

Mooring. Smaller yachts moor on the inner side of the breakwater (depth about 2.5 m); part of the head of the breakwater is used by passenger ships. The anchorage off the harbour (depth 8–20 m) is sheltered only from winds from the NE quadrant.

Facilities. Post office, medical service, several shops and restaurants. Provisions in local shops.

Local passenger line: see Zadar.

Sights. The fortification (Kaštel) at the har-bour entrance (17–18 C) built for defense against pirates; Sv Stošija church (St Anastasia, 17 C).

ISLAND OF SILBA

SILBA

(44°22,5'N; 014°42,4'E), village and east-ern harbour of the island.

Approach. Landmarks: the quadrangular red tower with a column and gallery (red light) on the head of the breakwater and the red tower in the village.

Mooring. The harbour is protected from all winds except the bora and tramontana. During these winds it is advisable to leave the harbour and seek shelter on the W coast of the island. Smaller yachts can moor along the inner side of the breakwater which is arranged as a marina (depth 2–3 m); at the head of the breakwater there is a sub-merged pile of stones (up to 5 m). Along the head of the inner quay there is a landing ground for local passenger boats. The anchorage for yachts is situated some 250 m off the harbour (depth 10–15 m).

Facilities. Harbour master's branch office, post office, medical service, chemist's, restaurants. Provisions in local shops, limit-ed water from the cistern and mains water supply.

There are two slipways for smaller ves-sels.

Coastal passenger lines: see Zadar and Mali Lošinj.

Sights. Uznesenje Marijino church (Assumption of the Virgin, 1637, paintings, the crown of the »peasant king« elected each year by the local population to reign from December 26 until January 6); parts of fortifications built against pirates (16 C), the Belvedere tower Toreta (19 C).

SVETI ANTE

(44°21'N; 014°42'E), cove on the SW coast of Silba.

Approach. Landmarks: the house on the Mavrova point and the chapel on the point between the N and S coves. Care should be taken of the shoals fringing the entrance points.

Mooring. The northernmost part of the cove is protected from all winds, the rest of the cove is exposed to W winds. The best anchorage for smaller yachts is in the S part of the cove, especially during the sirocco.

ŽALIĆ

(44°22,4'N; 014°41,8'E), cove and the western harbour of the village of Silba.

Approach. Landmarks: the white tower with a column and gallery (red light) on the head of the pier and the belfry in Silba.

Mooring. The harbour is sheltered only from the bora and the easterlies; yachts should leave when W and NW winds start blowing. The SE end of the pier is reserved for passenger ships. Smaller yachts can moor at both sides of the pier (depth 1.5–5.4 m) but only in calm weather and the bora; if all berths are taken, they should use the four-point moor. A good anchorage for larger yachts is NW of the harbour (depth 25–40 m); for smaller yachts a good shelter from the bora is some 400 m NW of the demolished part of the breakwater.

 IST

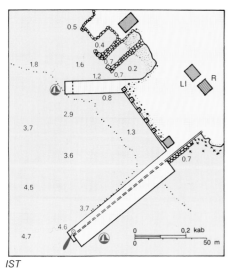

IST

Facilities. Limited water supply; provisions and other shopping in local shops.

ISLAND OF PREMUDA

KRIJAL

(44°20'N; 014°36'E), small bay on the W coast of the island. Above it, on the top of the island, there is the village of Premuda.

Approach. Landmarks: SW of the bay a string of rocks (Hripa, Masarine, Plitka Sika, Bračić, Mala Sika). The red tower with a column (red light) on the head of the N breakwater and the chapel.

One can enter the harbour from SE and NW keeping as near as the coast of the island. Sailing between cliffs is dangerous because of shoals and sunken reefs.

Mooring. The harbour is sheltered from all winds except the north-westerlies, which cause a moderate sea in it. The anchorage is sheltered only from the bora and southwesterlies. Small yachts can moor in the inner harbour, securing the boat alongside the inner breakwater or using the four-point moor. Larger yachts anchor NE of Hripa rock. With the bora or N winds, anchor WNW of the harbour, in other winds S of it.

Facilities. Post office in the village of Premuda (1 km). Provisions in a local shop.

There is a slipway for smaller vessels at the inner end of the harbour.

Coastal passenger lines: see Mali Lošinj and Zadar.

ISLAND OF ŠKARDA

GRIPARICA

(44°16,6'N; 014°43,4'E), cove in the S part of the island.

ŠTERNA

Approach. Landmarks: the abandoned house at the head of the cove, the summit of the hill (102 m) NE of the entrance to the cove and the lime-kilns on both sides of the entrance.

Mooring. The cove is sheltered from all winds except the sirocco which raises a heavy sea; leave the cove at the first sign of the sirocco. Good anchorage for yachts of all sizes (depth 6–25 m).

ISLAND OF IST

IST

(44°16'N; 014°46'E), small harbour at the head of Široka cove on the SE coast of Ist. The village of Ist is some 600 m away.

Approach. Landmarks: the green tower with a column (green light) on the head of the breakwater and the chapel on Straža hill (175 m); the shoal (2 m) at the entrance to the cove is marked by a spar with black and red bands surmounted by two black spheres.

Mooring. The anchorage is not safe; the bora blows heavily and the sirocco raises the heavy sea. Smaller vessels can moor on the inner side of the breakwater (70 m long); with the bora blowing, secure to the bollards on the opposite coast, which is partially protected from all winds. The head of the pier is reserved for passenger ships.

Facilities. Harbour master's branch office and post office. Provisions in local shops; water in limited quantities.

Coastal passenger lines: see Mali Lošinj and Zadar.

MARINA IST D. D. O. IST

(44°16'N; 014°6,6'E) lies on the SE coast of the island near the small port in front of the village (max. depth 4 m).

Mooring. On the S side of the main mole as well as on the inner side and the head of the inner mole. Anchorage on the buoys (40).

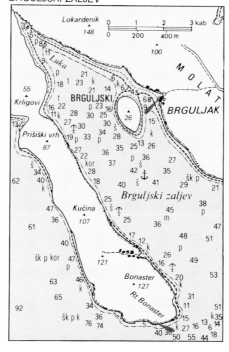

BRGULJSKI ZALJEV

Facilities. Marina reception office, water and electricity hook-ups, WC, exchange office and restaurant in the village Ist.

KOSIRAČA

(44°17'N; 014°45'E), cove on the NW coast of the island.

Approach. Landmarks: the chapel on Straža hill, three small houses S of Kok point and the houses at the head of the cove. When approaching from NW, take care of the shoal (3 m), rock and islet of Križica (the housing of the underwater cable), situated W of the Kok point.

Mooring. The cove is protected from all winds from the SE and SW quadrants, but is exposed to N and NW winds; the bora is strong and blows from various directions. Anchor off the root of the cove in 5–20 m.

ISLAND OF MOLAT

ZAPUNTEL

(44°15'N; 014°49'E), cove and village in the passage of the same name (between the islands of Ist and Molat).

Approach. From Virsko more: the conical white tower with a gallery (white light) on Vranač point (on the island of Molat) and Vrh gore and Straža hills (on the island of Ist); when approaching from the open sea take care of the islets, reefs and shoals off Ist and Molat.

In the straits (depth at midpoint 20–40 m) there is a strong current (up to 3 knots) coming from the open sea; with a strong bora and the current from the opposite direction there is a strong chop.

Mooring. A good allround shelter. Yachts can moor along the mole in the harbour (alongside it or using the four-point moor); depth 3.5 m. The head of the mole is reserved for passenger ships.

It is prohibited to anchor in the middle of the passage and in its narrow W part (an underwater cable).

Facilities. Very limited provisions and water available in the coastal part of the village.

Local passenger lines: see Zadar.

JAZI

(44°13'N; 014°53'E), cove on the SE coast of the island.

Approach. The islet of Tovarnjak off the cove and the church on the hill in the village of Molat can be easily identified.

Mooring. The cove is exposed to NE winds; with a strong wind blowing, anchor in Lučina cove (Brguljski zaljev). Smaller yachts can anchor some 300 m off the small pier bearing NNE (depth 5–8 m) or in Pržina cove (some 0.6 M northwest of the harbour, depth 4–6 m), where they can also moor (four-point moor). A good anchorage for larger yachts (depth 8–20 m) is on the alignment of the centre of Tovarnjak island and the church in the village.

Facilities. Limited provisions and water available in the village of Molat.

BRGULJSKI ZALJEV

(44°13,7'N; 014°52,6'E), small bay on the SW coast of the Molat island between Bonaster and Golubinjka points; with its

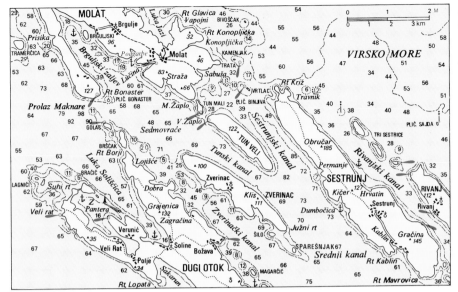

SEDMOVRAĆE

eastern Lučina, Podgarbe and Luka coves, it is the best natural shelter in this part of the Adriatic for vessels of all sizes.

Approach. Landmarks: the pyramidal stone tower (white light) on Bonaster point; the white tower with a column and gallery (white light) on the islet of Golac; the belfry and several houses in the village of Molat; the round red tower with a column and gallery (red sector light) in Lučina cove; the conical white tower with a gallery (white-green sector light) on Tun Veli islet; the red tower with a column and gallery (red light) on Tun Mali. When navigating through Maknare passage, larger yachts should keep in the white sector of the light on the islet of Tun Veli. Approaching from Zadar, keep in the second white sector of the light on Tun Veli; turn towards the bay after you have passed the light on Bonaster point.

Warning. About 1 M north of the light on Bonaster point is a buoy (no light) used by warships.

Mooring. Small yachts can moor at the mole in the Lučina cove. The best anchorage is NW of the islet of Brguljski in Studena cove (depth to 4.5 m) nearer the NE shore; there is good anchorage in the SE part of Podgarbe cove (sheltered from S winds) and in the Luka cove at the NW end of the bay.

Facilities. Provisions and water in Lučina.

Local passenger line: Ist – Molat – Zadar.

BRGULJE

(44°14'N; 014°50'E), small port in the N part of Brguljski zaljev, NE from the island Brguljski.

Approach. No problems, see Brguljski zaljev.

Facilities. Water and food shop in Lučina.

MOLAT

(44°13'N; 014°53'E), small port in the bay Lučina at the SE coast of the Molat island. The village Molat is 1 km away from the port.

Mooring. Protected from all winds except SW and W.

Facilities. Food shop, restaurant, post-office.

SEDMOVRAĆE,

sea area bounded by the islands of Molat, Tun Mali, Tun Veli, Zverinac and Dugi Otok. Access through the following straits: Maknare, between Bonaster point on Molat and Borji point on Dugi Otok; Velo Žaplo, between Tun Mali and Tun Veli; Malo Žaplo between Žaplo point on Molat and Tun Mali (see Brguljski zaljev). A high-tension overhead transmission line, with a vertical clearance of 10.5 m, spans the Malo Žaplo straits. In the Velo Žaplo straits and Sestrunjski kanal, the tidal stream sets eastwards and northwards respectively at a rate of 2.5 knots. The two streams meet at the islet of Vrtlac and form eddies. The ebb tide setting in the opposite direction attains a rate of up to 1.5 knots.

Warning. Approaching from the open sea from NW, care should be taken of Bačvica reef (some 0.5 M southeast of the islet of Tramerka); approaching from S, care should be taken of the islets of Lagnjići (about 0.7 M northwest of Veli Rat point), which are fringed by submerged reefs. In the passage of Maknare, between the islets of Golac and Bršćak is a 3 m deep shoal. By night, the passage of Maknare, between the light on Bonaster point (white flashes) and the islet of Golac (white flashes), is indicated by the white sector of the light on the Tun Veli island.

Vessels approaching from Zadarski kanal and Virsko more should take care to avoid Sajda shoal, situated about 1.5 M north of the Rivanj island. It is marked by a quadrangular masonry tower with black and red bands (white flashing light) surmounted by two black spheres. About 700 m NW of the group of islands Tri sestrice is a reef marked by a black-red-black spar on a concrete base surmounted by two black spheres. E of the NW extremity of Sestrunj island is a shoal (5.8 m), which is dangerous only for deep drawing yachts. By night, keep within the white sector of the light on Tun Veli (conical white tower with a gallery), which leads between Trata islet (red tower with a column and gallery, red flashes) and Vrtlac islet (white tower with a column and gallery, white flashes); Sedmovraće is entered between the islet of Tun Mali (red flashes)

and the NW point of Tun Veli (green flashes).

The best course from Sedmovraće to Srednji kanal is through Tunski kanal, where there are no obstacles for navigation.

ISLAND OF SESTRUNJ

HRVATIN

(44°10'N; 015°00'E), cove on the NE coast of Sestrunj.

Mooring. Good shelter (anchorage) from the sirocco. Smaller yachts can moor at the pier, where they are protected from all winds.

Facilities. Provisions and water in the village of Sestrunj.

Coastal passenger lines: see Zadar.

KABLIN

(44°08'N; 015°01'E), cove and point on the SW coast of Sestrunj, about 1.5 M northwest of Mavrovica point, which is the southernmost point of the island. Kablin serves as the harbour for the village of Sestrunj.

Mooring. Kablin affords good shelter from the northerlies and the bora to smaller yachts. During the sirocco, yachts should shift to the NE coast of the island. Mooring at the inner side of the piers, the first of which is reserved for local lines.

Facilities. Provisions and water in the village of Sestrunj (1 km inland).

DUMBOČICA

(44°08'N; 014°59'E), cove on the SW coast of Sestrunj. A good shelter from the northerlies and the bora for smaller yachts; anchorage closer inshore (depth 1–5 m).

Facilities. Provisions and water in the village of Sestrunj (1.5 km inland).

ISLAND OF RIVANJ

RIVANJ

(44°09'N; 015°03'E), small harbour on the W coast of the island of Rivanj; on the hill above the harbour is the village of Rivanj.

Approach. Landmarks: the white tower with a column and gallery (green light) on the head of the breakwater.

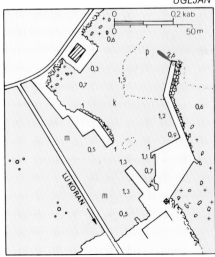

UGLJAN

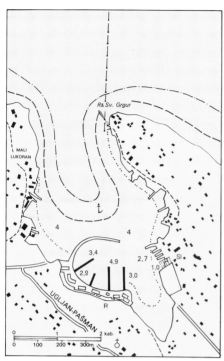

SUTOMIŠĆICA

Due to the strong currents in Rivanjski kanal (up to 4 knots) anchoring in it is not recommended.

Mooring. The breakwaters protect the harbour from the northerlies and partly from the sirocco. Smaller yachts can moor only along the inner end of the bigger breakwater (depth 3 m), the outer end being reserved for the coastal lines.

Facilities. Provisions and other shopping in local shops.

Local passengers lines: see Zadar.

ISLAND OF UGLJAN

UGLJAN

(44°08'N; 015°07'E), village and small harbour on the NE coast of the island.

Approach. Landmarks: the red column on the head of the breakwater and the monastery on the N entrance point. Care

should be taken of the rocky shoals (1 m) NW off the entrance.

Mooring. The harbour is protected from the sirocco but is open to the bora. Smaller yachts can moor along the inner end of the breakwater or moor (four-point moor) near the root of the breakwater (depth 0.5–1 m). The depth in the inner harbour (SW part) is about 1 m. The anchorage some 0.5 M south-east of the light (depth 6–10 m) is safe only in the sirocco but should not be considered in the bora.

Facilities. Post office, medical service, hotel, and restaurant. Provisions in local shops.

Sights. The Franciscan monastery (1430) with a cloister and Sv Jerolim church (St Jerome, 1447); next to the cove the ruins of a Roman villa rustica; at Stivan the ruins of early Christian buildings (4–6 C).

ČEPRLJANDA

(44°07'N; 015°07,5'E), small cove SE of the village of Ugljan (some 0.7 M); good all-round shelter except from the winds from the NW quadrant. The depth in the cove is up to 3 m and small yachts can moor by using the four-point moor or at the small moles.

LUKORAN VELI

(44°06,2'N; 015°10'E), cove on the NE coast of Ugljan; the village of Lukoran.

Approach. Landmarks: the church on the hill in the village and old pine-forest on the W part of the cove.

Mooring. The cove is well sheltered from all winds except those from the NW quadrant. Smaller yachts can moor along the pier off the village or anchor in the cove; good holding.

Facilities. Post office and medical service. Provisions in local shops.

Sights. Sv Lovro church (St Lawrence, Romanesque) at the cemetery; in the hamlet of Mali Lukoran the summer residence of da Ponte family (17 C).

SUTOMIŠĆICA

(44°06'N; 015°10'E), village and small harbour in the cove of the same name on the NE coast of Ugljan.

Approach. Landmarks: the red column (red light) on Sv Grgur point and the belfry in the village.

There is an underwater cable 370 m off the coast E of Lukoran light extending to Oštri rat point.

Mooring. The cove is exposed to the tramontana and protected from all other winds and seas. There are several small moles (depth up to 2 m). Smaller yachts can moor in the middle of the cove (depth 8–12 m). During the bora it is advisable to anchor off the NE coast.

Facilities. Provisions and water in local shops.

Sights. Sv Eufemija church (St Euphemia, 1349, renovated in 17 C), Sv Grgur chapel (St Gregory, renovated in 15 C), the ruins of the monastery and Lantana summer house (1684) surrounded by a park.

POLJANA

(44°05'N; 015°12'E), village and cove on the E coast of Ugljan, N of Preko.

Approach. Landmarks: the round green tower with a column and gallery (green light) on the shoal (2 m) some 100 m of Sv Petar point and the red iron column (red light) on the breakwater S off the entrance point can be easily identified.

When entering the cove care should be taken of the shoal SE of Sv Petar point. Vessels should not navigate between the round green tower (green light) and Sv Petar point. In the harbour care should be taken of the submerged rocks off the N coast, between the chapel and the first house.

The cove is exposed to E and SE winds. Limited provisions and water available.

PREKO

(44°06'N; 015°02'E), village and small harbour on the E coast of Ugljan, opposite Zadar.

Approach. The landmarks include the wooded islet of Galovac with the monastery, the red column (red light) on the head of the breakwater and the white tower (green light) on the ferry pier. The harbour consists of a northern and a southern part. A high-tension

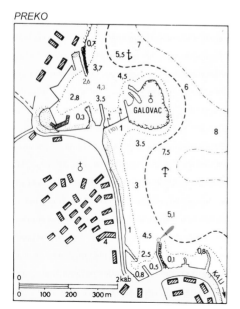

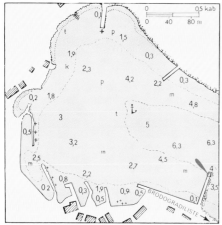

KUKLJICA

cable spans the passage between Galovac and Ugljan (10 m).

Mooring. The S part of the harbour is exposed to the bora; the N (inner) part is protected from all winds. Yachts drawing up to 1.2 m moor along the breakwater in the S part of the harbour and on the outer, S pier in the N part of the harbour. The ferry uses the pier 300 m SE off the village. The anchorage (depth 5–10 m), situated off the village N of Galovac, is exposed to the bora.

Facilities. Harbour master's branch office, post office, medical service and chemist's. Provisions from local shops, mains water supply; fuel at the pump on the pier, some 50 m from the ferry pier.

Car-ferry line: Preko – Zadar.

Sights. Remnants of ancient buildings (a cistern, mosaics) in the Gradina area; the Romanesque church of Sv Ivan Krstitelj (St John the Baptist, 12/13 C), Gospa od Ružarija church (Our Lady of the Rosary, 1765). – Galovac islet: Franciscan monastery (until 14/15 C Pauline, renovated in 16 C) with Sv Pavle church (St Paul, 1569) and library (from 15 C); park with subtropical vegetation. – Sveti Mihovil on the hill of the same name (256 m), first a Benedictine then a Dominican monastery, converted into a fortress by the Venetians in 1202, was their main observation post for the Zadar archipelago.

KALI

(44°04'N; 015°12'E), small town and fishing harbour on the NE coast of Ugljan.

Approach. Landmarks: the red column (red light) on the head of the E breakwater, the belfry in the village and the islet of Ošljak (white light) NE of the harbour.

Mooring. The harbour is exposed to N winds, which causes a sea in it. Yachts drawing up to 3.5 m can moor on the inner end of the masonry breakwaters and in the inner harbour (depth 0.5–2 m); the inner harbour is mostly occupied by fishing boats.

Facilities. Post office and medical service. Provisions and water available.

Minor repairs to marine engines can be undertaken at the local workshop. Hauling-out facility. »Zadar« repair shipyard in Lamjana Vela bay.

Each year on August 10 a fishermen's festivity (»Kaljska ribarska noć«) is held here with a fishing boat regatta and other competitions.

KUKLJICA

KUKLJICA

(44°02'N; 015°15'E), village and small harbour in the cove of the same name in the south-easternmost part of Ugljan.

Approach. Landmarks: the apartment settlement at the entrance to the harbour, the round green tower with a column and gallery (green light) on the head of the N breakwater, the islet of Mišnjak (some 0.8 M southeast of the cove) and the church in the village.

Mooring. The cove is sheltered from the bora and northerlies and the harbour from all winds. Yachts can moor along the breakwater or, using the four-point moor, along the quay. There are several small jetties in the W part of the cove. In the middle of the cove the depth is between 1.5 and 6 m. A good anchorage is in the middle of the harbour (depth 5–6 m).

Facilities. Post office and medical service. Provisions and water available; fuel at the petrol station in Preko.

A boatyard for wooden craft with a slipway for medium-sized vessels.

On August 5 each year there is a traditional religious ceremony of carrying Our Lady of the Snow from the chapel (Mali Ždrelac) to Kukljica; more than 100 vessels take part in it.

Sights. Sv Petar i Pavao church (SS Peter and Paul, 1666, Glagolitic inscriptions), the Romanesque-Gothic church of Sv Jerolim.

LAMJANA VELA and LAMJANA MALA,

two coves on the south-westernmost coast of Ugljan, in Srednji kanal. The bay Lamjana mala is protected from all NN and SE winds.

In **Lamjana Mala** there is a fish and mussel farm and navigation for vessels over 16 m in length and engine over 60 kW (81 HP).

In **Lamjana Vela** there is a shipyard »Zadar – Kali« with a breakwater 370 m long; there are two cranes (5,6 and 32 t) and two movable cranes (9 and 40 t).

MALI ŽDRELAC

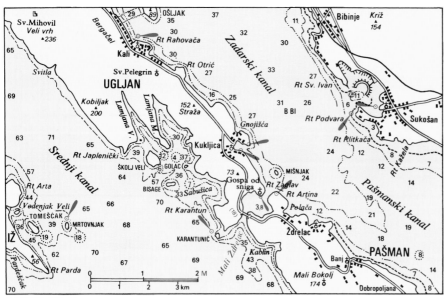

MALI ŽDRELAC

MULINE

(44°08,3'N; 015°04,5'E), cove and village on the NW coast of Ugljan in Veli Ždrelac passage; the fairway is not marked by lights and navigation is possible only by day.

Mooring. Yachts drawing up to 3 m can moor along the masonry part of the pier. The cove is protected from all winds and seas except those from the SW quadrant. During the SW winds it is recommended to anchor 0.4 M north off the SE point of the island of Rivanj.

Facilities. Limited provisions and water available in the village of Donje Selo (E part of the cove).

Sights. Remnants of a prehistoric fort and of early Christian buildings (basilica, small chapel, mausoleum, villa rustica).

ISLAND OF PAŠMAN

MALI ŽDRELAC

44°01'N; 015°17'E), passage between the islands of Ugljan and Pašman connecting Zadarski kanal and Srednji kanal. The bridge across it has a vertical clearance of 18 m.

Approach. The fairway is marked by 7 coast lights and two triangular reflecting marks (red or green); the bridge piers (3 m above sea-level) are painted in red or green reflecting colours (height about 1 m); they mark the sides of the passage (lateral system). Coming from Srednji kanal the starboard hand is marked by green towers (green flashes) and the port hand with red towers (red flashes); in the middle part of Ždrelac harbour, on the fairway axis (270 m N of the bridge) is a cardinal mark (a black and yellow tower, white flashes) surmounted by two black cones points downwards – keep S of the mark. Coming from Zadarski kanal, after passing the islet of Mišnjak, steer for the red tower on a base in the sea (white-red sector light) some 150 m off the chapel of »Gospa od Sniga« on Zaglav point and the green tower on a stone block in the sea (green light) on Artina point.

Warning. The speed limit in the passage is 8 knots. Anchoring, stopping and fishing is prohibited. Vessels coming from Zadarski kanal have right of way.

Mali Ždrelac passage is sheltered from all winds. Under the bridge the tidal currents may attain a rate of 4 knots.

ŽDRELAC

(44°01'N; 015°17'E), village and small harbour (Sv Luka) on the northernmost coast of Pašman.

Approach. Shape course for the chapel in the cemetery (E of the entrance) and the red column (former light) on the head of the breakwater.

Mooring. The harbour is a good allround shelter. Yachts drawing up to 1.5 m can moor at the mole. Good anchorage for vessels drawing less than 4 m.

Facilities. Post office. Provisions and water available.

BANJ

(44°00'N; 015°18'E), village and cove in the NE part of Pašman. Wooded slopes. Good anchorage for smaller vessels.

Facilities. Provisions and water available.

DOBROPOLJANA

(43°59'N; 015°20'E), village and small cove in the N part of Pašman.

Mooring. The harbour is sheltered from S and W winds. Along the waterfront are berths for vessels drawing up to 2.5 m only. E of the L-shaped pier is a 120 m long L-shaped breakwater made from piled stones.

NEVIĐANE

(43°58,5'N; 015°21'E), village and cove on the NE coast of Pašman.

Approach. Landmarks: the belfry and the houses in the olive groves, the red tower with a column and gallery (red light) on the head of the breakwater.

Mooring. The breakwater affords good shelter for smaller vessels from SE and SW winds; the cove is exposed to the bora and the northerlies.

Facilities. Post office. Provisions and water available.

Sights. Adjoining the church of Gospa od Zdravlja (Our Lady of Salvation, 19 C) are the ruins of a church (1670); in the cemetery the ruins of Sv Mihovil church (St Michael, 990), W of the village is Sv Martin church (St Martin, 11 C, ruins).

PAŠMAN

(43°57,5'N; 015°23,5'E), village and small harbour at the narrowest part of Pašmanski kanal.

Approach. Landmarks include the round green tower with an open framework structure (green light) on the head of the E breakwater and the belfry in Lučina cove, NE of the village. Entering and leaving harbour is difficult because of the strong currents at the entrance (see Pašmanski kanal).

Mooring. The harbour is protected from all winds except the north-westerlies. The inner harbour is mainly occupied by local fishing boats. Smaller yachts can moor along the breakwater. Depth in the harbour 1–4 m.

Facilities. Post office, medical service. Provisions and water available.

Sights. Rođenje Marijino church (Birth of Our Lady, 9 C, enlarged in 18 C); two early Croatian chapels in Pašman Mali.

TKON

(43°55'N; 015°25'E), village and small harbour on the SE coast of the island of Pašman.

Approach. Landmarks: the belfry and chapel with part of the monastery (90 m above sea-level), NW of the village; on the head of the breakwater is a red tower with a column and gallery (red light).

Mooring. The harbour is protected from all winds and seas. Smaller vessels can moor along the breakwater (depth 1.5–2.5 m). Some 200 m SE of the harbour is the landing-place (red tower with a column and gallery, red light) used by the car-ferry. A part of the quay (some 45 m) is damaged and cannot be used for landing or mooring.

Facilities. Post office. Limited provisions (self-service shop) and water; fuel at the petrol station in Biograd na moru. Repairs to marine engines can be undertaken.

Car-ferry line: Tkon – Biograd na moru.

Sights. The summer residence of the d'Erco family (17 C); on Čokovac Hill (90 m) the ruins of the Benedictine monastery with Sv Kuzma i Damjan church (SS Cosmas and Damian, 1367–1418).

TRILUKE

(43°53,5'N; 015°27'E), uninhabited cove on the southernmost coast of Pašman, some 0.5 M west of Borovnjak point.

Approach. When approaching from N and NE larger yachts should take care of the shoals S of Borovnjak point (4.8 m) and, near the E coast, of the islet of Žižanj (4.6 m).

Mooring. The cove is protected from all winds but the sirocco sends in a sea and makes it untenable. Good anchorage for vessels of all sizes.

SOLINE

(43°55,6'N; 014°21,6'E), cove on the SW coast of the island of Pašman.

Approach. Zaglav Hill (127 m) on the S side can be easily identified.

Mooring. The SE part of the cove is sheltered from all winds (the north-westerlies cause a swell). Smaller yachts anchor in the SE part of the cove (submerged reefs are visible during the low tide), and in the NW part of the cove (depth 2–8 m). Larger yachts anchor in the middle of the cove (depth 16–22 m). During the bora, vessels at anchor should secure ashore as well.

ISLAND OF ZVERINAC

ZVERINAC

(44°10'N; 014°55'E), village in the cove of the same name on the SW coast of the island of Zverinac.

Approach. Landmarks: the houses in the village and the belfry at the head of the cove can be seen from afar.

Mooring. The cove is sheltered from all winds except the south-westerlies, which cause a big sea in it and make it untenable.

The head of the L-shaped pier is used by passenger ships. Smaller vessels can moor along the head of the L-shaped pier (depth 2 m) or secure to the bollard, some 5 M east. Larger yachts can anchor closer inshore, securing ashore.

Facilities. Provisions in local shops.

Coastal passenger lines: see Zadar.

Sights. Palace of the Fanfogna family (1746) with chapel.

ISLAND OF IŽ

VELI IŽ

(44°03'N; 015°07'E), village and small harbour on the NE coast of the island.

Approach. Landmarks: the red tower with a column (red light) on the S side of the entrance and the »Korinjak« hotel on the N point of the harbour. Some 0.4 M off the harbour is the islet of Rutnjak. The spar surmounted by two black spheres marks the shoal some 400 m NW of the island of Knežak.

Mooring. The harbour is protected from all winds. Yachts can moor in Iž Marina on the E coast of the cove or anchor in Draga harbour (some 0.4 M north), Knež cove (some

VELI IŽ

1.4 M south-east) or Komaševa cove (the village of Mali Iž, 1.8 M south-east). During the sirocco, a good anchorage for smaller vessels is N of the narrowest part of the passage between Iž and Knežak and during the bora E of it.

Facilities. Post office, medical service, a hotel and two restaurants. Provisions and water in local shops.

Hull and marine engine repairs (wooden craft) at the local boatyard; hauling-out facility. Major repairs in the »Zadar« shipyard in Lamjana Vela on the island of Ugljan.

Veli Iž is the venue of the traditional »Iške fešte« (Iž Festival), held every year in late July.

Coastal passenger lines: see Zadar.

Sights. Remains of Illyrian and Roman settlements. Palaces of the families Canagietti and Fanfogna. Sv Marija (St Mary), church (9/11 C) above the village; museum collection.

VELI IŽ MARINA

(44°03'N; 015°6,8'E) is situated on the E coast of the island of Iž; belongs to Zadar marina (Borik).

The marina has 50 berths (with hydrants and electricity hook-ups) along the waterfront and the pier and 200 dry-berths. The depth along the waterfront is 2 m and in the middle of the cove 3 m. Sale of gas in metal cylinders.

Hauling-out of vessels on an automatic slipway (crane 50 t); security, rubbing down and maintenance of vessels the year round (see also Veli Iž).

ISLAND OF RAVA

RAVA

(44°02'N; 015°04'E), village and small harbour on the island of Rava, which stretches along the NE coast of Dugi otok.

VELI IŽ MARINA

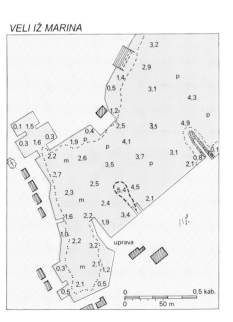

SOLIŠĆICA

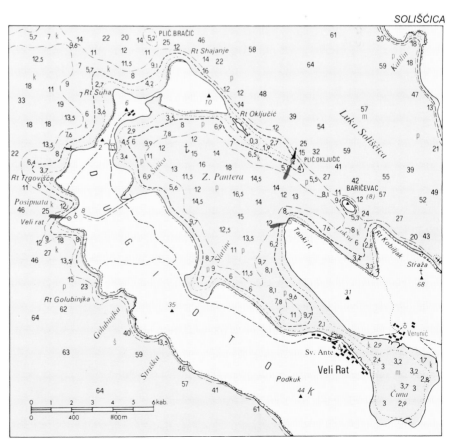

VELI RAT

Mooring. Medium-sized yachts can anchor in Marinica cove on the W coast of the island; it is open to SW.

Facilities. Post office. Limited provisions available.

Coastal passenger lines: see Zadar.

ISLAND OF DUGI OTOK

SOLIŠĆICA

(44°09'N; 014°52'E), spacious bay on the NW coast of Dugi otok; in its SE part is the village of Soline.

Approach. Solišćica can be identified from seaward by the round tower (41 m) of the Veli Rat lighthouse (white flashes, visibility 18 M). In the cove is the red tower with a column (white and red light with sectors) on Tanki point and the yellow church in Soline (see Sedmovraće).

Mooring. The bay is sheltered from all winds except the north-westerlies, during which smaller yachts anchor in Lučica cove (some 0.6 M northwest of Soline). A good anchorage for larger yachts (depth 24–30 m) is some 750 m NNW of the church in Soline. During the winds from the SW and NW quadrants Brguljski zaljev (Island of Molat) affords good shelter. The W part of Solišćica is the shallow cove of Pantera, which is sheltered from all winds and waves; in its NW part is a good anchorage (depth up to 16 m). At the head of the bay is the village of Veli Rat.

Facilities. Post office in Veli Rat; provisions and water available.

PANTERA

(44°09'N; 014°51'E), the bay is opened to the West towards Solšćica.

Max. depth is 16 m. It is protected from all winds and provides safe shelter.

Approach. From the bay of Solišćica one should be careful because of the shoal of about 0,4 square m from Oključić to SE. By night the red sector of the lighthouse on Tanki rt covers the shoal.

Mooring. In NW part of the bay Pantera there are 100 places for yachts and 40 more in the neighbouring bay of Čuna (44°04,4'N; 014°51,8'E).

BOŽAVA

(44°08'N; 014°55'E), village, small harbour and tourist resort on the NE coast of Dugi otok. Border crossing open only April 1 – October 31.

Approach. Landmarks: the white tower with a column and gallery (green light), the chapel on Sv Nedjelja point (pine wood) and the belfry in the village.

Mooring. The harbour is sheltered from all winds and seas except the SE wind and it is recommended to anchor in the Dragove cove (2 M SE of Božava). Along the N coast there is a landing ground for local passenger ships. Somewhat on the W side there is a breakwater which closes a small harbour (capacity ca. 20 yachts), depth along the breakway is 2–6 m. In front of the hotel to the south there is a quay; depth 2–3 m.

Facilities. Harbour master's branch office, post office, medical service, the »Božava« hotel complex.

Provisions in local shops; limited water (from the locals or the hotel). Fuel from the pump at the hotel.

Coastal passenger lines: see Zadar.

Sights. Two Illyrian (later Roman) settlements on the nearby hills. Sv Nikola church (St Nicholas, 9 C?, reconstructed) in the cemetery; old garden walls (18 C) near the coast with loopholes built for protection against pirates.

BRBINJ

(44°04,4'N; 15°00,6'E), village and cove on the NE coast of Dugi otok.

Approach. Brbinj may be identified by the white tower (white light) at the extremity of the N end of the cove (Koromašnjak point).

Mooring. The N part of the cove is protected from all winds, the outer part is exposed to the bora. Small yachts can moor at the quay (depth 1 m) and the mole fronting the village (N part of the cove), which is also used by local passenger ships. W from the village there is the Lučina cove (44°4,9'N; 015°00'E), good for anchoring of yachts of all sizes. Anchorage gives protection from all winds. In the cove there is a landing ground for car ferries. On the SE side of the village there is a small cove Bok (44°04,4'N; 015°0,7'E) with a possibility of shelter for 25 yachts.

Facilities. Post office. The boatyard in nearby Lučina bay undertakes the construction and repair of all types of boats and smaller vessels.

LUKA

(43°59'N; 015°06'E), village in the cove of the same name, some 4.4 M northwest of Sali on the NE coast of Dugi otok.

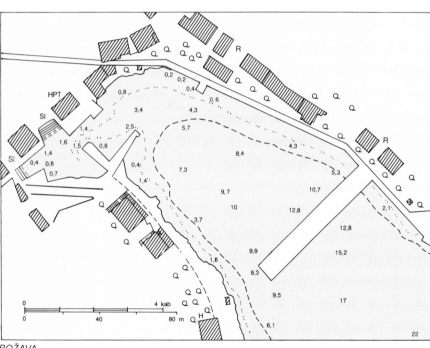

BOŽAVA

BOŽAVA

Approach. A point lying midway between the church (left) and the chapel (right) should be steered for.

The passage between the islet of Luški and Gubac point should be avoided because of the strong current and the shoal. About 200 m east of the islet of Luški is a reef marked by a conical masonry mark, painted black, red and white and surmounted by two black spheres.

Mooring. The cove is open to NW winds, which may cause a swell in it. Smaller yachts can moor at the mole in the village harbour (depth 1–1.5 m). There is a good anchorage SW of the islet of Luški (depth 24 m).

Facilities. Provisions; water from the main.

ŽMAN

(43°58,3'N; 015°7,3'E). Village in the small cove of Žmanišćica.

Approach. On the N coast of the cove there is a lighthouse (green light) Žmanšćica. On the SE coast there is a small island Krknata.

Mooring. Small boats can moor in the fishing harbour. Yachts can find well protected anchorage place on the SW coast of the small island of Krknata.

ZAGLAV

(43°57'N; 015°09'E). Village and harbour in the N of the bay Triluke.

Approach. There is a red lighthouse for orientation on the small island of Pohlib and a green lighthouse on the ferry pier of Zaglav.

Mooring. One can anchor at the place protected from all winds except the bora.

Facilities. Food and water in the shop. Petrol station on the quay.

SALI

(43°56'N; 015°10'E), largest village and fishing harbour on the NE coast of Dugi otok.

Approach. Landmarks: the quadrangular tower (green light) on Bluda point at the entrance to the harbour; the red tower with a column and gallery (red light) on the head of the outer breakwater; the belfry in the village and the factory chimney at the SE edge of the village.

Mooring. The outer part of the cove is exposed to SE winds. The inner part with the harbour is better sheltered. Secure by using the four-point moor. Most of the berths

UVALA TELAŠĆICA

in the harbour are occupied by the local fishing boats. Small yachts can anchor in the outer part of the harbour; during SE winds go to the anchorage in Sašćica bay (0.5 M northwest of the village of Sali; depth up to 26 m).

Facilities. Harbour master's branch office, post office and medical service. Provisions and water available.

The boatyard in Sašćica cove carries out hull and engine repairs. Marine engine maintenance and repairs at the workshop attached to the »Mardešić« fish cannery.

Sali is the venue of the annual fishermen's festival called »Saljske užance« (Sali party), which is held in August.

Sights. Uzašašće Marijino church (Assumption of Our Lady, 1465, altar 1584; collection of stone monuments), a number of patrician houses (from the Renaissance

onwards). Near the village remnants of a Roman villa rustica. At Stivanje polje Sv Ivan church (St John, 1060), on Citorij hill, Sv Viktor church (9/11 C). A fine olive grove at Saljsko polje (botanical reserve).

TELAŠĆICA

(43°55'N; 015°10'E), natural harbour in a deep uninhabited bay on the SE end of Dugi otok.

Approach. From open sea the following landmarks can be identified: Grpašćak hill and the lighthouse on the islet of Sestrice vele (white light); next to the lighthouse attendant's house there is an iron tower with spiral red and white bands; red tower (red light) on the Vidilica point.

Mooring. The bay affords good anchorage and shelter to yachts of all sizes; it is partic-

MIR, JEZERO

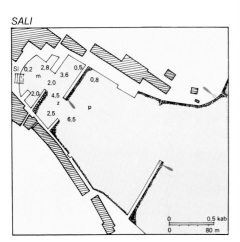

97

ularly attractive for a longer stay. The bora is violent and a strong sirocco may cause a considerable sea. During the bora larger vessels should anchor some 800 m WNW of the islet of Korotan, during the sirocco some 400 m S of the islet. Small yachts can anchor E or SE of Školjić rock but should take care of the remains of the masonry mark on the shoal some 200 m SW of the rock.

The buoy in the middle of Tripuljak cove (on the W coast) is reserved for naval vessels. There is an entrance fee for the park.

Facilities. Provisions are available in the village of Sali.

MIR

(43°54'N; 015°09,5'E), cove on the W coast of Telašćica.

SE of Mir cove is Jezero, a lake with brackish water (area 0.23 km^2, depth 5.6 m).

Mooring. The SW part of the cove is a good allround shelter. Yachts drawing up to 3 m can moor (four-point moor) off the »Mir« restaurant and campsite. A good anchorage in the middle of the cove. There are three moles on the E coast of the cove for boats with tourist parties.

ŠIBENIK HARBOUR MASTER'S OFFICE AREA

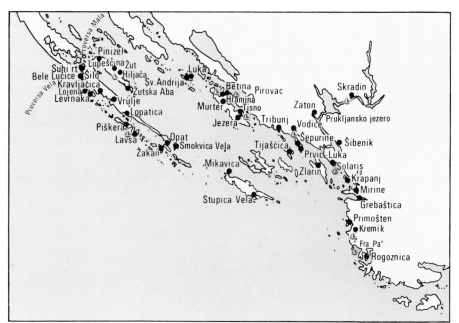

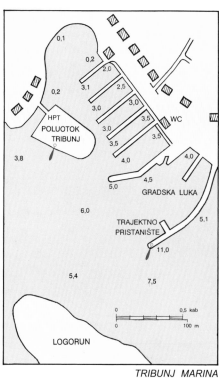

TRIBUNJ MARINA

	BETINA	KAPRIJE	KRAPANJ	PELEŠ/KREMI	PIROVAC	PRIMOŠTEN	PRVIĆ LUKA	ROGOZNICA	SKRADIN	ŠEPURINE	ŠIBENIK	TIJESNO	TRIBUNJ	VODICE	VRGADA	ZATON	ZLARIN	ŽIRJE	
	4	10	17	22	3	20	11	25	23	10	15	3	8	9	6	18	12	11	BETINA
		8	14	19	7	17	8	22	20	7	12	2	5	7	10	16	10	9	JEZERA
			11	14	12	12	7	17	19	8	11	8	8	7	14	15	8	4	KAPRIJE
				9	19	7	6	11	14	7	7	14	10	8	22	40	5	12	KRAPANJ
					24	2	12	4	21	12	13	20	16	15	28	17	11	14	PELEŠ/KREMIK
						23	13	27	25	12	17	5	16	11	8	21	15	14	PIROVAC
							10	7	19	10	12	19	13	12	25	15	10	13	PRIMOŠTEN
								14	12	2	4	9	4	3	16	8	23	8	PRVIĆ LUKA
									23	15	16	23	18	17	30	19	14	16	ROGOZNICA
										13	9	20	15	14	28	6	11	19	SKRADIN
											6	7	2	2	15	10	3	9	ŠEPURINE
												14	7	6	20	5	4	11	ŠIBENIK
													5	7	8	16	10	9	TIJESNO
														2	13	11	5	9	TRIBUNJ
															15	10	5	8	VODICE
																24	18	14	VRGADA
																	8	15	ZATON
																		9	ZLARIN
																			ŽIRJE

DISTANCES OF PORTS

HARBOURS ON THE COAST

PIROVAC

(43°49'N; 015°40'E), village and small harbour in the SE part of Pirovački zaljev.

Approach. Landmarks: round green tower with a column (green light) on the L--shaped part of the quay, which can be seen over the low point some 400 m W of the harbour and the belfry in the town. Care should be taken of the islet of Sustipanac (ruins) in the middle of Pirovački zaljev. West of the harbour is a shoal.

Mooring. The harbour is sheltered from all winds except the westerlies, which cause a sea in it. Yachts drawing up to 2 m can moor along the L-shaped pier or along the quay near the harbour light. There is a good anchorage for small vessels W of the harbour; care should be taken of the submarine cable extending between Sv Jure point and the opposite side of the bay. The harbour is not recommended for a longer stay during the sirocco or W winds.

Warning. Mooring is prohibited on part of the waterfront.

Facilities. Post office and medical service. Several hotels. Provisions (supermarket) and water from a hydrant available. Fuel at the petrol station near the Adriatic highway. A motel is also situated near the highway.

Sights. Sections of a defense wall (1505), Gospa od Karmela church (Our Lady of Carmel 1506, reconstructed in the Baroque style in 18 C); on the islet of Sustipanac remains of Roman buildings and the ruins of a monastery dating from 1511; near the village of Dazlin is Sopalj forest - a nature reserve.

TRIBUNJ

(43°45'N; 015°45'E), village and small harbour 1.2 M west of Vodice.

Approach. Landmarks: off Sv Nikola church on the hill (51 m) NW of the village; the round red and black tower with a column and gallery surmounted by two black spheres on Bačvica reef; the green column (green light) in the middle of the mole in the harbour.

The harbour is approached from SE but small vessels may pass through the narrow passage between the islets of Logorun and Lukovnik, S of the harbour. Care should be taken of the three shoals (2, 2.5 and 6.5 m) W of the harbour and of the shoal E of it.

Mooring. The harbour is exposed to S winds and seas; the bora is moderately

TRIBUNJ

the breakwater and the belfry of the church in the town. Care should be taken of the shoal (1.3 m) E of the entrance, marked by a black spar with two red bands and surmounted by two black spheres; by night the shoal is in the dark sector of the harbour light.

Mooring. The harbour is exposed to the bora, which is very strong, especially in the winter; the sirocco is also strong and may raise the sea level. The root of the L-shaped breakwater, which encloses the harbour from S, is reserved for passenger ships. Yachts drawing up to 3 m can moor elsewhere along the breakwater including its inner side, where there is no wall and where the four-point moor should be used, especially in the bora. Smaller vessels can moor (four-point moor) at the mole in front of the »Imperial« hotel. The inner harbour is mostly occupied by fishing boats and local craft. A good anchorage, although exposed to the bora and the sirocco, between the mark on the shoal and the point of Prvić island (depth 15–17 m).

Facilities. Harbour master's branch office, post office, medical service, chemist's; shipchandler's. To the SW, on Punta peninsula there are several good hotels with facilities for winter and summer sports and recreation.

Provisions at local shops, water from the hydrant at the root of the mole and the waterfront at the small breakwater; fuel from the petrol station near the Adriatic highway (some 800 m from the waterfront).

The local festivals include »Ribarska noć« (Fishermen's Night) on July 27, donkey races, a swimming marathon and other activities.

Local passenger line: Vodice – Šibenik.

Sights. Remnants of a defense wall (16 C) with Čarićev toranj tower (in the harbour), Sv Križ church (Holy Cross at the cemetery, 1421), Našašće Sv Križa church (Discovery of the Holy Cross, Baroque 1749); on the waterfront a monument to anti-fascist fighters killed in World War II (erected in 1971).

strong. Only yachts drawing up to 0.80 m can moor in the harbour; there is an anchorage SE of the village (depth 7–9 m).

NE of the harbour light there is Tribunj marina, 350 berths and 150 dry-berths (for boats up to 11 m length); semicircular breakwater (200 m long).

Facilities. Post office and medical service. Provisions and water available. The boatyard in Sovlje cove builds small boats and carries out repairs.

Sights. Sv Nikola church (1452). The ruins of a medieval fort in the old village of Jurjevgrad.

VODICE

(43°45'N; 015°47'E), town and tourist resort at the N end of Šibenski kanal.

Approach. Landmarks: the large »Punta« hotel (SW of the town), the red tower with a column and gallery (red light) on the head of

VODICE

VODICE MARINA (ACI)

(43°45,2'N; 015°47'E), is situated in the Vrulje cove (NE part of Vodice); it is protected by two breakwaters (120 and 80 m).

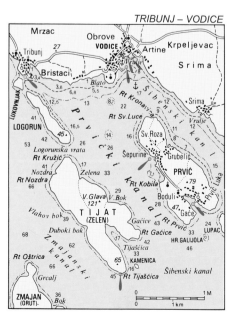

TRIBUNJ – VODICE

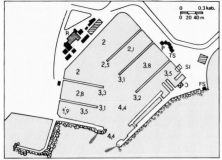

VODICE MARINA

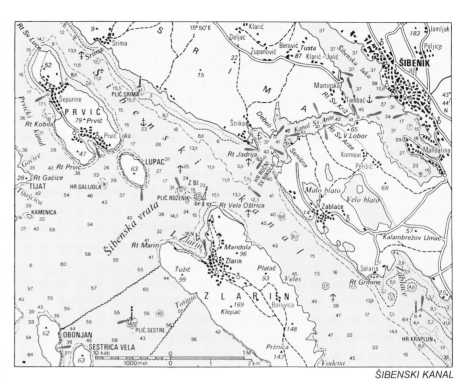

ŠIBENSKI KANAL

Approach. Difficult by night as there are shoals off the entrance and breakwaters without harbour lights (see Vodice).

Along the waterfront, the E pier and 5 floating fingers are 415 berths (depth 2.4—5.7 m) for boats up to 22 m length, and 150 dry-berths. The marina office is near the head of the E pier. Along the berths there are electricity, telephone and water hook-ups.

The marina operates all the year round.

The marina has: reception office, post office, bank, fish-market, tavern, grillroom, self-service cafe, snack-bar, pizzeria, supermarket, various shops, toilet facilities with showers and hot water; skipper's club; car park; petrol/diesel pumps, sale of gas.

Launching and hauling-out of vessels (10 t crane, 40 t travel-lift), slipway, general repairs, spare parts.

ŠIBENIK

(43°44'N; 015°54'E), town and commercial port. The port is entered through Sv Ante Channel (length 1.4 M, width at the entrance 220 m, width at narrowest part 140 m, depth 11–30 m, speed limit 6 knots).

The river Krka flows into the NW part of the port.

The port of Šibenik is a permanent border crossing for international traffic.

Approach to the channel. The channel is well marked by coast lights (lateral system): the green tower next to Sv Nikola fortress (green light) on the right side of the W entrance to the channel; the stone tower next to the house with the signal station (red light) on Jadrija point and the green tower (green light) on Ročni rock. The E entrance

is marked by the red tower (red light) on Sv Križ point and the green tower (green light) on Paklena shoal.

Navigation through the channel. The bora is violent. There is a constant current running towards the open sea of about 0.5 knots during the summer; in the winter, after heavy rains, it may attain a rate of 3 knots and even increase with the bora blowing. Vessels up to 50 GRT, except those with a barge in tow, and boats can navigate through the channel without special permis-

ŠIBENIK

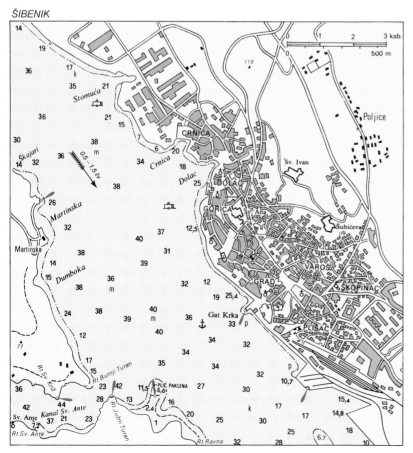

ZATON – PRUKLJANSKO JEZERO

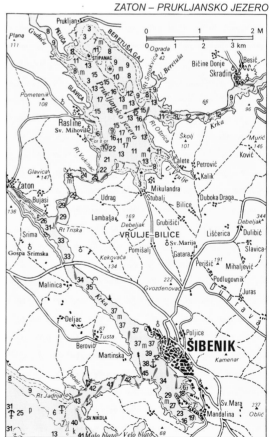

ŠIBENIK

ŠIBENIK, BAPTISTERY OF THE CATHEDRAL

sion. Such vessels and boats must keep to starboard and out of the way of vessels over 50 GRT. They are required to give way to larger vessels leaving or entering the channel. Senišna point is fringed by a shoal and should be given a berth of at least 10 m. Anchorage is prohibited in the channel and off the outer entrance to it in the area enclosed by the parallels passing through the light structures on Sv Nikola fortress (E) and Roženik shoal (W), and by the meridian passing through Sv Nikola lighthouse (E) and the meridian touching the E extremity of Lupac islet (W).

Mooring. Berths on the waterfront will be indicated by the harbour master's office. In the harbour yachts can anchor wherever convenient, with the exception of the narrow area about 100 m NNW of the harbour light on the pier Gat Krka (Krka mole). Poor holding ground; those vessels that decide to

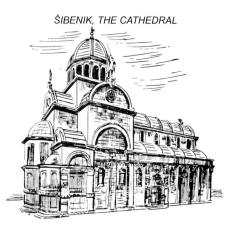

ŠIBENIK, THE CATHEDRAL

anchor should do so SW of the Sv Jakov cathedral (depth 25–30 m), not far from the waterfront and secure to the bollards ashore. Anchoring and mooring is prohibited in the area around Burnji Turan point and around Panikovac, Dumboka and Sveti Petar coves. Gat Krka and the quay SW of it (300 m) are reserved for coastal lines (depth 3.4 m); there are hydrants. The concrete wall stretching for 50 m from the Obala palih omladinaca quay is used for mooring boats. Dolac cove (quay, depth 2–3 m) is exposed to winds and a swell. Detailed regulations for places where yachts are forbidden may be obtained in the harbour office.

Facilities. Port of entry, harbour master's office, customs, post office, hospital, medical service, chemist's and railway station; »Slobodna plovidba« shipping company.

Water from the hydrant on the waterfront, fuel at the petrol station on Obala hrvatske mornarice quay; if larger quantities of fuel are needed, arrangements can be made to have it delivered by tank trucks. Navigation charts and other relevant publications available in the office of PLOVPUT – Plovno područje Šibenik.

»Brodoservis« carries out repairs (hull and engines, yachts up to 350 GRT); repairs and maintenance of vessels of all sizes at the »Šibenik« repair shipyard.

Local passenger lines: Šibenik – Zlarin – Obonjan – Kaprije – Žirje; Šibenik – Zlarin – Obonjan – Prvić Luka – Šepurine – Vodice.

Šibenik hosts the International Children's Festival (June, July) and many concerts and theatre performances. Excursions to Prukljansko jezero, Skradin, Skradinski buk

waterfall, a trip up the Krka river to Roški slap waterfall.

Sights. Sv Jakov cathedral (St Jacob, Gothic and Renaissance, 1431–1505, designed by Juraj Dalmatinac, who also made part of the carvings; after his death the project was carried on by Nicholas of Florence; altar, baptistry, portal with lions - »lavlja vrata«, and frieze with 71 portrait heads around the apse); Sv Frane church (St Francis, 14 C, coffered ceiling from 17 C), with a Gothic/Renaissance Franciscan monastery (collection of manuscripts and other valuable items); Nova crkva (New Church, Gothic/ Renaissance style); Sv Ivan church (St John, reconstructions in 1485, 1544 and 1643, external flight of stairs, bell-tower with Turkish clock); Sv Barbara church (1447–51, collection of sacral items, part of the Town Museum); the orthodox church of Uspenje Bogorodice (Assumption of the Holy Virgin, built around 1390, later reconstructed in the Baroque style, until the early 19 C part of a Benedictine convent); the Loggia (1534 –42, severely damaged during World War II, renovated); Kneževa palača (Rector's Palace, 14 C, later additions, renovated; it houses the Town Museum and its collections of old masters, archeological finds, ethnographic material, archives, modern art); numerous old patrician houses, styles ranging from Romanesque to Baroque (Rossini, Mišić, Fontana, Foscolo, Orsini –Juraj Dalmatinac, Divnić, Dragojević, Lavčić); the great cistern (velika čatrnja) dating from 1446. The forts:

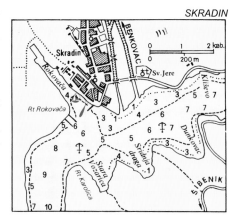

SKRADIN

102

Sv Ana (fortified in 16 and 17 C), Sv Ivan (St John, 1645–49), Šubićevac (17 C), Sv Nikola (1540–47), situated at the entrance to Sv Ante Channel.

ZATON

(43°47'N; 015°50'E), village and bay in the lower reaches of the river Zrmanja, some 1 M northwest of Triska point.

Approach. Landmarks: the green tower (green light) on Triska point, the green column (green light) on the SE end of the mole and the belfry at the head of the bay.

Mooring. The bay is sheltered from all winds except the sirocco, which causes considerable waves at the head of the bay. Yachts drawing up to 2.5 m can moor at the mole. There is a good anchorage in the outer part of the bay. During the sirocco use the four-point moor, bows-to SE.

Facilities. Post office. Provisions and water available.

Sights. Sv Juraj and Sv Rok churches (1533, renovated); the ruins of a medieval building at Bankovac.

SKRADIN

(43°49'N; 015°55,6'E), village and small harbour on the left bank (upstream) of the Krka river, some 4.5 M north of Šibenik. When entering the port note the lighthouse (red light) on Lukovo point and the lighthouse (green light) on Dut point.

Approach. The river Krka and Prukljanski tjesnac passage (marked by marks and lights) lead to the Prukljansko jezero lake. On the stretch between Prukljansko jezero and Skradin the Krka narrows at places to only 100 m (depth 7–13 m) in the first half and further on to 80 m (depth 7–8 m); the river is very shallow along the left bank. The stretch up to Skradinski buk waterfall is navigable for yachts drawing less than 2 m. At the point where the river branches into three channels, take the middle one; when it forks again, near the waterfalls, take the S (narrower) channel. Some 1 km upstream from Skradin is a bridge (vertical clearance 5 m).

The Krka cascades down from the Visovac lake over 17 tufa barriers (highest fall: 45 m). The Krka waterfalls (Skradinski buk), one of the most beautiful spots in Croatia and a nature reserve, are up to 36 m high

SKRADIN MARINA

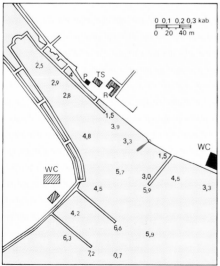

and 500 m wide. They can be reached only by small boat.

Mooring. Yachts can moor in Skradin marina.

Facilities. Post office, hotel, medical service, chemist's. Provisions and water available; fuel at the petrol station.

Sights. Remains of Roman buildings, tombs and inscriptions. Scardona: the capital of Illyrian Liburnia, later a Roman municipium. Remnants of Turkish and Venetian fortifications at Biskupija (above the town). Porođenje Marijino church (Nativity of Our Lady, 1745), the church at the cemetery (16 C), the Orthodox church of Sv Spiridion, reconstructed in 1754 (iconostasis and collection of icons in the new church) – Visovac islet with a Franciscan monastery (library with a collection of historic documents and artefacts) and church

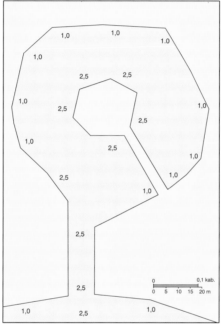

SOLARIS

VISOVAC, NEAR ŠIBENIK

(1576, later reconstructed); further upstream to Roški slap waterfall and the Orthodox Krka Monastery (14 C, destroyed and reconstructed several times); – Drniš (Sv Antun church, part of which is a reconstructed mosque; several sculptures by Ivan Meštrović) – 33 km; Otavice (mausoleum by I. Meštrović) – 42 km.

SKRADIN MARINA (ACI)

(43°49'N; 015°55,6'E), is situated in the cove NW of the pier in Skradin.

When entering the marina care should be taken of the fish and mussel farm off the S entrance point; the farm is marked by buoys.

The marina has 220 pontoon sea-berths along the SW and NE coast of the cove, two floating fingers at the S entrance to the cove and a shorter one at the N entrance (depth about 4 m), and 10 dry-berths. There are water, electricity and telephone hook-ups.

The marina operates the year round.

It has reception office, restaurant, shops, snack-bar, toilets and showers with hot water; general repairs. Fuel at the petrol station in Skradin.

SOLARIS

(43°42'N; 015°52'E), hotel complex at Grmine point (village of Zablaće) in Šibenski kanal.

SKRADIN MARINA

Mooring. The hotel harbour has two piers and is protected from all winds and seas, except the sirocco. Yachts drawing up to 2.5 m can moor at the S pier.

Anchoring is prohibited at both sides of the entrance (underwater cables).

Facilities. Provisions at a local shop, water and fuel available.

MIRINE

(43°38,5'N; 015°57'E), cove in the south-easternmost part of Šibenski kanal.

Approach. Landmarks: the stone cross at the E entrance point and the high old wall extending from the head of the cove across Vela Oštrica peninsula.

In the middle of the entrance is a shoal (6.8 m) and at the entrance to the adjoining cove a dangerous reef hardly covered by the sea.

Mooring. The anchorage is in the middle of the cove (depth about 7 m). The cove is a good allround shelter and can be used for a longer stay.

Sights. Old wall (6–8 m high, built in 15 C against Turkish raids) running across Oštrica peninsula.

GREBAŠTICA

(43°38'N; 015°58'E), village in Luka Grebaštica gulf, SE of the S entrance to Šibenski kanal.

Approach. Shape course for the quadrangular white tower with a column and gallery (green light) on the N side of the entrance on Oštrica Vela point; the old wall running across the peninsula.

Mooring. The cove is well sheltered from the bora but is exposed to W winds. Larger yachts can anchor SE of Oštrica hill (97 m), and smaller ones in the coves along the N coast (depth about 5 m). When anchoring closer inshore care should be taken to stay clear of the underwater cable.

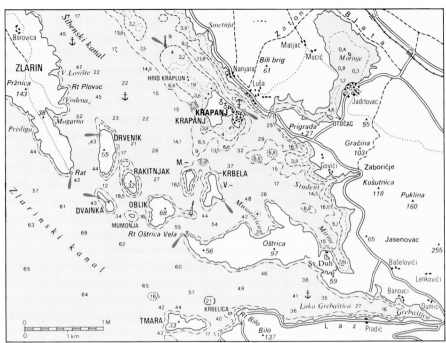

MIRINE – GREBAŠTICA

Facilities. Provisions and water in the village of Grebaštica (E of the harbour).

PRIMOŠTEN

(43°34'N; 015°55'E), small town, small harbour and tourist resort S of Šibenik.

Approach. Landmarks: the tall belfry among houses and the quadrangular red tower with a column and gallery (red light) on the head of the breakwater; red tower with a column and gallery (red light) on the head of the mole in Vojska cove; the fan-shaped marina Lučica hotel on the right side of the entrance.

Mooring. The harbour is protected from NE and NW winds. Yachts drawing up to

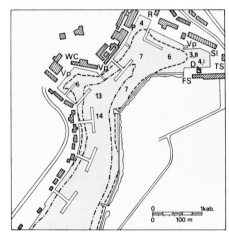

KREMIK MARINA

3 m can moor along the breakwater. The mole in Vojske cove, some 400 m E of the breakwater, is reserved for the car ferry (depth 5.5 m). The breakwater E of the old harbour is used by the coastal lines. Good anchorage ground inside the harbour (depth 14–30 m).

Facilities. Harbour master's branch office, post office, several hotels, campsite (3 km W of Primošten), medical service and chemist's.

General repairs to yachts and marine engines at the Primošten boatyard. Hauling-out facility on the waterfront.

Sights. Churches of Sv Juraj (St George, renovated in 1760), Sv Rok (1680) and Gospa od Milosti (Our Lady, first recorded in 1553); at nearby Kruševo – Sv Martin (medieval, surrounded by medieval tombstones); at Široke – Sv Jere (St Hieronymus, 1460); at Prhovo – Sv Juraj (St George, 11 C, renovated in 1724).

KREMIK MARINA

(43°34,2'N; 015°56,6'E) is situated in the sheltered N cove of Peleš bay, some 2 M south of Primošten. The Adriatic highway passes in its immediate vicinity.

PRIMOŠTEN

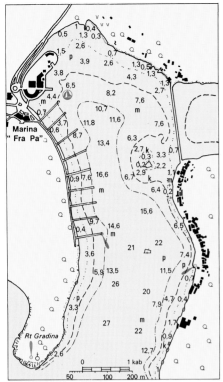

ROGOZNICA – COVE

PRIMOŠTEN

The marina has 280 berths (length up to 25 m) at the quay (450 m) and the floating fingers (depth 2–15 m); there are 140 dry-berths. All berths are provided with water and electricity hook-ups. The marina operates during the summer season only. During the season it is also a border crossing (April 1 – October 31).

It has reception office, customs, police station and harbour office; money exchange, phone booth, various shops (nautical equipment and tools). Parking lot for 200 vehicles nearby. Some 800 m from the marina there is a hotel, medical service.

A slipway (up to 50 t) and a hoist (5 t); repair of hulls, diesel engines and electrical installations; major repairs and overhaul at the boatyard in Trogir. Security and maintenance of vessels out of season.

ROGOZNICA

(43°31'N; 015°58'E), village and small harbour in the cove of the same name N of Ploča point; the safest shelter for yachts of all sizes in this part of the Adriatic.

Approach. Landmarks: Movar Hill (124 m) and the eight-sided masonry tower; Mulo lighthouse, a stone tower next to the house (white flashes). Other landmarks include the round tower with a column and gallery with black and red bands (white light) surmounted by two spheres on Kalebinjak reef (in the passage between Smokvica Vela islet and Konj point; the quadrangular red tower (red light) on Gradina point (in the cove); the green column (green light) ashore.

Mooring. The cove is protected from all winds. 300 yachts drawing up to 3.5 m can moor along the S part of the mole fronting the village or along its N part (four-point moor). An anchorage for larger yachts (indifferent holding ground) is in the E part

FRAPA MARINA – ROGOZNICA

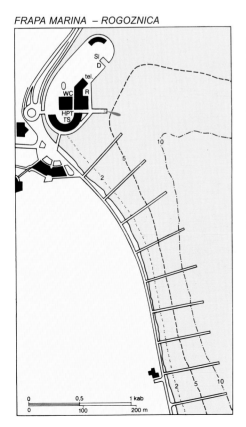

ROGOZNICA

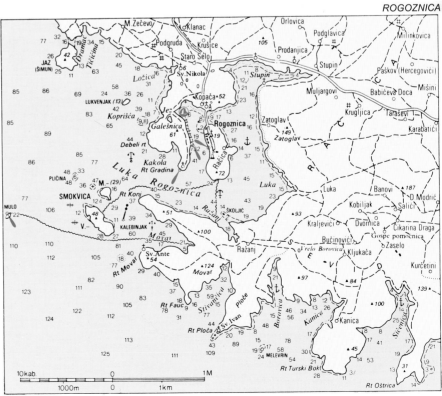

FRAPA MARINA – ROGOZNICA

MULO

ROGOZNICA

of the cove, NE of Artić point (depth 25–31 m). Smaller vessels can anchor in the W part of the cove, WNW of the harbour light (depth 21–23 m) or in Stupin cove, NNE of the village (depth 3–6 m).

Warning. Navigation and fishing are prohibited in the N part of Lozica cove (NW of Rogoznica) in the area delimitated by the line connecting: S point of Jaz islet and Lukvenjak islet, bearing of 30° from Lukvenjak islet to the coast. It is prohibited to anchor in the area bounded by lines joining: from NW point of Smokvica Vela islet in bearing 38.5° to the mainland coast; from Gradina point in bearing of 90° to coast of Rogoznica islet; from Varoš point (in the S part of the cove) in bearing 0° to the coast of Rogoznica islet; from SW point of

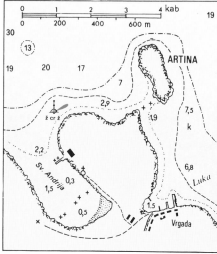

SVETI ANDRIJA

Smokvica Vela in bearing of 128° to the mainland coast.

Sights. Uznesenje Marijino church (Assumption of the Virgin, 1615, renovated in 1746); in Stara Rogoznica Sv Nikola church (medieval, a graveyard with old tombstones), above the village an old mill and the remnants of a fortress (1809).

FRAPA MARINA

A new yacht harbour on an artificial island in the bay of Soline, at the NW coast of the Rogoznica bay.

Approach. During the day one should note the danger signs on the point Kalebinjak. At night there is a lighthouse (red light) on the Gradina point.

Mooring. 300 berths alongside the piers, 30 more on the coast, and 150 dry-berths.

Facilities. Reception office, water and electricity hook-ups, telephone, showers, WC, restaurant, supermarket, apartments, disco, Captain's Club, tennis courts, swimming pool.

Service. Technical service, lift, repairs, spare parts, supplies.

ISLAND OF VRGADA

SVETI ANDRIJA

(43°51'N; 015°29,5'E), cove on the N side of Vrgada.

Approach. On the SW side of the cove, the reddish brown landslide is conspicuous; on the E side is an isolated chapel. The reef off the NE point of the cove (N coast of the island) is marked by a cylindrical concrete black and yellow mark and two cones point to point; the clear passage is W of the mark.

Mooring. The cove is open to NW but is protected from the bora; strong S winds cause a swell in it. Yachts drawing up to 2 m can moor on the inner end of the small pier (only 15 m from the root towards the head) in a depth of 2 m. At the head of the cove depth range between 0.5 and 1,0 m.

Sights. Sv Andrija church (St Andrew) at the cemetery.

LUKA

(43°51'N; 015°30'E), cove on the E coast of Vrgada, the harbour of the village of Vrgada.

Approach. Landmarks: Artina islet off the NE point and the church on the hill.

Mooring. The cove affords good shelter from W winds. Approach is difficult during the bora. Only yachts drawing up to 2 m can moor on the inner side of the long breakwater (four-point moor is recommended); poor holding.

Limited provisions and water available.

ISLAND OF MURTER

BETINA

(43°49'N; 015°36'E), village and small harbour on the NE coast of the island.

Approach. When approaching from Pirovački zaljev shape course for the white tower (white light) on Rat point and the stone column in the sea off the shallow point of Artić (N of the harbour); the green column (green light) on the breakwater.

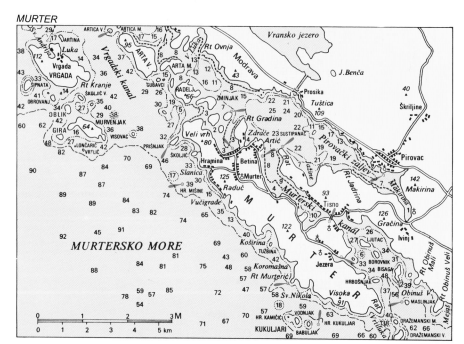

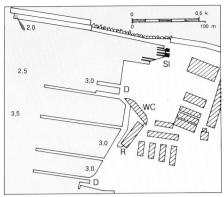

BETINA MARINA

Mooring. The harbour affords good shelter during SW and NW winds. Yachts can moor at the inner end of the breakwater. Anchoring is not recommended because of the poor holding (depth 3 m). The inner harbour is occupied by the local fishing-boats.

Facilities. Post office and medical service, restaurant, shop; parking lot for 100 vehicles; harbour office in Tisno. Provisions and water available.

The shipyard in the marina builds craft 7–40 m in length, carries out general repairs and maintenance of engines; they also look after and maintain yachts out of season. General repairs may also be undertaken at another, smaller boatyard.

Sights. Remains of an ancient settlement (stone fragments, tombstones, pottery), Sv Franjo Asiški church (St Francis of Assisi, 1601, expanded 1720).

BETINA MARINA

(43°49'N; 015°36'E) is situated NW from the village of Betina in the Zdrače cove at the N entrance to Murterski kanal.

Capacity: 190 sea-berths (up to 15 m length) and 80 dry-berths; the berths have water and electricity hook-ups.

It has reception office, grocery store, chandler's shop, toilet with hot water, laundry; building, renovating and repairing of craft (wooden, metal, fiberglass) up to 44 m; engine repairs.

Launching and hauling-out of vessels (crane 10 t, travel-lift 260 t); slipway (30 t); there are 6 more slipways in the nearby shipyard which can be used by the marina if necessary.

TISNO

(43°48,5'N; 015°39'E), village and small harbour on the island of Murter, at the narrowest part of Murterski kanal. A bridge links Murter with the mainland and divides the harbour into an eastern and a western part.

Approach. The western part of the harbour is approached from NW (Pirovački zaljev) and the eastern part from SE (Murtersko more); the landmarks include the coneshaped white tower with the green light on Maslinjak islet and the red column (red light) on the head of the breakwater.

The bora is strong and blows from various directions but does not cause big waves. The harbour is less exposed to the sirocco and affords better protection from it. There is a strong SE current, especially with the

BETINA

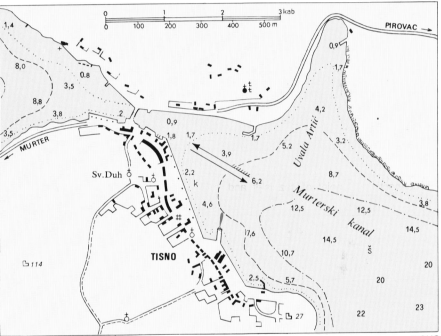

TISNO

TISNO

TISNO

JEZERA MARINA

Provisions and water available.

Repairs to boat and yacht hulls and repairs and maintenance of marine engines at Školjić boatyard. Post office.

JEZERA MARINA (ACI)
(43°47,1'N; 015°39'E) is situated in the S part of Jezera cove. It is protected by a breakwater (E) and a pier (W); depth 3–6 m.

The marina has 200 sea-berths at five floating fingers and 250 dry-berths. They have electricity, telephone and water hook-ups.

The marina operates the year round.

It has reception, restaurant, shop, toilets and showers with hot water; laundry; fuel pump, sale of gas. Boat rental and charter.

Crane (10 t); general repairs; the Školjić boatyard carries out repairs to hulls and engines.

MURTER
(43°49'N; 015°36'E), small town on the island of the same name, situated some 500 m inshore. In Hramina cove there is a marina, protected from all winds and a good allround shelter for smaller vessels. In Slanica cove is a beach and the »Colentum« hotel complex.

Facilities. Post office, medical service, several restaurants and shops, private guest houses and the head-office of the Kornati National Park. Provisions, water and fuel available. The »Slanica« boatyard carries out repairs of boats, small yachts and marine engines; security and maintenance for wintering yachts.

HRAMINA MARINA
(43°49'N; 015°36'E) is situated in the Hramina cove. It is protected from N and W by two breakwaters.

Along the quay and the four floating fingers there are 500 sea-berths (depth 1.5– 3 m up to 23 m length); 250 dry-berths (20 in the hangar).

The marina operates in season only.

Entering Hramina cove from Murtersko more (from W), go between the islands of Zminjak and Vinik Veli, round Tegina islet (white coast light; round white tower) and enter the cove shaping course SW. The passages between the islets of Vinik Veli and Vinik Mali and the islet of Tegina are shallow.

JEZERA MARINA

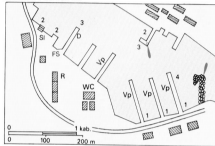

south-easterlies and north-westerlies, when it may attain 4 knots.

Mooring. Yachts drawing up to 2 m can berth on the inner end of the breakwater (SE of the bridge; the red column with a red light) or along the quay NW of the village (depth 2.5 m). There is a good anchorage in the SE part of the straits, NW of Ljutac i-water sewage pipe extends some 900 m E

of the harbour (under the level of 65 m), bearing 143°.

Facilities. Harbour master's branch office, post office medical service, and chemist's.

Provisions at local shops, mains water supply.

JEZERA
(43°47'N; 15°38'E), village in the cove of the same name on the NE coast of Murter.

Approach. Landmarks: the green column (green light) on the head of the L--shaped breakwater and the round tower with a column (red light) on the head of the breakwater in the marina.

The bay may be approached from both sides of Školjić islet.

Mooring. Good allround shelter for yachts of light and moderate draught. The four-point moor can be used at the inner end of the second pier.

Facilities. Harbour master's branch office, medical service and chemist's in Tisno.

HRAMINA MARINA

HRAMINA MARINA

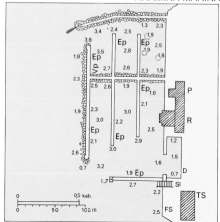

108

The marina has reception office, restaurant, toilets and showers with hot water, electricity hook-ups, shop selling nautical charts and publications, fuel pump and sale of gas (N part); water from tank trucks; harbour master's branch office in Tisno (6 km).

The marina issues weather reports and meteorological information. Crane (15 t), slipway at the root of the S pier, facility for mounting masts, travel-lift (50 t); general repairs to hulls, marine engines and electrical installations; maintenance of all types of vessels.

ISLAND OF TIJAT

TIJAŠĆICA

(43°42'N; 015°47'E), uninhabited cove on the SE coast of Tijat.

Approach. Shape course for the quadrangular stone tower (white light) on Tijašćica point (not visible when approaching from N).

Mooring. The cove is open to SE. Small yachts can moor off the E coast, securing ashore (bows to NW); depth 10–17 m.

ISLAND OF PRVIĆ

PRVIĆ LUKA

(43°43'N; 015°48'E), village and small harbour on the S coast of Prvić.

Approach. Landmarks: the green tower with a column and gallery (green flashes) on the breakwater can be easily identified. Give Galiola rock a berth of at least 50 m because of submerged reefs.

Mooring. The cove is open to SE. Yachts drawing up to 3 m moor on the inner end of the breakwater, where they are sheltered from the sirocco. Yachts drawing up to 2 m can moor (four-point moor) at the root of the breakwater. The anchorage is in the middle of the cove (depth 5–6 m).

Facilities. Post office and medical service. Provisions and water (from tank trucks) available.

Coastal passenger line: see Šibenik.

Sights. Marija od Milosti church (Our Lady of Grace, 15 C), memorial slabs, among which that of the historian and inventor Faust Vrančić (1551–1617); Franciscan monastery (1461).

PRVIĆ ŠEPURINE

(43°44'N; 015°47'E), village on the W coast of the island of Prvić.

Approach. Landmarks: the round white tower with a column and gallery (green light) on the head of the old pier.

Mooring. The small harbour is protected from the bora but is exposed to S wind and seas. Small yachts can moor at the inner end of the breakwater (depth 1.5 m) or of the old pier. With the S wind blowing it is easier to moor at the breakwater and with N winds at the old pier. Good anchorage for larger yachts is some 500 m W of the village (depth 18–20 m).

Facilities. Post office. Provisions and water available.

Coastal passenger line: see Šibenik.

Sights. Draganić-Vrančić Castle (historic and art collection, manuscripts), Sv Rok church (1620).

ISLAND OF ZLARIN

ZLARIN

(43°42'N; 015°50'E), village and cove (Luka Zlarin) on the NW coast of the island of the same name.

Approach. Approaching from N, care should be taken of Roženik shoal (1.5 M northwest) marked by a round green tower (white light); other landmarks include the white tower with a column (red light) on the head of the N pier and the church.

Mooring. Luka Zlarin cove is sheltered from the bora and sirocco, but is exposed to the north-westerlies. Large yachts can moor at the piers off the village; the N pier is reserved for the local line. Yachts drawing less than 3 m and shorter than 40 m can moor (four-point moor) between the third and fourth piers (looking from the N) and lying alongside. The inner harbour is occupied by the local fishing craft. There is a good anchorage off the E coast.

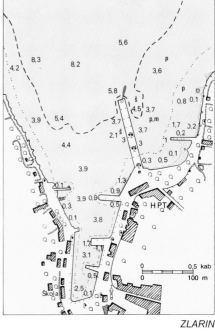

ZLARIN

Facilities. Post office and medical service. Provisions and water available.

Sights. The Baroque churches of Uzašašće Marije (Assumption of the Virgin), Sv Rok, Sv Šimun (St Simon) and Gospa od Rašelja (Our Lady of Rašelj); a number of summer houses (16/17 C); art gallery.

Some 2 M south-southwest of Zlarin, near the island of Zmajan, is the islet of Obonjan with an international training and recreation centre for young people. On its north point is a 20 m long mole (depth 3.5 m).

Zlarin is the venue of the annual festival Zlarin Evenings under the Clock-tower (»Zlarinske večeri ispod leroja«, July 27). The Zlarin art worskhop.

ISLAND OF KRAPANJ

KRAPANJ

(43°40,4'N; 015°55'E), village and small harbour in the S part of Šibenski kanal.

PRVIĆ LUKA

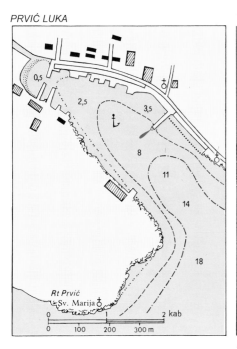

KRAPANJ

ŽUT MARINA

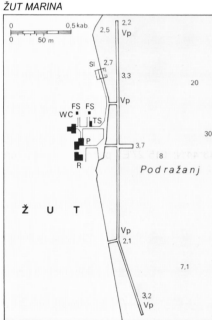

ŽUT MARINA

ISLAND OF ŽUT

PINIZEL

(43°53'N; 015°15'E), cove on the NW coast of the island, S of the islet of Pinizelić.

Approach. The shortest route from the open sea (from the W, the Sestrice lighthouse is conspicuous) is through the Proversa Vela straits, and from Zadar through Mali Ždrelac. It is not advisable to navigate by night.

Mooring. The cove is sheltered from all winds except the north-westerlies. Off the cove is an improvised breakwater, in the cove are two small moles; depth in the small harbour 1–1.3 m; yachts should anchor off the breakwater and closer to the islet of Pinizelić.

Some 0.5 km NW is the hamlet of Pinizelić, inhabited only during the summer.

ŽUT

(43°53'N; 015°18'E), wide cove on the NE coast of the island. *Approach.* See Pinizel.

Mooring. The cove is protected from all winds. A good anchorage for larger vessels is in the middle of the cove (depth 35–50 m). With the bora blowing, good shelter is afforded by the W cove of Pod ražanj (depth 3 m). In S wind, the best anchorages are the E coves of Strunac and Sarušćica (depth 19–22 m).

Provisions and other facilities in Žut marina.

ŽUT MARINA (ACI)

is situated in the cove of Pod ražanj (a part of Žut bay).

Capacity: 120 berths along the floating fingers running parallel to the coast (20 m length); depth 2.5–8 m.

The marina operates only during the summer season.

It has reception office, restaurant, shop, toilets and showers with hot water, water hook-up, fuel pump, sale of gas; general repairs. Three navigation and sailing courses organized by the Adriatic Nautical Academy (ACI).

HILJAČA

(43°51,5'N; 014°20'E), large cove on the N coast of the island.

Approach. See Pinizel.

Mooring. Good anchorage in the middle of the cove (depth 10 m). With the bora and westerlies the best anchorage is in the NW cove of Sabuni (depth 1–3 m) or off the coast of Gustac islet. The S part of the cove (Pristanišće cove; some twenty houses inhabited during the summer) is a good all-round shelter in all winds including the bora. There are two small piers; small yachts can moor at the outer end of the outer pier (depth 1.7 m).

PROVERSA VELA

passage between the NW coast of the island of Kornat and the islet of Katina; it links Srednji kanal with the open sea.

Approach. Shape course for the red tower (red light) on the breakwater.

Mooring. The bora blows with considerable force; the sirocco causes moderate waves. Yachts drawing up to 2 m can moor at the breakwater or the E end of the pier. It is also possible to moor along the quay of the small boatyard (depth 2.5 m), some 500 m W of the church (with the pointed roof).

Facilities. Post office, medical service, provisions (there is a supermarket in the village of Brodarica on the mainland). Water from tank trucks

Sights. Franciscan monastery and Sv Križ church (Holy Cross, 1446–1523, expanded in 1626, cloister, art collection).

Krapanj has a sponge refinery and a workshop for cutting corals (traditional local craft; sponge diving since 1704).

PROVERSA VELA AND MALA

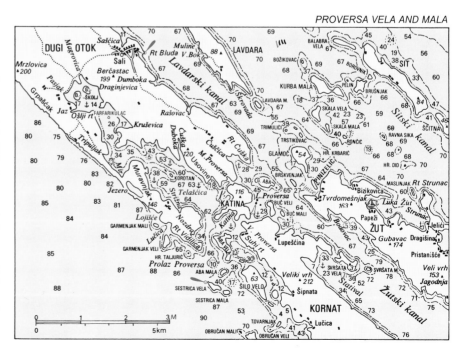

The passage is navigable for vessels drawing up to 2 m. Its narrowest part is marked by 4 stone marks; there are no navigation lights. The bora is violent and blows in gusts from various directions; the sirocco causes a sea. The current (up to 2.0 knots) sets eastwards; vessels navigating against the current should keep closer to the island of Kornat.

PROVERSA MALA

passage between Dugi otok and Katina. Navigation is temporarily prohibited because work on dredging the passage is under way.

It is advisable to use Chart 100–20 published by The State Hydrographic Institute in Split.

Mooring. Small yachts can anchor in Proversa Mala cove, E or SSE of Školjić rock (white truncated concrete pyramid). The shoal some 200 m of Školjić is marked by a spar surmounted by a cone (the whole mark is black). The small cove (with a small mole, depth 1.5 m) on the S coast of Katina island affords good allround shelter (»Kod Mare Tonine inn«). The W cove, which is somewhat larger, is a good anchorage with depth of 3–10 m; good holding; vessels can also secure to the rocks ashore.

KATINA

(43°53'N; 015°14'E) small port in the passage Proversa Vela (depth 2 m) between the islands of Kornat and Katina.

ISLAND OF KORNAT

The islands of Kornat, Žut and Sit and the string of islands off the SW coast of Kornat form part of the Kornati National Park.

It is advisable to navigate in the Kornati area only by day and with the help of Chart 100–20 published by The Croatian Hydrographic Institute in Split.

LUPEŠĆINA

(43°52'N; 015°14'E), cove some 1 M southeast of the northernmost point of the island of Kornat (see Proversa Vela).

KORNATI

Mooring. The cove is protected from the southerlies and exposed to the northerlies; it is not recommended for a longer stay. On the S coast of the cove are several seasonally inhabited houses and several jetties. The depth at the head of the longest jetty is 1.6 m. A shoal extends off the N coast (0.2–0.8 m) – in order to avoid it when entering the cove, steer closer to the jetties.

Facilities. No provisions. Water from the cistern.

OPAT

(43°44'N; 015°27'E), point and cove in the south-easternmost part of the island of Kornat.

Approach. The conical Mt Opat (108 m) and the stone cross on the S point of the point are conspicuous. SW of the cove is a shoal (2.3 m). Approach the cove from SE in order to avoid it.

Mooring. The cove is open to the southerlies and protected from the bora. The rocky coast is unsuitable for mooring. Smaller yachts can anchor in the SE part of the cove (depth 4 m) or along the small stone pier, S of the houses (depth 1.5 m); good holding. Larger vessels can anchor at the entrance to the cove (depth 28 m), securing stern-to the shore.

There are many fishing boats in the cove.

LOPATICA

(43°47'N; 015°20'E), cove in the central part of the W coast of Kornat, N of the island

KORNAT – KORNATSKI KANAL

SESTRICA VELA

of Piškera (Jadra); on its S side is the islet of Koritnjak.

Approach. From the open sea: the hill (84 m) at the NW end of Piškera is conspicuous. Larger yachts should steer closer to Piškera to avoid the shoal (5.7 m).

Mooring. The cove is exposed to the south-easterlies and south-westerlies. With a strong sirocco blowing, take shelter in the cove on the island of Lavsa or in Piškera marina. Closer inshore, off the house, is a mole for small yachts (depth 1–1.5 m). Larger yachts anchor in the outer part of the cove in 12–20 m, between the islands of Kornat and Koritnjak; good holding.

Provisions in Piškera marina.

VRULJA, also VRULJA VELA
(43°48'N; 015°18'E), cove with a seasonally inhabited hamlet, on the W coast of Kornat, at the NW end of Kornatski kanal.

Approach. The cove may be approached from the open sea or from the inner side of the Kornati islets. Between the islets of Rašip Mali and Mana are Kamičići reefs. A more interesting approach is through Kornatski kanal from the SE side. One of the landmarks when approaching the cove is the stone cross on Pivčena point, S of the entrance to the cove.

Mooring. The cove can be used for a longer stay. The anchorage is in the middle of the cove (depth 8–18 m), where there is also a small mole (depth 1.5 m). The E cove is shallow (depth at the heads of the small moles 1.5–2 m); fasten with rope ashore is possible. The SE part of the cove should be avoided (depth up to 1 m).

Facilities. Water from the cistern; other provisions in Piškera marina. Some 700 m north-westwards is a weather station.

Sights. Remnants of Illyrian structures (walls, tumuli) and a Roman villa rustica.

KRAVLJAČICA
(43°49'N; 015°17'E), cove on the W coast of the NW part of Kornat (NE of the southernmost point of Levrnaka).

BLITVENICA

Approach. The same as for Vrulja cove. The ruins of Toreta tower (at an elevation of 58 m), some 0.5 M north-west of the cove.

Mooring. The cove is sheltered from all winds except the south-easterlies. Off the houses are several jetties consisting of piled up stones (depth 0.7–1 m). Anchorage is obtainable off the outer end of jetties (depth 3–4 m). Larger vessels can anchor off the NE coast (depth 20 m), where it is also possible to secure the boat ashore. Smaller yachts can moor only in the SE harbour of Strižnja (depth 2–2.5 m).

Facilities. Water from the cistern; provisions and other shopping in Piškera marina.

Sights. On Tarac plateau (NW of the cove) is the church of Pohoda Marijinog (Visitation), late medieval, built amid the ruins of a medieval three-nave basilica (6 C?). Next to it are the ruins of a larger building. On the summit of Toreta are the ruins of an Illyrian fortress (about 1000 B.C.), tumuli and remains of Roman buildings. Venetian defense tower was built on the site.

BELE LUČICE
(43°50,6'N; 014°16'E), cove on the W coast of the NW part of Kornat (E of the northernmost point of the island of Levrnaka).

Approach. From the open sea: pass the island of Levrnaka and the neighbouring islets. For navigation through Kornatski kanal see Vrulja.

Mooring. The cove is protected from the bora and sirocco. In the inner, E part of the cove is a small harbour (depth 0.5–1 m),

protected by 2 small piers consisting of piled up stones. Yachts can anchor off the outer end of the pier (depth 3.5 m), but not off the entrance to the harbour. The anchorage in the outer part of the cove (depth 17–21 m) is not safe with the westerlies blowing, go to Kravljačica cove or the cove on Levrnaka.

SUHI RT
(43°52'N; 015°14'E), small cove and fishermen's village N of the point of the same name, in the north-westernmost part of Kornat (Proversa Vela).

Approach. Shape course for the two houses (inhabited in the summer).

Mooring. Gusts of the bora come from various directions. Off the houses are several jetties (depth about 1.5 m; at the head of the middle mole 1.3 m). Medium-sized yachts should use the four-point moor, larger yachts can anchor off the cove (depth 14 m).

ISLAND OF LEVRNAKA

LEVRNAKA
(43°49'N; 015°16'E), cove on the N coast of the island of the same name (Kornati).

Approach. The highest peak on the island is conspicuous (117 m). The cove is enclosed on the N side by the islet of Sušica; the narrow passage SE of the islet is not navigable. The sirocco is violent and the current strong in the passage between Kornat and Levrnaka.

Mooring. The cove is not exposed to winds. The best anchorage is in the SE part of the cove (depth 10–24 m); good holding; vessels can also secure to the rocks ashore. There is a small jetty of piled up rocks (four-point moor).

Facilities. There is a water cistern next to the two houses on the isthmus toward Lojena cove on the S coast ot the island; other provisions in the marina in Piškera.

LOJENA
(43°49'N; 015°15'E), cove on the S coast of Levrnaka.

Mooring. The cove is protected from the bora and exposed to the southerlies; it is not recommended for a longer stay. Larger

LOJENA

LEVRNAKA

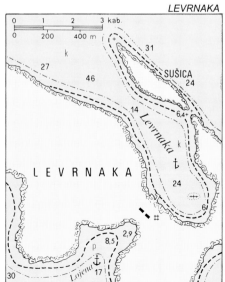

yachts anchor in the middle of the cove (depth 8–15 m), and smaller ones in the NE part (depth up to 3 m). With a strong sirocco blowing, go to Levrnaka cove on the N coast of the island.

Facilities. For provisions see Levrnaka.

ISLAND OF PIŠKERA

PIŠKERA, also JADRA
(43°45'N; 015°21'E), cove on the SE coast of the island of the same name (Kornati); protected from the open sea by the islet Panitula Vela.

Approach. Off the entrance to the cove are the islets of Panitula Vela and Panitula Mala and Škanji rocks. The cove can be entered only from SE; the NW passage between Panitula Vela and Piškera is shallow and full of dangerous reefs.

Mooring. The part off Piškera marina (depth 1.5–3 m) is sheltered from the bora. SE and W winds cause a slop. With SE and SW winds approaching, leave the anchorage and go to the cove on the N coast of Lavsa.

Facilities. Provisions in Piškera marina.

Sights. In the past Piškera was a centre for fishermen engaged in seasonal fishing. They had their houses and jetties and stored their catch there. It was also the seat of the Venetian administrator, who supervised the catch and collected a tax on it. Church (1560; renovated in 1968). Nearby there is the memorial ossuary of anti-fascist fighters who were killed or died (erected in 1956).

PIŠKERA MARINA (ACI)
(43°45'N; 015°21,2'E) is situated on the N coast of the islet of Panitula Vela.

Capacity: 185 berths at 6 floating fingers (depth 2.5–3.5 m).

The marina operates only during the season.

It has reception office, restaurant, shop, toilets and showers with hot water, sports equipment; small general repairs; water, fuel and gas available (in emergency).

ISLAND OF LAVSA

LAVSA
(43°45'N; 015°22,5'E), cove on the N coast of the islet of the same name.

Approach. From the open sea, the islet of Gustac can be identified by its reddish cliffs. The passage between Piškera and Lavsa is 6 m deep; in the N part of the passage, between Lavsa and the islet of Gustac is a shoal (5 m).

When approaching from SE, go between Opat point and Smokvica Vela island (coast light, red flashes) or between the islands of Smokvica Vela and Škulj and enter Kornatski kanal (consult Chart 100–20). The summits of these islands and Kurba Vela island are conspicuous from afar.

Mooring. The depth in the cove decrease from 30 m at the entrance to 3 m further inshore. The cove is a good anchorage and shelter, but with strong N winds blowing, go to the anchorage NE of the islet of Panitula Mala (depth 30 m).

PIŠKERA MARINA

In the inner part of the cove is the anchorage of Piškera marina with plastic buoys.

Facilities. Provisions in Piškera marina.

ISLAND OF RAVNI ŽAKAN

RAVNI ŽAKAN
(43°43'N; 015°26'E), cove on the S coast of the island of the same name, in the SE part of the Kornati Archipelago.

Approach. Shape course for the highest peak on the islets of Škulj (145 m), Opat (109 m) and Smokvica Vela (94 m; on the N point a quadrangular tower, red flashes) and the islet of Purara (a vertical cliff on the SW coast).

When approaching from S (the open sea) care should be taken of the shoal (6.3 m) SSE of the islet of Kameni Žakan

– pass between the islets Kameni Žakan and Škulj. The depth betweeen the islets of Ravni Žakan and Lunga is 6 m.

Mooring. The S cove is protected from the bora, but is exposed to SE and SW winds. The N cove is exposed to the bora. On the E coast of the cove is an L-shaped pier (length 35 m; depth at the head of the pier

PIŠKERA MARINA

1 m, the depth 2 m off it is 2 m). On its outer end is rock ballasting (depth 2.5 m) but it is possible to secure there by using the four-point moor. On the inner end of the pier is a small fishing harbour (depth 0.5–2 m). Larger vessels can anchor S of the island, closer to Kameni Žakan in depth of

LAVSA

15–30 m; the anchorage is sheltered from all winds except the bora.

Facilities. A restaurant near the harbour. In the NW cove of the island is the bungalow village of the Club Méditerranée; anchoring is possible only with the permission of the management.

ISLAND OF SMOKVICA VELA

LOJENA

(43°43'N; 015°29'E), cove with a seasonally inhabited village on the S coast of Smokvica Vela, at the SE entrance to Kornatski kanal.

Approach. The same as for Ravni Žakan cove. The best approach is from SE or from Murtersko more but not between Smokvica Vela and Smokvica Mala.

Mooring. The cove is sheltered from NE and NW but exposed to S. At the head of the cove is a fishing harbour (depth up to 1.3 m); moor stern or bows-to the jetty. At the first signs of a storm from the S go to Lavsa cove

or one of the anchorages between the islets of Ravni Žakan and Kameni Žakan.

Facilities. Water from the cistern in the village.

ISLAND OF ŽIRJE

MIKAVICA

(43°40,5'N; 015°36,5'E), cove on the NW coast of Žirje.

Approach. Shape course for the chapel at the head of the cove. Care should be taken of the shoal (2 m) extending up to 250 m S of the islet of Mikavica.

Mooring. The cove is sheltered from S winds but is open to NE and NW winds; W winds cause an unpleasant sea. Yachts drawing up to 2 m can moor at the small pier and the bollard in the E part of the cove. The anchorage is in the middle of the cove, closer to the mole (depth 6–8 m).

Žirje, the largest village on the island, is situated in the central part of the island, 5 km SE of Mikavica cove.

PRIŠNJAK

MALA STUPICA

a cove S of the island Žirje, where there used to be a military zone. It is however still a dangerous area because of possible mines.

ISLAND OF KAPRIJE

KAPRIJE

(43°41'N; 015°42'E), village and small port at the end of the bay on W coast of the island.

Approach. Secure approach through the middle of the bay.

Mooring. At the quay (depth 2 m) protected from all winds.

Anchorage. In the midst of the harbour (depth 5 m).

Facilities. Food shop, restaurant.

Warning. In the bay in front of the port Kaprije anchorage is prohibited except for emergency and without preventing official transport.

ŠIBENIK, FRIEZE AT THE APSE OF THE CATHEDRAL

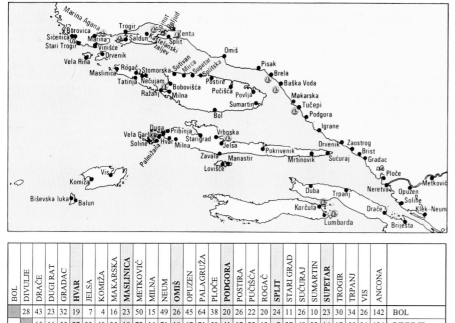

	BOL	DIVULJE	DRAČE	DUGI RAT	GRADAC	HVAR	JELSA	KOMIŽA	MAKARSKA	MASLINICA	METKOVIĆ	MILNA	NEUM	OMIŠ	OPUZEN	PALAGRUŽA	PLOČE	PODGORA	POSTIRA	PUČIŠĆA	ROGAČ	SPLIT	STARI GRAD	SUĆURAJ	SUMARTIN	SUPETAR	TROGIR	TRPANJ	VIS	ANCONA	
		28	43	23	32	19	7	4	16	23	50	15	49	26	45	64	38	20	26	22	20	24	11	26	10	23	30	34	26	142	BOL
			65	16	55	27	33	40	35	18	72	16	71	19	67	71	59	41	17	22	13	7	27	48	32	14	17	55	34	134	DIVULJE
				49	12	49	40	68	30	64	17	57	8	47	13	80	9	25	49	44	63	59	53	17	36	52	70	11	59	182	DRAČE
					38	28	27	40	19	21	55	15	54	3	50	73	44	24	4	8	15	10	28	33	17	5	23	40	34	138	DUGI RAT
						41	29	60	19	54	19	48	17	36	14	71	7	14	36	33	52	49	42	7	24	39	60	7	51	173	GRADAC
							23	23	34	18	57	15	55	30	52	48	45	37	27	32	20	23	15	35	29	23	28	39	14	133	HVAR
								38	16	27	47	21	46	25	42	69	35	18	27	23	25	28	15	23	11	28	34	31	30	147	JELSA
									49	25	77	28	74	43	72	41	64	52	39	44	30	36	30	53	43	36	33	58	13	121	KOMIŽA
										39	37	32	35	17	32	79	25	5	18	14	32	29	27	13	7	22	41	21	41	156	MAKARSKA
											72	14	70	24	73	61	59	42	21	26	7	14	22	48	33	17	10	55	22	121	MASLINICA
												63	22	55	5	87	14	32	54	49	69	66	60	24	42	57	77	19	68	189	METKOVIĆ
													62	18	58	59	52	35	14	19	9	11	14	42	26	11	17	48	22	132	MILNA
														53	17	86	13	30	55	50	69	65	59	23	42	58	76	16	65	188	NEUM
															50	75	42	22	5	6	18	14	30	30	14	7	26	38	37	141	OMIŠ
																82	9	27	49	44	64	61	55	19	37	52	72	14	63	184	OPUZEN
																	75	74	70	75	63	67	61	66	73	66	71	69	45	142	PALAGRUŽA
																		20	43	38	58	53	48	12	30	46	65	8	56	177	PLOČE
																			23	19	38	35	30	8	11	26	47	16	45	159	PODGORA
																				6	15	12	26	30	15	4	23	38	33	139	POSTIRA
																					20	17	31	26	11	9	29	33	37	144	PUČIŠĆA
																						9	20	45	30	11	10	52	26	125	ROGAČ
																							23	42	26	9	14	49	30	131	SPLIT
																								36	21	23	29	43	23	140	STARI GRAD
																									18	34	54	8	45	167	SUĆURAJ
																										19	39	26	35	150	SUMARTIN
																											19	41	29	135	SUPETAR
																												61	29	123	TROGIR
																													48	171	TRPANJ
																														125	VIS
																															ANCONA

DISTANCES OF PORTS

moor along the coast (four-point moor) or anchor in the middle of the cove (depth 12–19 m).

SIČENICA

(43°30'N; 016°01'E), cove some 1.5 M east of Ploča point.

Approach. Off the entrance to the cove is Muljica rock (4 m), and 0.5 M to the SE is the islet of Muljica (round white tower, white light).

Mooring. The innermost part of the cove is sheltered from all winds; its outer part is open to S and SW winds and seas. Larger yachts can anchor in the outer, E part of the cove (depth 25 m).

STARI TROGIR

(43°29,5'N; 016°02'E), cove N of the islet of Arkanđel, NW of the islet of Drvenik Mali.

Approach. Arkanđel islet and Muljica islet (white iron tower with a column, white light) off the entrance to the cove are conspicuous.

Mooring. The bora is very strong in the cove and SW wind causes a slop. The E part of the cove is well sheltered from the sirocco and the bora. Yachts should anchor with the ruined chapel on Arkanđel islet in alignment with Merara islet. During the bora they should secure ashore bows--to NE. Good anchorage in SW winds is off the N coast of Arkanđel islet.

VINIŠĆE

(43°29'N; 016°0,7'E), village and cove extending about 1 M in from the sea, on the N end of Drvenički kanal.

Approach. Shape course for the quadrangular stone tower (red light) on the S entrance of Artatur point. Care should be taken of the low Vinišće rock (3 m), which is hard to make out against the stony coast.

Mooring. Smaller yachts can moor at the inner side of the pier in depth of 0.9–3.7 m, on the NE coast. Here they are sheltered from all winds. The anchorage ground in the middle of the cove (depth about 15 m) is open to waves from the E. The bora is violent and anchoring yachts should secure ashore as well.

Facilities. Limited provisions and water in the village.

MARINA

(43°31'N; 016°07'E), village and small harbour in the bay of the same name, in the W part of Trogirski zaljev.

Approach. Landmarks: the chapel on Drid hill (177 m) on the N coast; the large tower (built in 16 C, now a hotel) on the SW coast;

HARBOURS ON THE COAST

BOROVICA

(43°30'N; 015°59,5'E), cove E of Ploča point, S of Rogoznica.

Approach. The ruins of Sv Ivan chapel on Ploča point and the low Melevrin rock SE of it (big waves wash over the rock) are conspicuous.

Mooring. The cove is sheltered from the bora; it is not safe in the sirocco. Yachts can

the conical white tower (red light) on Pasji rat (S coast); the red column (red light) at the head of the bay NW of the mole.

In Stipanov jaz cove care should be taken and speed reduced because of the floating cages for fish breeding.

Mooring. The bora is strong in the bay (it usually blows from the E) and causes waves. The sirocco, though also strong, does not cause waves. In the small harbour (depth at the mole under 2 m) boats are protected from all winds. In the bora small

yachts moor in the harbour in Šašina cove. Larger yachts should anchor closer inshore, SE of the chapel and S of Plokata hill.

Facilities. Post office, medical service, shops and a hotel. Provisions and water available.

MARINA

AGANA MARINA

(43°30,45'N; 016°7'E) is situated in the westernmost part of Marina bay. It is protected by the N breakwater (green light).

The marina covers an area of 25 ha; depth along the breakwater 3–8 m, along the waterfront 2.5–3 m, along the piers 3 m.

Capacity: 140 sea-berths (four-point moor) for foreign yachts (up to 40 m length) and 150 sea-berths for local craft; water and electricity hook-ups; 100 dry-berths (up to 25 m length); travel-lift.

The marina operates the year round.

It has reception office, hotel, restaurant, food and other shops. Parking lot for 200 cars.

Hull, equipment and engine repairs. The »Brodograđevna industrija Trogir« shipyard is in Trogir.

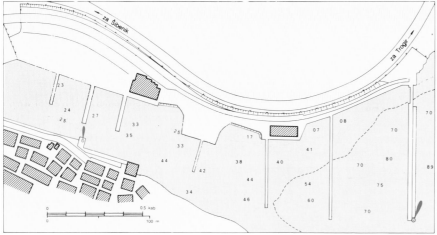

AGANA MARINA

TROGIR

(43°31'N; 016°16'E), city and harbour on an islet in the narrowest part of Trogirski kanal. It is linked with Čiovo island by a drawbridge (it is not opened; only small vessels without a mast can pass under it) and with the mainland by a stone bridge.

Approach. The W entrance should be approached with the belfry of the church of Sv Mihovil in line with the belfry of the Cathedral; after passing Čubrijan point (green tower with a column and gallery, green light) course should be shaped for the central part of the drawbridge, leaving the conical green buoy (green light) to starboard and the cylindrical red buoy to port. The E entrance to the harbour is marked on the N side by a cylindrical green buoy surmounted by a cone (green light), a conical green buoy (green light) and a conical buoy surmounted by a cone (green light). Approaching from S the fairway is marked by three cylindrical red buoys. The green

TROGIR

TROGIR, RADOVAN'S PORTAL

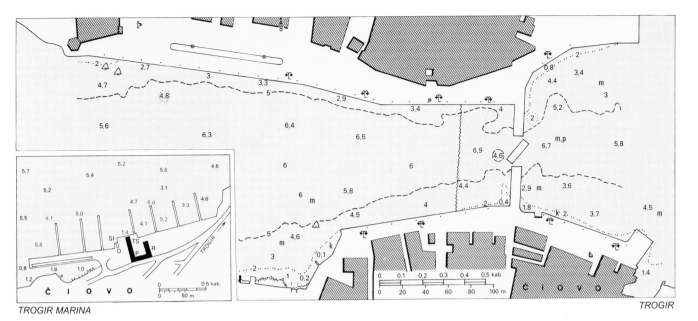

TROGIR MARINA

TROGIR

buoys should be left to starboard and the red ones to port.

Mooring. In Trogir marina.

Warning. Anchoring is prohibited in Trogirski kanal E of the line connecting Čubrijan point and the pier in Seget Donji harbour as far as the meridian 016°16,3'E. Landing is prohibited along the quay on the stretch (130 m) from the root of the drawbridge westward.

Facilities. Harbour master's branch office, post office, medical service, restaurants, chemist's, hotels, shops.

Provisions; water from the hydrant on the waterfront; fuel at the petrol station on the Adriatic highway and Trogir marina.

The »Trogir« shipyard undertakes all hull and engine repairs and has docking facilities.

The »Medena« hotels are situated in the village of Seget, 1 M west (1.5 km by road) of Trogir.

Trogir is the venue of the summer festival »Trogirski tjedni« (Trogir weeks).

Sights. Sections of old town walls with gate facing the mainland coast (13–15 C); the Kamerlengo Castle (1420–37); Kula Sv Marka (St Mark's Tower, 1470); Sv Lovro cathedral (St Lawrence, 13–15 C, famous Romanesque portal by Radovan, 1240), Baptistry, Ivan Orsini chapel (1468–97, works by I. Duknović, A. Aleši and Nicholas of Florence); small basilica of Sv Barbara (9–10 C), Sv Ivan Krstitelj church (St John the Baptist, 1270); the Benedictine convent (1064, renovated in 17 C) with Sv Nikola church, the Dominican monastery (14 C, museum of sacral art) with St Dominic

church; the City Loggia (1308) with the Clock Tower; the small Loggia on the waterfront (1527). Mansions: Čipico (Gothic, 15 C), Lučić (Renaissance), Gargani-Fanfogna (Baroque, houses the Archeological Department of the Municipal Museum, with the Greek relief of Kairos – god of the propitious moment, 1 C). On Čiovo island: the churches of Sv Ante na Dridu (St Anthony, 1432), Sv Križ (Holy Cross, with cloister from 15 C), and Gospa kraj mora (Our Lady by the Sea, early Romanesque). Park of the Fanfogna family – monument of garden architecture.

TROGIR MARINA (ACI)

(43°30,8'N; 016°15,2'E) is situated on the N coast of the island of Čiovo, between Trogir Bridge and Čubrijan point, opposite the W part of the town.

The marina has floating fingers with 205 sea-berths (depth 4–5 m; up to 18 m length) and 50 dry-berths on the coast (13 m length).

The marina is open the year round.

The marina has reception office, restaurant, snack-bar, shops, toilets and showers with hot water; water and electricity hook-ups, telephone; petrol station; car park.

Launching and hauling up of vessels (hoist 10 t), slipway, maintenance and general repairs. Major repairs can be executed at the »Trogir« shipyard.

KAŠTELANSKI ZALJEV (BAY of KAŠTELA),

a spacious bay closed from the S by the island of Čiovo and Marjan peninsula. On its N coast are 10 settlements, seven of which are Kaštela (settlements that developed around defense fortresses). The W part of the bay is linked by Trogirski kanal with the Bay of Trogir; In E part is the northern harbour of Split. The bora and sirocco are strong in the bay, the latter causing a heavy sea in the W part. Smaller yachts can moor in the following harbours: Nehaj, Kaštel Štafilić, Kaštel Novi, Kaštel Stari, Kaštel Lukšić, Kaštel Kambelovac, Kaštel Gomilica

HRID GALERA

TROGIR MARINA

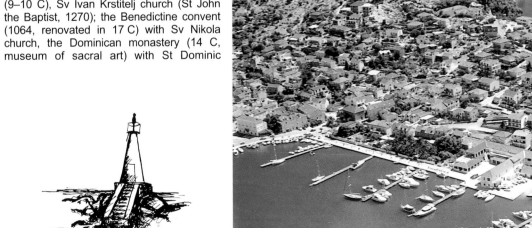

117

KAŠTEL NOVI

KAŠTEL STARI

KAŠTEL LUKŠIĆ

and Kaštel Sućurac. All these harbours are sheltered from the bora and Kaštel Novi, Lukšić and Sućurac from all other winds as well except the south-westerlies.

In the E part of the bay: Galija shoal (depth 3.6 m; yellow and black cylindrical light-buoy, a black column surmounted by 2 black cones points up); Galija rock (masonry mark, black and red spar with 2 black spheres) and Galija rock (cylindrical concrete house; the green sector of the light covers the rock and Galija shoal); Šilo shoal (cylindrical black and red tower with a column and gallery, 2 black spheres) E of the rock; Garofulin shoal (4 m; black and red spar with 2 black spheres) off Poljud.

Navigation and stopping is prohibited to all vessels (with the exception of naval vessels) in an area contained between the coast at the small harbour of Divulje and the lines joining: the floating mark 600 m offshore of the green light on the breakwater in Divulje harbour bearing 66°; the mooring buoy 250 m offshore of the same light, bearing 190°; the floating mark 600 m offshore of the above light bearing 260°.

Navigation is prohibited in the area between the coast and the 4 floating marks off the »Adriachem« factory (Kaštel Sućurac) and the green light-buoy (surmounted by a cone) some 500 m off Marjan point bearing 5° and the shore NE of that point; stopping, anchoring and fishing is prohibited in the E part of the bay marked by the following points: the root of the N breakwater of Lora harbour – Šilo shoal – Galija rock – Školjić islet – Rat point. Mooring in the small harbour of the Institute for Oceanography and Fisheries at Marjan point is allowed only with special permission of the Institute's management. All underwater activities are prohibited in the bay.

SPLIT

(43°30'N; 016°26'E), city and principal port of Dalmatia. It has two harbours: the North Harbour (cargo, in the E part of Kaštelanski bay) and the South (City) Harbour.

Approach. Landmarks when approaching the City Harbour: the belfry of the Sv Duje cathedral (St Doimus), the stony Sustipan point and Mt Marjan on the W side, the white stone obelisk of the Pomorac (54 m) at the root of the main breakwater, the eight-

KAŠTELANSKI ZALJEV

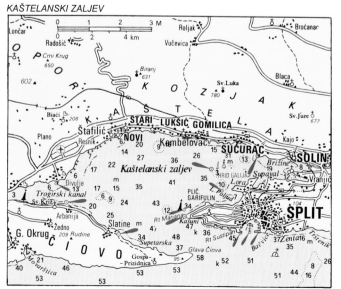

SPLIT

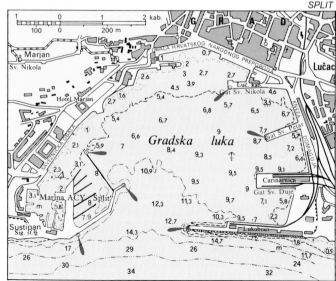

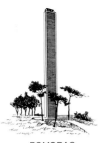

POMORAC

SPLIT, WOODEN DOOR BY A. BUDVINA, DETAIL

sided green tower with a gallery above the house (green light) on the head of the breakwater and the round red tower with a column and gallery (red light) on the head of the outer breakwater of Split marina (E of Sustipan).

The bora is rather strong in the City Harbour; the sirocco causes waves on the W coast only; the southerlies and south-westerlies cause an unpleasant swell and the flooding of the N sea-wall.

Mooring. Berths for yachts will be indicated by the Split harbour master's office. The E part of Obala hrvatskoga narodnog preporoda Street is reserved for motor-boats and sports boats.

In the W part of the City Harbour is the harbour of the »Mornar« Sailing Club (a few berths available for non-members), the »Labud« Sailing Club and »Split« marina. In Poljud cove on the N side of the city is the harbour of the RPŠD »Split« and PŠD »Spinut«; 1 M east of the City Harbour is the harbour of the »Zenta« Sports Club; the outer end of the pier in front of the »Lav« Hotel can be used for mooring by yachts drawing up to 2.5 m (four-point moor).

Anchoring is prohibited at the entrance to the City Harbour along the line joining the light on the head of the breakwater and the light on the outer breakwater of »Split« marina and E of the line joining the light on the outer breakwater of the marina and the NW corner of Gat Sv. Nikole (Sv Nikola pier) and inside the City Harbour; at the entrance to Supaval cove (shipyard area) in North Harbour on the line joining Šilo rock and the E entrance point of the cove.

It is prohibited to land in the City Harbour at Sv Duje pier without the permission from the customs office; landing is prohibited at Brižine pier (between the »Sv. Juraj« factory and the »Sv Kajo« factory in the North Harbour), in Lora harbour and at the mole NE of Marjan point (off which there is a light-buoy).

Stopping is prohibited in the North Harbour up to the distance of 1000 m off the red light on Galija rock; securing to the rock is also prohibited. Vessels passing Supaval cove (»Split« shipyard) are required to reduce speed so as not to create a wash.

Split is a port of entry with customs office and the sanitary inspectorate.

The coastal radio station SPLITRADIO forms part of the Maritime Service (see Part I of the Guide).

Facilities. Harbour master's office, two hospitals and the thermal spa Splitske toplice, several out-patients' departments, chemist's; post office, railway station, Split Airport (Resnik in Kaštelansko polje); »Split« Shipyard; the headquarters of the shipping lines »Jadranska slobodna plovidba« and »Splitska plovidba«; the Croatian Register of Shipping, Lloyd's Register, the institution responsible for the maintenance of maritime waterways (PLOVPUT), the Salvage Company »Brodospas«, the Institute for Oceanography and Fishing (at Marjan point), the Croatian Hydrographic Institute, the Maritime Meteorological Centre, Split University with several faculties (a department of the Dubrovnik Maritime Faculty), the Maritime School Centre (nautical and shipbuilding department).

Museums and galleries: Museum of Split, Ethnographic Museum, Museum of Croatian Archeological Monuments, Archeological Museum, Museum of Revolution, Maritime Museum, Art Gallery and Meštrović Gallery.

Supplies and services for yachts. Good shopping for provisions, water from hydrants in the harbour, fuel at the pump on the pier near the »Marjan« hotel (W part of the harbour). Nautical charts and relevant publications at the shop of PLOVPUT (Obala Lazareta 1), or at »Mladost« bookshop – »Znanstvena knjižara« (Trg Braće Radića 7).

Split is one of the major sports centres in Croatia, especially for water sports. It is the seat of the Sailing Federation of Croatia. There are »Labud« Sailing Society, »Mornar«, Split and »Spinut« Sailing Clubs and »Zenta« Maritime Sports Society.

Split is also the seat of the Croatian secretaries of the IOR – International Off-Shore Rule and of the international sailboat categories – »470«, »Finn«, »Laser« and »Optimist«; it is also the seat of the national secretary of the international sailboat class »Cadet«. Split is the starting point of many national and international regattas.

All repairs to yachts can be undertaken at the RŠPD »Split«. At the Labud harbour: slipway for yachts up to 14 m in length, facility for mounting masts, maintenance of marine engines; general repairs and maintenance at »Split« marina, hoists (2.5 and 5 t) at PŠD »Spinut« and in the »Mornar« Yacht Club's harbour (2 t). The »Split« shipyard and the »Brodoremont-Split« company (the latter in Vranjic, North Harbour) carry out repairs and maintenance of all types of marine engines and of yachts up to 750 t (including hauling out).

Tugboats, floating cranes and divers can be ordered through the firms »Luka« and »Brodospas«. Boating supplies and spares at »Brodokomerc«.

Car-ferry lines: Split – Vis; Split – Supetar (Brač); Split – Rogač (Šolta); Split – Stari Grad (Hvar); Split – Vira (Hvar); Split – Stari

SPLIT

119

SPLIT MARINA

In Sinj (35 km from Split) on the first Sunday of August the »Sinjska alka« equestrian tournament is held with medieval echoes in memory of the successful defense of Sinj from theTurks in 1715.

SPLIT MARINA (ACI)

(43°30,1'N; 016°26'E) situated in the SW part ot the City Port, N of the Sustipan Peninsula. Sheltered from S winds by a long L-shaped breakwater.

Capacity: about 400 sea-berths (up to 13 m length) at the inner side of the breakwater and at 5 floating fingers; depth 2.5–10 m. The wide inner pier affords room for 100 dry-berths; water, electricity and telephone hook-ups.

The marina operates all year round.

It has reception office, casino, skipper's club, restaurant, snack-bar, espresso-bar, shop, showers and toilets with hot water; car park. The marina offers pleasure crafts (charter fleet) for rent. Hoisting facility (10 t), slipway (50 t) and repair and maintenance workshop. The fuel pump is situated in front of »Marjan« hotel.

SPLIT RŠPD

(Worker's Nautical Sport Club/Radničko športsko pomorsko društvo), small yacht harbour on the NE shore of Marjan Peninsula, in the little bay of Poljud. Two L-shaped breakwaters offer protection from all winds and sea.

Approach. When approaching the bay of Poljud care should be taken to avoid the Garifulin shoal patch (depth of 4.4 and 4 m), which is marked by a red and black spar topped by two black spheres. Školjić rock, about 500 m off Rat point is marked by a green tower with a column exhibiting a green light. The entrance to the yacht harbour is marked by green and red harbour lights (see Split).

Mooring. The 2 breakwaters and 4 floating fingers afford 450 berths. The depth in the outer part of the harbour range from 2.5–4 m and in the inner part (alongside the quay) 1.5–2 m. There are 50 dry-berths outdoors plus 15–20 in a storage shed. Berths are indicated by attendants (reception office at the bent of the W breakwater). The yacht harbour operates all year round.

Facilities. Reception office, restaurant, toilets, a shop specialising in yacht equipment and spares. Sailing instruction available. Water and electricity are laid on. Aside from the berths used by club members, there are

Grad) – Hvar – (Vela Luka) – Ancona; Rijeka – Split – Dubrovnik (see Rijeka).

Local passenger lines: Split – Trogir – Drvenik Mali – Drvenik Veli; Split – Hvar.

Sights. Diocletian's Palace (built 295–395): Sv Duje cathedral (St Doimus, formerly the mausoleum of Emperor Diocletian, carved door by A. Buvina, 1214, altars by Bonino di Milano, Juraj Dalmatinac and G. M. Morlaiter, choir stalls, 13 C), the belfry (13–15 C, renovated in 20 C); Baptistry (formerly temple of Jupiter, font dating from 10 C); the Peristyle, the Vestibule, Diocletian's underground halls, the four town gates. In front of the N gate (Porta Aurea) the statue of Bishop Gregory of Nin (Grgur Ninski) by Ivan Meštrović, 1929. The Papalić Palace housing the Municipal Museum (15 C). Outside the Palace: W of the Palace

Narodni trg with the old City Hall (1443, now Ethnographic Museum), »Hrvojeva kula« (Hrvoje Tower, 15 C); on the waterfront Sv Franjo church (St Francis, 1213, renovated in 20 C, the pantheon of the famous citizens of Split), on the NW side of the city the Art Gallery; the Archeological Museum (contains Roman finds from the Solin area). Near the suburb of Poljud – the early Croatian church of Sv Trojica with Franciscan monastery and Sv Marija church (work of art). On the W edge of the city is Marjan Hill (178 m) which together with Sustipan peninsula is a protected forest park and viewpoint. It has a Natural Sciences Museum and Zoo; Sv Nikola (13 C) and Sv Jere (St Jeremy, 15 C) chapels. On the W slope of Marjan is the Meštrović Gallery and Kaštelet (17 C), and on Marjan point the Institute for Oceanography and Fisheries. On the E side of the city is a Dominican monastery and in the NE is the Venetian fortress Gripe. – Solin (Salona) was the central town of Roman Dalmatia, destroyed in the 5 C by the Huns and about 614 by the Avars. Since the 19 C it has provided an important site for archeological excavations: ruins of a theatre (2 C), forum and amphitheatre (2/3 C), Old Christian basilica, the Hortus Metrodori grave, urban basilica (4–6 C), Old Christian graves of Manastirina, Marusinac villa rustica, two pre-Romanesque churches on Gospin islet at the mouth of the Jadro river. – Klis (5 km), Turkish fortress on site of medieval one, key position for sweeping view – 11 km.

In June every year there is a Music Festival and every July the Split Summer Festival (opera, concerts, plays).

SPLIT MARINA

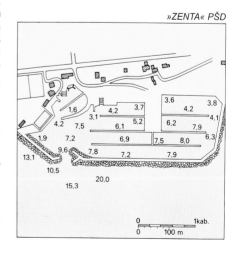

»ZENTA« PŠD

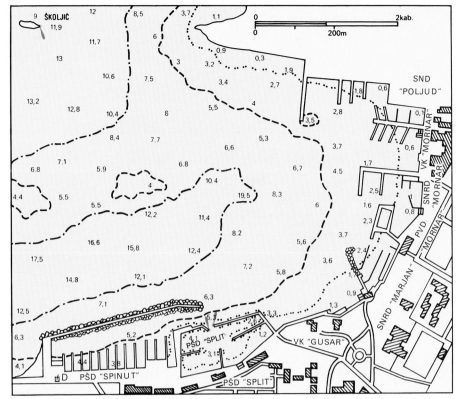

»SPLIT« RŠPD AND »SPINUT« PŠD

a number of commercial berths (for foreign and Croatian vessels). Parking lot for 60 vehicles. Hauling-out facilities (0.5 and 5 t), slipway, crane for shifting vessels inside the harbour, workshop for repairs to hulls, engines and electrical wiring, facility for mounting masts, storage of equipment, shed for laying-up vessels (up to 10 m in length) in winter. Maintenance, rubbing-down, painting and care of yachts.

SPINUT PŠD

(Nautical Sport Club / Pomorsko športsko društvo), small yacht harbour situated W of Split RŠPD.

For approaching see: Lučica Split RŠPD.

Mooring. The yacht harbour is protected from S and W winds by a 500 m long breakwater. There are 780 berths alongside the quay (the W portion of the breakwater up to its bend), and the 11 piers (in 12 basins). Depth inside the harbour ranges 2 m (along the shore) to 8 m (at the pier heads). Hoisting facilities (2.5 and 5 t). There are dry-berths (10 000 m of maintained area) for 250 yachts. The harbour has an office, a snack-bar and other facilities for a stay.

ZENTA PŠD

(Nautical Sport Club / Pomorsko športsko društvo);(43°30'N; 016°27'E), small yacht harbour situated about 1 M from the E of the City Port.

Approach (see Split). When approaching care should be taken to avoid a shoal patch (depth 0.4 m), about 20 m off the SW entrance point.

Mooring. The marina consists of an old and a new part. The W breakwater extending from the W entrance point and the L-shaped E breakwater afford protection from southerly winds, which are especially strong and frequent in the winter. The old harbour has about 170 berths. Depth in the inner part range from 0.3–1.5 m and in the outer part from 2–2.5 m. The new harbour has 710 berths. Depth range from 3 m (along the quay) to 8 m (towards the breakwater). There is accomodation for 120 vessels in dry-berths. The harbour has an office building with a snack-bar, a hoist (10 t) and two slipways.

Attached to the harbour is the POŠK Nautical Sport Club with an outdoor Olympic-size swimming pool, administrative office and other premises.

OMIŠ

(43°26'N; 016°42'E), town and harbour at the mouth of the Cetina River.

Approach. Landmarks include the steep cliffs flanking the Cetina gorge, a red metal structure mounted on the monastery wall (red light) and a white, round tower with a column exhibiting white-green sector light on the molehead. Vessels making and approaching from the W at night should keep S of the cylindrical light-buoy (in front of the Dugi Rat) till reaching the red sector of the light on the monastery wall. Course should be shaped for the harbour only after coming into the green sector of the light on the molehead. By day – after having passed S

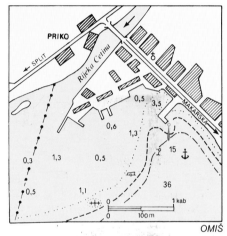

OMIŠ

OMIŠ

OMIŠ, CHURCH OF ST.PETAR IN PRIKO

of the light buoy fronting Dugi Rat – course should be shaped towards the harbour so that the two red cylindrical buoys marking the E edge of the big sand bank at the river mouth are left to port.

Mooring. The harbour is exposed to the bora. It can be especially dangerous during the tramontana. S winds also raise a heavy sea. Summer storms with winds blowing from the SW may be dangerous. Yachts drawing up to 3.5 m can lie alongside the inner end of the L-shaped mole in the harbour. They can also lie alongside the newly constructed quay on the E side of the river mouth (extending to the SE from Dugi Rat point). Anchorage for deeper drawing

BRELA

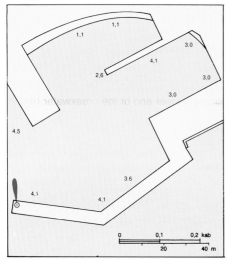

yachts may be found S of the monastery (depth 30–35 m). During a strong bora it is advisable to anchor with lines secured ashore, bows-to NE.

Facilities. Harbour master's branch office, post office, medical service and chemist's. »Cipal« Fishing Club. Provisions at local shops and on open market. Water from hydrants on the waterfront. Fuel at the petrol station on the Adriatic highway, across the bridge.

Minor repairs to yacht hulls at a privately owned boatyard for wooden craft.

Sights. Sv Petar chapel (St Peter) in Priko on the right bank of the Cetina (old Croatian architecture, 10 C), remnants of the town fortifications and tower on the Fošal promenade, Sv Ivan Nepomuk church (St John 17 C), medieval tower Stari Grad (Fortica, Mirabela) on a cliff, 311 m above the town. Regional Museum (Zavičajni muzej), collection of objects of cultural and historical interest in the house of the Radman family. The Ruskamen area, SE of town, has been declared a nature reserve on account of its geomorphological features. Up the Cetina River lie the islet of Šarin and ancient watermills, »Radmanove mlinice«, an excursion centre and nature reserve. Further upstream, near the village of Zadvarje, the river forms the Gubavica waterfalls.

Each year at the end of July Omiš hosts »Festival dalmatinskih klapa«, a competition of Dalmatian popular singing groups.

PISAK

(43°24'N; 016°52'E), village about 15 km E of Omiš.

Mooring. The small harbour affords good shelter to small craft from the bora, but is open to all other winds. Yachts are advised to seek more appropriate shelter (Kutleša, 2 M west). About 1.5 M east of Pisak a rare natural phenomenon may be observed in the cove of Vrulja. A powerful freshwater spring seethes up from the sea bottom forming a »mushroom« in the middle of the bay. The bora comes fiercely down into the bay, fanning out from it across the Brač Channel. Unsuitable for longer stays.

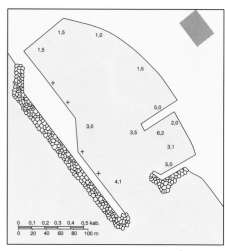

BAŠKA VODA

BRELA-SOLINE

(43°22'N; 016°56'E), village, small harbour and summer resort on the Makarska Riviera.

Mooring. The harbour is exposed to all winds and not recommended for longer stays, 100 berths (up to 15 m length). Anchorage is not allowed.

Facilities. Post office, medical service, chemist's. A number of high class hotels. Provisions and water in adequate supply.

Sights. The beaches and forest-parks around the village have been declared nature reserves. Ancient oak-tree in the village.

BAŠKA VODA

(42°21'N; 016°57'E), village and small harbour 5 M NW of Makarska.

Approach. Landmark include a round red tower with a column exhibiting a red light at the head of the breakwater and the village church.

Warning. A net extending for about 480 m is submerged in front of the bathing area 1 M southeast of the cove, about 100 m offshore.

Mooring. Both the bora and the sirocco are strongly felt in the bay. The small harbour is protected by a 200 m long breakwater (of which only the outward end has been com-

MAKARSKA

MAKARSKA

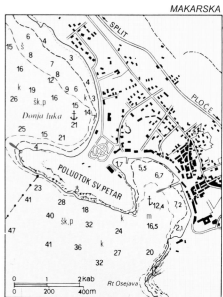

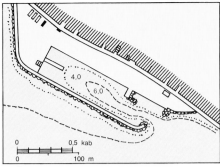

TUČEPI

pleted). Yachts drawing up to 5 m can lie alongside the masonry pier (50 m in length). Good holding ground.

Facilities. Post office, medical service. chemist's. Provisions at local shops, water from taps, fuel at the petrol station on the Adriatic highway (about 4 km NW).

Modern hotel complex in nearby Baško Polje, 3 km SE of Baška Voda. In its vicinity a convalescent home for children (»Dječje selo«).

MAKARSKA

(43°18'N; 017°01'E), town harbour and major summer resort on the Makarska Riviera.

Approach. Makarska can be identified from a distance by a square stone tower and dwelling exhibiting a light (flashing white), situated on the W extremity of the Sv Petar peninsula, by the television mast on the southern point Osejava and by its numerous hotels. A red light is exhibited from the white tower with a column situated at the head of the mole.

Warning. An underwater pipe lies on the seabed about 150 m SE of the light at the extreme end of Sv Petar Peninsula, on a bearing of 213°. Its end (about 1600 m offshore) is marked by a bouy. Anchorage is prohibited in the area between that buoy and the coast. Water-skiing and navigation with motor boats are prohibited within 200 m of the bathing beach Donja Luka.

Mooring. During the bora squalls are often violent, but the harbour offers good protection. With stronger SW and W winds an uncomfortable swell creeps in. The cove of Donja Luka, NE of the Sv Petar Peninsula is exposed to winds and waves from the NW. The quay measures 350 m in length. The

TUČEPI

mole extending from it (50 m) is used by regular lines (minimum depth 4.8 m). The NW part of the harbour (depth 1.5–2.5 m) is occupied by local craft. Between the fuel pumps and the ferry terminal there are berths (marked by yellow buoys) for 40 yachts (up to 12 m in length). Yachts can anchor in the middle of the harbour (depth 11–14 m) or in Donja Luka (7–12 m). In both places it is recommended to secure lines ashore as well. Attached to »Dalmacija« hotel, NW of the harbour, there is a small harbour for yachts drawing up to 3 m. Slipway and crane.

Facilities. Harbour master's branch office, post office, hospital, chemist's. Provisions and other necessities at local shops, water from hydrants on the waterfront, fuel from pumps in the harbour and the by-pass road of the Adriatic highway above the town.

Car-ferry line: Makarska – Sumartin (Island of Brač).

In the immediate vicinity of Makarska (to the SE, alongside the Adriatic highway) is a sports and recreational centre with a stadium and other sports facilities.

Sights. Churches: Sv Marko (St Mark, 1776, with a rich collection of sacral items), Sv Filip Neri (St Philip, 1757) and Uzašašće Marijino (the Assumption of the Virgin, 1540; construction of a new church building started in 1911), with Franciscan monastery housing a unique collection of shells and marine animal life of the Mediterranean area; the baroque Ivanišević mansion (Municipal reading-room).

TUČEPI

(43°11,5'N; 017°03,4'E), village, hotel complex and marina 2 miles SE from Makarska.

The marina is protected from all winds by its outer breakwater. A red light is exhibited

from a tower with a column situated on the breakwater.

Mooring. The quay is 40 m long. Alongside the inner end of the breakwater (depth about 4.5 m) there are 23 berths available for vessels measuring up to 15 m and 25 berths for boats (up to 5 m). The remaining 100 berths are occupied by locals. All berths have electricity and water hook-ups.

Facilities. Reception office, restaurant and shopping area (sports equipment, spares, provisions), showers and toilets. Fuel obtainable at the petrol station. Slipway with hauling-out facility for yachts up to 6 m in length.

PODGORA

(43°15'N; 017°05'E), village and small harbour 5 M southeast of Makarska. Off Podgora there are two small harbours: the eastern and the western one.

Approach. Podgora may be identified by a conspicuous white curved monument situated on the hill above Lijak point and by the light column (no longer in operation) on the molehead in the eastern harbour.

Mooring. The western harbour affords shelter from all winds and waves, the eastern one only from the bora. Winds blowing from the SE quadrant raise a heavy sea. Smaller yachts can berth in the eastern harbour (depth 2.7–4 m); the depth alongside the breakwater in the western harbour range from 1.1 to 2.5 m. Only small yachts can anchor in front of the town during the bora. Good holding ground.

In old harbour there is a small harbour under construction (for 140 yachts). Along the breakwater there are berths for fishing boats.

Facilities. Post office, medical service, chemist's. Food supplies at local shops.

PODGORA

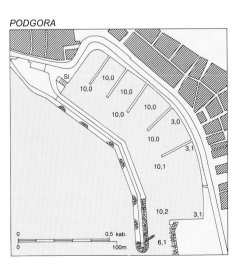

DRVENIK (MAKARSKO PRIMORJE)

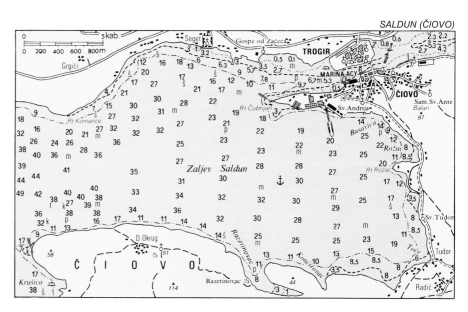

GRADAC

Water in adequate supply. Fuel at the petrol station at the Adriatic highway (above the town).

Sights. In the older, upper part of the town a number of defence towers erected as protection against the Turks and a church dating from 1764. The monument Seagull's Wings (»Galebova krila«) commemorate the formation of the partisan Navy of WW II.

IGRANE

(43°12'N; 017°09'E), village and small harbour in the NW part of the cove of the same name, about 4 M SE of Podgora.

Approach. The belfry on a steep hill above the village is a conspicuous landmark from seaward.

Mooring. The small harbour is protected by a breakwater from all winds except easterlies. Smaller yachts can berth alongside the breakwater (depth 1.3–3.4 m). During the bora yachts are well advised to anchor W of Igrane point (depth 20–25 m).

Facilities. The village has a post office, provisions and water.

Sights. Roman sarcophagus on the cemetery, the apse of a medieval chapel, baroque summer-residence of the Šimić-Ivanišević family. In the olive grove above the village is Sv Mihovil church (St Michael 11/12 C). – Živogošće (Franciscan monastery, 17 C); an epigram carved on the face of a cliff by the sea in late Roman times in the vicinity of the ruins of a Roman villa rustica – 4 km southeast.

DRVENIK

(43°09'N; 017°15'E), village in the cove of the same name on the Makarska Riviera, at the point where the Hvar Channel enters the Neretva Channel.

Mooring. The small harbour is exposed to southerlies and south-westerlies (the sirocco can be troublesome in its NW part). The pier is reserved for the car-ferry. Smaller yachts can anchor in the E part of the cove (it is recommended with lines secured anchore).

Facilities. The village has a post office. Food supplies and water (restricted). Repairs to smaller vessels in a privately owned boatyard.

Car-ferry line: Drvenik – Sućuraj (Hvar).

Sights. Ruins of defence tower and fortifications (17 C); the originally Gothic Sv Juraj church (St George) reconstructed in Baroque style.

ZAOSTROG

(43°08'N; 017°17'E), village and small harbour in a cove of the same name in the S part of the Makarska Riviera, on the shore of the Neretva Channel.

Approach. High steeple surrounded by cypresses is prominent from seaward.

Mooring. The harbour affords protection only from the bora. Untenable in all other winds which generally raise a heavy sea. Not recommended for longer stays. Only small yachts (boats) can lie alongside the pier (depth at E end 2.7–3.3 m, at W end 3.3–4.1 m). Smaller yachts may also berth at the SW coast using four-point moor. Good anchorage for larger yachts SW of the monastery (depth 26–30 m).

Facilities. Post office and medical service. Provisions in a shop; water and fuel.

Sights. Roman finds, Uznesenje Marijino church (Assumption of the Holy Virgin, Gothic, reconstructed in Baroque style in 1747), Franciscan monastery (1468, additions dating from 18–19 C) with Baroque church, ethnological collection, art collection and Roman mosaic in the monastery garden.

BRIST

(43°07'N; 017°20'E), village and cove on the S part of Makarska Riviera, on the shore of the Neretva Channel. Yachts drawing up to 3.5 m can find shelter behind the small pier.

Facilities. Provisions and water. Smaller yachts can be repaired at a privately owned boatyard.

SALDUN (ČIOVO)

GRADAC

(43°06'N; 017°21'E), village and small harbour NW of Ploče harbour. Known for the largest and most beautiful beach in the area.

Approach. Landmarks include the steeple of the church and the red iron tower (light no longer in operation) at the head of the L-shaped breakwater.

Mooring. The harbour is sheltered from all winds but open to waves raised by the sirocco. Untenable during S winds; currents running with considerable strength make it difficult to enter the harbour in such conditions. Yachts drawing up to 3 m can moor at the inner end of the breakwater. Due to the confined space inside the harbour it is advisable to use the four-point moor. Good anchorage ground for larger yachts in front of the harbour, somewhat to the S (depth 25–30 m). During the sirocco yachts should weigh and seek shelter (anchor) in Bošac cove NNW of the Gradac harbour.

Facilities. Post office and medical service. Provisions, water and fuel.

Sights. Remains of a Roman wall; two-storey tower built as defence against the Turks (1661).

ISLANDS OF DRVENIK MALI AND DRVENIK VELI

VELA RINA

(43°25,5'N; 016°04'E), cove on the S coast of Drvenik Mali. The cove is completely exposed to the sea, particularly to south-westerlies, and yachts are well advised to leave it at the first sign of wind. Good anchorage ground on the alignment of Kalafat point and the islet of Orud (depth 17–30 m). Smaller vessels can anchor in the proximity of the E coast.

DRVENIK

(43°27'N; 016°09'E), village and small harbour at the head of the cove of the same name on the NW coast of the island of Drvenik Veli.

Approach. Drvenik is identified from a distance by the red iron tower exhibiting a red light at the head of the landing place, the church on the hill above the W coast (elevation 93 m), and the church in the village.

On the W coast there is a sign warning of underwater cables.

Mooring. The cove affords good shelter from all winds. Yachts drawing up to 2 m can lie at the quay in the E part of the small harbour. The N part of the quay with greater depth alongside is reserved for coasting steamers. Larger yachts can anchor in the middle of the outer part of the cove (depth 30–40 m), with lines secured ashore, bows-to NE. Smaller yachts can anchor in Grabule inlet (about 0.2 M southwest) which provides good all-round shelter.

Facilities. The village has a post office. Limited supply of victuals and water.

Local passenger lines: see Split.

MARINA ZIRONA

(43°27'N; 016°08,9'E), a new marina in a long bay on the northwestern coast of the island of Drvenik Veli.

Facilities: There is only one breakwater on the northeastern coast of the bay (depth 3 m). Since most of the vessels land alongside there is room only for six. There are no other services. On the west from the breakwater there is a simple restaurant and other shopping possibilities only in the village.

ISLAND OF ČIOVO

SALDUN

(43°30'N; 016°13'E), spacious bay in the island of Čiovo in the E part of the Bay of Trogir.

Approach. Landmarks include Vlaška Hill (elevation 453 m), the belfry in Donji Seget village (on the N coast), a white conical tower on Čelice rock (flashing white) at the entrance to the Bay of Trogir, a green conical light-buoy (green light) off Čubrijan point. Vessels entering the bay through the passage between Okruk point and Čelice rock should keep on the alignment on a bearing of 65°, of the belfry of the Sv Mihovil church (St Michael) and the belfry of the Cathedral (both in the town of Trogir) in order to avoid the shoal patches extending off Okruk point.

A floating dock owned by the »Brodogra-đevna industrija Trogir« shipyard is moored 750 m SE of the light on Čubrijan point. Caution should be exercised E, S and W of the dock. Between Čelice rock and the coast there is a shoal (depth 4 m).

Mooring. The bay is exposed to winds blowing from the SW quadrant. Although strongly felt in the bay, the bora and sirocco do not raise big waves. Yachts with a draft up to 2 m can moor alongside the breakwater of Seget but only during the bora or in settled weather. Good anchorage ground for larger yachts 800 m S of Čubrijan point (depth 28 m). Smaller vessels can anchor in

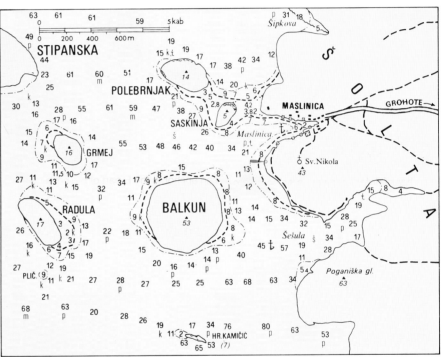

MASLINICA

MASLINICA

125

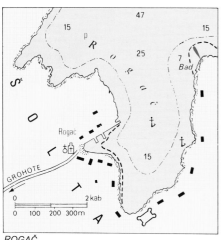

ROGAČ

the inlets in the S and E coast of Saldun Bay, the best anchorage ground for such vessels being that in Razetinovac inlet.

Sights. Finds from Roman times. In the village Čiovo the Early Romanesque chapel Gospa kraj mora (Our Lady by the Sea) with a 15 C polyptych, the Dominican convent and Sv Križ church (Holy Cross) with cloister, Gothic choir stalls.

ISLAND OF ŠOLTA

MASLINICA

(43°24'N; 016°12'E), village and inlet on the W coast of the island of Šolta.

Approach. Landmarks include the square masonry tower with a cupola exhibiting white and red light (sectors) on Sv Nikola point, the S extremity at the entrance to the cove; Sv Nikola chapel (St Nicholas, elevation 43 m), the hotel (old castle) at the head of the inlet. When effecting approach from

the S care should be taken to avoid Kamičić rock (S of Balkun islet). At night the rock is covered by the red sector of the light on Sv Nikola point. The passages between the Polebrnjak and Saskinja islets and between Saskinja and the coast of Šolta are shallow (depth up to 3 m) and passable for yachts of light draught only.

Mooring. The inlet is suitable even for protracted stays, since it offers protection from all winds. A reflected swell may creep into the harbour with westerlies. Smaller yachts can lie alongside the quay, the N part of which is reserved for passenger lines. A good anchorage ground for smaller vessels offering protection from the bora and the sirocco is situated S of the harbour in the adjoining Šešula inlet. Shelter from southwesterlies is to be found along the SE coast of the Balkun islet.

Facilities. Provisions and water in limited supply.

Sights. Tower with loopholes for firearms with adjoining Baroque residence of the Marchi family (1708), now converted into a hotel. On the islet of Stipanska – ruins of an Early Christian basilica.

ROGAČ

(43°24'N; 016°18'E), village and small harbour on the N coast of the island of Šolta. Road connection (2 km) with the village of Grohote.

Approach. Landmarks include the red quadrangular tower exhibiting a red light on Bad point. Care should be taken when approaching as a shoal extends on the E side of the entrance off Bad point (depth 4–5 m), the belfry in the village of Grohote and the reddish brown scar left by a land-slide near the W extremity.

Mooring. The cove affords shelter from all winds except northerlies and waves churned

up by them. Yachts drawing up to 3 m can berth at the heads of the two small piers on the W coast. Larger yachts can anchor in the W part of the cove (depth 12–16 m). Landing ground of the car-ferry.

Facilities. Food supplies at shops and water; fuel at petrol station.

Car-ferry line: Rogač – Split.

Sights. Remains from Roman times: fortifications, piscina (fish-pond). Defence tower built as protection against Turkish raids (late 17 C). In Grohote numerous Roman fragments built into the walls of the village houses. Early Christian sarcophagi in the cemetery. Frescoes (14 C) in Sv Mihovil church (St Michael).

NEČUJAM

(43°23'N; 016°19'E), cove on the N coast of Šolta and holiday centre.

Approach. See Rogač.

Mooring. The cove is exposed to N wind. Smaller yachts can land at the cement block connected with the coast by a timber pier in Supetar inlet (depth 4 m). Anchorage ground for larger yachts in the middle of the cove (depth 25–40 m). The four-point moor is recommended for smaller yachts berthing in the SW part of the cove.

An underwater pipeline (sewer) extends for 750 m from Gaj inlet (SE off Rat point) on a bearing of 156°.

Facilities. Food supplies and water at the holiday centre.

Sights. Remains of Roman walls in the E part of the harbour. The poet Marko Marulić (1450–1524) used to stay in the house adjoining the church. Column commemorating the poet Petar Hektorović (1487–1572).

SUPETAR

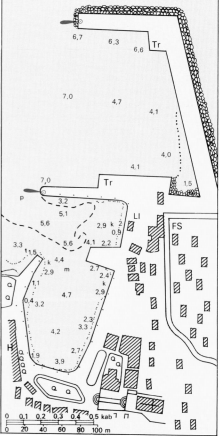

SUPETAR

STOMORSKA

(43°22'N; 016°21'E), village and small inlet on the N coast of Šolta.

Approach. Stomorska can be identified by the red iron tower with a metal framework exhibiting a red light on the E extremity at the inlet entrance and by the chapel on the N slope of Vela Straža hill.

Mooring. Sheltered from all winds but the bora is apt to raise waves inside the harbour. Smaller yachts can berth in the east part of the harbour along the quay (depth from 1–4.7 m).

Facilities. Post office. Food and water in limited supply.

Sights. Defence tower of the Cindro family. Fragments of antique sarcophagi.

TATINJA

(43°22'N; 016°17'E), the biggest cove in the middle of the south coast of the island of Šolta.

Approach. Caution must be exercised whilst entering the cove because of two small rocks: one situated off the W extremity, the other in the middle of the cove in front of the tiny peninsula. Yachts can anchor in the two inlets at the N end (depth 2–4 m).

Facilities. Shops at Grohote (2 km).

ISLAND OF BRAČ

SUTIVAN

(43°23'N; 016°29'E), village and small harbour on the N coast of the island of Brač.

Approach. Landmarks include the round red iron tower with a column exhibiting a red light at the head of the breakwater and the belfry in the little wood on the right side of the entrance.

Mooring. The small harbour affords shelter from all winds except the bora. With northerlies and north-westerlies an unpleasant swell creeps into the harbour. A high northerly wind (tramontana) can make it dangerous. Only yachts of small draught can moor in the harbour (depth 1.3–3 m). A good anchorage, but only in settled summer weather is situated in front of the small harbour (depth 20–30 m).

Facilities. Post office and medical service. Food supplies and water.

Sights. Early Christian church (6 C), the mansion of the Marjanović family (1777),

PUČIŠĆA

the residence of the families Natali-Boži-čević (1505) and Definis (early 19 C, art collection); summer residence of the poet Jerolim Kavanjin (built about 1700); old windmill by the sea.

SUPETAR

(43°23'N; 016°33'E), town and harbour on the N coast of Brač.

Approach. Landmarks include a red metal tower with a column exhibiting a red light situated on the head of the outer breakwater protecting the landing-place of the car-ferry, a green square tower with a column exhibiting a green light situated on the head of the inner (old) breakwater; the belfry in the town and the mausoleum surmonted by a white cupola on the small, low-lying, wooded peninsula W of the town.

Mooring. The sirocco, the bora and the N wind (tramontana) raise a heavy sea inside the harbour. Behind the breakwater yachts are protected from all winds but can stay here only for short periods since this is the landing-place of the car-ferry. Yachts drawing up to 2 m can berth here using the four-point moor. A good anchorage ground (but in settled weather only) is situated in front of the harbour (depth about 25 m).

Facilities. Harbour master's branch office, post office, medical service, chemist's. Food at local shops (self-service), water from the water supply system (taps), fuel at the petrol station (petrol and oil) 75 m from the waterfront.

Regular car-ferry line: Supetar – Split.

Sights. Remains of a Roman piscina (fishpond), Early Christian sarcophagi in the cemetery; Navještenje Marijino church (Annunciation 1738, enlarged in 1887); the mausoleum of the Petrinović family (Toma Rosandić, 1927) W of the town. – Donji Humac (remnants of the old Croatian churches Sv Luka and Sv Ilija (St Luke and Elias, 11/12 C) – 9 km; – Nerežišća (old administrative centre of Brač), Gospa od Karmela church (Our Lady of Carmel, Romanesque, renovated in Baroque style in 1593); a stone base for the town flag from 1545. Renaissance Loggia; Sv Nikola, Sv Juraj, Sveta Margareta churches (St Nicholas, St George, St Margaret, all three from the Romanesque-Gothic transitional period), Sv Petar church (St Peter) in Gothic style, Sv Tudor church (St Theodore), early Christian, reconstructed in 12/13 C. – Blaca (anchoretic settlement among cliffs founded in 1550); several buildings, church dating from 1558, collection of objects of cultural and historic interest, old observatory – 18 km, mountain path from Nerežišće. – Vidova Gora (highest peak on the Adriatic islands, elevation 778 m, sweeping view).

SPLITSKA

(43°23'N; 016°36'E), village in the cove of Zastup on the N coast of the island of Brač.

Approach. Landmarks include the red tower exhibiting a red light situated on the E entrance point and the belfry.

Mooring. Small yachts can anchor in the middle of the cove (pinewoods). Yachts should weigh and put to see at the first sign of northerly winds (tramontana). Anchorage is prohibited off its W part on account of an underwater cable.

Facilities. General store, restaurant and café in the village.

Sights. Uznesenje Marijino church (Assumption of the Virgin Mary, 1228, reno-

PUČIŠĆA

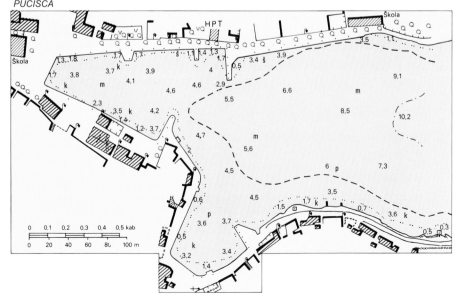

vated in Baroque style), the Cerineo castle (1577). Above the village there are quarries which supplied stone for the construction of Diocletian's Palace in Split.

Škrip, village, cyclopean masonry walls from Illyrian times; Roman remains; the Cerineo castle from 1618; the Baroque Sv Jelena church (St Helen); in the cemetery the Romanesque Sv Duh chapel (Holy Spirit) from 11/12 C; the Radojković castle housing the Museum of the Island of Brač (»Muzej otoka Brača«) with a collection of exhibits and documents from Brač – 3 km inland.

POSTIRA

(43°23'N; 016°38'E), village and small harbour on the N coast of the island of Brač.

Approach. The square masonry tower with a red cupola exhibiting a red light situated on the breakwater and the belfry in the town are conspicuous.

Mooring. The harbour is exposed only to N and NW winds which cause a moderate sea in it. Smaller yachts drawing up to 3 m can berth at the breakwater or use the four-point moor. In the S part of the harbour there is a slipway for boats.

Facilities. Post office, medical service and a fish cannery with its own fleet. Provisions and water.

Sights. Sv Ivan Krstitelj church (St John the Baptist, fortified apse, reconstructed 1776). At Lovrečina cove the ruins of an early Christian basilica (5–6 C). Roman finds and quarries in the Rasohe area.

PUČIŠĆA

(43°22'N; 16°44'E), village and harbour at the end of a deep cove on the N coast of the island Brač bearing the same name.

Approach. Landmarks: the square masonry tower with a balcony (white light), Sv Nikola chapel (St Nicholas) on the W entrance point and the white scars of stone-quarries on the hillside E of the entrance.

BUNJA NEAR PUČIŠĆA

Mooring. The bora is strongly felt and the small E inlet is especially exposed to it. Only yachts of light and moderate draught can land in the W inlet: At its entrance there is an anchorage ground (depth 2.5–4 m but care should be taken to avoid a number of submerged blocks). Yachts are recommended to secure their lines ashore as well.

Facilities. Post office, medical service, and a stone cutting factory. Food provisions and water available. Fuel in limited supply.

Sights. Sv Juraj church (St George, 14 C, in the transitional style from Romanesque to Gothic) in the Vela Bračuta area. Of the original 13 forts built for protection against the Turks only 4 have survived in reconstructed form; Sv Jerolim church (St Hieronymus, 1614). Monument commemorating the fallen fighters of the Anti-fascist War (1941–45). In the Batak area Uznesenje Marijino church (Assumption of the Virgin Mary, 1382).

POVLJA

(43°20'N; 16°50'E), village and wide cove on the NE coast of the island of Brač.

Approach. Landmarks include a square masonry tower (white light) situated on the E entrance point and the nearby Sv Ante chapel (St Anthony). Owing to shoal water the above E entrance point should be given a berth of at least 200 m.

Mooring. The harbour is protected from all winds except northerlies and north-westerlies. The bora often blows with violence but raises only a moderate sea. A

SUMARTIN

good anchorage ground is situated behind the E entrance point (depth 30 m). It is advisable to anchor with bows-to the NE and lines secured ashore. A good anchorage ground for smaller vessels (the best in this part of Brač) is situated in the westernmost arm of Luka inlet (in depth of about 14 m). Here it is also recommended to secure ashore (on the N shore). The inner part of Povlja harbour is occupied by local craft, while the outer end of the pier is reserved for passenger vessels.

Facilities. Post office and medical service. Food provisions and water.

Sights. Early Christian basilica (5/6 C) with baptistery. The latter has been incorporated into Sv Ivan Krstitelj church (St John the Baptist, 18/19 C); a defence tower (16 C) adjoining the church. Roman ruins in the vicinity.

SUMARTIN

(43°17'N; 016°53'E), village and small harbour in the E arm of the cove of the same name in the E coast of Brač.

Approach. Landmarks include Selca village above Sumartin, the square masonry tower with a cupola exhibiting a white light on the E entrance point and the red iron tower exhibiting a red light on the breakwater head.

Mooring. The bora and the sirocco (SSE) are only moderately felt. An unpleasant swell creeps in with S and SW winds, the E part of the cove being especially susceptible to it. Yachts drawing up to 2.5 m can lie alongside the breakwater. The W landing-place can accomodate only smaller boats (depth from 1.4–2.4 m alongside). Larger yachts can anchor in the middle of the cove (depth 30–38 m). During the bora anchoring yachts should secure their lines ashore as well.

BOL (ZLATNI RAT)

RT RAŽANJ

Facilities. Post office, medical service. Food provisions and water (in limited supply). Repairs to yachts and boats can be effected at the »Lučica« shipyard. Maintenance jobs and limited general repairs to marine engines at two local workshops.

Sights. Franciscan monastery (17 C, archives, collection of objects of historical and cultural interest), with a church dating from 18 C. – Selca (Sv Martin church – St Martin, from 1911, with a sculpture by Ivan Meštrović); in the park bust of Leo Tolstoj (by J. Barda) and of Stjepan Radić (by A. Augustinčić); in the vicinity the remains of a prehistoric hill-fort; old Croatian Sv Nikola chapel (St Nicholas) with a cupola, 11/12 C (a number of old, round stone shelters, called bunje) – 3 km inland.

BOL

(43°16'N; 016°40'E), village and small harbour on the S coast of Brač. Major tourist resort on the island.

Approach. The belfry of the monastery E of the town is prominent. Landmarks further include the grey building of the monastery, the square masonry tower with a green cupola exhibiting a green light situated on the head of the breakwater. If approach is effected from the W, care should be taken to avoid the shoal water extending off Dugi rat, point usually referred to as Zlatni rat (Golden point) in tourist literature.

Mooring. The harbour is protected from all winds except south-westerlies, which are apt to raise a heavy sea; the bora is strongly felt entering the harbour in gusts from different directions. Yachts drawing up to 2 m can lie alongside the breakwater. Its W side is reserved for local passenger lines. Larger yachts (20–25 m) can anchor in the harbour.

Facilities. Post office, medical service and chemist's. Large wine cellar and sardine salting plant. Food provisions and water. Fuel from the petrol station on the waterfront.

Sights. Roman finds (water reservoir); Early Christian sarcophagi; stone fragments with old Croatian interlaced patterns in Sv Ivan church (St John, 11 C). In the harbour the Jeličić Palace (15 C), the citadel (Kaštel, 17 C), Gospa od Karmela church (Our Lady of Carmel, built in the Renaissance period, reconstructed in Baroque style in 1785). E of the town a Dominican monastery (collection of objects of cultural and artistic value) with Sv Dominik church (St Dominic, after 1475, paintings of the Venetian school, coffered ceiling with paintings by Tripo Kukolja – about 1710); Modern Art Gallery »Branko Dešković«; – Murvica (above the town a deserted hermitage and »Dragonjina spilja«, a cave with figures carved in stone). Concerts and »Ribarske fraje«, fishermen's festivity in the summer months.

MILNA

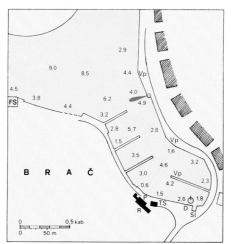

MILNA MARINA

MILNA

(43°20'N; 016°27'E), village at the head of the cove of the same in the W coast of Brač.

Approach. Landmarks: the white square stone tower exhibiting a red light on Bijaka point, the white metal tower with a column exhibiting a green light on the islet of Mrduja and the belfry at the head of the cove.

Mooring. The bora, hitting the harbour from the E, is strongly felt. The sirocco and south-westerlies also blow with violence but do not raise a heavy sea. Only the outer part of the cove is exposed to N and NW winds. Yachts can lie at the quay (depth 2.5–5 m alongside). During strong north-westerlies yachts are recommended to use the four-point moor or anchor in the inner part of the cove, which affords excellent all-round shelter. A good anchorage ground for larger vessels is situated in the middle of the outer part of the cove (depth 18–30 m). Smaller yachts can anchor off Bijak point.

Anchorage is prohibited in the harbour entrance.

Facilities. Harbour master's branch office, post office, medical service, fish cannery.

Food supplies in shops; water; fuel at the petrol station on the waterfront.

Repairs. The »Brodoremont« shipyard for smaller craft (up to 30 m in length) undertakes minor repairs to hulls and engines (situated on the S shore of the inlet; slipways).

Sights. Gospa od Blagovijesti (Our Lady of the Annunciation) church, 1783, baroque interior and liturgical objects.

MILNA MARINA (ACI)

(43°19,6'N; 016°27'E) is situated at the end of the SE inlet, opposite the village (depth 2.5 – 6.0 m).

Capacity: 170 sea-berths alongside the E and SW shore and at the 4 floating fingers; dry-berths for 30 vessels (up to 16 m length); electricity, telephone and water hook-ups.

The marina operates the year round. It has reception office, restaurant, snack-bar, shop, laundry, toilets and showers with hot water;

129

rental of sports equipment (excursions by sailing boats can be arranged); fuel at the petrol station.

Crane (10 t) and slipway. Maintenance and repairs in the boatyard. Safekeeping of yachts during the winter season. Storage of yachting equipment.

BOBOVIŠĆA

(43°21'N; 016°29'E), cove on the W coast of Brač with village of the same name; neighbouring village of Lozišća.

Mooring. The inlet affords good shelter to yachts of all sizes. The inner part is protected from all winds but during south-westerlies a disagreeable swell creeps in. A good anchorage ground for larger yachts (depth about 23 m) is situated in the outer part of the inlet but it is exposed to the bora. Smaller yachts can anchor closer to the coast, where they will find better protection.

Sights. Fortified summer residence of the Martinčević-Gligo family, Sv Juraj church (St George, 1693, reconstructed in 1914). Collection of old lace at the parsonage. On the hill above the village early medieval Sv Martin chapel (St Martin).

ISLAND OF HVAR

DUGA

(43°11,5'N; 016°25'E), cove in the N coast of Hvar fronted by an islet of the same name.

Provides shelter from all winds, especially those blowing from the NE and SE quadrants. Yachts of light and medium draught can anchor under the NE shore in depth of about 12 m.

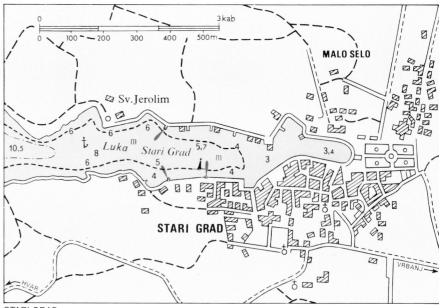

STARI GRAD

PRIBINJA, also VIRA

(43°12'N; 016°26'E), two-branched cove in the W coast of Hvar, 2.7 M east of Pelegrin point.

Approach. The white round tower exhibiting a white light on the western entrance point Galijola (marking the entrance). Landmarks further include the red iron tower with a column exhibiting a red light situated on Nezadovoljan point and the white iron tower exhibiting a green light on the molehead.

Mooring. The cove affords protection from all winds. The landing place in its W arm is reserved for the car-ferry. Anchorage ground (depth 15 m) in the middle of the cove.

Facilities. Limited food and water supplies at the restaurant beside the car-ferry landing place.

Car-ferry line: Pribinja (Vira) – Split.

STARI GRAD

(43°11'N; 016°35'E), small town and harbour at the head of Stari Grad Bay, on the north coast of the Hvar island.

Approach. Landmarks include the hotel complex on the left side of the harbour entrance, the belfry in the town, the white iron tower with a column exhibiting a white light on Kabal point, the green iron tower with a column exhibiting a green light situated on the new car-ferry landing place Zelenikovac (1.1 M W of the harbour), the white square tower with a column exhibiting a green light on Fortin point, the white column exhibiting a red light situated on the old car-ferry landing place (E corner), the green metal tower (green light) situated near the W end of the quay.

Caution must be exercised during landing operations: a submerged stone block with a depth of 1.5 m over it is situated some distance off the fourth bollard. A shoal patch extends in the vicinity of the landing place. It is marked by a conical buoy.

Mooring. The bay is sheltered from the bora. Only westerlies are apt to raise a disagreeable sea inside the harbour since the bay is open to the W. A violent sirocco may suddenly raise the sea level inside the harbour. Yachts can moor at the S shore in depth of about 3.5 m. Smaller yachts can berth at the E and N shores in depth of about 3 m, using the four-point moor. The waterfront is lined with bollards. A good anchorage ground is situated NE of Fortin point (depth 6–8 m). During the bora yachts can find shelter and anchor in Zavala and Tiha coves, whereas the coves Gračište, Sv Ante and Maslinica provide shelter from the sirocco.

The depth alongside the car-ferry landing-place and the breakwater is about 4.5 m.

STARI GRAD

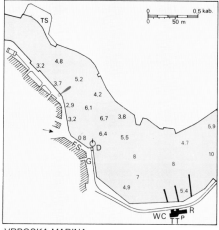

VRBOSKA MARINA

VRBOSKA

Facilities. Harbour master's branch office, chemist's, post office, medical service, wine cellar and grocery shops.

Provisions at local shops, water from the hydrant on the quay.

In the harbour on the N waterfront there is a slipway for smaller vessels. The local shipyard undertakes repairs to wooden and plastic hulls, while maintenance jobs and minor repairs to marine engines can be effected at two local workshops.

Car-ferry lines: Stari Grad – Split.

Sights. Remnants of a Cyclopean wall (4 C B.C.), remains of a Roman villa rustica at the locality called Pod Dolom; Early Christian baptistery beside Sv Ivan church (St John, 12 C); Tvrdalj (fortified summer residence of the Renaissance poet Petar Hektorović, about 1520, fishpond, ethnographical collection of objects of historical interest); monument to Petar Hektorović; Sv Stjepan church (St Stephen, 1605, valuabe liturgical and art objects), with bell-tower (1753); Dominican monastery (1482, reconstructed 1682, archives, library, art collection, numismatic collection, collection of fossils, lapidarium); baroque Škor square, residential houses of the families Gelineo Bervaldi (16–17 C), Bučić-Machiedo (17–18 C), Politeo (17 C). Maritime Museum and a collection of historical interest in the house of Juraj Biankini; »Josip Plančić« gallery.

VRBOSKA

(43°11'N; 016°40,5'E), village and small harbour on the N coast of Hvar, situated at the head of a long, narrow cove.

Approach. Landmarks include the greyish N entrance point Glavica, the square masonry tower exhibiting a white light on the E end of Zečevo islet; the red metal

JELSA

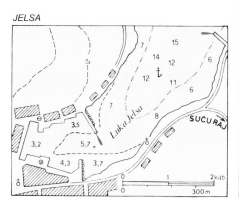

tower exhibiting a red light situated on the head of the E breakwater in Jelsa; the round white iron tower with a column exhibiting a white light situated on Križ point and the red light column exhibiting a red light on the SE corner of the quay.

Mooring. The bora and the sirocco are felt within the inlet but yachts at moorings are sheltered from them. South-easterlies raise a slight sea. A strong sirocco causes a rise of water (in exceptional cases up to 2 m), which enters the harbour with great velocity and may be dangerous to moored vessels. Smaller yachts can moor alongside the quay or use the four-point moor (depth from 2.5–3 m). The anchorage ground is situated in the outer part of the harbour under the N

shore (depth 24–27 m). Poor holding ground. During the bora yachts are recommended to secure ashore as well.

Facilities. Post office. Food provisions and water.

Sights. The churches Sv Marija (St Mary, 1465, fortified), Sv Lovro (St Lawrence, 1571, renovated in Baroque style in the 17 C, paintings by Venetian Renaissance painters), Sv Petar (St Peter, 1469).

VRBOSKA MARINA (ACI),

situated on the S shore of the outer part of the cove.

Capacity: 75 berths (16 m long) along the SE waterfront at the head of the cove (depth

JELSA

SUĆURAJ

up to 10 m); there is an area for 30 yachts in dry-berths; electricity, telephone and water hook-ups.

The marina operates the year round.

It has reception office, restaurant, shopping area, toilets and showers with hot water; laundry service; car park; maintenance and repair jobs.

Crane (5 t), fuel pump at the waterfront.

A small boatyard is situated on the opposite shore (0.3 km).

JELSA

(43°10'N; 016°42'E), town and small harbour on the N coast of the island of Hvar.

Approach. The town is easily identified from some distance by the prominent buildings of the hotel complexes flanking the harbour entrance, the road leading to the cemetery with a bell tower on the E side of the entrance, the round iron tower with a red light on the breakwater and the eightsided tower with a cupola with a green light on the head of the N breakwater.

Mooring. The inner harbour affords shelter from all winds, only its S part does not provide sufficient shelter during a strong bora. The outer part of the harbour is completely exposed to northerlies and to the bora and a dangerous surge develops in it with such winds. Only small yachts can moor using the four-point moor, at the quay (depth 1.6–3.4 m alongside). The inner harbour is

occupied by local craft. Passenger liners land at the S mole. An anchorage ground is situated 250 m NE of the breakwater (depth around 12 m), but not recommended in the winter bora.

Facilities. Harbour master's branch office, post office, medical service, and chemist's. »Zečevo« naturist hotel complex is situated N of the town, behind Glavica point.

Provisions at local shops. Water from hydrants on the waterfront. Fuel at the petrol station (about 300 m away).

A small slipway is situated in the S part of the harbour.

Each year at the end of August the »Jelšanska fešta vina« (Jelsa Wine Festival).

Sights. Sv Fabijan i Sebastijan church (St Fabian and Sebastian, 1331; renovated and fortified in 1535), Sv Ivan church (St John, in Baroque style); the square with Renaissance and baroque houses. Cemetery at the locality called Gradina with a church of the Augustinians (16/17 C) and remains of an old defence wall (11/12 C). On Tor hill an ancient Greek watch-tower (4 C B.C.).

POKRIVENIK

(43°09'N; 016°53'E), cove in the middle of the N coast of the island of Hvar.

Approach. It is entered between Tanki point and Zaraće point, which are foul and should be given a berth 300 m away.

Mooring. The inlet is sheltered from all winds except northerliess and the bora. Shelter from the bora, to some extent, can be found in its SE part. Smaller yachts can berth alongside the pier on the E coast of the cove. The best anchorage is in SE.

SUĆURAJ

(43°07,5'N; 017°11,5'E), village and small harbour in the inlet of the same name at the easternmost end of the island of Hvar.

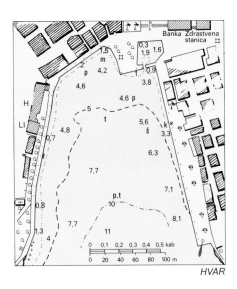

HVAR

Approach. Landmarks include the square stone tower with a balcony beside a dwelling with a white light on Sućuraj point; the red round iron tower with a white light on the head of the breakwater, the low white building with a green factory chimney on the N coast of the inlet in front of the village.

Care should be taken to avoid the underwater ballasting of the breakwater with shallow water over it and a submerged block off the SE side of the small pier.

Mooring. E and SE winds raise a heavy sea inside the harbour. Continuous northerly winds cause the depth in the harbour to decrease. Smaller yachts can berth at the ferry-pier using the four-point moor, or sidelong at the inner side of the breakwater. They can also lie sidelong and using the four-point moor at the quay in front of the harbour master's branch office (depth 2–3.5 m).

Facilities. Harbour master's branch office, post office, medical service, fish-cannery.

Food provisions and water.

Car-ferry line: Sućuraj – Drvenik (Makarska Riviera).

Sights. Parts of an Augustinian monastery (1573, now housing parsonage), Sv Ante church (St Anthony, 1664), and the picturesque small square in front of it. Fortifications dating from 1631.

MRTINOVIK

(43°07'N; 017°06'E), cove in the S coast of Hvar, about 4.4 M W of Sućuraj point. The cove is protected from all winds except those blowing from the SE and SW quadrants, which are apt to raise a moderate sea in it. The anchorage ground is in the middle of the cove.

Facilities. In Sućuraj.

ZAVALA, also PITAVSKA PLAŽA

(43°07,5'N; 016°42'E), village and small harbour on the S coast of Hvar, opposite the island of Šćedro.

Mooring. The small harbour is sheltered from all winds except south-westerlies. Smaller yachts can lie along the inner side of the breakwater (depth 2–6 m). Anchorage with sandy bottom (depth 3–4 m).

Facilities. Provisions at a local shop; a restaurant; water from cisterns.

HVAR

MILNA

(43°09,5'N; 016°29'E), inlet in the S coast of Hvar.

Mooring. The cove provides good shelter from N winds to smaller yachts. Depth up to 2 m.

Warning. Rocky shoal patches extend off the NW point.

Sights. Sv Marija Magdalena chapel (St Mary Magdalene, transitional Gothic--Renaissance style, 15 C); partly fortified summer residence of the Ivanić and Boglić-Božić families (17 C) with a chapel.

HVAR

(43°10,5'N; 016°27'E), town tourist resort and harbour on the S coast of the island of the same name.

Approach. Landmarks: the stone tower mounted on a pedestal exhibiting a white light on Pelegrin point, the square stone tower above a dwelling exhibiting a white light situated on the islet of Pokonji Dol, the red iron tower with a column exhibiting a red light on the NE edge of Jerolim islet, the forts Španjol and Sveti Nikola, the television mast W of the city, Gališnik islet with a square stone tower exhibiting a green light on its S side.

Anchorage is prohibited in the passage between Gališnik islet and Križni Rat point.

Mooring. The Hvar harbour is exposed to north-westerlies. Southerlies, especially the sirocco, raise waves and an unpleasant swell inside the harbour. The S part of the wharf is used by vessels on regular services. Yachts drawing up to 2.5 m can lie at the waterfront W of the small harbour Mandrač using four-point moor. Larger yachts anchor N and NW of Gališnik islet (depth 20–25 m). Smaller yachts can anchor in the middle of the harbour (depth 8–10 m) securing their sterns-to bollards on the W shore. Yachts can also sail into Palmižana marina on the islet of Sv Klement (Pakleni otoci).

Facilities. Harbour master's branch office, post office, medical service, chemist's.

Naturist beach on the islet of Jerolim S of the harbour.

Fresh food provisions at the shops and the self-service store. Water laid on to the NE waterfront (hydrant). Fuel obtainable from the pump on the pier in the E harbour – Križna Luka. Minor repairs can be arranged; slipway (width 5 m).

VELA GARŠKA

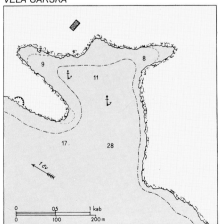

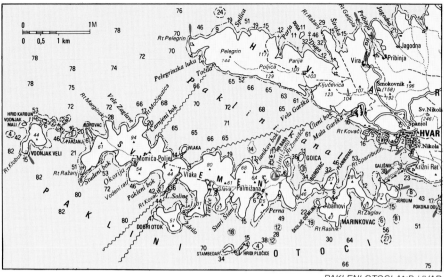

PAKLENI OTOCI AND HVAR

Sights. Town walls (built after 1278, additions in the 15 C). The »Palace« Hotel (1903) occupies the site of the demolished Rector's Palace; the Clock Tower (Leroj, 1476, reconstructed); Španjol (elevation 109 m, built 1551) and Sv Nikola forts (formerly: Fort Napoleon, built 1806, elevation 241 m); harbour (port development since 1455, the Venetian fleet of the Eastern Adriatic used to winter here); the Arsenal (1579–1611) into which galleys could be hauled up and the adjoining Fontik (housing historical archives, a Gallery of Modern Painting, the wooden figurehead of a dragon from the galley sent by Hvar to the Battle of Lepanto, 1571). Above the Arsenal a Theatre (built 1612, one of the oldest in Europe still extant, renovated in 1803 and 1900); Sv Stjepan cathedral (St Stephen, built in the 16–17 C on the site of an earlier cathedral dating from 14 C, liturgical objects dating from the 15–17 C, Gothic-Renaissance choir-stalls treasury) with the campanile from the 17 C. On the main square: the town well (1529); the residential homes of the families Paladini, Hektorović (unfinished, 15 C), Grgurić, Lucić, Vukašinović; the summer residence of the dramatist Hanibal Lucić; the City Loggia (by Tripun Bokanić, early 17 C); Sv Marko church (St Mark, preserved side walls and belfry from 1550, lapidarium; the tower of St Venerando on the extremity of the headland (now an open-air theatre); the Franciscan monastery (1461–64) in the SE part of the town (Renaissance cloister and refectory, collection of paintings, illuminated manuscripts, naval charts, old embroidery, archives, library), with Gospa od millosti church (Our Lady of Mercy, 1465, reconstructed 1571, three polyptychs, carved choir-stalls, paintings by Italian masters).

VELA GARŠKA

(43°11'N; 016°25'E), cove on the S coast of the westernmost part of Hvar, in the channel Pakleni kanal, about 1.6 M west of the town of Hvar.

Approach. The mouth of the cave on the W entrance point is conspicuous. Vessels

PAKLENI OTOCI AND HVAR

PALMIŽANA MARINA

PALMIŽANA MARINA

entering the cove should keep closer to the E coast.

Mooring. The small bay indented with several inlets affords good shelter, especially from winds blowing from the NE and SE quadrants. The sirocco blows violently but raises only a moderate sea. Yachts can moor at the small pier (depth up to 2 m) in the W part of the bay. Four-point moor with bows facing seaward recommended.

Facilities. In the town of Hvar in marina.

PAKLENI OTOCI

PALMIŽANA

(49°09,5'N; 016°24'E), cove in the N coast of the islet Sv Klement, about 2 M west of the town of Hvar.

Approach. When approaching the cove, care should be taken to avoid Baba rock (rising about 1 m above sea level; white flashing light) in front of the entrance to the cove.

MODRA ŠPILJA(BLUE CAVE) – BIŠEVO

Mooring. The cove affords good all--round shelter from all winds and the sea. Good anchorage grounds under the E shore and off the SW coast, where lines should be secured to the rocks of the shore. Depth 6–15 m. The pier in the SW part of the inlet is reserved for tourist lines.

Facilities. In Palmižana marina and Hvar.

PALMIŽANA MARINA (ACI)

is situated in Palmižana cove on the N coast of the island of Sv Klement, the largest in the island group of Pakleni otoci (Paklinski otoci).

Capacity: about 190 berths at pontoons extending parallel with the N shore and at the floating fingers at the W shore. The depth along the W shore is around 2 m, along the N shore 7 m, and in the middle of the cove between 12–20 m.

The marina operates through the summer season.

It has reception office, restaurant, shopping area, toilets and showers with hot water, rental of sports equipment; sale of butane gas; workshop for maintenance and repair jobs; taxi boat (Palmižana – Hvar).

SOLINE

(43°09,5'N; 016°22'E), spacious cove in the S coast of Sv Klement island.

Mooring. S and SW winds raise a heavy sea inside the cove. An anchorage ground for yachts of deeper draught is situated NE of the Dobri islet (depth 32 m). Only temporary stays recommended.

Facilities. Limited supplies at Vlaka hamlet (about 400 m inland).

ISLAND OF ŠĆEDRO

LOVIŠĆE

(43°06'N; 016°42,5'E), village and cove on the N side of the island of Šćedro.

Approach. The red iron tower exhibiting a red light E of the cove entrance is conspicuous.

Mooring. The cove affords good shelter from all winds except northerlies, which may blow with violence and send in a swell. During such winds smaller vessels seek shelter in one of the three small coves (Rake, Srida or Lovišće) securing their lines to the bollards or to rocks on the shore. A good anchorage ground for larger vessels is situated in the middle of the cove (depth about 26 m).

MANASTIR, also MOSTIR

(43°05,5'N; 016°42,6'E), cove in the N coast of Šćedro, E of Lovišće.

Like Lovišće it is open to northerlies but it affords good shelter from S wind and the waves. Only yachts of very light draught can berth at the small pier at the head of the cove using the four-point moor. The depth at the pier head is only 1 m.

Sights. Ruins of Dominican monastery (16 C, deserted in 18 C, later incorporated into a Renaissance church).

ISLAND OF BIŠEVO

BIŠEVSKA LUKA

(42°59'N; 016°00'E), cove in the W coast of Biševo. Suitable only as a temporary refuge from the bora. When other winds start blowing, especially westerlies or south-westerlies, yachts should leave without delay. It provides no adequate shelter from the sirocco either, since this wind is apt to change its

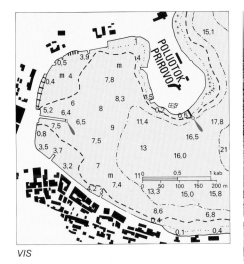

VIS

VIS

direction to the SW in these parts. Yachts of light and medium draught can anchor in the inner part of the cove (depth 5–10 m).

Polje hamlet inland.

BALUN

(42°58,5'N; 016°01'E), cove in the E coast of the island of Biševo. The famous Blue Cave (»Modra špilja«) is situated in this cove. At noon, when the sea is calm, sun-rays penetrating into the cave through an underwater opening are reflected from the white bottom, and illuminate the cave with a blue light while lending a silvery hue to objects under the water. The cave can be entered by small boats only.

ISLAND OF VIS

VIS

(43°04'N; 016°11'E), town and harbour on the N coast of the island of the same name. Border crossing during the season.

Approach. Landmarks: the lighthouse Stončica, a masonry tower on a dwelling exhibiting a white light, situated on the cape bearing the same name; the concrete tower with a balcony exhibiting a red light on Krava rock (E of the entrance); the eight-sided masonry tower exhibiting a white light on Host islet; the white tower with a balcony on Volići rock; the ruined Fort Wellington on an elevation on the left side of the entrance and Fort Torjan on its right side; the white tower exhibiting a red light on the head of the car-ferry landing place.

Care should be taken when making an approach to avoid the rocks Krava and Volići and the islet of Host.

Mooring. The harbour is open to the bora, which blows here with violence and raises a considerable sea. The sirocco also blows with heavy gusts. Protracted southerlies are apt to raise the sea level inside the harbour considerably. The E shore of the bay is exposed to waves coming in from the NW. Yachts can moor in the SW part of the harbour (depth 3–4 m). Yachts drawing up to 2 m can berth along the shore in Kut cove (to the SE). Deeper drawing yachts can also anchor in Kut cove except during northerlies and north-westerlies. During the bora and the sirocco it is recommended to anchor W of the small Pirovo peninsula.

Anchorage is prohibited in the W part of the harbour due to an underwater sewer pipeline. The pipe extends for 300 m from the shore, E of the »Issa« hotel.

Facilities. Harbour master's branch office, post office, medical service, chemist's.

Provisions at local shops and at self-service shop. Water in limited supply. Fuel at the pump on the small pier in the NW part of the harbour.

Car-ferry line: Vis – Split.

Sights. In the Gradina area remnants of the ancient Greek town of Issa; remnants of Roman walls, thermal baths and mosaics from the 1 C; on the small Pirovo promonto-ry remains of a Roman theatre and thermal baths (a Franciscan monastery with a church from the site in the 16 C). In the town of Vis the Garibaldi Palace (1552); the sum-mer-residence of the poet Marin Gazarović (early 17 C); the house of the Dojmi-Delupis family (with a collection of archeological finds); four defence towers on the outskirts

KOMIŽA

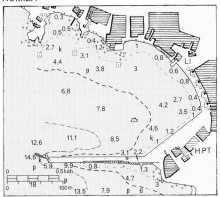

KOMIŽA

STONČICA

of the town (17 C); Gospa od Spilice church (Church of Our Lady, about 1500); Sv Ciprijan church (St Cyprian, 1 C, renovated 1742, coffered ceiling); Sv Duh (Holy Spirit, early 17 C); the British forts: George, Wellington, Bentinck, Robertson (early 19 C). Old Austrian barracks Baterija housing, the Archaeological Museum (Arheološki muzej).

During the Anti-fascist War, from 1943–44, Vis was the main base of the naval forces of the National Liberation Army, and from June 8 to mid September 1944 seat of the Supreme Command and the Committee of the Liberation of Yugoslavia headed by Marshal Tito. Vis served as the base for the seaborne assault operations that ultimately led to the liberation of Dalmatia.

KOMIŽA

(43°03'N; 016°05'E), town; harbour and spacious bay on the W coast of the island of Vis.

Approach. The harbour is easily recognized from seaward by the white masonry tower exhibiting a white light on the small islet of Barjak Mali; Sv Nikola church (St Nicholas) SE of the town (elevation 57 m); by the square masonry tower exhibiting a white light on Stupišće point; the red tower

PALAGRUŽA

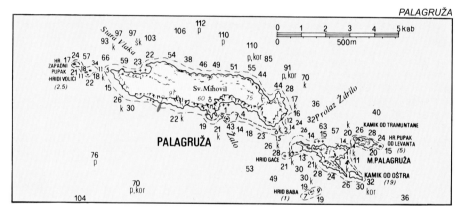

PALAGRUŽA

PALAGRUŽA

with a balcony exhibiting a red light on the island of Biševo (Kobila point); the green metal framework tower with a column and a balcony exhibiting a green light on the head of the breakwater.

Mooring. The bay is exposed to westerlies and south-westerlies, which raise a heavy sea. Behind the breakwater (depth 3–5 m) vessels are protected from these winds, as well as from the bora and the sirocco. Yachts can moor at its inner side, but it

should be borne in mind that the area around its head is reserved for regular passenger lines. Smaller yachts can berth at the quay NE of the breakwater using the four-point moor. A good anchorage ground (depth around 30 m) is situated 500 m W and 850 m S of the harbour light, but a bora renders it untenable.

Facilities. Harbour master's branch office, post office, medical service, chemist's, »Neptun« fish-cannery with its own fleet.

Provisions from local shops and the self-service shop. Fresh water (limited supply) and fuel on the quay.

Wooden hulls can be repaired at the »Neptun« boatyard (slipway). Maintenance jobs and repairs to marine engines can be effected at the workshop of the »Neptun« cannery.

Sights. The fortress (Kaštel) in the harbour built 1585; »Zanetova kuća« (house built in late 16 C), Gospa Gusarica church (of Our Lady, fishermen's endowment, late 16 C); Sv Nikola church (St Nicholas, 11–15 C, renovated 1696) forming part of the abandoned Benedictine monastery (also called Mustar, defence walls and tower, collection of liturgical objects); Sv Mihovil church (St Michael, 10/11 C) situated on a ridge (elevation of 310 m); the Art Gallery »Đuro Tiljak«; Fishing Museum (Riblji muzej).

ISLAND OF PALAGRUŽA

PALAGRUŽA

(42°23,5'N; 016°15,6'E), biggest island in the string of islands bearing the same name, situated about midway between the island of Lastovo and Italy. Rocky island, rising precipitously, devoid of vegetation.

The Volići and Pupak rocks are situated on its W side. Only small boats can find shelter in the coves Stara Vlaha and Žalo. A light is exhibited on the summit of the island at an elevation of 103 m (white flashes, visibility 26 M). About 20 m east of it there is a white column on a dwelling exhibiting a red isophase light; the sectors of which cover all dangers situated ESE of the island.

MALA PALAGRUŽA,

island situated SE of Palagruža. It is surrounded by a number of above-water and submerged rocks and shoals. In the neighbourhood are the islets: Kamik od Tramuntane and Kamik od Oštra.

The islet of Galijula is situated 3 M east-southeastward of Palagruža. Among the many dangers around its shores, the most dangerous is Pupak rock (identifiable from a distance, because the sea breaks over it).

PLOČE HARBOUR MASTER'S OFFICE AREA

HARBOURS ON THE COAST

PLOČE

(43°03'N; 17°25,6'E) town and commercial port NW of the delta of the Neretva.

Approach. Landmarks: the red tower with a column and a balcony (white light) on the S extremity of Višnjica headland (Rt Višnjica); the lightbuoy topped by a red cylinder on top with a red light marking Gumanac shoal about 0.8 M south of the light on Višnjica headland; the light-buoy (green light) about 0.3 M south of the light on Višnjica headland; the light-buoy (green light) about 300 m east of the light on Višnjica headland; the red tower with a column and a balcony (red light) about 300 m north of the light on Višnjica headland; the red square tower with a pyramidal construction (red light) on Bad point; Gubavac islet in the small cove between Bad point and the red tower situated about 300 m N of Višnjica headland (Rt Višnjica); the tower with a column and a balcony exhibiting a green light on the westernmost part (Bosanska obala).

The port is entered through a marked approach channel, the tower on Višnjica headland (white light) marking its beginning; two light-buoys (green) on the NW end of the wharf mark its right side; the red light-buoy on the Gumanac shoal marks the beginning of Vlaška channel, which leads to the tanker terminal.

In times of heavy rainfall, S winds and strong currents, yachts should keep as close to the buoys as possible.

Mooring. The harbour affords good protection from winds and waves, although the bora and the sirocco are strongly felt, in the winter. In summer the prevalent wind is a north-westerly, which blows with greater force than in the Neretva Channel and lasts late in the evening. Attention should be paid to the direction in and at the rate at which the current is setting in the harbour approaches, particularly in the vicinity of Višnjica headland. Yachts moor either in the city port which encompasses the Mala pošta bay (the E arm) and the area S of the connecting line defined by the following points on the coast: 395 m off the green light on Bosanska obala on a bearing of 335° and 870 m off the same light on a bearing of 22°.

Yachts are forbidden from entering the N part of the bay, outside the limits of the commercial port unless previously permitted.by the harbour master's office.

The port is open to international traffic as a permanent port of entry.

Facilities. It has harbour master's office, customs, post office, medical service, chemist's, bus and railway station.

Provisions at local shops, water from the hydrants on the waterfront. Fuel at the pump on the waterfront. Naval charts may be obtained at the office in Ploče.

Repairs to yacht and boat hulls andmaintenance of marine engines are possible.

Car-ferry line: Ploče – Trpanj.

NERETVA,

river flowing into the Neretva Channel; navigable for yachts drawing up to 4.5 m (up to 14 m) from the river mouth to the bridge in Metković.

In the valley the bora blows with violence, particularly around Kula Norinska village. In summer in the morning hours there is usually a breeze blowing seaward, down the valley and in the afternoon a wind blowing in from the sea. Under settled weather conditions the current is not strong (about 2.5 knots) but it can attain a rate of 6 knots when the river is carrying a great amount of water.

Approach. Landmarks: the hexagonal red cement hut with a column exhibiting a red light on the head of the N mole at the river mouth, the green square hut with a column exhibiting a green light on the head of the S mole, the guardian's house on the S embankment and the cross on Galičnik Hill.

PLOČE

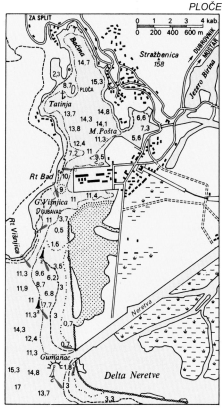

PLOČE

137

In the river mouth: the red light-buoy Gumanac topped by a cylinder (about 0.8 M south of the light on Višnjica cape headland); the green cylindrical light-buoy topped by a cone (785 m from the red light on the head of the N protective mole on a bearing of 294° from the red light on the head of the N protective mole); about 100 m from the red light on the head of the N mole, at a bearing of 240°, there is a green cylindrical buoy with a conical topmark, which should be left to starboard by incoming yachts (see Ploče).

The river mouth is entered S of the red Gumanac buoy. After clearing the lightbuoy yachts should shape course north of the green light-buoy (small vessels as close to it as possible). When abreast the buoy, course should be altered so as to lead between the N molehead (red column on hut, red light) and the green cylindrical buoy topped with a cone. After passing the N molehead (red light) yachts should take a sharp turn towards the middle of the river mouth, between the N and S protective moles (green hut with column, green light).

Warning. Due to banks formed by deposits in the river mouth, it is advisable to keep in dredged channel. It is necesarry to start changing course between the two moleheads (with lights on them) on time as the current at the river entrance is stronger. Yachts are recommended to reduce speed before changing course (when abreast the green buoy topped by a pyramid). About 4 km upstream the Gospa shoal extends off the right bank. Another shoal is situated at the E end of the quay in Opuzen (near the spot at which Mala Neretva branches off). The NW edge of this shoal is marked by a black buoy, which should be left to starboard by yachts proceeding upstream. A road bridge of the Adriatic highway crosses the river at Rogotin village, about 4 km upstream from the mouth (at highest water level the bridge has a vertical clearence of

14 m in the middle, reducing to 11 m at the piers). A high-tension cable with a vertical clearance of 15 m at highest water level spans the river 9.2 km upstream from the mouth, near the small town of Komin.

Care should be taken to avoid collision with the numerous local craft (»trupice«), passing up and down the river or entering it from the side arms.

Special Regulations for Navigation in the Neretva River. Vessels may navigate in the Neretva any time of the day or night. Yachts must keep to the starboard side. Navigation in fog is prohibited. Yachts proceeding downstream must have an anchor ready for instant use astern. At night, anchoring yachts are required to display an additional white position light astern, as well as the white position light on the bow prescribed by the International Regulations for Prevention of Collision at Sea. Yachts passing other navigating or floating objects, installations on the river banks, places at which hydrotechnical operations are in progress, or inhabited places are required to reduce speed at least within 200 m of such objects, installations and places so as not to endanger their safety or cause damage. Vessels proceeding upstream (with the exception of towing tugs) must give way to vessels navigating downstream. Boats must give way to ships. A yacht which loses its manoeuvering capacity is required to drop anchor at a place where it will not obstruct other vessels. Moored yachts and yachts at anchor are forbidden to keep dinghies, rafts, etc. or any other protruding objects secured alongside.

OPUZEN

(43°01'N; 17°34'E), town and harbour on the left bank of Neretva, about 6.5 km upstream from its mouth.

Approach. The green tower on a pedestal on the W bank (downstream) is conspicuous.

All vessels are prohibited from navigating, anchoring and landing at the section between the point at which Mala Neretva bifurcates and the iron bridge crossing it higher upstream when the water level rises 1 m above normal.

Mooring. Yachts can berth at the town quay (depth 2.4-2.9 m). A shoal patch with depth up to 4.5 m over it is situated at the NW end of the harbour. It is marked by a black conical buoy.

Facilities. Post office and medical service; the »Neretva« agricultural enterprise has citrus fruit and vegetable farms in the vicinity.

Food and water in adequate supply. Fuel at the pump about 20 m from the river bank.

Sights. Fort Koš (late 15 C), renamed by the Venetians in 1685 to Fort Opus – in ruins on a hill above the town; a collection of archaeological finds from Vid village, which occupies the site of Roman Narona; monument to the national hero Stjepan Filipović. On a hill above the nearby village of Podgradina the ruins of Brštanik castle built in 1373, during the reign of the Bosnian King Tvrtko (restored in 15 C and in 1878). Up to Neretva (on its left bank) Kula Norinska with a cylindrical defence tower (1550).

METKOVIĆ

(43°03'N; 17°39'E), town and principal harbour on the Neretva, situated about 11 M upstream from its mouth.

Approach. Landmarks: two red towers exhibiting red light are situated downstream from the bridge: one 1.1 M (Jerkovac), the other 0.4 M.

Mooring. Yachts can berth at the lower part of the S bank, at the quay fronting the harbour office (downstream from the harbour light). Attention should be paid to the underwater reinforcements of the quay, which extend at places up to 0.7 m offshore. The N quay is reserved for commercial operations.

Warning. Yachts are forbidden to land at certain portions of the quay.

Metković is a permanent port of entry.

Facilities. Harbour master's branch office, post office, hospital, chemist's and railway station (regular line to Sarajevo). Food supplies at local shops. Water from the water main (taps on the quay), fuel (diesel oil) on the N bank, 25 m downstream from the bridge.

»Mehanika« undertake repairs to and maintenance of marine engines.

Sights. Vid (village on the site of ancient Roman Narona) with numerous archaeological finds (remnants of town walls, stone fragments bearing inscriptions, mosaics, graves, Roman fragments built into the walls of village houses; Museum collection).

Ornithological collection– one of the most comprehensive in Europe (more than 300 stuffed specimens of birds and game)– represents the endemic and migratory wild life of the Neretva delta.

OPUZEN

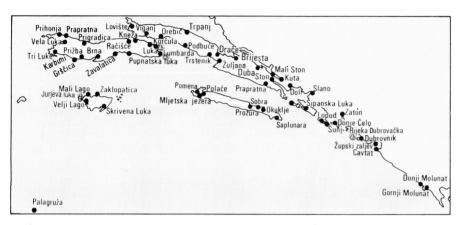

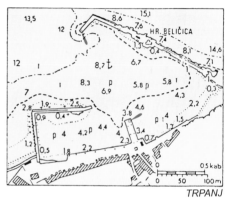

TRPANJ

DISTANCES OF PORTS

CAVTAT	DUBROVNIK	GRUŽ	KORČULA	UBLI (LASTOVO)	LUMBARDA	MOLUNAT	OREBIĆ	POLAČE	RAČIŠĆE	SLANO	SOBRA	STON	SV. ANDRIJA	ŠIPANSKA LUKA	TRSTENIK	TRSTENO	VELA LUKA	ZATON	
	6	11	55	65	51	15	54	40	59	21	28	28	12	22	45	13	78	11	CAVTAT
		6	49	59	46	21	48	34	50	15	22	22	8	15	39	18	72	6	**DUBROVNIK**
			48	60	45	23	46	33	53	13	23	20	6,5	14	27	6	71	3	GRUŽ
				27	3	57	2	16	55	38	26	39	31	35	13	41	28	44	KORČULA
					24	78	26	31	32	52	40	53	55	51	30	56	18	61	UBLI (LASTOVO)
						55	3	13	8,5	34	23	36	29	33	10	39	31	42	LUMBARDA
							56	53	63	35	24	42	26	34	46	27	90	24	MOLUNAT
								14	7	35	24	37	30	34	12	40	29	43	**OREBIĆ**
									22	23	11	23	28	22	7	27	41	31	POLAČE
										23	31	44	47	41	18	46	22	50	RAČIŠĆE
											14	10	9	5,5	26	7	64	11	SLANO
												15	16	12	15	17	50	21	SOBRA
													16	10	28	14	65	18	**STON**
														8,5	30	4	65	5,5	SV. ANDRIJA
															24	10	61	13	ŠIPANSKA LUKA
																30	40	33	TRSTENIK
																	67	4	TRSTENO
																		71	**VELA LUKA**
																			ZATON

TRPANJ

HARBOURS ON THE COAST

DUBA PELJEŠKA

(43°01'N; 017°10'E), village and small harbour on the N coast of Pelješac Peninsula.

Mooring. The small harbour affords protection for small yachts from the bora and the sirocco. It is open to waves raised by north-westerlies. Yachts are recommended to moor at the inner end of the breakwater (depth 2–3.5 m).

Facilities. Provisions and water are limited.

Sights. Remains of a Roman building with mosaics. The summer residence of the poet Dinko Ranjina (1536–1607) from Dubrovnik was in nearby Divna cove (1 mile E).

TRPANJ

(43°0,5'N; 017°16'E), village and small harbour on the N coast of Pelješac Peninsula in the Neretva Channel.

Approach. Landmarks: two chapels on two cone-shaped hillocks; a red tower exhibits a red light on the head of the E breakwater; a white column exhibits a red light on the head of the pier.

Care should be taken while approaching the harbour to avoid a shoal patch with depth of about 3.5 m over it, about 0.4 miles WNW from the head of the N breakwater. Shallow water extends off the outer end of the S breakwater, which should be given a berth.

Mooring. The harbour is protected from winds from the NE and SE quadrant. Northerlies and winds from the NW quadrant raise a heavy sea in the E part of the harbour. Yachts can moor along the quay or W of the pier (depth 1–3 m) using the four-point moor. The four-point moor with bows facing the second arm of the north, L-shaped breakwater is also recommended. This position affords protection from westerlies and from waves.

Facilities. Harbour master's branch office, post-office, medical service and a chemist's.

Provisions at local shops. Water from the hydrant on the pier. Fuel at the pump on the waterfront.

Car-ferry line: Trpanj – Ploče.

»Trpanjske glazbene večeri« (Trpanj Music Evenings) are held here in July.

Sights. Remnants of a Roman summer residence (villa rustica) at the cemetery; near the ruins of a medieval castle a Roman »piscina«; the Baroque church Gospa od Karmela (Our Lady of Carmel); a private art collection in the house of the Salacan family.

DRAČE

(42°56'N; 017°27,4'E), village and small harbour in Bratkovica cove on the N coast of Pelješac Peninsula. It serves as the harbour of the village of Janjina situated about 2 km inland.

Approach. The stone mark on Bililo shoal with a topmark (two cones turned base to base) and the white tower with a column (sector light) on the head of the N breakwater are discernible from a distance. Care should be taken when making an approach to avoid the numerous rocks and shoals E of Rat point and around the islet of Galičak. The red sector of the light on the N breakwater covers the clear passage to the harbour.

Mooring. Behind the breakwater yachts are protected from all winds. Smaller yachts can moor inside the harbour (depth 1.3–3). The anchorage ground ENE of the harbour becomes untenable in a bora.

Facilities. Post office and medical service. Provisions and water in limited supply.

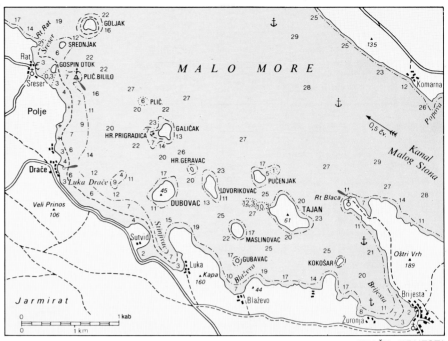

DRAČE - BRIJESTA

BRIJESTA

(42°54,2'N; 017°32'E), village in the cove of the same name on the N side of the Pelješac Peninsula.

Approach. Brijesta may be identified by the white tower with a balcony exhibiting a white light on Blaca point and by the old tower and the belfry at the head of the cove.

Mooring. The cove is protected (partly by a string of islets) from all winds and affords good shelter to yachts of all sizes. A good anchorage ground for larger yachts is situated about 700 m SSE from Blaca point (depth 17–23 m). Smaller yachts can anchor in the inner part of the cove. During the bora yachts at anchor are well advised to secure their lines on the NE shore.

Provisions and water in limited supply.

Sights. Defence tower built 1517 for protection against pirates; Baroque chapel of Sv Liberan (St Liberanus) at the cemetery.

KUTA

(42°50'N; 017°45'E), cove at the head of Mali Ston bay, between the Adriatic highway and the Pelješac road.

Approach. Vessels aproaching from the NW should take care to avoid the shoal (with a depth of 3 m over it) situated in the straits between Govanj islet (recognizable by a few buildings scattered in a sparse forest), also known as the island of Life (»Otok života«) in tourist literature, and the village of Hodilje. The cove is fronted by a string of islets (Crkvica, Veliki školj and Bisaci). Between them the sea is shallow. A dark rock is visible SW of Crkvice islet, and W of Veliki školj there is a low-lying rock seen only when closely approached.

Mooring. The anchorage ground (depth 6–8 m) off the NE shore affords shelter from all winds.

ZALJEV MALOG STONA,

bay situated between the mainland coast and the Pelješac Peninsula, is a continuation of the Mali Ston Channel. In some places it is narrow and shallow. Between the small harbour of Hodilje and Mali Ston there are a number of submerged rocks. Only yachts drawing up to 3 m can navigate from the islet of Govanj to Kuta cove. A bridge spans the entrance to Bistrina cove.

From Čeljen point (white tower with a column and a balcony exhibiting a white light)

MALI STON

course should be shaped towards the middle of the entrance into the narrow part of the bay. At night course should be shaped towards the middle of the line connecting the green light (white tower) on the molehead at Hodilje and the red light (red tower) marking Vranjak shoal. North of the harbour light at Hodilje, yachts should gradually change course so as to leave Vranjak to port and proceed closer to the islet of Ostrog in such a way that the green light (green tower on a cement base in the sea) marking the Školjić shoal (1.4 m) is left to starboard and the red light (red tower) on Mali Voz point to port. Oyster beds are marked with marker buoys. An underwater cable is laid between the islet of Govanj (sparsely wooded) and Pelješac Peninsula.

The bora blows violently, especially in the winter season. In the summer months the area is subject to frequent storms. Sudden changes in the water level, the so--called »seš« (1 to 2 m) which may occur when S winds suddenly start blowing but occasionally also in calm weather and during storms, are accompanied with strong and changing currents (whirlpools and fierce eddies). This phenomenon is rather rare, but when it occurs it is dangerous.

An underwater pipeline is laid on the seabed between the mainland and the shore of the Pelješac Peninsula (100 m NW of Čeljen point).

Mooring. Mali Ston, Kuta cove (depth 6–8 m at the anchorage ground), but care should be taken to avoid the islets, rocks, shoals and rocky patches. Miševac cove (S of the islet of Škrpun) has a good anchorage ground for small yachts.

MALI STON

(42°51'N; 17°42'E), village and small harbour on the NE side of the Ston isthmus, in an indented inlet in the Mali Ston Channel.

Approach. Landmarks: old fortifications (5 towers) above the village and on the slopes of Mt Bartolomija. A white tower with a column and a balcony exhibiting a white light on Čeljen point.

Mooring. The harbour is sometimes subject to sudden change in the waterlevel (»seš«); the sea level falls suddenly and immediately starts to rise again, at times even to 2 m above normal. Only smaller yachts can enter the harbour through the passage between Govanj islet and the village of Hodilje (depth of about 3 m), as the depth inside the harbour ranges from 0.7 to 2.4 m. The harbour provides shelter from all winds.

Facilities. Provisions at local shops, water from the main; fuel at Zamaslina on the Adriatic highway (4 km by road).

Sights. Town walls (1336–58) with Sea Gate; Fort Koruna (with 5 towers) above the village; the cylindrical Toljevac tower (1478) on the quay. The medieval defence system of Mali Ston is linked with that of the town of Ston (long walls transversing the isthmus and linking both towns with the fortress on Podzvizd (built in 1335) summit (elevation 224 m).

Oyster beds in Bistrina cove in the Mali Ston Channel; hotel complex on nearby islet (»Otok života«).

STON or VELIKI STON

(41°49,5'N; 017°42'E), village and small harbour in the NW part of Ston Channel (Stonski kanal).

Approach. Landmarks: the ruined medieval defence walls above the town; a round red tower with a column exhibiting a red light is situated on the quay at Ston.

Due to a submerged stone block at the beginning of the fairway, about 80 m NNW of the light on the molehead at Broce, yachts should keep closer to this light. The fairway leading to Ston is marked on the right side by two towers (green light) mounted on concrete bases in the sea. The left side of the fairway is marked by 4 towers (red light) on concrete bases in the sea and by a red tower (red light) in the small harbour of Broce. From the light on the molehead (Broce), yachts should proceed between the first pair of the lights on concrete bases, then closer to the red tower on a concrete base in the sea (about 1030 m on a bearing of 299° from the light on the molehead at Broce); then S of the line connecting the red light with the red light of the second pair of lights. On account of the shallow sea (up to 1.5 m) yachts should keep close to the middle of the channel and then pass between the second pair of lights. After passing it, they should shape course for the molehead at Ston, on which there is a red tower (red light). An incoming yacht must wait in front of Broce for any vessel navigating through the fairway. A yacht wishing to leave Ston must wait for any vessel coming through the fairway to reach Ston harbour.

Mooring. The harbour is protected from all winds and waves. Tides may cause a strong current which can make manoeuvering difficult. Yachts lie sidelong the mole or at the quay. The four-point moor may also be used. An anchorage ground is situated in the outer part of the inlet, SE of Broce (depth 10–50 m). Good holding ground.

Facilities. Harbour master's branch office, post office and medical service. Provisions in local shops; water from the main; fuel at the petrol station in the village.

Sights. City walls (890 m in length) in the form of a pentagon encompass the old town, the streets of which intersect at right

MALI STON

STON

OREBIĆ

LIRICA

angles. From the town walls the 5 km long Veliki Zid wall extends (1333–1508), which runs up to the Podzvizd summit (224 m), whence it links with the defence walls of Mali Ston. Remnants of the castle (Veliki Kaštel), the Rector's seat in the time of the Dubrovnik Republic; the Sorkočević--Đurđević residence (Gothic); the former bishop's residence (1573, with Gothic windows); a Franciscan monastery and Sv Nikola church (St Nicholas, 1347, old liturgical objects), town well (1571), Sv Vlaho church (St Blaise, 1878, with items from an older church). On Gorica hill above Ston Sv Mihajlo chapel (St Michael, 9/11 C, mural paintings from that period). Solila (salt pans), were in use even before the Dubrovnik Republic gained possession of Pelješac Peninsula (1333). They occupy an area of over 429 860 m2 and have an annual output of 2800 tons of salt.

STONSKI KANAL,

deep and narrow channel leading from the Koločep Channel (Koločepski kanal) to Ston. Its sides up to the village of Broce are steep and covered by dense brush or wooded (sparse pine-woods). The depth in the outer (wider) part of the channel range from 10 to 57 m. The inner part is narrow and shallow. The fairway leading from the harbour of Broce to the harbour of Ston is 25 to 60 m wide with depth ranging from 2 to 3 m. Its left side is marked by five red lights and the right one with two green lights (see Ston).

Approach. The village of Kobas on the S shore of the inlet with a quay and the big masonry column of the transformer station in a pine-forest are conspicuous. A round white tower with a column and balcony, on a pedestal, exhibiting a white light stands on a concrete base at the right entrance point (Pologrina); a round red tower with a column exhibiting a red light is situated at the molehead of Broce.

The bora and the sirocco are strongly felt but do not interfere with navigation. The direction and the rate at which the current sets in depend on the tides. Sudden S winds may cause the sea level to drop suddenly only to immediately rise again (sometimes up to 1.25 m). This phenomenon sometimes occurs in calm weather. The strong currents and waves pose a danger for navigation in the channel.

PRAPRATNA

(42°49'N; 017°41'E), cove in the SW coast of the Pelješac Peninsula.

Mooring. The cove affords good shelter to smaller yachts from E winds. Indifferent holding ground (depth about 20 m). During a bora it is recommended to secure lines ashore as well.

Warning. The stone mark E of the entrance indicates the place where an underwater cable comes ashore. A pipeline extends from Prapratna point at a bearing of 200°.

Limited supplies at the campsite.

ŽULJANA

(42°53,5'N; 017°27'E), village and small harbour in the E part of Žuljana bay.

Approach. Landmarks: a white tower exhibiting a white light on the islet of Lirica; a green tower with a column and a balcony exhibiting a green light on the head of the breakwater.

When entering harbour care should be taken to avoid the low-lying islet of Kosmač, the shallow rocky bank Mirište and the above-water rock lying W of it.

At night all these dangers are covered by the dark sector of the green light on the breakwater.

Mooring. Inside the harbour yachts are protected from all winds but not from waves sent in by strong SW and NW winds. Smaller yachts can moor at the end of the breakwater, behind the head of which the depth is 4 m shelving rapidly towards its root. The E part of the harbour gradually shelves towards a pebbly beach. During the bora, smaller yachts can also anchor in the first two coves W of the harbour, but with lines secured ashore.

Facilities. Post office and medical service. Some provisions and limited quantities of water.

Sights. Remains of Roman graves; Sv Martin church (St Martin, Baroque style, built on the site of a 12 C chapel), and Sv Julijana chapel (St Juliana, transitional style from Renaissance to Baroque).

TRSTENIK

(42°55'N; 017°24'E), village and small harbour in the NW part of Žuljana bay.

Approach. Trstenik may be identified by the red metal tower with a column and balcony exhibiting a red light on the head of breakwater and Sv Mihovil chapel (St Michael) on the right side.

Mooring. The harbour affords shelter from W winds, but strong S and SW winds raise a heavy sea in it. The bora blows violently here, but does not raise waves. Yachts can moor at the inner end of the breakwater (depth 2–4.6 m) or anchor SE from its head

STON

OLIPA

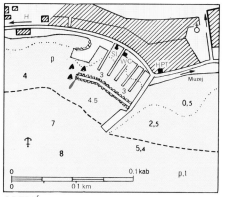

* OREBIĆ*

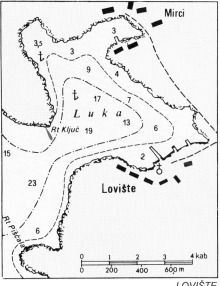

LOVIŠTE

(depth of about 30 m) with lines secured ashore, bows facing NE. The head of the breakwater is reserved for car-ferry.

Facilities. Post office and harbour master's branch office. Some provisions and limited quantities of water. Minor repairs are possible at the workshop on the N shore of the small harbour.

Car-ferry line: Trstenik – Polače (Island of Mljet).

PODOBUĆE

(42°57'N; 017°17'E), village and cove on the S coast of Pelješac Peninsula.

Mooring. The cove affords shelter from all winds except southerlies. The landing-place can only accomodate smaller yachts as the depth alongside range from 2–4 m.

Facilities. Limited provisions and water.

OREBIĆ

(42°58,5'N; 017°11'E), small town in the Pelješki kanal. Popular tourist resort.

Approach. Landmarks: the green square tower with a column exhibiting a green light on the head of the long breakwater and the buildings of the hotel complex.

Mooring. In the SE part of the harbour the local »Peliška Jedra« Sailing Club maintains a yacht harbour with 240 berths. About 30 of them are available to passing yachts. Most of them are situated alongside the breakwater in the E part of the harbour. The depth ranges from 2.5–3.5 m. The entrance is marked by marker-buoys.

Facilities. Post office, hotels, a hotel complex, restaurants, medical service, chemist's. Sandy beaches. The harbour master's branch office for the area is located at Korčula.

Provisions at local shops, water from the main, fuel at the petrol station in the town.

Car-ferry line: Orebić – Dominča (Island of Korčula).

Sights. Pomorski muzej (Maritime Museum) and two private collections at the homes of the families (sea captains) Župa and Fisković. – In the surroundings: hillforts and tombs dating from prehistoric times; remnants of a Roman villa rustica; the Franciscan monastery (1470, in Gothic-Renaissance transitional style); Gospa od anđela church (Our Lady of the Angels, with Renaissance marble reliefs, with adjoining cemetery and interesting gravestones of Orebić seamen). Above the town in the hamlet Karmen (elevation 178 m), Gospa od Karmena church (Our Lady of Karmen,

Gothic, renovated in Baroque style), surrounded by Roman sarcophagi and old cypress-trees; further on the ruins of the Rector's residence and a Loggia.

VIGANJ

(42°59'N; 017°06'E), village and small harbour in Pelješki kanal, on the S coast of Pelješac Peninsula, about 3.5 miles W of Orebić.

Approach. Landmarks: the buildings of holiday centre on the low-lying »Sv Liberan« promontory, the monastery and the belfry in the village.

Mooring. Yachts of light and medium draught can moor on both sides of the small pier or along the village jetty using the four-point moor (depth 1.9–4.2 m). The best anchorage ground for deeper drawing yachts is situated SW of the monastery (depth 20–28 m). It is sheltered from the sirocco but exposed to W winds and the bora.

Facilities. Provisions and water.

Sights. In the surroundings: Illyrian tumuli; Roman finds, Franciscan monastery (cloister) with the Gospa od ružarija church (Our Lady of the Rosary, 1671); Sv Mihovil church (St Michael, Gothic, enlarged in 1760).

LOVIŠTE

(43°02'N; 017°02'E), village and sheltered anchorage ground in Luka cove, on the westernmost part of Pelješac Peninsula, between the small promontories Lovišće (N) and Osičac (S). In the N part of the cove is the hamlet of Mirce.

Approach. The village may be identified by the white tower exhibiting a white light situated on Osičac; the white square masonry tower with a balcony on Lovišće point, the spar buoy on the S entrance point and round red tower with a column (red light) on Ključ point.

Mooring. The cove affords good allround shelter. Only its S part is exposed to waves sent in by W and SW winds. Small yachts can moor on both sides of the pier in front of the village of Lovište (depth from 1 to 3.2 m). A good anchorage ground is situated in the N part of the cove, E of Ključ point (depth 17 m). Another anchorage is in Mirce cove (a few houses) in its NE part.

Facilities. Post office. Food (restaurant) and water (from the main).

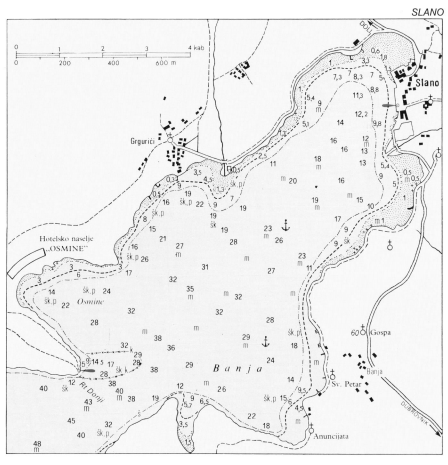

SLANO

Sights. Remnants of a Roman villa rustica. In Roman times Lovište was a stopping-off point for seaborne traffic between Korčula (Corcyra nigra) and Vid (Narona) on the Neretva River.

DOLI

(42°48'N; 017°48'E), cove and village in Budima bay (Koločep Channel), about 3.5 miles NW of Slano.

Approach. Landmak: a red iron tower with a column (a red light) on the head of the breakwater.

Mooring. The cove affords protection from all winds except the sirocco. Only small yachts can moor at the breakwater in the small harbour (depth 1.2–3.8 m). Larger yachts can anchor in the inlet, Budima cove, between the coves of Janska and Budima, about 500 m offshore (depth 40–60 m). As this anchorage is exposed to the bora and to southerlies, it is suitable for temporary stays only.

Sights. Remnants of the Roman castrum Pardua at Zamaslina (5 km NW). In the village the church Gospino Uznesenje (Assumption of the Holy Virgin), with several medieval tombstones around it, defence tower (late 16 C) built for protection against pirates.

SLANO

(42°47'N; 017°52'E), village and small harbour at the head of a spacious cove in Koločep Channel.

Approach. It may be easily identified by the light coloured buildings of the hotel complex at the head of the cove, the grey pointed spire with a clock, the masonry tower with a balcony exhibiting a red light on Donji cape, W of which is »Osmine« hotel. A green column exhibits a green light on the S corner of the quay.

Mooring. The inlet affords shelter from the sirocco and, partly, from the bora, which blows here with violence. Yachts drawing up to 2.5 m can berth at the landing-place with lines secured to bollards (depth 4–6 m). The four-point moor is also recommended. Good anchorage grounds abound within the inlet. During the bora and the sirocco it is best to anchor on the lee of the E shore in the small Banja cove. Osmine cove (to the SW) is occupied by naturists from the naturist »Osmine« hotel. Yachts of deep draught can anchor in front of the entrance to the inlet, SW of Gornji point (depth 50 m).

Facilities. Post office, medical service, harbour master's branch office. Provisions and water.

Sights. Remnants of Illyrian settlement and tumuli in the immediate surroundings; traces of Roman castrum in the village. Along the road to Zavala »stećak« medieval tombs. The Rector's residence (reconstructed in the 19 C); the summer residence of the Ohmućević family, Franciscan church (1420, with Roman sarcophagi around it); Sv Vlaho church (St Blaise, 1758).

A traditional fair is held at Slano every year on August 2. It is attended by villagers in folk-costumes. The famous folkdance »Linđo« is danced on that occasion.

ZATON

(42°41'N; 018°03'E), deep bay 3 miles NW of Dubrovnik. Three villages are situated in it: Veliki Zaton on the west side, Štikovica on the east side and Mali Zaton on the north coast.

Approach. Landmark: a white iron tower with a column and a balcony (red light) is situated on the SW entrance point (Bat) of the bay.

Mooring. In the winter season the bay is exposed to strong S, SW and N winds (especially to the bora) and it is not recommended for longer stays. Yachts drawing up to 2.5 m can moor at the pier fronting Veliki Zaton. Anchorage grounds in the middle of the bay and in its N part (depth 19–23 m). Owing to the bora, it is advisable that anchoring yachts secure their lines to bollards on the E shore.

Facilities. Post office and medical service in Mali Zaton. Provisions at the self-service shop; water. Fuel at the pump on the Adriatic highway. Minor repairs can be undertaken.

Sights. A number of Renaissance and Baroque summer residences of the Dubrovnik patrician families, Sv Stjepan church (St Stephen, 1050, reconstructed several times); old water-mill at Mali Zaton. – Orašac (Arapovo, fortified summer resi-

VELIKI AND MALI ZATON

dence allegedly built for the Florentine gonfalonier Pietro Soderini, now housing a restaurant) – 5 km NW. – Trsteno (two giant plane trees Platanus orientalis – on the village square; summer residence of the Gučetić family with beautifully laid-out park and arboretum dating from 1502; great number of exotic trees, nature reserve) – 8 km NW.

DUBROVNIK MARINA - »MIHO PRACAT«

(42°40,3'N; 018°7,6'E) is situated at Komolac (Rijeka Dubrovačka), about 2 M from the entrance into Gruž harbour. A long breakwater protects the marina from the river current.

Up to the prominent monastery in Prijevor village the inlet (river) has a width of 170 to 400 m and is navigable for craft of all sizes. From Prijevor onwards the river narrows and its depth gradually decreases. Anchoring is allowed only to small vessels (yachts) NE of the village of Čajkovići (depth 5–11 m).

The bora is strongly felt, at times blowing down the river valley with gale force. NW and SW winds sometimes raise a heavy sea at the river mouth.

ZATON

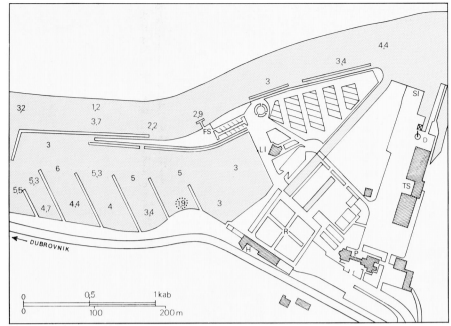

»MIHO PRACAT« MARINA - DUBROVNIK

Yachts berth at the breakwater, at the embankment, and at the floating fingers. There are about 450 sea-berths with water, electricity and telephone hook-ups. Dry-berths for about 150 vessels (up to 25 m length). The depth inside the marina is 5 m; max. speed allowed is 5 knots.

The marina is open all year round as the port of entry; customs.

It has reception office, harbour master's branch office, hotel, restaurant, super-market, shop selling nautical items and spares, nautical charts and other relevant publications, camping and sports equipment; tennis court. Nearest post office in the village of Komolac. Fuel pump and sale of bottled gas (500 m).

Crane (5 t) and launching and hauling-up facility (25 t and 60 t travel-lift), slipway, wintering (outdoors), safe keeping, cleaning and rubbing down of laidup vessels. Repairs to wooden and plastic hulls, repair and maintenance of all types of engines, installation of engines and electric installations, painting and varnishing. Nearest ship-yard at Mokošica (downstream on Rijeka Dubrovačka).

DUBROVNIK,

city, town, port and major tourist centre of the eastern Adriatic. The Port of Dubrovnik consists of the Old City harbour in the E part of the Old Town, the commercial harbour

DUBROVNIK, VILLA SORKOČEVIĆ

Gruž NW of the Old Town, and Rijeka Dubrovačka, the inlet which houses the Dubrovnik Marina (Komolac).

OLD CITY HARBOUR

(42°38,5'N; 018°07'E) protected by the Porporela breakwater (red square iron tower with a column exhibiting a red light) and by the masonry sea-wall Kaše.

The City harbour can accomodate yachts drawing up to 3 m. The small pier is reserved for local passenger ships. Smaller

yachts can anchor in Gornja Bočina cove (S of Križ point); moderate waves and winds.

GRUŽ HARBOUR

(42°40'N; 018°05'E), commercial port 2.5 km northwest of the Old City.

Approach. When approach is effected from Koločep Channel, landmarks include the »Babin Kuk« hotel complex on the Lapad peninsula, the round white tower exhibiting a white light on the N extremity of the islet of Daksa, the round red tower with a column and a balcony (red light) on Kantafig point. When approach is effected from the open sea, landmarks include Mt Srđ (elevation 403 m) with a conspicuous grey radio mast and cable car installations on its slopes, the two conical wooded hills (Velika Petka, 197 m and Mala Petka, 146 m) on the Lapad peninsula below which are the white buildings of housing developments, the lighthouse on the islet of Sv Andrija (square masonry tower on a dwelling, flashing white, visibility about 22 miles), the square masonry tower on a dwelling exhibiting a white light on the westernmost rock of the Grebeni rocks, the conical masonry tower with a balcony exhibiting a white light on the island of Koločep (Bezdanj point), the tower (white light) on the islet of Daksa.

The shoal patch Vranac which extends off the N coast of Lapad is marked by a square stone mark with a conical topmark (peak turned upwards). Between this mark and the coast the depth is about 0.8 m.

Special Regulations. Vessels of all descriptions are required to reduce speed to 4 knots inside the line joining the light on Daksa islet and Leandar point (Lozica).

»MIHO PRACAT« MARINA - DUBROVNIK

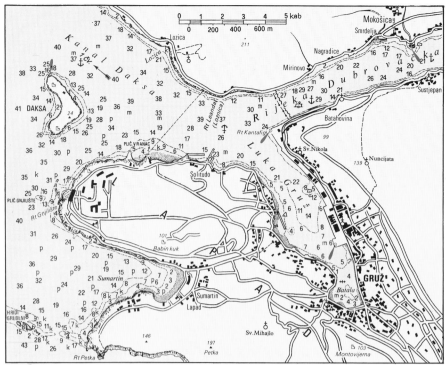

GRUŽ

Anchorage is prohibited SE of the line joining Vranac shoal (off the N coast of Lapad) and Leandar point. Navigation is prohibited between the islet of Daksa and the Lapad peninsula from April 1 to October 1.

Mooring. The harbour is protected from all winds except westerlies, which raise waves and cause a swell to creep in. The bora blows violently. Its full impact is felt at the harbour entrance and in the area around Kantafig point (at the mouth of Rijeka

Dubrovačka). The Petka pier (Gat Petka) is reserved for liners and the car-ferry service (Dubrovnik–Bari). Moorages for yachts are laid out S of Petka pier (in depth of about 4 m) to the Radeljević factory (berths are indicated by the Luka company). Smaller yachts may moor at the breakwater or in the small harbour of the »Orsan« Sailing Club, if prior permission has been obtained and dues paid at the club. The depth range from 4 to 5 m.

DUBROVNIK,
PATIO OF THE RECTOR'S PALACE

Dubrovnik marina »Miho Pracat« (ACI) is situated at Komolac (Rijeka Dubrovačka). Yachts can anchor (with lines secured ashore) in Lozica cove, NW of Leandar point.

The port is open to international traffic as a permanent port of entry.

The Gruž area houses the harbour master's office (with a branch office in the Old City harbour), post office, customs house, the Maritime Faculty and Maritime School, the headquarters of »Atlantska plovidba« shipping line, central post office, hospital and the »Atlas« Travel Agency, which owns a fleet of tourist ships. The »Orsan« Sailing Club.

The coastal radio station RADIODU-BROVNIK is a station of the mobile maritime radio service (see Part I of the Guide).

Facilities. Food provisions and other supplies at big shops and at the open market. Water from the hydrant on the waterfront and in the small harbour; fuel at the pump on the small wooden jetty (yachts drawing up to 3 m) in the boat harbour of the »Orsan« (E coast of the Lapad peninsula), and at the pump at Sustjepan (Rijeka Dubrovačka, yachts drawing up to 8 m). Navigation charts and other relevant publications may be obtained at the office of PLOVPUT – Plovno područje Dubrovnik.

Hauling-out of yachts up to 200 GRT at the slipway; mobile crane for yachts up to 12 and 13 m. The »Orsan« Sailing Club provides moorage and lying-up of yachts and boats during the whole year; also care and maintenance of engines.

Car-ferry lines: Dubrovnik – (Mljet – Vela Luka) – Hvar – Split – (Primošten) – Zadar – Rab – (M. Lošinj) – Rijeka; Dubrovnik – Bari.

Local passenger line: Dubrovnik – Koločep – Lopud – Suđurađ – Luka Šipanska – Okuklje – Sobra – Polače.

Sights. (Old City). City walls (10 C, reconstructed and reinforced between 12 C and

DUBROVNIK

GREBENI

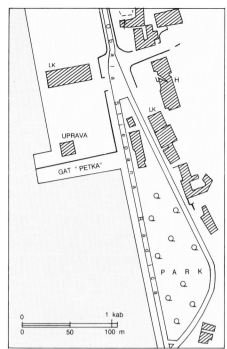

PORAT MARINA

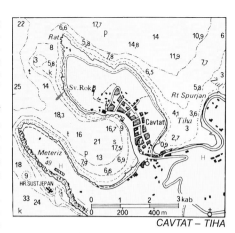

CAVTAT – TIHA

additions 1623–24). Churches: Velika Gospa cathedral (Our Lady, 1672–1713, rich treasury; the remains of an earlier, Romanesque cathedral, which stood on the same site, were discovered after the earthquake of 1979); Sv Vlaho (St Blaise, 1706–14), Sv Ignacije (St Ignatius, 1725, mural paintings; adjoining the church there is the building of the former Jesuit college, Collegium Ragusinum), Sv Spas (the Holy Saviour, 1520-28). Monasteries: Franciscan (Minorite) monastery (1317, cloister with 14 C hexaphores, pharmacy from 1317, Sv Frano church (St Francis, 1343), Dominican monastery (14 C, cloister from 15 C, art collections, Sv Dominik church, 1315, with later reconstructions); the nunnery at Danče (1457, important paintings in the church). Skočibuha Palace (1549–53). Summer residence of the Pucić family at the Pile Gate (now housing the »Atlas« Travel Agency).

Gruž summer residences of the Dubrovnik nobles: The Bunić-Pucić-Gradić residence (Gothic-Renaissance transitional style); the Gundulić residence (16 C, with boat house); the Natali residence (Renaissance); the Getaldić-Gundulić residence (Gothic and Renaissance); the residence of Petar Sorkočević (1521), now housing the Historical Institute of the Croatian Academy of Arts

DUBROVNIK, ST. BLAISE

17 C) with the forts: Sv Ivan (St John, housing the Maritime and the Ethnographic Museums, the Aquarium, the Biological Institute), »Minčeta«, »Revelin« (with a stage for performances) and »Bokar«. The town gates »Pile« and »Ploče«. Fort »Lovrijenac«, the Sponza Palace (1312, reconstructions 1516–22, housing the State Archives), the Rector's Palace (Knežev dvor, 1435, reconstructions in 1465 and after 1667, housing the Municipal Museum - Dubrovački muzej), the Clock Tower (first recorded in 1444, renovated in 1929), Rupe (granary of the Dubrovnik Republic, 1542—90, housing part of the Municipal Museum and ethnographic collection); Orlando's Column (1418, renovated), the Onofrio Fountain (1428), the Lazarettos (quarantine hospitals near the Ploče Gate, 1590 and

and Sciences (Zagreb) and a collection of objects of cultural and historical interest.

In the surroundings. Fort Impérial on Mt Srđ (elevation 412 m), cable car (from the Konal area N of the Old Town). – Lokrum islet (0.5 M from the City harbour): Benedictine monastery (14 C, later reconstructions) housing the Museum of Natural Sciences and the »Ruđer Bošković« Memorial Museum. On the S side of the islet there is an interesting natural phenomenon called the »Dead Sea«. The whole islet is under protection as a national park.

PORAT MARINA D.O.O.

(42°39,3'N; 018°5,6'E). Harbour for yachts belonging to the neighbouring harbour Gruž (180 m away) E of the mole Petka. Max. depth 5,6 m. Yachts can use the border crossing.

Mooring. 40 berths for yachts up to 40 m length. Larger yachts can stay at the commercial quay. There are 30 dry-berths for yachts 6–12 m of length.

Facilities. Reception office, water and electricity hook-ups, medical service, hotel, restaurant, bank, post office, coffee bar, several shops.

ŽUPSKI ZALJEV

CAVTAT

147

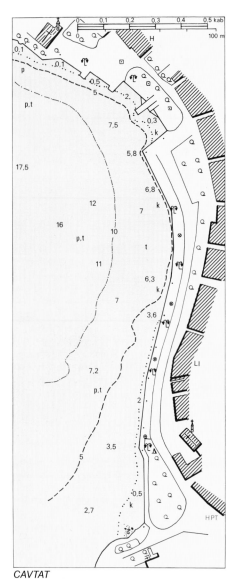

CAVTAT

Crane (10 t), lift (15 t), slipway, repairs and technical service for mechanical electrical and electronic equipment.

GORNJI MOLUNAT

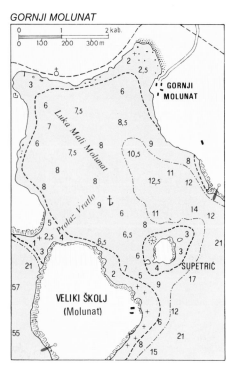

ŽUPSKI ZALJEV (BAY of ŽUPA)

This large bay NW of Cavtat opens between the capes Pelegrin and Sustjepan in the area of Župa Dubrovačka. In the bay (2,3 M long 1,3 M wide) max. depth is 44 m. The signs of bora are either small clouds around the peak of the mountain called Malešnica or above the village Mlini or an unexpected rainfall. The largest places within the bay are Srebreno and Mlini.

SREBRENO

(42°37,2'N; 018°12,2'E), small harbour, protected on the S side by the breakwater. At the head there is a lighthouse (red light). The length of the quay is altogether 70 m, max. depth 3–4 m. The harbour is protected only from W wind. The bora is very stormy here, and the S wind brings large waves over the breakwater.

MLINI

(42°37,3'N; 018°27'E), small harbour, protected by a 70 m long breakwater. The length of the quay is 25 m, max. depth about 4 m. It is well-protected from the bora, but the W and SW winds cause choppy sea.

CAVTAT

(42°35'N; 018°13'E), town and small harbour with a quayed shore situated in a well-protected cove about 18 miles SE of Dubrovnik.

Approach. Landmarks: the white mausoleum surmounted by a cupola on the summit of the Sv Rok hillock (elevation 42 m). Navigational marks include the round tower on a concrete base painted in red and black stripes, topped by two black spheres exhibiting a white light on the shoal Seka Vela and the white round tower with a column (sector light) on the NE entrance point.

When entering harbour care should be taken to avoid two shoal patches fronting the entrance Seka Vela (3.7 m) and Seka Mala (3 m); Seka Vela is marked by the black-red-black striped tower topped by two black spheres. SE of the Sustjepan point there is a rock and a shoal (9.3 m) of the same name. The white sector of the lights on the NE and SW entrance points covers the safe passage, while the red and the green sectors cover the off-lying dangers.

Mooring. The harbour affords shelter from the sirocco and the bora. With NW and W winds an uncomfortable surge develops inside the harbour and yachts are recommended to leave under such conditions; the occurrence of this surge (»seš«) is a characteristic feature of this harbour. Yachts can moor at the quay in the E part of the harbour (depth 1.5–4.7 m). A good anchorage ground affording shelter from E and SE winds is situated in the S part of the harbour (depth 10–20 m). An alternate anchorage is situated under the NE shore of the Sustjepan peninsula. During NW winds it is advisable to berth in front of the church using the four-point moor. Yachts can also anchor in the middle of Tiha bay (depth 6–8 m), NE of Cavtat (Bay of Župa), as well as in its W part (with lines secured ashore).

Facilities. Harbour master's branch office, post office, medical service, chemist's, hotels of all categories, and various tourist objects. Provisions at local shops, water from the hydrant on the waterfront. Fuel at the pump E of town.

Sights. Remains of defence wall (1461), remains of Roman thermal baths, aqueduct, inscriptions; the Rector's residence (1555–58, housing a library, archives, a museum collection, a graphic arts collection assembled by the scientist Baldo Bogišić, and a lapidarium). The churches: Sv Nikola (St Nicholas 1484; reconstructed 1732), Sv Vlaho (St Blaise, with adjacent Franciscan monastery from 1483). The residence of the Kaboga family. The gallery (former studio) of the painter Vlaho Bukovac. On the hillock Sv Rok above the town a cemetery with the mausoleum of the Račić family by the sculptor Ivan Meštrović (1920–22). – Mlini (remnants of Roman buildings, summer residence of the Stay family) – 7 km to the N. – Konavle (a 22 km long fertile valley), known for its folklore and national costumes, which may be admired at the village of Čilipi after Sunday mass.

DONJI MOLUNAT

(42°27'N; 018°26'E), village and cove on the N side of Rat peninsula. Affords good shelter to yachts of all sizes (in depth up to 16 m). It is open to NW winds, which raise heavy sea. In order to protect the underwater telephone cable, yachts should anchor as close to the peninsula as possible.

GORNJI MOLUNAT

(42°27'N; 018°26'E), village and cove on the SE side of Rat peninsula, about 13 M southeast from Cavtat.

Approach. Navigational marks include the round tower with a balcony (white light) on the SW side of Veli Školj islet.

Approaching yachts should give a berth to the rocky patch extending off the NNE coast of Veli Školj islet and keep closer to the mainland coast (tower with a column and a balcony white light).

Mooring. The cove is well protected from all winds. The bora is strong but does not develop a sea. Waves make entrance to the cove very difficult in a sirocco. Yachts draw-

PRIGRADICA

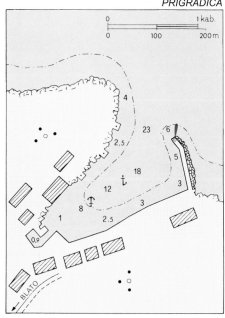

KORČULA, THE CATHEDRAL

KORČULA

ing 2.5 m can moor alongside the quay in front of the village. There is anchorage in the middle of the harbour (depth 9 m), N of islets Veli Školj and Supetrić.

ISLAND OF KORČULA

PRIHONJA

(42°59,5'N; 016°42'E), cove in the N coast of Korčula, sheltered from S winds. The E part of the cove provides some shelter from the bora, too. Smaller yachts can berth at the small pier in the E part of the cove using the four-point moor. A wreck dangerous to navigation (with a depth of 6 m over it) lies N of the pier.

PRAPRATNA

(42°59'N; 016°43'E), cove in the N coast of Korčula, adjoining the Prihonja inlet.

Mooring. The cove affords shelter from southerlies but is open to northerlies. Only smaller yachts can moor at the small break-water (depth 1.5–2 m). Care should be taken when anchoring on account of an underwater power cable.

PRIGRADICA

(42°58'N; 016°49'E), village and small har-bour in the N coast of Korčula, at the foot of the Veli Vrh hill (190 m).

Approach. Landmarks: the marks of a measured mile and a chapel; a red iron tower with a column and a balcony (red light) is situated on the head of the break-water (E shore). If approaching from E, care should be taken to avoid the Naplovci rocks.

Mooring. The cove is completely open to the bora and to E winds, NW cause a reflected swell. Good anchorage grounds for smaller yachts (depth 12–18 m); yachts can moor alongside the quay (depth 2.5–3 m) and at the inner side of the break-water (depth 5 m).

Facilities. Hotel and restaurant. Water from the main.

RAČIŠĆE

(42°58'N; 017°0,16'E), village and small harbour on the N coast of Korčula, W of Kneža Vela islet.

Approach. Landmarks: the village houses at the head of the cove; the white monu-ment on its E coast; a green tower with a column and a balcony (green light) on the head of the breakwater.

Mooring. The harbour affords shelter from all winds with the exception of northerlies. Smaller yachts can moor at the inner end of the breakwater (depth 2–3.5 m), which is from time to time used by local liners sup-plying the island population. A good anchor-age ground is situated in the middle of the cove, N of the breakwater (depth 14 m). It is open to northerlies and yachts should weigh and leave when such winds start blowing.

KORČULA, THE LAND GATE

KORČULA

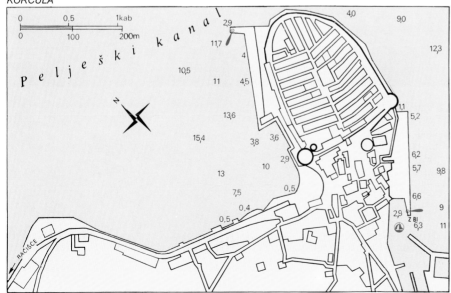

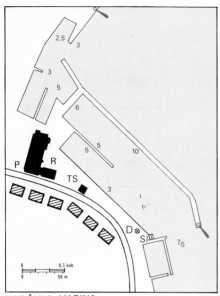

KORČULA MARINA

Facilities. Post office, medical service. Provisions in local shops, water from the main.

KNEŽA

(42°57'N; 017°04'E), cove in the N coast of Korčula in Pelješac Channel.

Approach. Landmarks: the islet of Kneža Vela and the masonry tower (white light) on its NE extremity are conspicuous. Shoal water extends betwen the islet Kneža Mala and the coast of Korčula.

Mooring. The islet is protected from winds blowing from the W and NW quadrants. Good anchorage SW of the island of Kneža Mala but during the bora it is better to anchor W of the islet.

KORČULA

(42°58'N; 017°08'E), town and harbour on the NE coast of the island of the same name. The harbour consists of W and E parts.

Approach. The city walls and the belfry of the cathedral are conspicuous. Landmarks:

LUKA

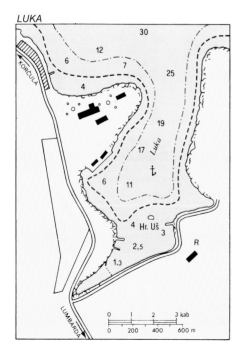

the red square tower with a column exhibiting (red light) on the breakwater head in the W harbour and the green round tower with a column and balcony (green light) on the quay in the E harbour.

Mooring. The W harbour affords shelter from winds blowing from the SE and SW quadrants. North-westerlies raise a sea in this harbour and it is advisable to shift to the E harbour or to Luka cove, when such winds start blowing; mooring for yachts are laid out alongside the S waterfront below the fortress walls (depth 3–4 m). The E harbour is protected from winds blowing from the SW and NW quadrants; mooring for yachts are also available alongside the quay (depth 4–6.7 m), S of the harbour light.

Warning. Underwater power cables cross the channel between the coves E and W of the town and Pelješac Peninsula and anchorage is prohibited in these areas.

The harbour is open to international traffic as a permanent port of entry.

Facilities. Harbour master's branch office, medical service, chemist's, post office; head-office of »Mediteranska plovidba« shipping line; »Inkobrod« shipyard.

Provisions at shops, water from the main. Fuel at the pump in the E harbour. Navigation charts and relevant publications

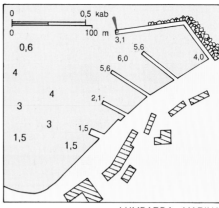

LUMBARDA MARINA

at the office PLOVPUT - Plovno područje Dubrovnik - office in Korčula.

Repairs to hulls and engines at the »Inkobrod« and the »Brodograditelj« shipyards, as well as at a number of privately owned workshops.

Car-ferry line: Korčula (Dominča) – Orebić.

A traditional sword dance, the »Moreška«, is performed at Korčula in July 28 and 29 when St. Todor is celebrated, also during the season (July and August) during the festival of Moreška, Kumpanija and Moštra.

KORČULA – LUMBARDA

Sights. City walls (13 C onwards, partly demolished 1875) with the forts: Zorzi (1449), Balbi (1483), tower next to the Balbi fort (1449), Zakerjan (1481–83), Bokar (1485–88), Barbarigo (1485–88), Capello (1493), and the Land Gate (Kopnena vrata) Revelin (14 C, renovated, with sculptural decorations). Loggia on the waterfront (1548), Sv Marko Cathedral (St Mark, apse from the 14 C, naves from the 15 C; Sv Rok chapel from 1525; ciborium, altar-pieces by Tintoretto, L. Bassano, C. Ridolfi, old tombs), Abbey Treasury (Opatska riznica, collection of liturgical items and church furnishing, art and other objects of cultural and historical interest), Gabrielis Residence (16 C, housing Municipal Museum, with exhibits and collections illustrating Korčula's development through history), abandoned Arneri Palace (florid Gothic, with Renaissance patio), Town Hall (1515, additions from 1866): Sv Mihovil church (St Michael, 1408, art objects, the hall of the Confraternity), the All Saints' Hall of the Confraternity (with church from the 15 C, renovated, coffered ceiling, collection of icons), the so-called Marco Polo House with a turret, the Dominican monastery with the Sv Nikola church (St Nicholas, about 1505, renovations in 1573 and 1655, baroque inventory). Outside the town, on a hill, the round Sv Vlaho (St Blaise) fort (also called Fort Wellington) built by the British in 1813.

KORČULA MARINA (ACI)

(42°57'N; 017°07'E) is situated in the small bay E of the town.

From the SE the marina is protected by a breakwater (green tower with a column and a balcony exhibiting a green light on its head).

Capacity: 160 sea-berths (four-point moor) (up to 12 m length) are laid out alongside the waterfront, the pier and the breakwater. About 50 dry-berths (up to 15 m long) are available. The depth is about 3 m along the waterfront and up to 10 m alongside the breakwater.

The marina operates all year round. The marina has reception office, restaurant, coffee-bar, apartments, shopping area, rent-a-car and rent-a-boat, toilets and showers with hot water, laundry, car park, fuel station

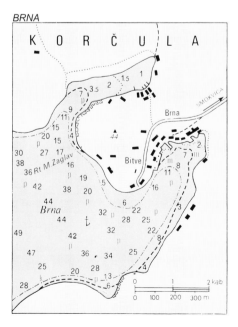

BRNA

LUMBARDA MARINA

nearby. Slip (35 t) and crane (10 t); technical services.

LUKA

(42°57'N; 017°07'E), deep inlet about 0.5 miles SE of the Korčula harbour. Affords shelter from all winds with exception of the bora. Small yachts can moor of the landing place in the NW part of the inlet. Food and water at the restaurants on the S shore.

LUMBARDA

(42°55,5'N; 017°11'E), village and small harbour situated on the easternmost part of the island of Korčula.

Approach. The white masonry tower (white light) on Ražnjić point, on the E extremity of the island, is conspicuous. Care should be taken to avoid the low-lying Knežić rock E of Tatinja cove and the Bili Žal shoal (depth 5 m over it) extending E of Knežić rock.

Mooring. In the marina. There are more anchorages. Bufalo cove (depth about

14 m) affords protection from all winds but is open to waves from the sirocco. Tatinja cove is open to winds blowing from the NE quadrant.

Facilities. Post office, medical service, chemist's, self-service store. Provisions and water.

»Berba naranača« (Orange-picking festival) is held in February.

Sights. Archaeological finds from a colony founded by Greeks from Issa (Vis) in the 4 C B.C. The most important of the finds, an inscription in stone (»Ploča iz Lumbarde«) is now in the Archaeological Museum in Zagreb. The medieval church of Sv Petar (St Peter) and the church of Sv Rok (1561); partly fortified summer residences of patrician families (Kršinić, Nobilo and Milina). Art collections: sculptors Frane Kršinić, Ivan Lozica and Ivan Jurjević-Knez.

LUMBARDA MARINA

(42°55,5'N; 017°10,6'E), is situated in Lumbarda cove (depth 5–7 m at the entrance; fixed mark, 1.6 m).

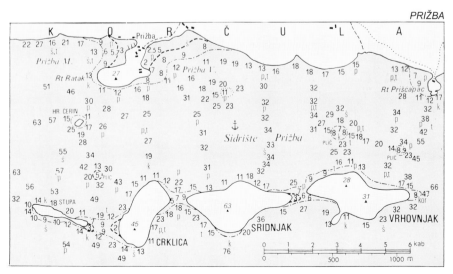

PRIŽBA

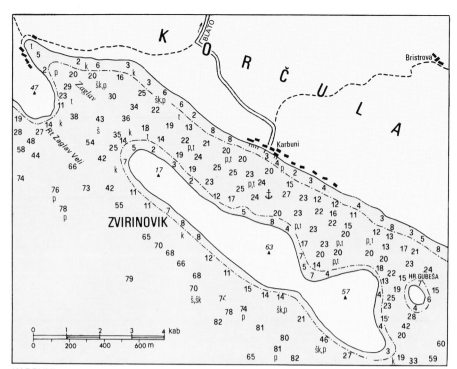

KARBUNI

VELA LUKA

There are about 90 sea-berths (for yachts up to 35 m long, depth 6–2 m) and 40 dry-berths (for yachts up to 14 m long).

It has reception office, restaurant, hotel, supermarket, shop; slipway, mechanical work; charter fleet.

PUPNATSKA LUKA

(42°56'N; 017°00'E), cove in the S coast of the island of Korčula. The village of Pupnat.

Mooring. The cove provides shelter only from northerlies. Yachts may anchor (depth 10–15 m) only in settled weather.

Facilities. Provisions and water in limited supply.

ZAVALATICA

(42°55'N; 016°56'E), cove in the S coast of the island of Korčula.

Mooring. Yachts (drawing up to 3 m) can berth behind the small breakwater using four-point moor. As the inlet affords shelter

from northerlies only, yachts should leave when southerlies start blowing.

Facilities. Water from the main, provisions in local shops.

BRNA

(42°54'N; 016°52'E), village in the spacious bay of the same name; harbour for the village of Smokvica situated further inland (4 km).

Approach. Landmarks: the round white tower with a column and a balcony (white light) on the wooded Veli Zaglav cape and the hotel building. When approaching the harbour from the W, care should be taken to avoid a number of shoals, rocks and islets.

Mooring. The bay is sheltered from all winds except westerlies and south-westerlies, which cause unpleasant sea, especially in the winter months, and it is recommended to seek shelter in the small cove of Kosirina. With the bora blowing, yachts should secure their lines on shore. Yachts

can moor along the mole (depth 4–5 m) or anchor in the middle of the cove.

Facilities. Provisions in local shops. Fuel not available.

PRIŽBA

(42°54'N; 016°48'E), fishing village and anchorage on the S coast of the island of Korčula; S of it lies Blato town and harbour.

Approach. The anchorage ground is surrounded by a string of islets (Stupa, Crklica, Sridnjak, Vrhovnjak) and by a number of above-water rocks (Čerin) and submerged rocks.

Mooring. The anchorage is exposed only to SE and SW winds. Smaller yachts can find shelter from S winds in the small cove of Prižba Mala or under the N coast of the islet of Sridnjak. The depth at the molehead in Prižba Mala is only about 1 m.

Facilities. Hotel, restaurant. Provisions and water.

GRŠĆICA

(42°54'N; 016°47'E), small fishing village and cove on the S coast of Korčula, about 1 M west of Prižba. Care should be taken when entering to avoid the shoal (about 1.2 m) situated in the middle of the cove by keeping to the N coast.

VELA LUKA

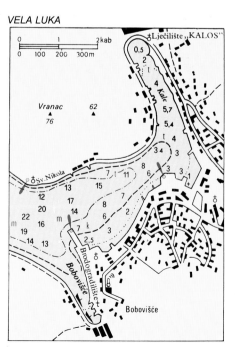

VELA LUKA

STRUGA

Mooring. The cove affords good shelter to yachts drawing up to 4 m in all winds with the exception of south-westerlies.

KARBUNI

(42°55'N; 016°44'E), village and anchorage on the SW coast of Korčula, about 2 M west of Grščica; fronted and protected by the islet of Zvirinovik.

Mooring. Good anchorage along the N coast of the islet of Zvirinovik (depth 14–25 m). Smaller yachts are recommended to use four-point moor in the small cove of Zvirinovik.

TRI LUKE

(42°55'N; 016°40,5'E), spacious cove on the SW part of Korčula.

Mooring. The cove is open to winds and waves from the SE quadrant but provides shelter from all other winds. During the sirocco small yachts can shelter between the islets of Pržnjak Veli and Pržnjak Mali.

VELA LUKA

(42°58'N; 016°43'E), town and harbour in the bay of the same name on the W coast of Korčula.

Approach. Landmarks: the white hexagonal masonry tower (white light) on the western extremity of the island of Proizd; the octagonal masonry tower (white light) on Velo Dance point and the square masonry tower (red light) on the islet of Kamenjak; the pyramidal stone tower with a red balcony (red light) on Vranac point; the belfries and the chimney of the fish cannery; the white tower with a column and a balcony (green light) on the head of the car-ferry landing place; the white tower (green light) on the W end of the quay in Vela Luka.

JURJEVA LUKA

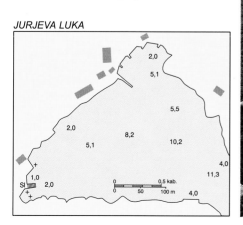

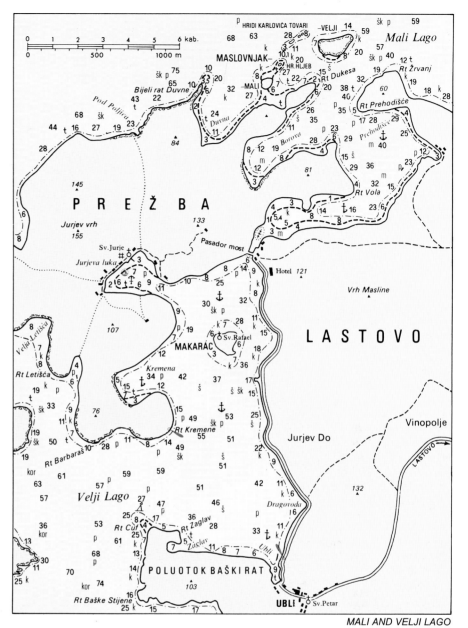

MALI AND VELJI LAGO

ZAKLOPATICA

SUŠAC

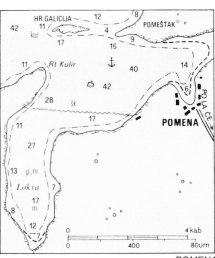

POMENA

The passage between the islands of Proizd and Korčula is shallow (3 m). The rocks Izvanjska and Prva are situated N of this passage. In the proximity of the low-lying point of Velo Dance, which should be given a berth of at least 400 m, there is the barely visible Čančir rock.

Mooring. The harbour is sheltered from all winds but stronger westerlies send in waves. Yachts can moor alongside the quay, a part of which is reserved for local passenger ships (depth 2.1–4.8 m). Smaller yachts can use the four-point moor along-side the small jetty E of the quay (depth 1.3–2.1 m).

The bay affords good protection to yachts: the anchorage ground E and ESE of the Ošjak islet (depth 30–50 m); Plitvine cove (where smaller yachts can use the four-point moor); Gradina cove (good anchorage for yachts drawing up to 4 m) and alongside the shore in Bobovišće cove.

Facilities. Harbour master's branch office, post office, hotels, rest-homes, numerous espresso-bars and restaurants, medical service, chemist's, fish-cannery.

Water from the hydrant. Fuel at the pump on the waterfront. Repairs can be undertaken at the »Greben« shipyard.

Car-ferry lines: Lastovo (Ubli) – Vela Luka – Hvar – Split; Lastovo (Ubli) – Vela Luka – Split.

Every four years Vela Luka is the venue of an international club (workshop) of architects, sculptors, painters and mosaic artists. The works of art produced are donated to Vela Luka.

In Kale cove, situated at the head of the harbour, there is the »Kalos« sanatorium (treatment of joint inflammations, sciatica and female disorders with radio-active water and mud).

LASTOVO

ISLAND OF LASTOVO

MALI LAGO or MALO MORE
(42°46,5'N; 016°50'E), small bay between the W coast of Lastovo and Prežba island.

Approach. Žrvanj point on the small cone-shaped peninsula on the E side of the entrance and the islet of Maslovnjak Veli N of it are easily identified from seaward. Approach should be made between the islet of Maslovnjak Veli and Žrvanj point because of the Karlovića Tovari and Hljeb rocks situated between the islets of Maslovnjak Veli and Maslovnjak Mali.

Mooring. The cove is sheltered from all winds. Good anchorage for larger yachts S of Žrvanj point (depth 38–40 m). Smaller vessels can anchor at the head of the cove (depth 14–16 m).

Facilities. Limited provisions in the passage Most (Pasadur) or in the harbour of Ubli.

VELJI LAGO or VELJE MORE
(42°45'N; 016°49'E), spacious bay and harbour on the W coast of Lastovo. The village of Ubli is situated in the SE part of the bay.

Approach. Landmarks: approaching from the W: the islet of Kopište, the hills Hun

(417 m) and Pleševo (415 m), the islets of Bratin and Vlašnik. On the S side of the entrance is Cuf point and on the N side Kremene point - a white concrete tower with a column and a balcony (sector light); a red tower with a column and a balcony (red light) is situated on the wharf at Ubli (SE part of the bay).

Warning. In order to avoid the rocky shoals N of Cuf point yachts should approach on the aligment: Kremena point (white tower) and the SE extremity of Makarac islet. By night the fairway lies within the white sectors of the light on Kremena point.

Navigation is prohibited in the small cove of Jurjeva luka (the islet of Prežba). All sailing and underwater activity is forbidden in the area within the radius of 500 m round the point Velje More.

Mooring. Kremena cove on the SE coast of Prežba island is sheltered from all winds. Smaller yachts can moor along the wharf in the harbour of Ubli (depth 4.5–6 m) in the SE part of the cove or in front of the »Solitudo« hotel (depth 1.5–2 m). They can also anchor in Kremena cove. Jurjeva port , a bay north from Kremena, also on the island of Prežba is completely sheltered from all winds. There is a chance for landing on both sides and anchorage for fishing boats. One can anchor also in the middle of

GLAVAT

POLAČE

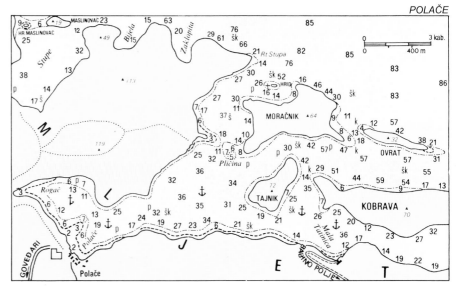

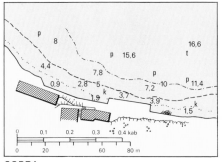

SOBRA

the bay since it is 8 m deep.; that is why the bay is attractive for nautical torists.

Facilities. Harbour master's branch office in Ubli. Provisions, water and fuel (on the agricultural estate).

Sights. Remains of Roman and early medieval buildings, foundations of an early Christian basilica (5/6 C), sarcophagi and foundations of farm buildings. – Lastovo (the largest village on the island: ruins of the Romanesque Sv Ivan church (St John), of Sv Kuzma i Damjan church (St Cosmas and Damian, built in 1473, reconstructed in the 16 C, with collection of liturgical items); Loggia; defence wall (early 17 C), Sv Vlaho church (St Blaise, reconstructed in the 14 C). Folklore and carnival celebrations – 10 km by road.

ZAKLOPATICA

(42°46'N; 016°52,5'E), islet, village and cove on the N coast of Lastovo.

Warning. The W passage between the coast of Lastovo and the islet of Zaklopatica is only 1.4 m deep; E passage is 20 m wide and about 5 m deep.

Mooring. The cove is protected from all winds except those from the NE quadrant. Best anchorage during the bora on the lee of Zaklopatica islet.

SKRIVENA LUKA (PORTORUS - locaL name)

(42°44'N; 016°53'E), village and cove on the S coast of Lastovo.

Approach. Landmarks: the round masonry tower above a dwelling on Struga cape and

PROŽURA

the red iron tower with a column and a balcony (red light) on Stražica point (at the entrance to the cove). Approaching from the W, care should be taken to avoid the rocky shoal W of Velje More point.

Mooring. The cove is sheltered from all winds and suitable for longer stays. The best anchorage in a sirocco is in front of the cove entrance. In a rock (0.5 M of the entrance to Skrivena Luka cove). A good anchorage for smaller yachts is in the inner part of the cove (depth up to 15 m).

Facilities. Limited provisions and water.

ISLAND OF MLJET

POMENA

(42°47,5'N; 017°20'E), village and cove on the W extremity of the island of Mljet. It is protected from the N by the islet of Pomeštak. Between that island and the Galicija rock there is a shoal patch.

Approach. When approaching from SW, care should be taken to avoid Šij rock N of Goli rat point and the rocky patch near the rock; Crna Seka rock fronts the cove entrance (should be given a berth of at least 200 m; shoals). Approaching from the NE, course should be shaped NW of the islet of Glavat in order to avoid Crna Seka and Borovac rock, two rocky patches and a shoal (depth 3 m).

Mooring. The cove is sheltered from all winds and suitable for prolonged stays. Good anchorage for larger yachts S of Galicija rock and Pomeštak islet (depth about 40 m). Smaller yachts can anchor in the S of the bay (depth 20–30 m). Moorings along the waterfront in front of the hotel (depth 2–4.5 m). In the middle of the bay there is a mooring buoy.

Facilities. Limited provisions and water.

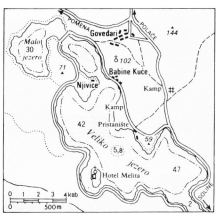

MLJETSKA JEZERA

POLAČE

(42°47'N; 017°23'E), village and cove on the N coast of Mljet.

Approach. The string of small, almost bare islands, among which the islet of Ovrat stands out, is easily discernible from seaward. A round white tower mounted on a pedestal exhibiting a white light is situated on Kula cliff. In the W part of the passage between the coast of Mljet and the islet of Moračnik, shoals extend around Stupa point and both sides of its S part.

Mooring. The inner part of the cove, particularly Mala Tatinica cove, affords protection from all winds and sea. Yachts can moor along the pier in Polače harbour (depth 4.7–5.2 m) or use the four–point moor along the NW part of the landing-place (depth ca. 2.5 m). Good anchorage for larger yachts NE of the ruins of the old palace near the village (depth 22 m), W of Tajnik islet (depth ca 35 m) or W and SW of Kobrava islet (depth 43 m). The best

MLJETSKA JEZERA (SOLINE CHANNEL)

VELIKO JEZERO

anchorage for smaller yachts is in the W part of Rogač cove (depth 14 m).

Car-ferry line: Polače – Trstenik (mainland).

Local passenger line: see Dubrovnik.

Facilities. Limited provisions. Shops in the village of Goveđari – 1.5 km inland by road.

Sights. Walls of a palace, according to tradition of Agesilaius of Anzarbo, dating from the late Roman period (3/4 C), remnants of an early Christian basilica (5/6 C). Starting point for visit to the Mljet lakes (2 km by road).

SOBRA
(42°45'N; 017°37'E), village and cove on the N coast of Mljet. Main harbour of the village of Babino Polje, 7 km inland.

Approach. Landmarks: the white octagonal concrete tower (white light) on Pusti point (should be given a berth of at least 500 m; shoals), the low-lying Seperka rock in its vicinity and part of the road leading to Babino Polje can be seen from seaward.

Mooring. In the harbour yachts are exposed to the bora and the sirocco and it cannot be recommended for longer stays. Yachts can moor along the landing-place in front of the village (depth 3.2–4.1 m). The best anchorage, even in a sirocco, is situat-

ed S of the islet of Badanj, in the small cove of Zaglav (E part). In NW winds Klačna Luka cove affords a good anchorage (W part), but care should be taken to avoid submerged rock (depth about 0.8 m).

Facilities. Harbour master's branch office, shop, car-ferry landing ground in Zaglav cove (the E part of the cove). Limited provisions. Post office and medical service in the nearby village of Babino Polje.

Car-ferry line: see Dubrovnik.

PROŽURA
(42°44'N; 017°39'E), village and cove on the N coast of Mljet.

Approach. Landmarks: the islet of Borovac fronting the cove entrance and the islet of

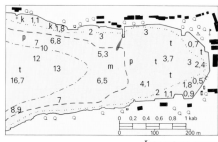

ŠIPANSKA LUKA

ŠIPANSKA LUKA

Planjak situated S of it, are easily identifiable. When approaching from E, care should be taken to avoid a submerged rock (depth 4.5 m) in front of Maharac point, as well as the Senjevci rocks.

Mooring. The cove is exposed to the bora and to north-westerlies. Smaller yachts can use the four-point moor at the smaller mole in the S part of the harbour (depth 4–5 m). Good anchorage off the SW coast of Planjak islet (where yachts should anchor with lines secured to the shore, bows facing NE).

Facilities. Limited provisions.

Sights. Ruins of a Benedictine monastery, Sv Trojica church (Holy Trinity, 15 C).

OKUKLJE
(42°44'N; 017°41'E), village and small harbour on the N coast of Mljet.

SVETI ANDRIJA

Approach. Landmarks: navigational marks include the round white tower with a column and a balcony (white light) on the E entrance point (Stoba), the green tower standing on a cement block in the sea in front of Okuklje point and the green tower (green light) on the molehead.

Mooring. The cove is protected from all winds and it can be recommended for longer stays. Yachts drawing up to 3.5 m can moor alongside the mole on the NE coast (green light) or use the four-point moor in its vicinity. Anchorage for smaller yachts in the harbour entrance (depth 4–6 m). Poor holding ground. The SW part of the harbour is shallow.

Facilities. Restaurant on the N coast of the small harbour.

SAPLUNARA
(42°42'N; 017°44'E), village and cove on the E extremity of the island of Mljet.

Mooring. The cove is sheltered from the sirocco and the bora but open to southwesterlies. It should be taken into account that the sirocco (SE) is likely to turn into a south-westerly (»lebić«), which makes the cove untenable. An anchorage ground for smaller yachts is situated at the head of the cove.

Warning. All sailing and underwater activity is forbidden in the area with the radius of 500 m round point Gruj (42°41,2'N; - 017°45,2'E).

MLJETSKA JEZERA
(42°46'N; 017°23'E), sea lakes situated in the W part of the island of Mljet. There are two lakes, Veliko jezero and Malo jezero (Big Lake and Small Lake), linked by a narrow channel. The lakes are part of the

»Mljet« National Park. They are connected with the open sea by the 0.6 M long Soline Channel (depth up to 2 m), width at narrowest part 10 m. The tide produces strong currents.

Warning. Speed limit in the channel and in the lakes is 4 knots. Yachts are forbidden to enter the channel and the lakes except in cases of force majeure.

Facilities. Shopping for provisions in the village of Govedari – 5 km by road.

Sights. On the islet in the S part of Veliko jezero there is a Benedictine monastery (12/13 C), enlarged in the 15/16 C, with a cloister (16 C) and Uznesenje Marijino church (Assumption of the Virgin, 12/13 C, later additions).

ISLAND OF ŠIPAN

ŠIPANSKA LUKA
(42°44'N; 017°52'E), village and cove in the NW part of the island of Šipan.

Approach. The cove can be entered either through the Mali Vratnik passage, between the SE extremity (Vratnik point) of the Pelješac Peninsula and the island of Olipa, or through Veliki Vratnik (between Olipa and Jakljan). It can also be entered through the Harpoti passage (between Jakljan and Šipan). Yachts approaching through Veliki Vratnik should navigate past the SE extremity of the islet of Olip (square masonry tower, white light) and the three islets off the NE coast of Jakljan: Tajan (round red tower with a column and a balcony, red light), Crkvina and Kosmeč (between them is Goleč rock). The harbour light: a white iron column (red light) on the molehead.

Warning. All sailing and underwater activity is forbidden here in the area within the

LOPUD

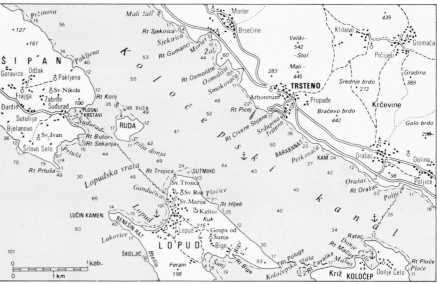

KOLOČEPSKI CHANNEL

RT OŠTRA

radius of 500 m round the point Debela Glava (42°43,2'N; 017°52'E).

Mooring. The harbour is sheltered from all winds with the exception of »lebić« (southwesterlies). The anchorage it affords is one of the best sheltered in Koločep Channel. Smaller yachts can use the four-point moor

SUĐURAĐ, SUMMER RESIDENCE STIJEPČEVIĆ-SKOČIBUHA

along the waterfront in the inner part of the cove. Depth along the mole 1–3 m. Larger vessels will find good anchorage between Mišnjak point and the small peninsula of Brag (depth 30–60 m).

Facilities. Post office, hotel and medical service. Food supplies at local shops; limited quantities of water.

Local passenger line: see Dubrovnik.

Sights. Summer residence of the Sorkočević family (15 C), remains of the Rector's Palace (Gothic, 1450), Sv Stjepan church (St Stephen, 10 C, later reconstructions).

ISLAND OF LOPUD

LOPUD
(42°41'N; 017°57'E), village and cove on the NW coast of Lopud.

Approach. The cove can be entered through Lopudska Vrata (from the S) or through the Koločep Channel. When approaching from the N, care should be taken to avoid the shoal patch and Sutmiho rock in front of N Sv Mihajlo point; in its vicinity there is a monastery with a belfry. A red iron tower (red light) is situated on the breakwater.

Mooring. The cove is well protected from all winds except north-westerlies, during which waves break strongly against the coast. Smaller yachts can moor alongside the L-shaped breakwater fronting the village, when it is not used by local liners (depth 1.3–4.3 m). Good anchorage, especially for bigger yachts, off the E coast (depth 20–40 m).

Facilities. Post office and medical service. Provisions and water.

BROTNJICE, MEDIAEVAL TOMBSTONE

LOPUD, CLOISTER OF THE FRANCISCAN MONASTERY

Local passenger line: see Dubrovnik.

Sights. Remains of ramparts (15–16 C), the Franciscan monastery (1483, fortified in 1516, tower dating from 1592), Sv Marija od Špilice church (Our Lady of Špilice, 12 C, later additions), the ruins of Miho Pracat's and Bishop Brautić's summer residences (16 C), Sv Trojstvo church (Holy Trinity, 16–17 C, collection of sacral art objects), the Đurđević-Mayneri summer house with a park.

ŠUNJ

(42°41'N; 017°57'E), cove in the SE coast of Lopud.

Approach. When approaching from the N, care should be taken to avoid the Čavalika shoal (depth about 3.5 m), W of the point cape of the same name. When approaching from the S, care should be taken to avoid Skupio islet (shoal extends E, depth about 5.8 m), and the Skupjeli rock near the S entrance point.

Mooring. As the cove is exposed to southerlies and to waves, it is not recom-

mended for longer stays. Provisions in the village of Lopud (2 km).

Sights. Gospa od Šunja church (Our Lady of Šunj, 15 C, reconstructed in the 17 C).

ISLAND OF KOLOČEP

DONJE ČELO

(42°41'N; 018°0,1'E), village and cove on the NW coast of the island of Koločep.

Approach. Yachts approaching from the open sea pass beside the Sv Andrija lighthouse (white flashes); between the islands of Šipan and Lopud care should be taken to avoid shoals extending from the shores of

Skupio islet and the shoal patch (2 m) in the vicinity of the W extremity of Koločep.

Mooring. The bay is sheltered from S winds and waves; it is protected from the bora by a limestone ridge. Smaller yachts can moor alongside the pier (depth 0.9– 3.2 m). The anchorage under the NE coast affords protection from the bora; yachts are advised to secure lines ashore as well.

Facilities. Some provisions and limited quantities of water. Better shopping for provisions at Zaton Mali and Gruž (Dubrovnik).

Local passenger line: see Dubrovnik.

Sights. Uznesenje Marijino church (Assumption of the Virgin, 13–15 C), defence towers at several localities on the island.

INDEX